Carl Menger

WIENER ARBEITEN ZUR PHILOSOPHIE

Reihe B: Beiträge zur philosophischen Forschung

Herausgegeben von Stephan Haltmayer

Band 17

PETER LANG

Frankfurt am Main · Berlin · Bern · Bruxelles · New York · Oxford · Wien

Gilles Campagnolo (Hrsg./ed.)

Carl Menger

Neu erörtert unter Einbeziehung nachgelassener Texte

Discussed on the Basis of New Findings

Mit Beiträgen von / With Contributions by
G. Campagnolo, S. Haltmayer, P. Livet, A. Lordon, J. Magnan de Bornier,
H. Mayerhofer, K. Milford, M. Ohana, P. Rosner, W. Wilke

PETER LANG
Internationaler Verlag der Wissenschaften

Bibliografische Information der Deutschen Nationalbibliothek
Die Deutsche Nationalbibliothek verzeichnet diese Publikation in der Deutschen Nationalbibliografie; detaillierte bibliografische Daten sind im Internet über <http://www.d-nb.de> abrufbar.

Gedruckt mit Förderung
des Bundesministeriums für Wissenschaft und Forschung
in Wien.

Gedruckt auf alterungsbeständigem,
säurefreiem Papier.

ISSN 0948-1311
ISBN 978-3-631-51634-8

Printed in Germany 1 2 3 4 6 7

www.peterlang.de

List of Contributors / Verzeichnis der Mitarbeiter

Dr. Gilles Campagnolo, French National Center for Scientific Research (CNRS) / Center for Comparative Epistemology, Paris / Aix-en-Provence

Pr. Dr. Stephan Haltmayer, Universität Wien, Fakultät für Philosophie und Bildungswissenschaft, Institut für Philosophie

Pr. Dr. Pierre Livet, University of Provence, Center for Comparative Epistemology, Aix-en-Provence

Dr. Aurélien Lordon, University of Rennes

Pr. Dr. Jean Magnan de Bornier, Department of Applied Economics Aix-Marseilles, Research Unit in Quantitative Economics, Aix-en-Provence

Dr. phil. Herta Mayerhofer, Wien

Pr. Dr. Karl Milford, Universität Wien, Fakultät für Wirtschaftswissenschaften, Institut für Volkswirtschaftslehre

Dr. Marc Ohana, ESC Group School of Management and Business, Troyes

Pr. Dr. Peter Rosner, Universität Wien, Fakultät für Wirtschaftswissenschaften, Institut für Volkswirtschaftslehre

Dr. phil. Dr. rer. soc. oec. Werner Wilke, Wien

Thanks / Dank

This volume is the result of a joint-work between researchers in the fields of philosophy and economics, and between Institutes in Vienna (Austria) and in Aix-en-Provence (France), together with associated researchers in Vienna and in French institutions. All contributors focus on Carl Menger's works and ideas, and the history and concepts of the "Austrian School of Economics".

On the French side, cooperation was financially supported by the French National Center for Scientific Research (CNRS) within the frame of a project entitled "Carl Menger and the Austrian School", coordinated by Dr. Gilles Campagnolo, the Editor of this volume. Special thanks to Ms Martine Fize (CNRS personal assistant) who helped in formatting this volume, with care and interest much beyond her duties. On the Austrian side, publishing was made possible through the activity of Pr. Dr. Stephan Haltmayer and the office of Peter Lang Verlag in Vienna and Frankfurt/Main.

Table of Contents/ Inhalt

Introduction

Gilles Campagnolo

It is a major problem with all histories of economic thought to establish evidence for the transmission of ideas. The stuff that history of scientific thought (history of economic thought, HET, in particular) is made of, and the issues it deals with, those are directly related to links between ideas, concepts, authors, and to which extent one may soundly assess them.

Carl Menger was born in 1840 in the Galician parts of the old Austro-Hungarian Empire. He is undoubtedly one of the major characters in the History of the science of economics, as well as of well-known so-called "Marginalist revolution". Menger was also later recognized as the founder of the Austrian school of economic thought. As such, he has been an object of academic study in "sound HET" for more than one century now. The present volume deals with him and with economics as the science of material exchange related to individual needs and the satisfaction thereof. As such; economics is often regarded as a somehow "strange" and inaccurate science with respect to the *natural* sciences. But economists have invented their own guidelines and made their methods relevant to analyze the exchange of goods in the frame of human behaviour. In that respect, not all of economics comes from mathematics. Menger's certainly does not. But, if it is at all possible to find economic "laws" of "human action" (a term coined by Menger's heirs), then Menger lies in the foreground.

Menger's biography has been told and retold by commentators.[1] Since his death (in 1921), and given the re-emergence of a "Neo-Austrian" school in the last third of the 20th century, Menger's fame has re-acquired a place in the economic *Pantheon*. "Neo-Austrianism" (as it is sometimes called) is now represented by numerous living authors whose influence on the mainstream of economics spreads all the more as the crisis in the "positivist" method proposed by Milton Friedman (himself deceased in 2006) seems to deepen. But one should remember that Menger had already a place of great renown during his lifetime, in the last third of the 19th century. He was not regarded only as the leader of "Anti-historicism" in the "Dispute over methods" (*Methodenstreit*), but mostly as a contender for international leadership in his discipline.

---

[1] It can neither be the goal of this Introduction, nor that of the present volume, to assess the literature about Menger, the Austrian school and their relationships. Part of that literature (now quite extensive) is selected and quoted in the final bibliography. The criterion of the selection in this list of references is what the contributors in this volume have deemed useful for their respective chapters. It is in no way complete or exclusive. Readers of the present volume will undoubtedly have ideas about whom to add, and neither the editor nor the contributors of this volume hold any prejudiced opinion *pro or contra* possible additions.

One should point out that Menger benefitted from a large recognition among the academic leaders in economics, although he was hated by the Historicists. He was reckoned throughout numerous national Academies outside Austria and Germany. He was, for instance, an official correspondent of the French "*Institut des sciences morales et politiques*", where he had succeeded Wilhelm Roscher in the "Economics and Statistics" section. He was, later on, also offered the Presidency of the International Sociological Institute in 1901.

Menger always preferred to emphasize the importance of a "pure" science of economics (*reine Wirtschaftslehre*) than what was then known under the terms used for "political economy" in German: *Nationalökonomie* and *Volkswirtschaftehre*. Menger especially rebuked in them the implicit acceptation of the ontological stand according to which collective entities like the "people" (*Volk*) would *truly* exist *as such* within the frame of economic analysis. That was erroneous in Menger's eyes. He also avoided the politically-oriented definition of the "nation" – especially in the context of the building of German unity along a path deemed "particular" by German social scientists (what was then called *ein Sonderweg der deutschen Nation*).

Menger would rather stress the existence of a general substratum of consistent methodology for economics, based upon a thorough subjectivist foundation. His name has thus become a rallying cry for the advocates of what was later on called "Methodological individualism" (let us stress the fact that, in Menger's own vocabulary, the texts never yield that term). Also important to remind the reader is the fact that Menger founded his school of thought before 1900 in the capital-city of *Mitteleuropa*, Vienna. Therefore, while reckoning the interest of the individualistic revival in North-American intellectual circles since the 1970's, the contributors of this volume preferably hold firm to the context of "old-style" 1900's *Mitteleuropa* – known as the "*Belle époque*" or the "Viennese apocalypse" along opposite views of the same reality. Menger was naturally immune to later ideas and interpretations. He must therefore be set again in the context where his own ideas developed and where his works flourished. They were anchored in his birthplace, as was the current of economic thought that he introduced. They were originated in Central Europe, although the material available *today* to assess its value and its extent has been disseminated.

In order to trace back Menger's "work-in-progress" in the theoretical field, one must then first get a thorough knowledge of the *present* state of the sources to take into account. Too much has been said about the Austrian economist's ideas *without* taking into sufficient account his *Nachlass* and it is indispensable to assess first what one may really use in order to discuss Menger's thought. It is true that specialists of his works have sometimes heard that evidence could be gathered from the contents of Menger's own private collections – especially his library now located at the *Hitotsubashi Center for Modern Western Social Sciences* (Japan). But how many did travel there? One commentator had begun to truly inquire on location: Emil Kauder was the first to carefully examine the Archives in Japan.[2] In 1997 and 1998, I could resume his meticulous work where he had left it, thanks to a Grant by the Japanese *Monbusho* Ministry of Research. Next step was to display commentaries that bear *directly* on some of the material that I shared with colleagues within the frame of a project entitled "Carl Menger and the Austrian School" for the French National Center for Scientific Research (CNRS) to which I belong. One result is the present volume. It shall contribute to present scholarly debates and significantly improve some arguments that would otherwise remain intuitive – although sometimes insightful, debates on Menger usually lack pieces of evidence required for hard cases in the sciences.

Another issue is at stake: the intellectual origins of some major traits in present-day economics (as regards the role of many "Austrian" concepts, but even more widely) seem naturally quite close to issues raised by Menger in his times. One may say that economic phenomena are explained by scientifically interpreting how individual agents face specific institutional constraints. Nevertheless that is not enough to characterize "Austrian-*ness*". The label of "Methodological individualism" was later spread by Josef Schumpeter (although not coined by him) and not, as mentioned above, in Menger's vocabulary. Thus, an insufficient characterization of Menger's thought has had many undesirable consequences: first, many economists who claim themselves to be "Neo-classics" would sincerely approve of some Austrian ideas, *but* without ever thinking in the least their work to be "Austrian". Secondly, many Austrian claims are too narrow and leave aside other major facets of Menger's influence in the HET. On both sides, insufficiencies in studying Menger's *Nachlass* and the deep interest in the philosophy of science it shows is responsible for that account.

Specifically, let us ask: what can be proven about Menger? And what might, on the contrary, be said of his followers (at times, of very few of them only)? What is "his" "school", so to speak? Much of Menger's ideas had to do with central questions of philosophy, theory of knowledge (*Erkenntnistheorie*), methodology (especially in the social sciences: *Sozialwissenschaften*) and "sciences of the mind" (as they are called in German: *Geisteswissenschaften*). Among the latter, psychology was the triumphant science in the 1900's. But did Menger rely on Wilhelm Wundt's *experimental* psychology? We shall ask that question. The self-denominated "Austrian school" of economists includes the followers of Menger, from Eugen von Böhm-Bawerk and Friedrich von Wieser, to Friedrich von Hayek and Ludwig von Mises, down to Ludwig Lachmann and Murray Rothbard (only to quote a few names in a long list). Those seemingly rallied some core-creeds found in Menger. But such a "core" is also much in debate.[3]

---

[2] One must also quote various works by Japanese scholars: see the final bibliography.

[3] Here, we must establish the rule of referring the reader to the final bibliography where texts quoted and used by contributors of this volume are listed. Let us point out, among other

Thus, we shall not deal with them in this volume, but conscientiously get back to the fundamentals of *Mengerian* economics in *Menger's texts*, whether philosophical, methodological or theoretical. Menger (and almost Menger only) shall here be our concern in relation to his interest for those topics.

The inquiry made by contributors in the following chapters is not only historical. Some of the issues discussed are *today* at the heart of economics – not only of the "Austrian" or "Neo-Austrian" school, but more at large in the profession. For that matter, interest may even come from outside the profession, as "Austrians" have reached a devoted audience outside *Academia* too. Although the present volume is written by renowned specialists, it is thus both intended for specialists *and* for a larger audience. The former may already know much about Menger, but they shall find here new material unearthed from the Archives. Among the latter wider audience, many of those who may sometimes feel somewhat by the (almost) exclusively econometrics approach of today's *mainstream* economics will here find information on an author whose work and thoughts were indeed deeply by and large *cross-disciplinary*.

For that matter, we shall here point out that we will leave political matters aside. Such affinities are a strong bone of contention between specialists and we shall not take stands, but rather try to consider Menger in the tradition of "true" liberalism in the second part of this volume. The reference to a "true" liberal creed will unavoidably raise comments in the readers' minds. Contributors chose to rely on the British Classics. Other choices are possible. Anyway, let us repeat that this volume is written for a wide and open-minded audience, and that it is a study in economics and philosophy (not politics). Hence, it belongs to the Series *Wiener Arbeiten zur Philosophie*, in which its Director, Prof. Dr. Stephan Haltmayer has wished to retain it.

Once again, let us ponder about Menger. To make a hard case that there was an influence between two authors, who lived at different periods and could neither meet nor exchange correspondence, it is neither enough to point out that both cherished the same view upon some given topic, nor that one had read the works of the other, nor even that this author had read the works of the other one *before* writing his own book. It might be the case that the later author developed his views quite independently and, only then, found comfort and a confirmation of those views in the works of the earlier thinker. It follows that, short of an explicit acknowledgement, it is almost impossible to make a hard case for the transmission of any ideas. Without such evidence, there is only speculation.

Even though that speculation may be of much help in clarifying the standpoints of both authors, one may call on commentators for more caution. As a matter of fact, particularly well-inspired commentators have often established

---

works, that of Bruce Caldwell (1984), where he attempted to define such an "Austrian core" distinguishing between *apodictic* and *empirical* creeds within Austrian thought.

connections between fine pieces of economic thought. Still, one reason to be cautious, however interesting such speculation might be, is that evidence remains *always needed* by a commentator as well as by a scientist, and indeed by a philosopher. In some cases, the proofs for earlier intuitions are only provided in the end by commentators who thus show how well-grounded their intuitions really were. But, in order to make a strong case of "influence", we will argue that evidence must come *first*. To do so, many kinds of evidence can be used, like claims assessed by the later writer when acknowledging that he got his ideas from an earlier thinker. It may appear in public declarations, published material, etc. Non-published manuscript annotations, when available, may even better show the extent of inspiration and influence and how they melt. If unpublished (as with Menger), notes are the historian's game to seek and display.

Such material left unknown for decades is indeed a godsend to the researcher!

Our purpose here would then be useless if it were only to rehash what has already been written in numerous works on Menger.[4] On the contrary, we shall focus on a limited number of "hot" issues, discussed *nowadays* in circles aware of Menger's significance in the history of modern and contemporary economics, in philosophy and in some neighbouring sciences. On those topics, specialists gathered in the present French-Austrian joint-work will unearth material left in oblivion and use those *new* findings. Three sets of issues are raised:

- I. What are the sources left unknown (or little-known), Menger's *Nachlass* in particular, that we may count upon?
- II. To what extent and in what sense was Menger a thinker in the "true" tradition of Liberal economics?
- III. Four major issues in Epistemology and the Philosophy and Methodology of economics: Menger and the role of psychology, Menger and the issue over Cardinality *vs.* Ordinality, Menger and the methodo-logy of experimental economics, Menger and the Theory of Capital.

After recalling the history of Menger's life in an *Einleitung zu Carl Menger* (chapter 1, Herta Mayerhofer), we shall detail the results of our philological inquiry within the Archives (chapter 2, Gilles Campagnolo). The link with earlier traditions will clearly appear thanks to the work done on first-hand material: as one may expects, Menger was of course neither foreign to the German tradition, nor merely though a part of it, but he has his own place in it, deserving a qualified understanding. The history of the publishing and editing of his works is of much help, such as, when necessary, the philosophy that he acknowledged. Be-

[4] Again, the reader is invited to see the final bibliography, as we shall not here quote the works on Menger – first, for lack of space, unless we should only allude to them (which would be disrespectful regarding their endeavours and achievements), or leave aside too many of them (as those authors are also worthy of attention and as they have found devoted readers among the contributors of this volume, it would be a pity to leave them aside).

cause this volume is also intended to put light onto less known facets, the role of Comte and the French philosophical tradition will be discussed (chapter 2), and also, besides Menger's fight with the German Historicists, his inheritance from previous German thinkers such as Hufeland (chapter 3, Karl Milford – Milford's works on Menger's methodology are well-known. Here, he presents a new insight with respect to Menger's predecessors). When dealing with authors more often quoted, such as Aristotle, the present volume seeks to set them into a new light, from the philosopher's point of view (chapter 4, Stephan Haltmayer).

A somewhat odd debate about Menger and British-style economic liberalism has been going on almost since the origins of the Austrian School. Its solution has long been embittered by political stands. Here, we mean to placate the issue and, in the second part, three contributions by Austrian researchers question usually accepted views on the topic. After reminders on the authors at stake and how Menger related to them (chapter 5, Mayerhofer), the analysis is pursued in depth based on Menger's writings and teachings (chapter 6, Peter Rosner) as well as the posterity of Adam Smith (chapter 7, Werner Wilke). In line with the general rule for this volume, original and clarifying remarks come from new material gathered. Some insights may undoubtedly raise more questions than the authors here have attempted to solve. In any case, the goal sought after is reached, that is to discuss the issue with available material at hand.

In the third part, aspects of the "theory of knowledge" that Menger dealt with are selected, each a major issue in present-day economic literature:

- The role played by psychology. In the incipient Austrian marginal school, the extent to which one may have adequately (or not) used the denomination "*Psychologenschule*" is much more than a matter of "words". Whether it is an overstatement, a misunderstanding, some strategic or rhetoric, or something else, it reveals the essence of the school (chapter 8, Campagnolo)
- The debate around ordinality or cardinality within Menger's framework. That opens up the issue of the compatibility between Neo-classic and "Austrian" frameworks (chapter 9, Pierre Livet)
- The place and nature of experimental methodology in Menger questions *a-priorism* within Menger's own works (an issue which is often discussed with regard to Menger's heirs gets here focused on the founder) (chapter 10, Aurélien Lordon and Marc Ohana)
- The debate about the theory of capital between Menger and Böhm-Bawerk is a tribute to a question that was never really solved: once it is said that they disagreed, how to account *accurately* for that matter? (chapter 11, Jean Magnan de Bornier).

At last, this Introduction will not be complete in this prelude without a few words about the main character in the play: Menger himself. If it may seem too much to call him a "*hero*" of his times (another *Held* for Vienna's *Heldenplatz*?), he has undoubtedly at least been a major player in the science and power games of the 1900 Imperial city.

Once again, our purpose is *not* to rehash Menger's biographical facts here.[5] In the following pages ending the Introduction, we will only briefly try to set the reader back within the environment of the thinker in his times. For that purpose only, suffice then to remind the reader of a few facts in the context in which Menger wrote his works, as well as regarding his own destiny.

Second of three brothers, Carl Menger became famous as a *Kameralwissenschaften* Professor at Vienna University, and then as the unanimously recognized founder of the "Austrian School of Economics" (as it was called later on). Yet, one must keep in mind that Menger was *also* a high civil-servant, a counsellor to the Government of one of the major European Empires and the private preceptor to the Crown-Prince Rudolf. Incidentally, he was also a fierce collector and a bibliophile, a brilliant reader of the Classics in the Humanities and a passionate lover of exotic travel-books. Although the Austro-Hungarian Habsburg Monarchy might have appeared ancient and decaying in the 1900's, there were hopes for renewal. Carl Menger was one of those brilliant restorers of hope in 1900 Vienna – before the final collapse came with the First World War.

Amidst innumerable artists (painters, musicians, poets, writers, all of whom changed their fields with visions lasting until today), scientists and inventors (from the most theoretical minds, like Boltzmann, to a genius like Tesla who had to go into exile to get recognition in the United States) as well as philosophers (Brentano, Mach among others) and "social scientists" (*Geisteswissenschaftler* – one of the most controversial being the "analyst" of the *psychè*, Sigmund Freud), the Menger brotherhood accordingly incarnated the chances and expectations of modernizing Austria in its own way. Max, the elder brother, was to become a successful *entrepreneur* and the leader of a section of the National-Liberal party at the Viennese Parliament, ceaselessly advocating the modernization of the economic structures of the Empire. Anton, the younger brother, was a Professor of jurisprudence at the Vienna University, and most famous throughout Europe for his book: *The Right to the Whole Produce of Labour* (*Das Recht auf den vollen Arbeitsertrag in geschichtlicher Darstellung*, 1886). He raised a large scientific debate about private property (which he condemned), fighting

---

[5] Among other biographies, the reader may here refer to numerous authors, among which, in English, the forgotten essay by Bloch, H, "Carl Menger: the founder of the Austrian School", *Journal of Political Economy*, 1940, 48, p. 428-433; the famous Introduction by Hayek to his reprint of the *Grundsätze*, in *Gesammelte Werke*, vol. 1, reprinted 1968, Mohr, Tübingen; also by famous later economist Hicks (with W. Weber), ed. *Carl Menger and the Austrian School of Economics*, Oxford, Clarendon Press, 1973.

against both the tenants of free-trade (*Freihändler*) and the Marxists. The book was translated in English by Herbert Foxwell (London, 1900), and in French by Alfred Bonnet (with an Introduction by the renowned philosopher Charles Andler: *Le droit au produit intégral du travail*, Paris, Giard & Brière, 1900).[6] The name of Menger evoked at least as much Anton as Carl to the educated public. All three brothers (Max was less known outside of Austria) were honoured and admired, but for very different stands and by different audiences. They illustrated the Vienna of 1900, where there were many possible paths towards the future in what was still the capital of an Empire, before its dismantling.

Vienna was not only the capital city of that Empire, but *the* main city of Central Europe, entitled to the phrase "*Paris of the Mitteleuropa*". At the same time, it was also said (in a proverbial stance that hints at the mixture of hopes and decay displayed there) that "Vienna's streets [were] more paved with theories than with asphalt"! Great expectations could be cherished in Vienna, but many of those chances were left by, gone away before they ever truly realized. To some extent, the same happened with Menger's works: the high civil-servant of the Empire and the willing founder of an indigenous school of pure political economy would see his dreams only partly realized before the whole structure of the Empire got crushed into the War. Carl Menger's own wish was to build a school of thought that would restore the science of economics in the direction of pure and solid theory to serve as a sound basis to expected implementations in the economic policies, in touch with the reality of the times.[7] Still; the historical parallel with the German Historical School displaying the German "special path" (*Sonderweg*) is fragile, because Menger's school was never dominant in the German-speaking countries. In his fight against Gustav Schmoller's anti-theoretical stand, Menger purposefully advocated theoretical works rather than monographs and compilation works. He laid the ground for the Austrian School of Economics in the 1880's in order to counterbalance the dominant position of the Historicist German School of Economics during the fight called *Methodenstreit*. But he could not achieve the same kind of influence the Germans had.

---

[6] Foxwell was the distinguished economist who succeeded Jevons in 1881 at the Political Economy Chair of University College in London. The English translation of Anton's book was reprinted in 1962 in New-York (Kelley Publishing House.). The English translation of Carl's 1871 *Grundsätze* would be translated as the *Principles of Economics* by Dingwall and Hoselitz for New York U. Press in 1950 and the *Untersuchungen* of 1883, by Nock in 1963 under the title *Problems of Economics and Sociology* (Urbana, U. of Illinois Press). Carl's main works would have to wait much longer for a translation in English… and, let us point out that there exists still none in French! (a French translation of Menger's *Untersuchungen* by the editor of this volume is forthcoming in 2008, one of the *Grundsätze* later).

[7] As gives proof his letter of March 19, 1903 (Wiener Staatsverwaltungsarchiv) to the *Kultusministerium* then in charge of Universities and high-level education, Menger intended to build a counterpart to the German School and counterbalance its influence in raising his claim to a science directed towards theoretical matters, and their practical implementations, rather than a "realistic-historical" approach. We shall come back on that matter.

Menger indeed paved the way for a modernized theory (Marginalism) and an analytical scientific framework in economics (a pure science of economics). In doing so, he contributed to the reform needed in science and to the birth of epistemology. The *Wiener Kreis* tried (but half a century later!) to solve some of the issues at stake with a radical proposal, the so-called in logical positivism. That cannot be understood properly without referring to Menger's dispute with the Historicists (the *Methodenstreit*). Further on, Menger's son, the mathematician Karl Menger opened new ways for modern analytical economics. But the son resolutely fought metaphysics. The father had paved the way – although not *against* philosophers. The son followed a different path with logical positivism in the 1920's. In the same years, his father's ideas got stressed through endeavours of disciples like Ludwig von Mises, whose seminar was next to Menger Jr.'s *Mathematisches Kolloquium* (again chapter 2, Campagnolo).

Political upheaval also explains that members of those circles then had to flee Europe and got scattered around the world. Exile was not only for people, but also for material and sources. The carefully gathered book collection of Menger Sr., his own *Library*, left Austria. It was sold by his widow in the 1920's (in order to survive Austrian misery and hyperinflation after the First World War). Exile was thus the fate of Menger's disciples and of his *Nachlass*. It was a miracle that they remained safe from the destructions many times during the travel (last but not least the Great Kanto earthquake that shook Tokyo in 1923). During World Wars and the rise of totalitarianism (Stalinism, Fascism, and Nazism), academic circles were indeed among the first to feel the consequences in the 1930's. A major one, due to hostile politics or troublesome unrest, was the migration and exile of scientists and of Austrian economists.[8] The Vienna of the scientists disappeared twice with the World Wars…

As exile also brought oblivion, Mengerian views remained unpopular until, in the 1970's, Friedrich Hayek won the Prize for economics in the Honor of Alfred Nobel by the Bank of Sweden (1974) and a handful of Misesians in the United States attracted renewed attention at the occasion of a successful Congress in South Royalton. That brought back interest for Menger's works and topics related to them. Yet, Menger was regarded only as a starting-point, and not always studied for his own sake. In this volume, we shall not venture besides discussing Menger. Our work is thus also intended as a tribute.

---

[8] Career goals were also influential in such a context – for instance, going to the *London School of Economics*, for instance, was for some Austrians the best self-promotion About Friedrich Hayek in *LSE* upon the invitation of Lionel Robbins, see chapter 2 of this volume. The reference dictionary in that respect is: Hagemann, Harald & Krohn, Claus-Dieter (eds), (with H.U. Eßlinger), *Biographisches Handbuch der deustchsprachigen wirtschaftswissenschaftlichen Emigration nach 1933* (Biographical Handbook of the Emigration of German-speaking Economists, post 1933), 2 vols. Munich, Saur Verlag, 1999.

Those reminders about our focus character being said, let us add to conclude that the contributors to the present volume were called upon their expertise to enter debates that are "hot" at the present time, and not for any position they may take.

Also, there exists no guarantee that those debates would still be the same in years from now (except that they were already discussed in years past). They deserve all the more attention here as they are based on new investigations. No purpose of exhaustiveness is aimed at. Nor is there any intent of being "final" on approached topics. As the Editor, I insisted that each and every statement made in the following pages be based upon some piece of probing material. "Where there is no evidence, make no statement" was the motto given to contributors, and the warning kept in mind when discussing texts and preparatory versions. Whether we have followed that path thoroughly enough is up to the reader to decide – but the ideal regulating research was always in that line.

More specifically, it seemed to us that commentators are too often tempted to say that they provide their readership with path-breaking news... In the present volume, contributors were simply asked to systematically call upon arguments that can be proven and that may be counterchecked with the relevant documentation, provided that material looked at is as *complete* as possible. That implied to refrain from excess of enthusiasm. It was good to placate issues. It was also a condition to boldly face the fact that we know some things for certain, while acknowledging that others we cannot know. Such caution seemed to the Editor the price for all the more useful contributions.

It is reassuring to note that our caution echoes the motto of neutrality and seriousness in scientific work that was Menger's own. Even more than other major characters in HET, Menger is often deemed to be "hot" matter. We hope we could placate the debate, but also fuel it with sound arguments. More generally speaking, dealing with economics appeared as not enough: *philosophy* of science was at stake. One more proof of the importance of Menger lies precisely in the fact that he discussed *economics and the philosophy of economics*. It is impossible to "do" the one without acknowledging the other. Contemporary commentaries upon Menger must be done in that spirit and by calling upon Archives systematically. It is up to the reader to judge whether we were up to the task.

I.
Carl Menger:
Leben, Werke und *Nachlass* /
Life, works and source materials

Einleitung zu Carl Menger

Herta Mayerhofer

Carl Menger (1840 – 1921) entwickelte seine subjektive Wertlehre während eines Zeitraumes wirtschaftlichen Aufschwungs, der mit dem Begriff „Gründerzeit" bezeichnet wird. Diese Periode dauerte in Österreich von 1850 bis zum Ausbruch des ersten Weltkrieges im Jahr 1914.

Nach der gescheiterten Märzrevolution von 1848 wurde Wien unter der Regentschaft von Kaiser Franz Josef als Haupt- und Residenzstadt zum wirtschaftlichen und kulturellen Mittelpunkt der Monarchie. Durch den Einsatz neuer Produktionstechniken setzte um 1850 eine verstärkte Industrialisierung, besonders im Großraum Wien, in der Obersteiermark, Vorarlberg und den Sudetenländern ein. Der Ausbau von Eisenbahnlinien erleichterte die Verbindung zwischen den Länden der österreichisch-ungarischen Monarchie und eine Anbindung an die Verwaltungsmetropole Wien. Die alte Stadtmauer rund um Wien wurde geschleift und durch die Ringstraße ersetzt, die mit Prachtbauten in unterschiedlichen Stilen ausgestattet wurde. Durch die Eingemeindung der bisher außerhalb der Stadtmauer liegenden Vorstädte und den Zuzug von hunderttausenden Arbeitskräften, besonders aus Böhmen und Mähren, wurde Wien zur sechstgrößten Millionenstadt der Welt.

Handel und Gewerbe erlebten ein Zeitalter der Blüte, das Bürgertum erlebte einen politischen Aufstieg und setzte dadurch seine liberalen Ideale durch. Vor 1871, dem Jahr als Carl Menger sein erstes Hauptwerk veröffentlichte, gab es im österreichischen Wirtschaftsleben noch keine Beschränkung der unternehmerischen Tätigkeit, es herrschte die von den Klassikern der Nationalökonomie empfohlene vollkommene Konkurrenz. Die Bauern mussten noch nicht mit Schutzzöllen geschützt werden, die Unternehmer hatten sich noch nicht in Kartellen zusammengeschlossen, die Arbeiter noch nicht in Gewerkschaften organisiert. Noch war es nicht nötig, persönliche Interessen gemeinsam zu vertreten und gegenüber der „Gegenseite" abzusichern.[9]

Auf dem Gebiet des Bildungs- und Hochschulwesens trafen sich die Interessen von Staat und Bürgertum. Nach der Aufhebung lokaler Feudalprivilegien übernahm ein zentralisierter Verwaltungsapparat die vakant gewordenen Rechte

---

[9] Der erste Höhepunkt des mit viel Optimismus verbundenen Liberalismus fand in Österreich mit dem Börsekrach 1873 seinen Abschluss. Es folgte eine wirtschaftliche Depression, der man mit Sozialpolitik und einer dirigistischen Wirtschaftspolitik zugunsten des Bauerntums und Kleingewerbes zu begegnen suchte. Gegen die Jahrhundertwende setzte durch die Entwicklung des Maschinenbaus, der chemischen Industrie und der Elektronik erneut eine Epoche des wirtschaftlichen und kulturellen Aufschwungs ein. Dieser Zeitraum war allerdings politisch durch die Separationsbestrebungen der einzelnen Völker der Habsburgermonarchie und kulturell durch ein mit einem unbestimmten Weltschmerz verbundenen Lebensgefühl gekennzeichnet: das Fin de siècle und mit ihm der Untergang einer Epoche zeichneten sich ab.

und Befugnisse. Dazu wurde ein gut geschultes Fach-Beamtentum notwendig, das von den Vertretern des Bürgertums erstellt wurde. Von den im Staatsdienst tätigen Beamten erwartete man rechtliche und wirtschaftliche Erneuerungen, freilich in einem vom Kaiser bestimmten Rahmen. Zu Beginn der 1850er Jahre erfolgte eine Schul- und Universitäts-Reform, durch welche die vorher getrennten Bereiche Lehre und Forschung vereinigt wurden. Die universitäre Lehre erlangte auf diese Weise immer mehr Unabhängigkeit vom bürokratischen Bewertungsschema. Die Wiener Universität versammelte 43% der Hörerschaft der Monarchie, wodurch sie einen entscheidenden Einfluss auf die Entwicklung der Lehre an den anderen Universitäten der Monarchie gewann.

Carl Menger habilitierte sich 1872 mit seiner Schrift *Grundsätze der Volkswirtschaftslehre* an der Rechts- und Staatswissenschaftlichen Fakultät der Wiener Universität und wurde nach der Approbation seiner Schrift Privatdozent für Politische Ökonomie. Im Jahr 1873 wurde er sowohl zum Ministerialsekretär im kaiserlich-königlichen Ministerialpräsidium als auch zum außerordentlichen Professor an der Wiener Universität ernannt. Zwei Jahre später beendete er allerdings seine Beamtenlaufbahn, um seine volle Arbeitskraft der Forschung widmen zu können. Bereits 1879 erlangte er den Rang eines ordentlichen Professors und war damit der erste österreichische Professor, der einen Lehrstuhl für Politische Ökonomie innehatte.

In der Zeit, als sich Menger wissenschaftlich mit wirtschaftlichen Fragen zu beschäftigen begann, hatte die klassische Nationalökonomie in der von John Stuart Mill entwickelten Form ein in sich geschlossenes Theoriengebäude erstellt. Menger sollte einen entscheidenden Beitrag dazu leisten, Grundthesen dieses Systems in Frage zu stellen.[10] Bereits vor dem Abfassen seiner Habilitationsschrift war Menger als Wissenschaftsjournalist tätig und machte dabei Beobachtungen, die ihn an der Richtigkeit der zu seiner Zeit üblichen wissenschaftlichen Preistheorien zweifeln ließen. Immer wieder musste er feststellen, wie Theorie und Praxis diametral auseinander fielen: wollte man als Unternehmer Erfolg haben, musste man sich seinem eigenen Gespür und seiner Erfahrung anvertrauen und den gängigen Preistheorien misstrauen. Außerdem präsentierten sich die aus dem Kostenprinzip der klassischen Nationalökonomie entwickelten

---

[10] Drei bedeutende Strömungen meldeten – weil durch die wirtschaftliche und soziale Entwicklung die Mängel der klassischen Theorie immer deutlicher erkennbar wurden – berechtigte Zweifel an der von der klassischen Theorie beanspruchten Lösungskompetenz an: der Marxismus, der Historismus und die Grenzwerttheorie. Während der Marxismus das Theoriengebäude der klassischen Ökonomie uminterpretierte und für seinen Kampf gegen die kapitalistische Marktwirtschaft in Anspruch nahm, lehnte der Historismus jede aus Prinzipien entspringende deduktive Methode ab und suchte wirtschaftliche Phänomene deskriptiv zu erfassen. Die Grenznutzenschule, der Menger als einer der drei Gründungsväter angehört, suchte ebenso wie die klassische Ökonomie, allerdings unter anderen Voraussetzungen, eine umfassende Theorie zu entfalten, um daraus relevante Anweisungen für die wirtschaftliche Praxis zu gewinnen.

Preistheorien so unterschiedlich, dass sich die Zweifel an der Gültigkeit an dem Prinzip, aus dem diese deduziert wurden, immer mehr verstärkten.

Um dem Problem der Preisgestaltung auf die Spur zu kommen, beschloss Menger, das von den Klassikern gelehrte Prinzip der Produktionskosten beiseite zu lassen und seine Aufmerksamkeit auf die Veränderung der Nachfrage zu richten. Dabei stellte er sich die Frage, durch welche Fakten ein Mensch dazu veranlasst werde, ein bestimmtes Produkt zu wählen und sein Geld für dessen Erwerb auszugeben. Da Menger erkannte, dass bei Wissenschaftern und Praktikern der Wunsch nach einer einheitlichen Preistheorie, aus der alle Preiserscheinungen erklärt werden konnte, immer dringlicher wurde, sah er seine Aufgabe als Nationalökonom darin, eine einheitliche Theorie zu entwickeln, die der Forderung nach Vollständigkeit, Einheitlichkeit und Praxis-Relevanz standhalten konnte.

Damit wurde Carl Menger zum Gründungsvater der „Österreichischen Schule der Nationalökonomie“, die die Volkswirtschaft unter einem neuen, bisher nicht beachteten Aspekt betrachtete: aus der Sicht des „wirtschaftenden Subjekts“, wie Menger den für seine materiellen Bedürfnisse sorgenden Menschen nennt. Im Gegensatz zur klassischen Volkswirtschaftslehre rückt mit den Bedürfnissen des Menschen ein subjektives Element auf den Platz, den in der als objektiv verstandenen Werttheorie die Arbeits- bzw. Produktionskosten eingenommen hatten. Freilich bildete sich die von Menger gegründete „Österreichische Schule der Nationalökonomie“ nicht spontan, sondern baute auf einem bereits von anderen Wissenschaftern errichteten Fundament auf. Während der Studienzeit Mengers an der Wiener Universität wurde die Volkswirtschaftslehre noch nicht als eigener Lehrgegenstand vorgetragen, sondern im Rahmen der Rechtswissenschaften gelehrt.

Der seit 1821 an der Wiener Universität lehrende Professor der Rechts- und Staatswissenschaften Joseph Ritter von Kudler hatte 1846 ein volkswirtschaftliches Werk mit dem Titel *Die Grundlehren der Volkswirtschaft* verfasst. Mit diesem Werk suchte Kudler die österreichische Volkswirtschaft, die noch unter dem Einfluss des Merkantilismus stand, zu reformieren und an die Regeln der klassischen liberalen Nationalökonomie in der Tradition Smiths, Ricardos und Mills anzupassen. Mit seinem Werk beabsichtigte Kudler, der bereits durch seinen Vorgänger im Lehramte, Joseph von Sonnenfels, empfohlenen „Wohlstands-Politik“ durch die Ausarbeitung einer theoretischen Volkswirtschaftslehre ein solides theoretisches Fundament zu errichten. Mit der Widmung „Seiner kaiserlichen Hoheit“, die dem österreichischen Erzherzog Wilhelm zugeeignet ist, warb Kudler um Beachtung seiner Vorschläge beim österreichischen Hof. Kudler unterscheidet drei moderne Wirtschaftssysteme: das Merkantil-System, das Physiokratische System und das System Adam Smiths. Gemeinsam mit Smith spricht sich Kudler gegen den Merkantilismus und dessen Prohibitiv-System aus. Ebenso wie Smith ist Kudler davon überzeugt, dass alle wirtschaftlichen Tätigkeiten, nicht nur die Produktion in der Landwirtschaft, Werte schaffen. Die Arbeit bilde das grundlegende Element für den Wert eines Gutes. Alle wirtschaftlichen Prozesse, die auf Arbeit basieren, wie die Erzeugung von Rohstoffen, deren Verarbeitung und Umgestaltung, sowie der Handel mit den fertigen Produkten, seien an der Schöpfung von Werten beteiligt. Obwohl Kudler an der Kosten- und Arbeitswerttheorie der klassischen Volkswirtschaftslehre festhält, richtet er bereits sein Augenmerk auf die Bedeutung der menschlichen Bedürfnisse im Zusammenhang mit dem Wirtschaftssystem. Er betont, wie sehr die Nützlichkeit eines Gutes in seiner Funktion für die Bedürfnisbefriedigung des Menschen die Festsetzung des Tauschwertes mitbestimme (Grundlehren S. 43ff.). Damit schafft sich bereits eine bemerkenswerte Abweichung von der bisher gelehrten Werttheorie der klassischen Nationalökonomie Raum: ein subjektiver Faktor beeinflusst den bisher als objektiv betrachteten Wert eines Gutes. Menger hatte Anfang der 1860er Jahre Kudlers Buch gelesen und das oben erwähnte Kapitel über den Tauschwert – allerdings ohne Kommentar – exzerpiert.

Erst die Überlegungen von Karl Heinrich Rau, eines in Heidelberg lehrenden Professors, veranlassten Menger zu selbständigen Kommentaren. Rau, ein zu seiner Zeit sehr bekannter und geschätzter Professor, hatte 1826 ein *Lehrbuch der politischen Ökonomie* verfasst, dessen erster Band den Titel *Grundsätze der Volkswirtschaftslehre* trägt. Carl Menger hatte 1864 ein 1863 in siebenter Auflage in Leipzig und Heidelberg erschienenes Exemplar erworben. Carl Mengers Studienexemplar befindet sich in „Mengers Bibliothek“ auf der Hitotsubashi Universität in Tokio, wohin Mengers bedeutender Bücherbestand 1923 nach dem Verkauf durch seine Witwe gelangt war. Zahlreiche Unterstreichungen und handschriftliche Notizen an den Rändern des Exemplars, die nahezu auf jeder Seite von Menger angebracht worden waren, geben uns die Möglichkeit, Mengers Gedanken zu verfolgen, die später in der Ausarbeitung seiner eigenen Theorie einen Abschluss gefunden haben. Emil Kauder unterzog sich im Auftrag der japanischen Hitotsubashi Universität, wo sich das Exemplar Raus mit den Anmerkungen Mengers befindet, der Mühe, die Anmerkungen zu entziffern, in einem Sammelband „Carl Mengers erster Entwurf zu seinem Hauptwerk *Grundsätze*“ zusammenzustellen und 1963 der Öffentlichkeit zugänglich zu machen. Im so genannten „ersten Entwurf“ finden sich – freilich noch nicht ausgearbeitet – bereits alle Überlegungen, die Menger in seinem Hauptwerk der klassischen Volkswirtschaftslehre entgegenhalten wird. Besonders interessant sind die Vermerke (S. 70 in der Ausgabe Raus, S. 29 in der Veröffentlichung Kauders), wo Menger eindeutig zu Raus Werttheorie Stellung nimmt. Er verwirft diese aus dem Grund, weil darin der individuelle Wert keinen Platz findet.[11] Immer wieder

[11] Menger merkt an: „Da Rau die folgenden Sätze vollständig verkennt, so ist seine ganze Darstellung wertlos: a) Es gibt nur einen individuellen Wert [...] b) Dieser ist nicht messbar [...] c) Die Messung dadurch dass man diesen Wert in Relation zu anderen bringt ist höchst unvollkommen [...] Rau hat vom individuellen Wert keine Ahnung. Allerdings kann das

bringt Menger seine Interpretation des Wertes zum Ausdruck und wendet sich entschieden dagegen, den Wert als ein Maß aufzufassen: „Er [sc. der Wert] ist nur ein Verhältnis, nicht aber ein Mass." (S. 70 Rau/ S. 29 Kauder.) „Übrigens ist der Wert nur das Gefühl der Abhängigkeit der Bedürfnisbefriedigung von einem Gute." (S. 86 Rau/ S. 40 Kauder.) „Rau behandelt den Wert wie etwas Körperliches." (S. 87 Rau/ S. 41 Kauder.) Menger erkennt, dass der Wert eines Gutes außer dem individuellen Ermessen davon abhängig ist, welches Quantum zu einem bestimmten Zeitpunkt dem Menschen zur Deckung seines individuell unterschiedlichen Bedarfs jeweils zur Verfügung steht:

> „Auch richtet sich die Wertschätzung nach dem Verhältnis des Quantums zum Bedarf und ist in jedem Zeitpunkt und bei jedem Menschen eine andere, wenn auch das Gut das nämliche ist." (S. 71 Rau/ S. 30 Kauder.)

Wert dient Menger als gemeinsamer Oberbegriff für Produktionsmittel und Konsumgut: „Wert ist Wert. Im Wert einigen sich Erzeugungsmittel und Genussmittel zu einer Gruppe." (S. 72 Rau/ S. 30 Kauder.) Menger sieht in der Volkswirtschaft das organische Zusammenwirken von Privatwirtschaften: „Es ist ein grober Fehler die Volkswirtschaft als etwas anderes als einen Organismus von Privatwirtschaften anzusehen." (S. 81 Rau/ S. 38 Kauder.) Aus den Randbemerkungen geht bereits Mengers Auffassung vom Menschen hervor, an der er in seinen eigenen Schriften festhalten wird:

> „Das Ziel der Menschen ist darauf gerichtet, ihren Zustand in wirthschaftlicher Hinsicht zu erhalten, wo möglich zu verbessern. Dazu sind Hilfsmittel, Erhaltung, Vermehrung nötig (Capital)." (S. 92 Rau/ S. 45 Kauder.)

Im Vorwort zu seinem 1871 in erster Auflage erschienen Hauptwerk, das er als Habilitationsschrift eingereicht hatte, *Grundsätze der Volkswirtschaftslehre* betont Menger, dass die „Reform der höchsten Prinzipien unserer Wissenschaft", welche er durch sein Werk anstrebe, nicht nur sein eigenes Verdienst sei, sondern auf der Grundlage aufbaue, „welche fast ausnahmslos deutscher Forschergeist geschaffen hat" (1871 S. X). Menger bezeichnet sich selbst als „Mitstrebenden aus Österreich". Um seine Wertschätzung der deutschen Tradition der Nationalökonomie zum Ausdruck zu bringen, widmete er sein Werk „in achtungsvoller Verehrung" dem „königlich sächsischen Hofrathe Dr. Wilhelm Roscher, Professor der Staats- und Cameralwissenschaften an der Universität Leipzig etc.". Den Mitgliedern der Tradition, der sich Menger verpflichtet sah, war das Anliegen gemeinsam, die Grundsätze der klassischen Volkswirtschaftslehre in Frage zu stellen. Der Münchner Friedrich Hermann hatte bereits in seinem 1832 erschienenen Werk „Staatswirthschaftliche Untersuchungen" den engli-

---

Mass eines Wertes nur in Beziehung zu einem anderen Gut bestehen, da wir den individuellen Wert zu messen noch nicht gelernt haben." Der Aufgabe, nach einer Darstellung des individuellen Wertes zu suchen, wird sich Menger in seinem Hauptwerk stellen.

schen Klassikern insofern widersprochen, dass er nicht die nachfrageunabhängigen Kosten, sondern die nutzenorientierte Nachfrage des Käufers und dessen Zahlungsfähigkeit als bestimmend für die Preisgestaltung erklärte. In den Fußnoten seiner „Grundsätze“ zitiert Menger häufig außer Wilhelm Roscher seinen eigenen Vorgänger auf dem Wiener Lehrstuhl, den Schwaben Albert Schäffle. Beide Professoren hatten bereits stichhaltige Einwände gegen die englische Nationalökonomie vorgebracht, die Menger in sein Denken aufnahm. Roscher verwirft jeden objektiven Maßstab für die Bestimmung des Wertes eines Gutes, für ihn ist die menschliche Psyche die Quelle aller Werte. Der Wert habe keinen vom menschlichen Bewusstsein getrennten Status, das menschliche Bewusstsein setze die Güter untereinander in Beziehung und erteile ihnen einen dem Relationsgefüge entsprechenden Wert.

Obwohl bereits – wie oben ausgeführt – andere Ökonomen das klassische Kostenprinzip abgelehnt hatten, kommt Carl Menger das Verdienst zu, die Kritik an diesem Prinzip konsequent und auf nachvollziehbare Argumente gestützt zu betreiben. Durch ihn wird die von deutschen Ökonomen geschaffene Grundlage erweitert und zu einem System ausgebaut. Wie er uns im Vorwort seines Werkes berichtet, stellt er sich die Aufgabe, „alle Preiserscheinungen (somit auch den Kapitalzins, den Arbeitslohn, den Grundzins u.s.f.) unter einem einheitlichen Gesichtspunkt zusammenzufassen“ (1871 S. X). Um dies zu erreichen, will er sich der Methode bedienen, komplexe Erscheinungen des Wirtschaftslebens auf „ihre einfachsten, der sicheren Beobachtung noch zugänglichen Elementen zurückzuführen“, um dann die Gesetze zu entwickeln, nach welchen sich aus den einfachen Elementen komplexe ökonomische Prozesse „gesetzmäßig“ entwickeln (1871 S. VII). Mit diesem Ansatz fordert Menger – im Gegensatz zu der damaligen Volkswirtschaftslehre – eine empirische Grundlegung einer wissenschaftlichen Preistheorie. Das Ziel seiner wissenschaftlichen Tätigkeit sieht er darin, wichtige Aufschlüsse über wirtschaftliche Vorgänge zu gewinnen, die vorher nicht analysiert und erklärt werden konnten.

Mengers *Grundsätze* enthalten acht Kapitel, wobei die Kapitel zwei bis sieben seine neu entwickelten Thesen enthalten. Nach einem Einführungskapitel unterbreitet uns Menger in den Kapiteln zwei und drei seine Überlegungen über den menschlichen Bedarf und dessen Zusammenhang mit dem Wert der Güter, im Kapitel vier erläutert er die Motive und Faktoren, die für den Austausch von Wirtschaftsgütern relevant sind. Daraus ergibt sich die Frage nach dem Preis, der bei einem Güteraustausch eine entscheidende, bei Menger allerdings nicht die ausschlaggebende Rolle spielt. Das Kapitel fünf enthält die Lehre vom Preis, wobei die Preisbildung bei „isoliertem Tausch“ (zwischen zwei wirtschaftenden Subjekten ohne Einflussnahme durch Dritte), im Monopolhandel und bei beidseitiger Konkurrenz behandelt wird. Im Kapitel sechs entfaltet Menger seine Interpretation von Gebrauchswert und Tauschwert eines Gutes, Kapitel sieben handelt über die Ware. In den bisher genannten Kapiteln legt Menger seine zur

Tradition des Liberalismus in Widerspruch stehende Ansichten über den individuellen Wert eines Gutes und dessen Auswirkung auf die Volkswirtschaft dar. Kapitel acht enthält die Lehre vom Geld, worin sich Menger zwar noch der metallistischen Auffassung anschließt, aber bereits die Grundlage für eine neue Interpretation legt.

Gemäß seiner im Vorwort angekündigten Methode geht Menger von einfachen Elementen aus, um dann zu zeigen, wie sich komplexe Phänomene daraus entwickeln. Als einfaches Element gilt Menger die Erfahrung, dass jeder Mensch Güter braucht, um damit die Aufrechterhaltung seines Lebens zu sichern. Menger klassifiziert die Güter in ihrem Zusammenhang mit der Befriedigung menschlicher Bedürfnisse: „Güter erster Ordnung" finden für die unmittelbare Bedürfnisbefriedigung des Menschen Verwendung (1871 S. 8). Alle Mittel, die zur Herstellung der Güter erster Ordnung, der Konsumgüter, erforderlich sind, wie Rohstoffe, Zwischenprodukte und Arbeitsleistungen, zählt Menger zu der Gruppe der „Güter zweiter Ordnung". Darüber hinaus gibt es „Güter dritter [und weiterer] Ordnung", wie zum Beispiel Getreideäcker, die ebenfalls, wenn auch nicht mittelbar, zur Befriedigung menschlicher Bedürfnisse dienen. Mit „nicht-ökonomischen" Gütern, wie Luft und Licht, beschäftigte sich (zur Zeit Mengers) die Wirtschaft nicht (1871 S. 53f.). Die Erfahrung lehrt uns, dass die Güter, die zur Bedürfnisbefriedigung notwendig sind, knapp sind. Um an diese Güter in für uns zufrieden stellendem Ausmaß heranzukommen, ist wohlüberlegtes, „ökonomisches" Handeln erforderlich. Die Gesamtheit der von den Menschen ausgeführten Handlungsweisen, die dahin zielen, ihre mittelbaren und unmittelbaren Bedürfnisse mittels wirtschaftlicher Güter zu decken, bezeichnen wir mit „Wirtschaft".

Wie bereits in den oben erwähnten Randbemerkungen im Exemplar Raus betont Menger seine Auffassung vom individuellen Wert eines Gutes. Diesmal präzisiert er:

> „Derselbe [sc. der Wert] ist ein Urtheil, welches die wirtschaftenden Menschen über die Bedeutung der in ihrer Verfügung befindlichen Güter für die Aufrechterhaltung ihres Lebens und ihrer Wohlfahrt fällen, und demnach außerhalb des Bewusstseins derselben nicht vorhanden." (1871 S. 86)[12]

Bei der Erstellung seiner bekannt gewordenen Bedürfnisskala (1871 S. 93, 1923 S. 123) orientiert sich Menger an den menschlichen Bedürfnissen nach „Erhaltung des Lebens" und nach dem Streben des Menschen nach einem natürlichen und angenehmen Dasein. Beide Werte werden bereits in der Aristotelischen Ethik als zentrale Werte bestimmt. Menger unterteilt die menschlichen Bedürfnis-

[12] Hier zeigt Menger besonders deutlich den Zusammenhang des Güterwertes mit dem menschlichen Bewusstsein auf. Ähnlich lautende Bestimmungen finden sich auf den Seiten 2, 3, 10 und 81 der „Grundsätze".

se in zehn Gruppen, die der Bedürfnisbefriedigung dienenden Güter in Einheiten. Danach untersucht er, bei welcher Einheit eines Gutes sich für den Menschen noch Nutzen einstellt, und wo die Grenze liegt, bei deren Überschreitung eine weitere Einheit desselben Gutes keinen individuellen Nutzen mehr erbringt.

Im Jahr 1923 wurden Carl Mengers „Grundsätze" postum von seinem Sohn Karl in der zweiten, auf den doppelten Inhalt erweiterten, Auflage herausgegeben. Wie uns Menger jun. im Vorwort des Herausgebers berichtet, fand er im Nachlass seines Vaters nicht nur das dritte Kapitel „Über das Maß der menschlichen Bedürfnisse und der Güter", sondern auch große Teile der Wertlehre und die Kapitel sechs bis neun („Die Lehre vom Tausche, Die Lehre vom Preise, Die Lehre von der Ware, Die Lehre vom Gelde") in druckfertiger Form vor. Alle anderen Teile lagen fragmentarisch vor und wurden hinsichtlich der Wahrung des von seinem Vater gewünschten systematischen Charakters aus den übrigen nachgelassenen Schriften ausgewählt und in die druckreif vorliegenden Teile eingegliedert (1923 S. X).

Mengers 1871 vertretene Theorie fand in Deutschland zunächst wenig Aufnahme[13]. Um seine eigene Methode zu rechtfertigen, veröffentlichte Menger 1883 sein zweites, umfangreiches Werk unter dem Titel „Untersuchungen über die Methode der Socialwissenschaften und der Politischen Ökonomie insbesondere". Darin übt er an der Methode der älteren und der jüngeren historischen Schule der Volkswirtschaftslehre Kritik und stellt der von ihm beanstandeten Methode dieser Schulen seine eigene Systematik gegenüber, die auf der Grundlage des „methodischen Individualismus" beruht. Dieses Werk wurde besonders von Schmoller („Jüngere Historische Schule") kritisiert, die daraus resultierende heftige Kontroverse ging unter dem Titel „Methodenstreit" in die Geschichte der Wirtschaftswissenschaften ein. Mengers Schule erhielt die Bezeichnung „Österreichische Schule", die die lokale Beschränktheit seiner Thesen zum Ausdruck bringen sollte. Trotz der Anfeindung von deutscher Seite gelang es Menger, zusammen mit den Arbeiten von Léon Walras und Stanley Jevons, die fast zur gleichen Zeit fertig gestellt wurden, eine neue Bestimmung des wirtschaftlichen Wertes zu entwickeln. Alle drei Wissenschafter entdeckten die marginalistische Methode, die Grenzwertmethode, die um den subjektiven Nutzwert eines Gutes zentriert ist.[14] Allerdings war es Menger noch nicht möglich, eine seinen eige-

[13] Die „Historische Schule" (die ältere historische Schule wird hauptsächlich von W. Roscher, die jüngere von G. Schmoller vertreten) in Deutschland hatte sich von den herkömmlichen Methoden des wirtschaftlichen Liberalismus abgewandt und suchte durch Anwendung einer historisch deskriptiven Methode die Wirtschaft in den Zusammenhang einer Volksgemeinschaft zu stellen. Mengers abstrakt-deduktive Methode stellt in der Sicht dieser Schule lediglich eine Analyse traditioneller Begriffe wie Gut, Wert, Tausch, Preis und Geld dar.

[14] Der Ausdruck „Grenzwertschule" stammt von Mengers Schüler Friedrich v. Wieser; sie umfasst drei Richtungen: 1. die Österreichische Schule: Carl Menger, E. von Böhm-Bawerk, F. v. Wieser, J.A. Schumpeter, 2. die Lausanner Schule: Léon Walras, V. Pareto, E. Barone,

nen Theorien gemäße Geldwerttheorie zu entwickeln. Erst Mengers Schüler, unter ihnen Ludwig von Mises, bedienen sich des von ihrem Lehrer entwickelten Gesetzes des subjektiven Güterwertes und des Grenznutzens und vereinigen die Theorie des Geldes mit der Grenznutzentheorie.

Wenn auch seit dem wissenschaftlichen Wirken Mengers zahlreiche andere Volkswirtschaftslehren entwickelt worden sind, kann der von ihm entwickelte Aspekt hinsichtlich der Bedürfnisse und der Wertzuschreibung durch den Konsumenten aus den nationalökonomischen Überlegungen nicht mehr ausgeklammert werden. Aufgrund der Thesen Carl Mengers muss die Nationalökonomie der subjektiven Interpretation der Umwelt durch das Individuum und dessen Reaktion darauf Rechnung tragen, um gültige Aussagen machen zu können. Auch wenn dies expressis verbis nicht immer betont wird, findet Mengers Leistung in allen modernen Volkswirtschaftstheorien ihren Ausdruck.

M. Pantaleoni, 3. die Angloamerikanische Schule: W.S. Jevons, A. Marshall, F.Y. Edgeworth, J.B. Clark. Alle drei Schulen werden der „Neoklassik“ zugerechnet.

Carl Menger: from the works published in Vienna to his *Nachlass*

Gilles Campagnolo

The context in which Menger elaborated his works was reminded to the reader in the previous chapter. It was also shown that, in order to have a thorough knowledge of Menger's ideas, one must not only read his published works but also retrace the destiny of his archives (*Nachlass*). What was their fate? How did it influence the knowledge we have of the thinker's ideas? Those are the issues to deal with now. Our perspective in the following chapter is not only historical. What counts more is the accuracy of the inquiry, but also the questioning of the methodology used in our approach of the past. It is not only some kind of "archeology of thought" *à la Foucault* that is required here, but also the demonstration that hot-button present-day debates shall get light from discussing changes that were operated in the theory thanks to Menger's works published in Vienna, but also now that his *Nachlass* is made available today. To rediscover little known (or downright unknown) points is not only exciting, it is a facet constitutive of a serious commentator's task. The fate of archives is thus of major significance for theory itself, how it was built and how it is still in use.

Upon examination, one might say that if most step-stones of Austrian economics philology have first been carved in Europe, not only in Vienna but in the capitals of *Mitteleuropa* (like in Prague, for instance), hidden parts of that intellectual construction have also disappeared from its heritage in the course of the turmoil of the 20th century. Some traces remain though, but far from Europe. From recalling the origins of the evolution followed since then, one may wish to reconsider the *distortion* of the original facts and ideas in Menger's theory. Menger could have been read otherwise by his inheritors, if only some papers of his that were left aside could have been used. We shall not imagine a fictitious history of what was not the case, but we shall rather leave the issue open, showing that commentators could have displayed more interest in the task that is today made possible by work on archives – for the material does still exist! that was just not of easy access. Nonetheless a few scholars unearthed them. We shall point out at some examples regarding what can be done with archives. In order to measure the extent of the shift between Menger's original thought in the earlier works, and later interpretations, the best tool at our disposal remains such written documents. What has then Menger fortunately left us?

The answer is as follows: manuscripts, handwritten annotations on the volumes he owned, as well as upon his own books. If all that had disappeared from the sight of scholars for quite a long time – as well as from the bibliographies of most of their works, especially in the texts published in English, a reason is that Menger's documents were "exported" from Europe and thus quite difficult to gather until recently: the *Menger's Papers* are for the most part located in Japan (roughly for two-thirds of it, at the University of Hitotsubashi),[15] and in the U.S.A. (Perkins Library, Duke University, North Carolina, for the last one-third, with the papers of Menger's son, the mathematician Karl Menger).[16] Ironically, there is almost nothing left in Europe, but for administrative papers (such as Menger's attendance sheets in the University of Vienna).[17]

Those foreign archives are very rich, and it is all the more a pity that they had so long been left in oblivion, especially by the alleged heirs of Menger. Before us, they had been examined in detail only by historian of marginal utility Emil Kauder (himself in exile from Austria to Illinois), who rediscovered them in 1959! Menger had written down many lengthy annotations on the books he owned as well as on his own copies of his works, especially his master-copy of his 1871 *Grundsätze der Volkswirtschaftslehre* (*Principles of Economics*). The copy sent to him by his publisher, Wilhelm Braumüller, thus bears remarks and comments of great value to scholars if those are willing not just merely to quote their existence, but to search them closely and at length.

From a purely historical point of view, it can also be stressed that it was in his own private Library room that Menger held his *Privatseminar* which Böhm-Bawerk, Wieser, Neurath, etc. attended. The books that were there at hand for use are the ones annotated and available in the collection in Japan. Although notes seem to be only due to Menger, their abundance really allows considering some "work-in-progress", as it can rarely be seen. In the case of the founder of a major stream of economic thought, those notes, excerpts, etc. certainly acquire a major importance. For that purpose, it is indispensable to work, as we have done, on first-hand material. Having conscientiously examined them on location for almost two years, I could here raise (and answer) a few questions about the consequences of their absence in "Austrian Studies": what did in fact belong to Menger Sr. and what to his heirs? We shall begin with his own son, the mathematician Karl Menger and mention, besides, those who claimed to be faithful disciples, like Friedrich Hayek and Ludwig Mises, as well as later less known characters. How could many aspects, originated in the heart of Europe, Vienna, be understood in the light of later emigration, in particular to the USA?

---

[15] That material left Vienna for Japan on the year following the death of the Viennese Professor and academics that made the trip are scarce. Emil Kauder did so during two stays at the Archives Center in 1959 and 1960. We were on location for a longer period (from October 1997 to May 1999) made possible by a Research grant from the *Monbusho* Japanese Ministry for Research, handling thus a lengthier study of those until now unpublished papers, and of a number of volumes Menger had read.

[16] To present those resources in America, Bruce Caldwell edited a special volume, *Carl Menger and his Legacy in Economics*, as the annual supplement to the journal *History of Political Economy,* in 1990.

[17] To his disappointment, a Japanese scholar found out precisely that when he inquired upon the background of the author of the *Grundsätze der Volkswirtschaftslehre*. See Ikeda, Yukihiro: *Entstehungsgeschichte Mengers Grundsätze* (1997).

We shall also ask: How were established links with other disciplines and upon other grounds than those that were *en vogue* in Vienna? How can the notes by Menger himself help clarify his views on many kinds of topics and other streams of thought? With the manuscripts, and also the whole material left by Carl Menger, one may understand his reflection in a way that was not retraced for almost a century – it is now time that Menger's inheritance be put to the fore.

One most important work was to transcribe the archives, at least partly.[18] Until that work is completed and published, *all* reprints of the 1871 edition of Menger's *Grundsätze* thus remain *incomplete* with regard to the corrections and changes that Menger himself wanted to bring to his masterwork. In particular, the reprint given by Friedrich Hayek at the *London School of Economics* (thanks to the facilities offered by Lionel Robbins)[19] is based *only* on the original published text, thus lacking much material.[20] Hayek was not endorsing the divergences shown by the *second* edition of the *Grundsätze*, published in 1923 by Karl Menger (son) out of filial faith. That posthumous (Menger father died in 1921) second edition came out from pieces brought together that were only partly what Menger (Sr.) had in mind, and wished to re-publish. The son did not have in his possession any more the manuscripts sold by his mother, Menger's widow, to the Japanese (namely to the University of Trade – *Kanda Shoka Daigaku* – later to become *Hitotsubashi University*).

Another sequel is the bibliography drawn by Hayek. Although it is faithful, the reprinted texts were selected and some works published by Menger and not reprinted (even when the references were given) became hard to find for the "Menger scholar", including the one text in French published by Menger.[21] Intellectual exile and dispersal of material went hand in hand. The dominant English language was then incorporated in the works of post-WWII Academia German-speaking exiles. But this came at a price. It was the disappearance of many themes previously discussed within the Austrian circles, notably among economists. The School that Menger had tried to build persisted in a distorted way that the continuous reference to the character of its forefather can no more hide once the archives are put to the fore.

---

[18] The work of transcribing and mimeographing the notes had been undertaken by Emil Kauder. It has been completed by a team of researchers on location (along with a Japanese *Monbukagakusho* program) and in France, headed by Gilles Campagnolo for the *National Center for Scientific Research* (CNRS / CEPERC) and the "Menger and the Evolution of the Austrian School of Economics" Project (ACI-HDS-2003-2007).

[19] The *Gesammelte Werke* were then reprinted in four volumes (the *Grundsätze* being volume I) by J.C.B. Mohr, Tübingen, from 1968 to 1970.

[20] Hayek's pretense to a faithful inheritance from Menger may thus be questioned already from a strict philological point.

[21] See Campagnolo (2005): «Money as Measure of Value. An English Presentation of Menger's Essay in Monetary Thought»; together with the English translation of the same essay by Campagnolo: *History of Political Economy*, 37/2, p.233-262.

1. From Carl Menger Sr. to Karl Menger Jr.

In order to discuss issues of contemporary relevance in rediscoveries of Menger's texts, the history of the *Grundsätze* is important regarding both *exile of books* and *exile of men*. The story leads from Carl Menger to us. Right after her husband's death in 1921 and to get through the hard times of everyday life in Austria after World War I, Menger's widow had sold almost the entire Library collected by her husband together with some of the manuscripts – except for a few notebooks, which will *later* prove very useful as they will be part of the archives that her son took with him in his exile to the States and that have thus reached us – they were presented to the academic audience in the annual supplement of the journal *History of Political Economy* by Bruce Caldwell in 1990 under the title: *Carl Menger and his Legacy in Economics* (more precisely, that was the "legacy" available in the States).

The reason why Menger's readers have never read the *complete* text of the major work of the Austrian School is twofold: 1. Menger did not publish the revised version he intended to give; 2. His *Nachlass* virtually vanished from the available data. In the following section, we will discuss the significance of the lack of availability of those archives sold and sent to far away Japan. It will allow us to assess the alterations between the first edition of the *Grundsätze der Volkswirtschaftslehre* (original text of 1871) and the second one, published by his son as a revised version under the same title in 1923.

1.1. Karl Menger the son and his father's works

Carl Menger's son, Karl, became the famous mathematician well-known today to scholars in logic, didactics, epistemology and… economics. Karl created the *Mathematisches Kolloquium* in Vienna where mathematicians of all kinds confronted their ideas. Economics were discussed there and Karl furthered the line traced by his father. But he also repositioned it significantly. For instance, while the father had always rebuked the use of mathematics as an essential tool of economic analysis and recognized (at the best) its convenience as *symbolic*, or illustrative, the son argued in favor of its value and he saw in it a tool, a heuristic device relevant for theoretical analysis.

The position of the father may be made more understandable when one remembers that the use of mathematics in the 1870's was still often merely reduced to a compilation of statistical data (like some "history made into figures"). Developing mathematics later on made major results possible, and a few of them regarding economics came out of the *Mathematisches Kolloquium* held by Menger Jr. We may mention here the first mathematical proof of the Walrassian general equilibrium that was presented by Abraham Wald in 1934. The *Ergebnisse eines Mathematischen Kolloquiums* that Menger Jr. published then displayed well enough the richness of the apparatus then used.

Without entering into detail here, we had to mention that fact in order to see that, despite the son's claims of allegiance, father and son were clearly acting on different grounds. One must not forget that their works were also a world apart, even if both anchored in Vienna. Between the capital of the Austro-Hungarian empire and the oversized city (for a country diminished to a regional size), and after a half-century, the difference was enormous. At last, with the *Anschluss*, the son departed Austria, resigning from his professorship in Vienna and accepting a permanent position at the University of Notre-Dame, where he was already staying when German troops crossed the border. Although not a Jew, the new regime was not of his liking. After 1946, he became a Professor of Mathematics at the Illinois Institute of Technology in Chicago. There, he edited in English the second series of the *Reports of a Mathematical Colloquium*.

As far as the Library of the father is concerned, apart from the archives sold to Japan, the remaining notebooks the widow had kept were also brought to the States with him by the son. Those, too, are of major importance for scholars as part of a *Nachlass*. In his father's notebooks, the son found hints of things that he could unfortunately not check with the notes his father left for republishing his masterwork. The existence of that part of the archives was later acknowledged by Hayek, who did not find them in 1934 usable enough:

> "Much more, however, remains in the form of voluminous but fragmentary and disordered manuscripts, which only the prolonged and patient efforts of a very skillful editor could make accessible. For the present, at any rate, the results of the work of Menger's later years [to which pertains the most part of the archives] must be regarded as lost".[22]

It is then only in 1990 that those remaining papers reappeared.[23] It is thus possible to retrace much of the way the son himself worked, but for our purpose here, it is both the "work-in-progress" of his father and the second edition of the *Grundsätze der Volkswirtschaftslehre* that his of our concern. A comparison between the two editions will show noticeable divergences.

1.2. Close-up on the two editions of the *Grundsätze der Volkswirtschaftslehre*

It is well-known among Austrian economists, as well as among historians of economic thought that Menger (the father) had first intended that his 1871 mas-

[22] Hayek, Friedrich, Introduction to his reprint of Menger's *Grundsätze*, in the LSE Reprint Series, 1934, p.xxxiii.

[23] Karl Menger (son) had kept them in the basement of his American home. When he died, his daughter, now a Professor in Virginia, called for help with those papers and Roy Weintraub, the son of the economist Sidney Weintraub, an acquaintance of Menger Jr. and a well-known economist. His son, himself an economist and a historian of economics at Duke University, went to explore the basement and brought the material back to Duke. As said before, they thus became a major part of the Perkins Library of "Special Books" at Duke University.

terwork, the *Grundsätze der Volkswirtschaftslehre*, be the first part of a much larger project, that was never achieved, as Menger had to devote himself to fighting the Historical School. Still, he kept wishing to revise his edition. When he died, in 1921, a half-century later, that was not done either, but he had abundantly annotated his own copy of his masterwork. The new edition was done by his son and, although the latter introduced himself as having "*two souls residing within [his] breast*"[24] and with a total sense of duty dedicated to the memory of his father, what he achieved *without having at his disposal* many of the archives is *different* from what his father had wanted.

Now, that point can be assessed with certainty by using the archives, as we have done, because that piece of evidence exists. And it allows at the same time to see how interesting the second edition is, as an *interpretation* of the first, and also how it distinguishes itself from it.

To show the point better, let us show only a few of the differences between the two editions by comparing the tables of contents. That will already sufficiently show the extent of the differences between the two versions (reproduced also in Annex 2):

The two versions of the *Grundsätze der Volkswirtschaftslehre* by Carl Menger

1. *Die allgemeine Lehre vom Gute* **(The general Theory of good)**	**1. *Die Lehre von den Bedürfnissen*** **(The Theory of needs)**
2. *Die Wirthschaft* [sic] *und die wirtschaftlichen Güter* (The Economy and the economic goods)	**2. *Die Lehre vom Gute*** **(The Theory of good)**
3. *Die Lehre vom Werthe* [sic] **(The Theory of Value)**	**3.*Über das Maß der menschlichen Bedürfnisse und der Güter*** **(Measuring human needs and goods)**
4. *Die Lehre vom Tausche* **(The Theory of Trade)**	**4. *Die wirthschaftlichen* [sic] *Güter* (The economic goods)**

5. *Die Lehre vom Preise*
(The Theory of Price)
6. *Gebrauchswerth und Tauschwerth* [sic]
(Value-in-use and value-in-trade)
7. *Die Lehre von der Waare* [sic]
(The Theory of Wares)
8. *Die Lehre vom Gelde*
(The Theory of Money)

In the last four chapters, there are changes in the titles of the subsections.

[24] Karl Menger, Introduction (*Einleitung der Herausgeber*), but also: 1973 "Austrian Marginalism and mathematical economics" in Hicks and Weber (eds), *Carl Menger and the Austrian School of Economics*, Oxford, Clarendon Press.

What Menger the father *wanted to publish* and what was in fact published by his son are two different things, and they bear witness to different intellectual and (the word seems appropriate) *philosophical* backgrounds. In the annotations of the volume of the *Grundsätze* kept in Japan, as well as in the *marginalia* of his Library, what the father wished to see published is apparent, as well as what he used as source of reflection. Menger the son published a different version, as we shall see, because his ideas were born in a different context.

Although there is no question about how sincerely and conscientiously the son performed what he regarded as his task and duty of filial piety, there is no doubt either, however, that major differences can be pointed between the two editions. The difficulty is to trace them back: does any given point belong to the father's revising wishes, or to the son's own interference? Lacking textual evidence, it was impossible to decide what should be attributed to whom. This is precisely why commentators usually preferred to use the 1871 edition rather than the 1923 edition which is, too, useful and *despite* the fact that Menger (Sr.) was willing to revise his own text

As is clear from the comparison, the structure of the *Grundsätze der Volkswirtschaftslehre* has thus undergone changes *unwanted* by Menger Sr. when one looks at his original manuscript annotations. Neither did he desire to change the order of the chapters in the architectonics of his work, nor to introduce new ones. Conversely, he wanted to modify the title of his book, choosing that of *Allgemeine theoretische Wirtschaftslehre*, which his son did not do, as he could neither know that wish! Substituting a new title for the so-common *Grundsätze der Volkswirtschaftslehre*, which appeared on almost every textbook of the times implied a conscious refusal of the *collective* nature of the concept of economics that *Volk* in the word *Volkswirtschafts-lehre* unconsciously implied.

Menger denied that economics could study any collective body as a whole, but only as the combination of *individual* behaviors (which tend to satisfy each individual's needs). That methodological belief led him to fight against the German Historical School from the 1880's on, and it probably ultimately prevented Menger to publish himself the second edition of his book as well as the rest of the *opus magnum* as he had planned it at first (the *Grundsätze* being intended as only the first step of a much larger undertaking). While changing the title, Menger wished to keep the same structure that he had first designed. The 1923 edition shows on the contrary alteration in that respect, as well as within chapters and subsections themselves – for instance, regarding the determination of the motivation that makes a good an *economic* one. Some changes are identifiable within the papers Menger the son had in his possession (now kept with his own legacy at Duke University). Most interesting are the additions by the father that did not make it to the new edition for that obvious reason that the Library had gone to Japan.

Moreover, changes inserted by Menger the son reorganized the work at the conceptual level. Besides architectonics, issues rooted in the terminology of the economic concepts used can be traced. While Menger the father titled his first chapter "The general Theory of Goods" (*Die allgemeine Lehre vom Gute*), the 1923 version begins with "The theory of needs" (*Die Lehre von den Bedürfnissen*). Other concepts than the notion of *Gut* also play a significant role in Menger's system. Let us mention the notion of "availability" (*Verfügung*) of those goods. The notion of "needs" is also clearly a key one. Now, Menger the son felt for some reason entitled to put it even further forward than his father had done, but also maybe to shift its significance (*Bedeutung*). The meaning that the German word "*Bedarf*" conveys is a bit differently specified when using "*Bedürfnisse*". It is not easy to distinguish between the uses of both words (*Bedürfnisse* in the 1923 edition and *Bedarf* in the 1871 editon). And it is also true that in modern everyday German language, those terms are synonymous (we refer to the dictionary *Weis Mattutat*). Both obviously carry the meaning of needs that require some satisfaction (*Bedürfnisbefriedigung*). Still, on closer inspection, *Bedürfnisse* is more widely used in the 1923 edition in order to specify quantities that are used so as to satisfy needs, and, as a result, to convey *demand* (*Nachfrage*) and consumption (equivalent to *Verbrauch*). The stress from the original meaning, strictly individual, is slightly diverging.

Such a shift may be unintentional, but that does not make it insignificant, on the contrary. It may even show how deeply anchored in different approaches to the subject-matter, both thinkers were. That may seem far-fetched but it is supported by textual evidence and hints that the son was aware of the possible importance of the question – which he acknowledges while rebuking it at the same time in a footnote of the 1923 edition. One still gets thus gradually shifted from the purely subjective understanding that Menger the father had put forward and bends towards an *objective* idea according to which given quantities obtain as objectively measurable and quantitatively computable from an external viewpoint. All in all, subjectivism has perhaps become less clear and more confusion was introduced. This new ambiguity also authorized readings of Austrian views by *mainstream* economists to whom Menger the son was closer than his father had been in his times.

Conversely, some of the criticisms made by later so-called "*radical subjectivists*" became possible,[25] and that may derive from such an evolution of the significance within that key-notion of "needs". The same could be argued about some other concepts, such as *Nützlichkeit* (that is felt subjectively on an individual basis and meant as of subjective "significance" – *Bedeutung*) but can easily derive to a more general kind of signification, shared common knowledge and it could actually even end up within collective *explanantes* rather than private *explananda* in terms of mere *Bedeutung*.

---

[25] See Lachmann, L. (1978), «Carl Menger and the incomplete revolution of subjectivism».

As a first step of inquiry in the nature and causes of the incomplete and delayed reception of Menger's *authentic* conceptions of economics, it is of course not our purpose to analyze here the whole fundamental scientific *credo* of Menger Jr. Besides, logicians and historians of mathematics are keen on doing that work. We shall merely remind how it accounted for economics too, and sum up what seems to be two major causes of those divergent directions:

- First of all, let us repeat that Karl Menger did *not* have at his disposal the volumes of his father's Library: neither the author's copy of the *Grundsätze*, nor all the manuscript annotations written by his father on other books, which are proof of what the father wanted to see published.
- Second, despite his good faith, Menger the son was not inspired by the same views as his father. As a mathematician and a member of the Vienna Circle, more than fifty years after his father's edition of the *Grundsätze*, the son shared *neither* his father's "*Weltanschauung*" *nor* his philosophical creeds. Whereas the father was Aristotelian and a realist [26], his son was espousing the hypothetic-deductive nomological standpoint.

The misunderstanding of the fundamental differences between father and son regarding that philosophical background may, by the way, also be responsible for the fact that it was later taken for granted, in a rather naïve way, that Menger the father had "anticipated" viewpoints that belonged in fact to the *Vienna Circle*. Menger may have sparked some disputes of 20th century epistemology with his Dispute over Methods against the German Historicists (*Methodenstreit*), but he could certainly not yet foresee what logical positivism would achieve. And he was certainly not willing to go in that direction.

The way the son re-edited his father's work was then surely useful in order to remind the economists of his time of how much they were indebted to his father in the concepts they were using, but it was not accurate as to the contents of those very concepts. What had thus really become needed at the time was a presentation of Menger's works as a whole within their own age. Friedrich Hayek undertook precisely that. He, too, could only count with the available material, that is *without the archives*. It is essential to remember that point and to see what he did in editing the *Carl Mengers Gesammelte Werke* – which was to become the standard reference edition and the source of a revival of interest in Menger's thought. It would also authorize Hayek to claim himself the legitimate heir of Menger – which is, as we shall show, a somewhat questionable point.

---

[26] It is not here the place to come back on the debate upon Menger's Aristotelianism. However, whatever one's standpoint, one must at least specify in what sense to consider Aristotelian concepts one may use *and also upon which piece of archival evidence* one forms an opinion. As to us, the reader may refer to our article «Une source philosophique de la pensée économique de Carl Menger: l'*Éthique à Nicomaque* d'Aristote», *Revue de philosophie économique,* n 6, 2002/2, born from research on location with, in hand, the volume of the *Nicomachean Ethics* that Menger owned and annotated.

2. Reediting Menger's *Works*: the task and role of Friedrich Hayek

What did Hayek reedit and what got spread from what Menger had written? How if the Archives were to show us two different things? On the one hand, Menger the son had tried his best to "reconstruct" something that his father would have wished for, but retrospectively and in the light of the *Nachlass,* that appears to be different in the end from his father's intentions. Can we now guess from the archives what to think of the work achieved on the other hand by Hayek? Hayek did not embarrass himself with research of archives, or rather he thought what existed was hardly usable.

Therefore, Hayek was merely happy with *reprinting* the originally published works and, first of all, the masterwork of 1871. Hayek knew that Menger had wished for a new edition, but he deemed impossible to provide it. Therefore, he gathered Menger's works and merely had them reprinted from 1934 to 1936 at the *London School of Economics* (*LSE*) where the facilities were offered to him by Lionel Robbins. That was of course also a means to reinforce his reputation and his fight against the incipient Keynesian school and "Cambridge". The respectable Viennese Menger was thus recruited into a new fight – but was it his own? In any case, it was Hayek's. Although faithful to the literacy of the Mengerian text, Hayek was also a canny lad.

2.1. Menger's work edited by Hayek: emphasis and oblivion

In 1934, Menger was more often quoted by economists than read, but for a few German-speaking *aficionados*. Still, the so-called "Socialist Calculation Debate" had brought back some Austrian themes to the fore – such as the pricing mechanism *without* any central planner or auctioneer. But Mises' criticism of socialism from the point of view of price-theory also seemed to have been defeated in the 1920's, and interest had shifted to parts of debate where "Austrian economics" was secondary, or even not much existing. After all, Menger's own theory did not have the purpose to fight socialism, although it may be used with that purpose. Menger had wanted to build a *theoretical* science of economics, and getting rid of collective concepts (*Kollektivbegriffe*) was only a part of it. Max Weber had recaptured it in his own sociology.[27] Just as Weber had done (or less well), others would use Menger's views. They could also (like Weber in some cases) be recruited into fighting socialist and communist views, but to view such works *only* in that respect would be most partial and unilateral. That would neither respect such approaches, nor display perhaps their most interesting parts.

Besides arguing over socialism, the "Socialist Calculation Debate" could be of interest when considered as evidence of the discrepancy between two forms of Marginalism, represented by Walras and by Menger. On the one hand,

[27] Letter to Liefmann, March 9, 1920. A copy of the typed letter could be obtained from the *Geheimes Staatsarchiv, Preussischer Kulturbesitz*, copy seemingly due to Marianne Weber.

Lange argued in favor of socialism, but from a strict Walrassian equilibrium standpoint, while, on the other hand, Mises was building a path to "praxeology" and Hayek, in the Great-Britain of the Thirties was fighting Keynes. Neo-classical economics were in jeopardy due to Keynes, but were they common with Austrian theory? Not only Keynes, but Hayek was drawing attention to points that Classical and Neo-classical authors could not explore or were unable to answer. Divergent assumptions had also been made by Menger and Walras. At the time that Hayek was at *LSE*, at the request of Lionel Robbins, an answer to the new challenge was needed. As the story is well-known, we shall not retell it here, but insist on how Menger's works were thus reedited and used.

Hayek needed to base himself on sound pure theory and also to build his legitimacy against renowned Cambridge fellows. Since Menger's son had published the second (1923) edition of the *Grundsätze*, attention for the work of the Viennese had decreased. Moreover, as already said, the son's edition was a clumsy defense of his father's memory in that it used some different patterns. Hayek undertook a reprint of the founder's works as he was then in an open conflict with the Keynesian thought. As in the Cambridge circles, epistemology was given much attention (since Russell and Moore), he asked for help by Karl Popper and had him come to *LSE*. He kept for himself the field of economic theory, and began collecting, selecting and reediting Menger's *Gesammelte Werke*:
- I: *Grundsätze der Volkswirtschaftslehre*, 1871, Wien
- II: *Untersuchungen über die Methode der Socialwissen-schaften und der politischen Œkonomie insbesondere*, 1883, Leipzig
- III: *Kleinere Schriften über Methode und Geschichte der Volkswirtschaftslehre*
- IV: *Schriften über Geld und Währungsreform*, writings from 1886 to 1909. At the end, a complete Bibliography of Menger's published texts.

As Hayek's Introduction shows blatantly, his aim was also to establish himself as Menger's heir. For that purpose, he remained more faithful to the literacy of the original Mengerian text than the 1923 version of the *Grundsätze* by Karl Menger, but at the same time he did not use the *unpublished* material of Menger the father. He shared with the son the same disadvantage, and even more in a sense, as the son had acknowledged his father's will to make changes within the original text. Hayek said that he was lacking material although he knew well of the existence of the archives (including those of the son), but he got around the difficulty by pledging that they were of no practical use:

> "An inspection of his [Menger's] manuscript has shown that, at one time, considerable parts of the work must have been ready for publication. But [pursued Hayek] even after his powers had begun to fail, he continued to revise and rearrange the manuscripts to such an extent that any attempt to reconstruct this would be a very difficult, if not an impossible task".[28]

[28] Hayek, Friedrich: introduction to his reprint of Menger's *Grundsätze*, as appears in the LSE Reprint Series, 1934, p. xxxiii. Yet, archives yield plenty of very interesting material..

On the contrary, as the pages that follow will show, it seems to us that Hayek was over-pessimistic in tone. His refusal to consider those texts had a considerable influence on Austrian studies for decades, in a bad way. The Archives which the son had taken with him are of much help when we used them, as they had been to Bruce Caldwell when he analyzed the "legacy" of Menger. As said *above*, the most useful material to understand Menger's ideas was already kept in stacks in a Japanese Library, and more stacks were leaving for the States with Menger the son. We also found that the archives remaining in Japan are the indispensable key to piece all that puzzle together. Still, Hayek was content with a mere collecting and reprinting work.

Now, there is even more to it, because not all the texts listed by Hayek in the final bibliography, which is quite exhaustive, were selected for reprint. For reasons of keeping a reasonable number of pages, maybe, but some articles on the statistics of the *Valutareform* of old Imperial monies were already of scarce interest. On the contrary, a significant example of what was *not* reprinted by Hayek seems to us to be the article given by Menger in the *Revue d'économie politique* (1892) entitled "La monnaie mesure de valeur" (*Money as Measure of Value*).[29] This article clarifies much of Chapters X and XI in the first version of the article *Geld*, which Menger had written for the *Handwörterbuch für Staatswissenschaften* and first published in the same year (1892) – he subsequently revised it until the last version was published in the 1909 edition of the same "Dictionary of the social sciences". In his French article, Menger dealt much with theoretical views, distinguishing between an "inner" and in "outer" value of money, discarding "objective" theories of value that measure prices by reference to some allegedly inherent quantity of value in goods and inside money itself.

The *rationale* behind that distinction is explained in depth by Menger, who already characterizes in some way inflation and "purchase-power parity" (although the phrasing is different). That is all the more a pity that, besides the above concepts, the text also contains a phrase according to which Menger supports the issuance by the State (or by "a group of States") of "the quotity of money in use" thus deciding to give markets (and observers like economists) a fixed point of reference to see how prices move, due to the currency and/or to the merchandise own increase / decrease in value. This is only one example…

[29] A philological question of curiosity for the archives-lover is whether Menger had given the text already in French to the *Revue d'Économie politique* which published it in its volume VI. It is hard to say, especially as we could not find a rough-copy of that specific paper in German in the Menger Archives (neither in Japan, nor at Duke University where the son's papers are kept). But evidence gathered both from the work on the article *Geld,* and also the fact that Menger mastered French, plus the fact that the *Revue d'économie politique* was at the time very active internationally and directed by able German-reading young Frenchmen (philosophers and economists Halévy, Secrétan, etc.) leads us to think that Menger may have given the paper in French and received some polishing as to the language from the Editorial Board before publishing it under the signature of "*Charles* Menger".

Hayek's own choices orientated later readings. Following the fact that Hayek did not reprint that text on money, this reference has almost vanished from all English-language bibliographies on the topic.[30] True, the texts that Hayek had reprinted texts were in German, and the fact that the text quoted here was written in French is; in that respect, "unfortunate". But, as to further reading of Menger, its absence should not be under-estimated. Many British academics such as Marshall had, in their times, practiced German almost as well as their own language. But that was rapidly vanishing. Also, later on Menger would *not* be read in German, but only when his works would be translated into English, which was to happen much later.[31] In between, Hayek was able to enforce his own interpretation in the English-speaking world. He had then certainly in mind the needs for his own purpose, both career-wise and in academic fights. Let us now give one detailed example of one transformation that he brought.

2.2. An example of the distortion of Menger's thought

Money and the concept of "rise and fall of monetary nationalism" formed by Hayek will illustrate how, although claiming Menger's inheritance, the latter forged concepts much beyond what can be soundly assessed from Menger's texts. It will also show that such "supplements" endanger Menger's coherence.

The first English translation of Menger's article *Geld* was due to Monika Streissler and Leland Yeager in 2002.[32] The chapters of comments on contemporary payments systems and monetary issues that follow in the same volume, still, are more influenced by the later evolution of the theme within the Austrian school than by the founder's ideas. Although that may not have been the aim of the editors, the volume shows well the gap between Menger's original thought and the subsequent tradition.[33] For instance, George Selgin and Lawrence White concentrate on "monetary nationalism", a concept brought in by Hayek, not Menger, and interestingly criticize short-sightedness in general (or even partial) equilibrium theories. It is significant that, while the comments are meant to bear on Menger, they clearly refer to a concept *not* present in Menger's framework, but put forward by heirs, like Hayek. While examining thoroughly the future of retail payments, Selgin and White[34] raise the question of private monies.

[30] The French text by Menger was translated by us in the Summer 2005 issue of *HOPE*.

[31] Menger Carl [1871], 1950 reprinted 1981: *Principles of economics*, translated by James Dingwall and Bert Hoselitz. New York, New York University Press.

[32] Latzer, Michael; Schmitz, Stefan (eds.) 2002: *Carl Menger and the evolution of payments systems*. In volume IV of Hayek's *Mengers Gesammelte Werke*, the text is edited in German.

[33] See our 2003 book-review for the *European Journal of the History of Economic Thought*, London (Routledge), 10/3, p. 505-509.

[34] In line with previous works: see Selgin, G., *The Theory of free-banking*, Rowman & Littlefield, Totowa, 1988, only *one* reference in a field where the reference list is now long!

True, Menger paid attention to institutions, and one may refer to many passages in his 1883 *Untersuchungen*, regarding his research on methodology, as well as his action as a counsellor in the Austro-Hungarian Imperial Government deserves mentioning. And Menger indeed fought the idea that institutions (the Prince) *cause* the phenomenon of money. But he also rebuked theories where the institutions are merely *given data* –an idea too strange to a bureaucrat's mind bent on *organizing* power. Let us recall that Menger was one highest civil-servant in Austria, close enough to the Emperor that he served as private tutor to the Crown Prince (*Kronprinz Rudolf*). Although Menger's analysis may not so easily be called "institutionalist" (depending on the definition one gives of such a term), yet he certainly had major concerns for institutional dynamics, concerns that later Neoclassical approaches often lack.

Therefore, in commenting Menger on payments systems, one should feel estranged in bringing forth something quite different, something for which economists are undoubtedly indebted to *Hayek*, the concept of "rise and fall of monetary nationalism". Interesting when evoked by Selgin and White, yet it cannot easily be traced back to Menger who worked in Vienna for the Imperial Government in its authoritative monetary reform (*Währungsreform*). Menger stressed a purely economic definition of money as 'intermediary of exchange' – that is, *before* any existing State could force it upon its subjects. Still, he held the view that such a State, once existing, may decree the quantity of money it issues, and had better do it (*once* Governments have taken charge) because the resulting standardization tends to facilitate money's "marketability" (*Absatzfähigkeit*).

No movement of "rise and fall" of State intervention is thus envisaged, but rather a general trend towards some stricter accordance between the essence of money (*Wesen des Geldes*) as a tool of interpersonal exchange (*Tausch*) and its existence as a *economic* good. Opposing German Historicists, Menger always stressed how untenable the idea was that money be "created" by the Prince's *imprimatur* (legal tender). But he also showed the State's intervention helped "perfecting" money as a standard that made it all the more *absatzfähig* ("marketable") as it was at first hardly differentiated from other goods, but got specified, and even standardized by the State, and then issued under Government's guidance. Free-banking supporters argue in favor of competition between credit institutions and money issuers. Help lies in Hayek's ideas, not in Menger's.

Let us conclude that the detailed history of the editing work of Hayek at *LSE* still has to be written. We could not undertake it here. Still, it is clear that reediting the *Works* was orienting the way of reading Menger afterwards. The removal of the Menger Library had unfortunate effects again – since a mere reprint was given by Hayek, whereas Menger had wanted a revised edition of his *Grundsätze* for instance, different from that of 1871: one should not forget that the Viennese founder had worked on it until his death, some fifty years later!

Clearly, shifts in the direction of the interpretation of Menger's ideas were due to some of the choices that Hayek had made. From them, Hayek also gained recognition as Menger's heir, and could all the more force upon foes as well as supporters one image of Menger's that he endorsed, while at the same time he indeed introduced his own new, original and diverging ideas. Whereas many titles were little accessible, the logical consequence of the reprint was to spread to many "Austrian economists" the image of Menger tinted with Hayek's concerns (be it anti-Socialism in the Calculation Debate or the "rise and fall of monetary nationalism" in money theory). It is impossible to know whether that would have been accepted by Menger – but it is sure it was not in his own texts. So, what there is in them has to be found by exploring the Archives? In the last section of this chapter, we shall present two examples of that wealth of resources, one in economic theory and the other in a tradition he studied.

3. Examples of the rediscovery of Mengerian ideas from the Archives

The latter two sections of the present chapter have sufficiently shown why it would be highly unsatisfactory for serious academic historical research to confine to the published papers of Menger – a "Menger in print" that is limited to available editions reedited by followers with their own ideas. Be they guided by the best thoughts, or by career concerns, later editors could not avoid to be unfaithful to the thoughts Menger had matured during a half-century after he had first given his masterwork, the book that we know as the *Principles of Political Economics* (*Grundsätze der Volkswirtschaftslehre*) of 1871 and that he would have re-titled *A General Theoretical Doctrine of Economics* or *A General Theory of Economics* (*Allgemeine theoretische Wirtschaftslehre*). In order to appreciate the true extent of Menger's ideas on such a theory, as well as on other disciplines, and to assess what he truly brought to science and the achievement of a scientific "revolution", one must rediscover what there is in the Archives.

Obstacles are numerous as Hayek had reckoned: one must go through the deciphering of Menger's abundant notes scattered on the volumes he owned (in the Library now located in Japan), on his own copies of his works (like the *Grundsätze* and the *Untersuchungen*). One must explore the "voluminous" cardboard boxes of other books, correspondence etc. scattered through the archives of his son, too. Still, some tracks are more easily traced: for instance, between the annotations left on his copies of his own *Grundsätze* and the annotations on the margins of his Library's volumes. That is true, for example, of his copy of Aristotle's *Nicomachean Ethics* in the German translation in the archives: that permits the scholar to solve the riddle of Menger's "Aristotelianism".[35]

[35] A point of view that was much supported by some commentators, like Barry Smith – and more or less evicted by others, like Erich Streissler. We showed how evidence came from the

Also, Menger kept regular notebooks of his activities and ideas at various periods of his life and they are of great help, when available. Those taken to his American exile by his son are now kept at the Perkins Library (Duke University) and that material allows the careful inquirer to re-assess much more accurately part of the "*Menger-Lehre*", as well as many of the sources whose influence can be felt in Menger's doctrine. Some are surprisingly (but understandably, given what we said of the Archives) still little known. We shall select two of them: on the one hand, a table of concepts underlying his views, shown in an astonishingly clear-cut graph; on the other hand, a point sometimes acknowledged, but rarely demonstrated: how Menger was influenced by the *French*, with regard to philosophical considerations of 19th century authors and economic liberal views.

3.1. An example of rediscovery of the structure of Menger's concepts

We have previously shown, through the comparison of the Table of Contents of the 1871 and the 1923 editions of the *Grundsätze*, that it was of great significance for Menger's theory to explain the original terms. The following table of key-words is taken from an early notebook[36].

ZWECK (ends or goals)	MITTEL (means)	VERWIRKLICHUNG (achievement)
MENSCH (human being)	AUßENWELT (environment)	LEBENSERHALTUNG (subsistence)
BEDÜRFNIS (desire or need)	GUT (good)	BEFRIEDIGUNG (satisfaction)

Menger only used terms that he had accurately chosen, or even coined, to deliver his thought. The table shows how he organized them. It reads vertically and horizontally as follows: a good (*Gut*) is a means (*Mittel*), for the satisfaction (*Befriedigung*) of a need (*Bedürfnis*) subjectively felt in a given environment (*Außenwelt*). Each term asks for more explanatory inquiry and the analysis of terminology was always for Menger a matter of tremendous significance (see

archives. See Campagnolo (2002): «Une source philosophique de la pensée économique de Carl Menger: *Éthique à Nicomaque* », *Revue de philosophie économique*, 6, p. 5-35.

[36] It was taken to the States by his son. The page of the notebook was entitled by Menger "*Geflügelte Wörter*". It is now located in the Carl Menger papers at the Perkins Library (Box 2); a folder filed under the same title by the librarians, and pointed out by commentators as being of much significance – for instance: by Yagi, Kiichiro (1993).

the Appendixes to his 1883 *Untersuchungen*). The concepts he used are reflected with accuracy in the words he intended to substitute to his fellow economists' imprecise wording.

Menger's new theory of science thus deserved attention and caution with the precise combination of meanings that he used. In the above table, Menger is in fact *mapping* "human action" (although he does not use the word) concerning *material life* (within an environment– *Außenwelt*) and in a rational way (that is, according to his epistemology based on causal analysis). It is consciously limited to the individual man (*Mensch*) who seeks survival and subsistence (*Lebenserhaltung*) in a way shown on the second horizontal line of the table (linked with the Aristotelian principle that each being tends to survive). The first column will also read: in order to survive, human being tends to realize their goals according to their representations of their own individual needs. Such a "representative" mechanism could possibly be studied by psychology (or the then incipient phenomenology) but Menger held those as *not* being parts of the economist's task.[37] Menger started from the *fact* that one's feelings are only *subjective* (as Descartes had said about pain) and that fact brings economics to remain within the *individual* reality.

Menger believed strongly that the economist should not decide whether individuals are fools or wise, moral or immoral, when they choose what they choose in the environment at their disposal, but that *relationship* to his surroundings itself (between the individual and «things») is the very basis of economics as a science. For example, the question of the «price of things» would otherwise have no meaning whatsoever. The understanding of why wares are manufactured and/or exchanged (if not immediately available, but still desired by individuals) derives from there too. From the characteristics of that basic relation derives what makes of a "thing" an "economic good". Material things in the world make sense (*Bedeutung*) for human subjects as they are available (*vorhanden, verfügbar*) means for their (material) life-ends. The concepts of *Verfügung* and *Verfügbarkeit* (availability) are key-notions, as much as satisfaction of needs (*Bedürfnisbefriedigung*). The above table, as scribbled down by Menger, presents the combination of all of those conceptual elements.

Without even knowing its existence, the work of reconstruction from the lengthy dissertations of the 1871 *Grundsätze* could of course be undertaken (for example, by Henri Simon Bloch, in his PhD *Theory of needs by Carl Menger* dating back to 1937).[38] The countercheck may be worked out of the above table, whereas the need then felt for the analysis of language itself was obviously left

---

[37] See our chapter: "Was the Austrian School a *Psychological-School* in the realm of Economics in Carl Menger's view?" further on in this volume.

[38] Bloch, Henri Simon, 1937: *La théorie des besoins de Carl Menger* (Introduction by Gaëtan Pirou), Paris.

into oblivion by economists who began reading Menger in English (where the word "needs" covers up all nuances in the translation by Dingwall and Hoselitz).

3.2. An example of rediscovery of historical influence: the perception of French philosophical and epistemic ideas of the 19th century by Menger

After considering aspects of economic theory structured in Menger's doctrine, one may insist on the wealth of information brought by archives about influences that Menger had consciously received. As we mentioned in the Introduction of the present volume, the concept of "influence" itself is rather dubious and, if it were only for the sake of quasi-paleontological interest, then the field of the history of economic ideas may well be of little meaning. Still, through material made available in archives and following the relations that it is actually subsequently possible to establish, the "portrait" of a man and his works can be retraced. That is what Hayek aimed at. But such an endeavour brings about more documentation than he cared to use. Strictly historical knowledge is not enough, but it is also needed. Therefore, whereas we gave in the previous example parts of theoretical concepts the archives provide us with, we shall here seek for not less significant, although historical, matter. Any enlightenment about Menger's philosophical and epistemic fundamentals may bear consequence upon his theory, and here we may put to the fore Menger's reading of the French authors, not only in economics but in philosophy as well.

Menger did neither confine himself to confront the German Historicists, nor did he only criticize the British Classics of Political Economy. He was also a careful reader of French economists and philosophers. The link between Say and Menger has at times been commented upon, and the influence of French Liberal Thought of the Enlightenment and the first half of the 19th century on Menger has recently received much attention from the Austrian School in the USA. Israel Kirzner was first to pay attention to it within the frame of his theory of the *entrepreneur* (a word of French origin). Kirzner traced his topic back to the works of Jean-Baptiste Say (1767-1832) and stressed how close Menger was.[39] Murray Rothbard also focused on the vivid 19th century French Liberalism in his *History of Political Economy in an Austrian perspective*.[40] Other erudite commentators also pointed out the same facts, leading to re-appreciate studies on French economic thought with regard to facets of the Austrian tradition. For instance, the long neglect suffered by such studies was denounced by Joseph Salerno already in 1988. Numerous reasons may explain such neglect, including the fact that Say had long been regarded as *very* compliant with Classical Politi-

[39] See Kirzner (1978) in particular, but his theory of the *entrepreneur* dates back to 1973. Recently, he insisted on entrepreneurial *discovery* in competitive markets (Kirzner, 1997).
[40] The link is essentially to be found in the first and last chapters (resp. entitled: "J.B. Say: the French tradition in Smithian clothing" and "After Mill: Bastiat and the French *laissez-faire* tradition"), volume II titled *Classical economics* (Rothbard, 1995, resp. p. 1-46 and 439-476).

cal Economy. To some extent, there were good reasons to make believe so, but Say had also often confronted British Classics, especially Ricardo and Malthus. That fact was subsequently often ignored, although many French Liberals had distinct pre-Marginalist insights as Rothbard had written (Rothbard, 1995 and Campagnolo, forthcoming). It was then conceivable (and, to some extent, palatable) to link French Liberal economists with later-coming "Austrians".

Now, it is necessary to give substantial proof of the true extent of that influence through documentation with proper archives. Menger's reading of the French authors other than Say is much less known. For instance, Count Pellegrino Rossi (who succeeded Say as Chair of Political Economy at the Collège de France) had written a handbook of economics that Menger extensively annotated while correcting his own copy of his first edition of the *Grundsätze der Volkswirtschaftslehre*. It supplemented the work done by Menger upon Karl Heinrich Rau's famous handbook (see the previous chapter in this volume). Menger used Rau's text *before* 1871, and Rossi *after* that publication – as he did not give the second edition of his work, those notes were left unknown to his followers. Upon the basis of the archives, we have shown elsewhere the deep interest of such a reading, as well as the necessary limitations of drawing on it, however true and important as it was.[41]

Both from the Menger Collection in Japan and the Perkins Library at Duke University, first-hand information also enables us to briefly hint at philosophically-oriented studies by Menger with respect to French philosophy. Menger had some solid knowledge of 19th century French philosophy in two major directions: on the one hand, in the "psychological" trend of science (as we have just seen), and on the other hand, in its "positive" orientation (with regard to Auguste Comte). But before coming to Comte, Menger's readings at the crossroads of French economics, politics and philosophy began with Frédéric Bastiat. And one must immediately stress how *hostile* Menger was to the methodology followed by the advocate of *laissez-faire*. Menger saw no more sense in Marxian or Utopian socialist projects than in the opposite views, all inspired as they were by the advocacy of a cause rather than by the pursuit of scientific truth. On that point, Menger wrote clearly that:

> "Bastiat on the one hand, and the Socialists on the other, do not want to display things, and respectively explain them as they are but, on the contrary, they follow practical goals and the former wants to *legitimize the situation as it is* (which is not a scientific issue), while the latter display glaring wrongs, hence their falsifying facts, not to say anything of their laws! As to Bastiat, he wants to conflate the conceptions that are fundamentally different of "what is" and "what ought to be". That is a wrong

---

[41] We refer the reader to our detailed analysis (Campagnolo, forthcoming: "Origins of Menger's Thought in French Liberal Economists", *Review of Austrian Economics*).

> methodology (Socialists of the Chair as well as free-traders in Germany!). Bastiat is only the champion of a cause [*ein Advocat*]". [42]

Menger's opinion was final, never to change about the character of pure science that he deemed sacred. But one would be misled in thinking that was also the end of his interest in philosophical positions. Trends of thought that had importance on the political and/or social order of his time interested him and works of the French Enlightenment and their followers are present in his archives: Guérard-Dupont, Destutt de Tracy, Montesquieu or Condillac. The latter philosophers participated in the incipient science of economics of their times, but Menger paid more attention to their philosophy than to their economics.

Menger also had some interest in British philosophy, mostly documented by his reading of German historian of philosophy Friedrich Überweg's in his *Philosophy of Modern Times* [43] and his numerous quotes from British philosophers and economists, from Bacon to John Stuart Mill. Yet, Menger's liking for French philosophy is certainly less known while equally impressive. [44] Whereas Menger's manuscript notes on the handbook by Überweg make blatant the attention Menger paid to British and French thoughts, the latter can be seen also in another account that Menger read (in the German translation), the *History of 19th century French philosophy* by Félix Ravaisson. On the other hand, the annotations Menger left on Comte in his unpublished manuscript papers shall also be useful here. On those influences, there exists in the current literature, no study that we know of. From the archives, we thus bring forth new material.

Before developing that theme, it may be useful for the reader to know that there were in Menger's times three largely well-known accounts of French philosophy, one by Hippolyte Taine, another by Paul Janet, and the *History of French philosophy in the 19th century* by Félix Ravaisson. While Taine applied his own

---

[42] We translate from the following passage: "Bastiat einerseits und die Socialisten andererseits wollen nicht die Dinge darstellen, bez.[iehungsweise] erklären wie sie sind, sondern dieselben verfolgen praktische Zwecke und ersterer will die *Thatsachen rechtfertigen* (das ist kein wissenschaftliches Problem), die letzteren sie als schreiende Ungerechtigkeiten darstellen, daher ihre Fälschung der Thatsachen, ganz zu schweigen von ihren Gesetzen! Bastiat will die grundverschiedenen Anschauungen von "Thatsache" und "Recht", "das was ist" und "das was sein sollte" in einander zu verschmelzen. Das ist eine falsche Methode (Kathedersocialisten u. Freihändler in Deutschland!) Bastiat ist ein Advocat." lines written in front of the page of *Vorrede*, in Menger's own copy of his *Grundsätze* kept in Japan.

[43] Überweg, Friedrich, 1892: *Grundriss der Geschichte der Philosophie der Neuzeit von dem Aufblühen der Althertumsstudien bis auf die Gegenwart*. Berlin. The volume is in Menger's Library under number *Philos 26.*

[44] Menger's comments on the British tradition are studied in detail (in French) in our *Critique de l'économie politique classique*, *op. cit.*, chapter "Menger et la tradition britannique".

theory of the *milieu*,[45] Janet and Ravaisson were more *mainstream* – Janet did not bear the same resentment against the French *Academia* that Taine had felt.[46] Menger mostly knew Ravaisson's work. He heavily annotated the translation that he owned.[47] His reading is a most significant piece of evidence of the interest Menger had for the specificity of French philosophy regarding the German or the English thoughts of the times.

That specificity was stressed by the translator in his foreword (*Vorwort*) as he wrote that the French brand of thought could not be compared to anything existing in the English world. He stressed one most significant difference, which is of interest regarding Menger too. It relates philosophical tendencies to the controversy of religion in the Enlightenment, and the divide within the German-speaking world, between German Protestants (in particular Prussian circles which had given birth to Criticism and Idealism, since Kant, Fichte and Hegel), and German (Bavarian, for instance) and Austrian Catholics is notable. According to Ravaisson, a source of inspiration for any "psychological philosophy" was the Catholic background. It was found *also in Austria*. But Menger was certainly no true believer and he had even had troubles at times with the Imperial Court on that matter. Notes show that he must have thought something like the following: religion could not bargain its authority to comment upon science, but the least acceptable philosophy is that which makes use of divine authority. Menger praised French philosophy for clearly displaying the "independence of philosophy from any authority besides that of evidence and proof".[48].

Ravaisson also paved the way towards *new* understandings of how the mind functions. Menger also kept in mind the key word (which appears often in his *marginalia*) of "*Causalismus*". For instance, he underlines a passage about the Leibnizian view according to which body and mind are strictly separated and follow two strict sets of causes in their own domain.[49] Menger's position (here about the link of the soul and body) is reaffirming a rigorous causalism that is

---

[45] Hippolyte Taine (1838-1893) wrote *Les Philosophes français du 19ème siècle* (*The French Philosophers of the 19th century*) in 1857 and applied therein his own systematic and rigorous triadic theory of *race*, *milieu* and *moment*, meaning the human, geographic, social, and historical factors which determine the nature of the work of a given author (literary, philosophical or even scientific).

[46] That was because Taine had been rebuked by the Sorbonne University at the *agrégation*. Conversely, Paul Janet (1823-1899) was an heir of Sorbonne's long-time leading master Cousin. He learnt from his eclecticism and spiritualism, and his works tended towards a "psychological philosophy". He gives the state of knowledge of his times in introspection in *La Morale* (1874) and *Psychologie et Métaphysique* (1897).

[47] Koenig , Edmund, 1889: *Die französische Philosophie 19 Jhdt.* Eisenach, Baumeister.

[48] Menger underlines „*Unhabhängigkeit der Philosophie von jeder Autorität außer derjenigen der Evidenz und des Beweises*", in the translation of Ravaisson's book, p. 183. In the French context, "evidence" refers to Descartes to whom Ravaisson dedicated his introduction.

[49] Menger shows interest for Leibniz who assumed that God has set their respective clocks exactly the same "parallel synchronicity" so that they perfectly coincide.

evidenced in such extreme standpoints.[50] The same causality will likely be found in modern medically-proven cognitive results. It does not mean that Menger would ground economics upon any such *experimental* truths, but his interest in medical psychology, as illustrated in his reading of the French philosophers, remains, although strictly apart from economic comments. That distinction is not the case with another branch of French philosophy Menger is interested in: if "causalism" cannot be strictly identified with positivism – as other philosophical currents would claim it may be, it is nevertheless emphasized in the fact that causes can be identified with *non*-metaphysical principles, a completely different view from that which was dominant in the Prussian philosophy (whose influence pervaded even Austria, although there emerged an anti-Kantian and anti-Idealistic line , with Brentano and other philosophers who were, like Menger, at the University of Vienna).[51]

To enter into some detail of the argument followed, let us display the structure of Ravaisson's textbook, with the four directions he points within modern French philosophy, with regard to the metaphysical contents implied in the "psychology" trends espoused by philosophers:

1) Sensualism. Still inspired by 18th century Enlightenment and Condillac. Let us note that Menger owned a copy of Condillac's *Complete Works*, which he scarcely annotated.[52]
2) Catholic ontology and introspection. That is based on faith and the emotional quest related to it, purposely far from any kind of rationalism.
3) Materialism. It must be considered as different from sensualism, although also inherited from the Enlightenment (works like those of Diderot, d'Holbach). In the course of the 19th century, that kind of analysis of the individual body was extended to the social body and issues like poverty and economic freedom melted with it to bring forth various kinds of French socialism (that in turn inspired Marx).
4) Medical psychology. Due to the incipient research on the cognitive power of the mind, considered as expressing the brain itself in a specifically clinical and experimental way, Ravaisson put many hopes in separating that trend from old phrenology and the renowned 17th century and 18th century Moralists.

As said above, the trend to which Menger seems to feel close to, somehow following Ravaisson, is the last "scientific" approach. Ravaisson refers at length to the renowned physiologist of the brain Vulpian, who started with the distinctive criteria of vegetative, animal and human (conscious) life and then discovered

[50] In the translation of Ravaisson's book, p. 176: "according to Leibniz, the soul has no direct influence upon the body and directs only moves of its will and conscience, etc."
[51] Menger noted in the margin of the chapter on Kant in Überweg's textbook: "Kant sees no pure reason in political economy" ("*Kant sieht in der Nat. -Ökonomie keine reine Vernunft*".)
[52] In the Menger Collection, it appears under number *Philos 6*.

relationships between the nervous system and the brain, also giving the first standard clinical descriptions of neuro-sclerosis. Menger shows interest for Ravaisson's descriptive style, seeking useful information on famous physicians like Bordas-Dumoulin, Boullier, Jaumes and Laprade, for instance. In France, the University of Montpellier has a Faculty of Medicine older than the one at the Sorbonne and physicians like Jaumes regarded themselves as "philosophers of the mind" united their efforts in understanding how the mind works. Furthermore, some wished they could extend study of the individual to the collective body through studying inter-individual relationships.

Exploring the mind was also a topic of research in the German Academia in particular with Wundt's experimental psychology. Menger knew of it and wrote about it in his notebooks. Yet, he insisted that to ground economics upon *experimental* laws would be erroneous. For instance, if one inferred the marginal utility argument in economics from the famous Weber-Fechner "Fundamental Psycho-physical Law" (*Psycho-physisches Grundgesetz*) that defined *satiety* (*Sättigung*), one would only impair theoretical research in economics. Along with his realistic and causal method, Menger thus aimed at building a kind of reasoning specifically designed for economics, acknowledging the legitimacy of different *independent* levels of knowledge. Conversely, to try to ground economics in the results of some other science would do good neither to one, nor to the other. As the experimental nature of the new psychology created the temptation to do so, the warning was all the more necessary. Both sciences agreed in confining to the individual the results obtained from their observed behavior, but one started with a given set of facts in order to deepen them, whereas the other would take them as granted working on the reasoning implied by material exchange, seeking *general validity* of results of a theoretical nature. Menger wanted economics to become scientific for its own sake.

The archives show that Menger acquired a large part of his knowledge of psychological topics from a volume by physician Pr. Stricker on the medical studies of consciousness.[53] Menger carefully underlined excerpts about the "threshold of stimulus" (*Reizschwelle*), the differential threshold (*Unterschiedschwelle*) and the layers (*Stufen*) of consciousness regarding stimuli. Such concepts revolutionized experimental psychology in particular in Wundt's works.[54] Whatever the results obtained though, Menger only used for his own works a notion of *psyche* inherited from the much older Aristotelian formulas. That understanding of the economic behavior of man kept Menger away from the idea

---

[53] Stricker, 1879: *Studien über das Bewusstsein.* Vienna, Wilhelm Braumüller. In the Menger Collection, it is registered under *Philos 23*. Chapter 4 bears upon *stimuli* and reactions.

[54] Menger evoked them in his notebooks, partly located at Duke University. Reference numbers of the boxes where archives show this topic are: 1-3 for notebooks falling in the period 1910's; 14-20, *e.g.* There is much material refuting Wundt ("*Gegen Wundt*"), but the notes show that Menger also thought of revising some passages from his own *Untersuchungen* while thinking over Wundt's results.

that "pure economic theory" (*reine Wirtschaftslehre*) be in some way established upon factual knowledge of psychological phenomena. Both sciences should get established as autonomous, but their subject-matters would respectively be informative for both kinds of scientists. Pointing out Menger's interest towards medical psychology and the incipient cognitive sciences of his times is thus significant, also with regard to the atmosphere of "Vienna 1900" and whereas Freud also studied French thought (even completing, as his well-known his education in Paris hospitals under Pr. Charcot). Economics and psychology, not to speak of psychoanalysis then, took part in a similar revolution in the story of the sciences of the mind (*Geisteswissenschaften*), although dealing with the topic in strictly different ways – and we may suggest that Menger got that impression from enthusiastic Ravaisson.[55]

In connection with those questions but also with Menger's fight within the Dispute over Methods (*Methodenstreit*) against the German Historical School, Menger rebuked the so-called "ethical studies" ("*ethische Studien*"), a direction of research that justified socially-oriented economic policies upon self-proclaimed "ethics and morality" of behavior. Followers of Schmoller and his *Verein für Sozialpolitik* had often implicitly (and sometimes explicitly) substituted it to the theory of science and Menger fiercely objected. Socialist materialism was in any case repulsive to Menger,[56] just as the doctrine of religion when called upon for grounding scientific work. As much as the religious views mentioned above, Menger also rebuked materialistic "ethical" claims. His attitude towards French philosophy, where "enlightened" materialism plays a major part, shows well how Menger learnt to distinguish medical scientism from materialism. The philosopher Paul Janet (an uncle of famous neurologist Pierre Janet) wrote extensively on the methodology to access metaphysical realities of the mind. Ravaisson's book stresses how he reacted against Materialism (chapter "*Janet gegen den Materialismus*"). However, spiritualism *à la Cousin* (the master of the Sorbonne University of the 1860's) is not the solution either and the only "material" view that Menger seemed ready to espouse was medical (let us note that Pierre Janet too studied with Charcot).

Drawn back to "psychological philosophies" explored by Ravaisson, one may wonder to which extent they corresponded to the German *Geisteswissenschaften* "philosophies of the mind". Was sensualism (as designed in the spirit of the Enlightenment) another kind of the same? One should remember Condillac himself had introduced sensualism in France from the Scots like Hutcheson, who had in turn influenced Adam Smith's *Theory of Moral Sentiments*. Economics are again at stake and, if one accepts the terms posed by

[55] For more details and warnings on that relationship, see our chapter in the present volume: "Was the Austrian School a Psychological School in the Realm of Economics?".

[56] In the case of Marx, one may say that French Materialism could be regarded as inspiring "dialectical Materialism"– the story not being that simple though. Menger rebuked both.

German historian Oncken about "*Das Adam Smith Problem*" in Menger's times; that is: how to link Smith's moral philosophy in his 1759 *Theory of Moral Sentiments* where "sympathy" played a major role to the key-notion of "self-love" in his *Wealth of Nations* that was reckoned as grounding Classical economics?[57] Then the question naturally rises as to what relationship exists between sensualist themes (like the idea that "all knowledge comes to man through his senses") and basic Mengerian economics. For instance, may the individual expect to obtain from that idea a *substratum* for the most important reference to "satisfying his/her needs" (*Bedürfnisbefriedigung*)?

From Menger's comments on Ravaisson's work, it seems clear that those themes are neither mutually exclusive nor foreign, but that one should not draw inferences from one field to another, both approaches are distinct to his mind. His refusal to see economics based upon psychology is clear, as he cannot believe that "sciences of the mind" could benefit from such unwarrantable interference. The general conclusion to draw is that, whatever the field, Menger held that various objects must be dealt with by different sciences, causality being the only method for all different facets of the human mind.

Another aspect of Menger's reading of the French authors was his interest in Comte's "positive" philosophy of science. Last but not least, it must be mentioned here. Was that major French trend of philosophy at the origins of Menger's thought and Auguste Comte a favorite author of the Viennese? Was "positive" philosophy a basis for "Austrian" marginalist economics? A key element to Menger's attitude towards modern science was not only the refusal of political economy in the historical German style, but also in the British Ricardian way. Both erred according to Menger and his interest in Say was partly dictated by the intuition that if others were wrong, he might have been on the right track, had he only followed it all the way. A few notes by Menger deal with Comte, maybe not enough to make a hard case, still showing a fitting pattern between Mengerian methodological causalism and French positivism. Yet, Menger remained an Aristotelian realist according to enough evidence in the archives and a more accurate characterization of his attitude is needed.

Menger's reading of Auguste Comte is helpful, although notes are not numerous.[58] Menger had read Comte, but also accounts of his ideas, in *Essays on Political Economy, Theoretical and Applied* by J. E. Cairnes, especially the critical essay entitled "M. Comte and Political Economy",[59] Menger underlines:

[57] The article by Gustav Oncken was: « Das Adam Smith Problem », *Zeitschrift für Sozialwissenschaft*, 1898, 1.

[58] Among the notes one must also be careful that some refer to Comte and some to Charles Comte Guizot (*Comte* being French for the lord title of Count). Guizot wrote a *Traité de législation* that Menger had read.

[59] J.E. Cairnes, *Essays on Political Economy Theoretical and Applied*, London 1873. In Menger's Library, it is listed under "Eng.234". The paper on Comte (p. 265-307) had been

> "It was M. Comte's opinion that Political economy, as cultivated by the school of Adam Smith"s successors in this country [Great-Britain] and in France, failed to fulfil the conditions required of a sound theory by Positive Philosophy, and was not properly a science. He pronounces it to be defective in its conceptions, "profoundly irrational" [Cairnes translates Comte's words] in its method, and "radically sterile" [Cairnes translates Comte's own words again] as regards results (p. 267)".

Such a definitive statement by Cairnes, then a major author though not an innovative theoretician, must be examined into detail. The arguments by Cairnes on Comte's "positive" philosophy come, first of all, from the idea that Comte regarded the phenomena of wealth as deserving a science of their own but were unable to obtain it. Note that the question whether "political economy" in the *Ricardian* style was adequate is a different one. Comte did not believe in the tools presented by the Classical economists. Cairnes shows Comte's disappointment. But he ridiculed it, saying that Comte must have missed a clear understanding of the great achievements of the Classics.

Menger's notes show that the Viennese professor regarded things otherwise: Comte's expectations must be acknowledged to a large extent, being neither out-of-place, nor malformed. Yet, Comte diagnosed that a science dissociating economic and social phenomena and economics from sociology was impossible. That, in Menger's eyes, was desperately wrong. While he did not discard Comte's criticisms, Menger was confident in building such a separate theory.

One key-word, often stressed by Cairnes about Comte, was the French "*ensemble*" ("altogether") meaning that phenomena regarding social activities of various kinds should be treated as intrinsically mixed and bounded together. Menger refused that view and the Comtian standpoints that followed from it. But whereas Cairnes refused it too by arguing from the history of natural sciences (at each period of time, scientists had divided their domains and obtained better results), Menger bought Cairne's argument only by supporting the idea that causality is *always* the key-element to scientific analysis. Other analogies, that Comte denied, are only vague and Menger agrees with Comte in rebuking such *analogon*. The French philosopher's arguments were worthier than that.

The demonstration should then be that the kind of thought that stressed the notion of "*ensemble*" (togetherness) *cannot* be pertinent for a pure and general theory of economics. Comte had put forward the argument of a scale of complexity in social phenomena. Menger answers that a strict analysis starts from elementary trading units (individuals) and goes, by degree, up the scale of

---

previously released in the *Fortnightly Review* (May 1870). Menger was interested in the paper and we take from him the quotes given in the following lines. Cairnes (1823-1875) was famous for his *Leading Principles of Political Economy newly expounded.* He had always taught the purest kind of Classical political economy, deliberately distancing himself from any new kind of theory, such as Marginalism presented, in Great-Britain, by Jevons

phenomena through combinations. Against Cairnes, Menger agreed with Comte in saying that Classical economists had failed to acknowledge complexity, but there existed no reason why such an analysis could not succeed if done properly, according to the causal method that was, after all, advocated by Comte himself!

Again, according to Cairnes, Comte's idea that "the *ensemble* of the subject [of political economy] is better known to us and more accessible than the parts (*op. cit.*, p. 277)" aggravated considerably the trouble for a science of political economy. Menger simply refused that statement. Economists must not deal with complexity by following the principles of historicism. But whereas Cairnes concluded that "the [Comtian] argument against Political Economy [is] that phenomena in proportion as they are complex are more *solidaires* [in French in the original]", Menger linked the words "*ensemble*", the term "*solidaires*" (joint, interdependent) as either obvious (and banal) statements, or as grave obstacles if one despairs of the success of the analytical method in science. In the *marginalia*, the word "*Causalismus*" is the repeated key-notion to assess that confidence in the future of analytical science.

The hypothetico-deductive approach, or even the nomological one, was later preferred by the members of the "Vienna Circle". That only confirms that Menger belonged to the world *before* logical positivism. Menger's times were that of *Comte's positivism*, although he did not endorse it for his philosophy of science. Anyway, Menger avoided strange readings like those Cairnes' criticism displays at times (provoking disputes with defenders of Comte in England, like Frederic Harrison, in his reply (July 1870) to Cairnes' article. Cairnes reprinted that dispute in the volume that Menger read but the argument gets confuse and Comte is seemingly misinterpreted by both Britons. In Menger's eyes, however, the system of Comte relied upon causality, and that was no failure. But Comte did not see how it could work for the benefit of separate sciences of the social phenomena. Contrary to Comte, isolating a pure science of political economy is possible and necessary for Menger. Just like about Kant,[60] Menger thought that, unfortunately, Comte did not believe in a science of social phenomena based on pure reason to understand trade, exchange, etc. Menger wanted precisely that.

Menger's notes referring directly to Comte's writings (and not Cairnes' account of the latter) indeed stress the same point, and confirm the idea that, to Menger, if there was a contradiction between Comtian methodology and Smithian political economy, both were in their own respect defective. Menger thought that their followers (like Cairnes) were either over-enthusiastic about what had really been achieved, or over-pessimistic when, like Comte, bluntly calling the whole thing "deceptive" and "impossible". The "true" method of economics was not absent from Smith's works, but intertwined with arguments

---

[60] See above footnote 37 in this chapter.

that a truly "positive" attitude should do away with.[61] Menger was confident that he could precisely practice that attitude.

[61] Menger quotes at the back of the dedication page of his volume of the *Grundsätze*: "Comte (bei Cairnes p. 267, 285) denies that the Smithian Political Economy is a science. He finds that the economic facts are intertwined with facts of many other kinds and the science of society must therefore be considered as a *whole*" (we translate from: "Comte (bei Cairnes p. 267, 285) leugnet dass die Smithische Nationaloe[konomie] eine Wissenschaft ist [.] Er findet dass die wirtschaftlichen Thatsachen von verschiedenartigen andern Thatsachen durchwoben sind und die Gesellschaftswissenschaft deshalb als ein *Ganzes* betrachtet werden muss".

Inductivism and Anti-essentialism in Menger's work

Karl Milford

I. Carl Menger's intellectual biography shows an unexpected turn in the 70ies and beginning 80ies of the 19th century. Although he intended to publish a four volume treatise on economics he obviously discarded that plan after having published its first volume, *Grundsätze der Volkswirthschaftslehre* in 1871[62]. Instead of writing the three remaining volumes he started to work on epistemological and methodological problems of the theoretical social sciences and published a rather small volume, *Untersuchungen über die Methode der Socialwissenschaften und der Politischen Oekonomie insbesondere*[63], 12 years later. Actually both volumes are devoted to the discussion of economic and methodological issues but with much different emphasis. Whereas the former primarily discusses open problems in economic theory, such as value and price theory, the latter explicitly considers methodological and epistemological problems that form the basis of the former.

The main problem Menger wants to solve in his *Grundsätze* is the problem of finding a satisfactory explanation of exchange and relative prices. The state of contemporary price theory was quite unsatisfactory because of its heterogeneity and incompetence of explaining exchange. Neither of the existing labour and cost theoretical explanations nor the existing subjectivist explanations was able to explain exchange and relative prices satisfactory. But Menger was aware that the explanatory power of economic theory is almost zero unless it provides satisfactory explanations of exchange and relative prices and therefore emphasises that a solution of these problems is most urgent. Since he believes that the progress of economic theory is seriously impeded unless such a theory exists, he states that the primary aim of his analysis consists in providing

> "… a price theory based upon reality and placing all phenomena (including interest, wages, ground rent, etc.) together under one unified point of view."[64]

The solution of the price theoretical problem which Menger suggests is embedded in a problem situation which basically can be described by four different positions. Each position is a combination of a behavioural and a methodological theory. Whereas the behavioural theories explain the evaluating behaviour of individuals and on that basis exchange and relative prices, the methodological theories ascertain something about science, for instance, about the structure of a satisfactory explanation in the theoretical social sciences. The behavioural theo-

---

[62] Menger (1871/1981); quoted in the text as *Grundsätze*.
[63] Menger (1871/1985); quoted in the text as *Untersuchungen*.
[64] Menger (1981, p. 49).

ries in turn can be classified into objective and subjective value theories. Objective value theories assert that individuals evaluate physical objects as goods because they are labour products; subjective value theories explain that individuals evaluate physical objects as goods according to their preferences only.

The methodological theories of those combinations can be classified into the positions of methodological individualism on the one hand and into the positions of methodological essentialist inductivism or methodological collectivism on the other. Methodological individualism requires that social institutions and processes are explained as the unintended results of the interplay of individual intended actions; in contrast methodological essentialist inductivism or methodological collectivism maintains that there exists at least one social fact that can not be explained on an individualistic basis and therefore requires an explanation along different methodological principles such as those of methodological essentialist inductivism or methodological collectivism.

It is interesting to note that in the history of economic ideas the four logically possible combinations of value and methodological theories were in fact developed by different authors. Smith's position can be regarded as a combination of objective value theory and an individualistic approach; the positions represented by many neoclassical authors and by the representatives of the so called Austrian school of economics as well, as for instance by Menger, Mises[65] or Hayek[66] – and long before them, Hufeland[67] – are combinations of subjective value theories and methodological individualism; In contrast the positions developed by the authors of the so called German historical school of economics, like Roscher[68], Hildebrand[69], and Knies[70] represent combinations of subjective value theories and methodological essentialist inductivism. And the positions of Marx and to some extent of J. S. Mill[71] can be regarded as combinations of objective value theories and methodological essentialist inductivism or methodological collectivism.

However, it is not only worth noting that those logically possible combinations were in fact developed in the history of economic ideas. It is also of much interest to note that the history of economic ideas shows internal relations existing between them. Frequently the different positions are the result of critical investigations scrutinising the validity of existing combinations. For instance, Hufeland's position results from his critique of Smith's position: it retains Smith's individualistic approach but substitutes his objective value theory by a radical theory of subjective evaluations. His position, however, was to become a

[65] Mises (1933).
[66] Hayek (1979).
[67] Hufeland (1807).
[68] Roscher (1842), (1843).
[69] Hildebrand (1848).
[70] Knies (1853).
[71] Mill (1843/1974), (1848/1974), (1848/1965).

major factor for the ensuing development of economic ideas by German authors such as Rau[72] and Hermann[73]. His theory of subjective evaluations as a basis for explaining exchange and relative prices triggered a special German tradition (Gebrauchswertschule) which later was continued by the authors of the German historical school. But the authors of that school, although retaining different kinds of subjective value theories as a basis for explaining relative prices rejected individualistic explanations of social and economic institutions and substituted methodological individualism by methodological essentialist inductivism. Yet their price theories remained unsatisfactory and Menger replaced their position of methodological essentialist inductivism by one of methodological individualism. He thought that the German methodological position here is a major cause for their unsatisfactory price theories. By substituting methodological individualism for methodological essentialist inductivism and by combining that position with an improved theory of subjective evaluations, Menger basically reanimated Hufeland's position developed about 60 years earlier.

II. According to Menger a satisfactory explanation of exchange and relative prices can only be found on the basis of a relational behavioural theory. In contrast to essentialist theories such a theory investigates the behaviour of humans (or in the natural sciences for instance that of physical objects) by analysing their behaviour under different conditions and by establishing regularities or laws on that observational basis.[74] Menger maintains that

> "... economic theory is concerned ... with the *conditions* under which men engage in provident activity directed to the satisfaction of their needs. [and that it investigates] ... under what conditions a thing ... is a *good*, whether and under what conditions it is an *economic good*, whether and under what conditions it posses *value*, ... and how large the *measure* of this value is ... [and] whether and under what conditions an *economic exchange* of goods will take place between two economizing individuals, and the limits within which a *price* can be established if an exchange does occur ... [and that on that basis]... the phenomena of economic life, like those of nature, are ordered strictly in accordance with definite laws."[75]

In Menger's view, however, such a relational behavioural theory of economic behaviour can only be developed within a framework that combines a theory of subjective evaluations and the principles of methodological individualism. As a behavioural theory explaining the evaluating behaviour of individuals under different conditions, the theory of subjective evaluations has more explanatory

---

[72] Rau (1826).
[73] Hermann (1832).
[74] Popper (1979, sec. 10 and 29).
[75] Menger (1981, p. 48).

power than other theories have; but without combining it with methodological individualism it remains rather blind, since by applying other methods social regularities or laws are not established on the basis of economic behaviour. The idea of developing a relational behavioural economic theory has then to be discarded. Accordingly, Menger develops the structure of his *Grundsätze* along those considerations. After having developed a relational behavioural theory in chapter I which states the conditions under which individuals regard things as goods, Menger proceeds in chapter II to develop a theory of the hierarchical order of goods in order to show that the demand for inputs is derived from the demand for final goods and that the conditions of economic behaviour uncovered in the previous chapter apply here as well. In the chapter on value (chapter III) Menger investigates the conditions and principles that determine the evaluating behaviour of individuals by applying systematically the ideas of marginal utility and the equimarginal principle in order to explain demand. And chapters IV and V are devoted to explain exchange and relative prices as the unintended outcome of the interplay of individual intended actions. Having thus established the social laws of individual economic behaviour and shown how they determine and regulate other social processes, institutions and structures, Menger proceeds to clarify on that basis issues that in other theories were considered as important.

According to Menger his relational behavioural economic theory is an empirical theory derived from observation. He shares the prevailing contemporary epistemological and methodological views that empirical science is characterised by the so called method of induction. According to that method there exist content enlarging and truth preserving valid inferences. Thus the conclusions of such inferences entail more information than the premises and the authors defending this method thought that only by applying inductive methods genuinely new synthetical and empirical knowledge can be acquired. In contrast it was emphasised that the conclusions of deductive inferences can not form genuine new additions to synthetic and empirical knowledge because they are analytic only.[76]

According to inductivism, science starts from singular observational statements describing observations or personal experiences (introspection) and infers from that empirical basis strictly universal regularities or laws by content enlarging and truth preserving inferences. Sharing that view Menger states that

> "… [he] endeavoured to reduce the complex phenomena of human economic activity to the simplest elements that can still be subjected to accurate observation, to apply to these elements the measure corresponding to their nature and constantly adhering to this measure, to investigate the manner in which the more complex economic phenomena evolve from their elements according to definite principles."[77]

[76] Cf. For instance Mill (1843/1974) or Schlick (1974).
[77] Menger (1981, pp. 46, 47).

In Menger's view, this method of inferring regularities from an observational basis has "... mistakenly be[en] called the natural scientific method". [78] But in his view it is "... a method common to all fields of empirical knowledge, and should properly be called the empirical method."[79] (p. 47) He readily concedes that the different areas of research of the social and the natural sciences require specific methods which can not be uncritically transferred; but the basic principle according to which the findings of the empirical sciences must be based on observation is the same for both disciplines. According to him the German authors' attempts of providing satisfactory explanations of relative prices on the basis of a theory of subjective evaluations faltered and ultimately failed because they mistakenly took history to constitute the empirical basis of theoretical social research and not singular statements describing observable behaviour and personal experiences (introspection). He maintains that the German authors influenced by the general principles of historism, tried to transfer Bacon's inductive method into the social sciences without, however, having realised that Bacon's aim was to establish relational behavioural theories in the natural sciences. According to Menger the German's view that the natural and the social sciences are empirical sciences and that they are characterised by the method of induction is true; but their views that history constitutes the empirical basis of social science is false. He writes:

> "Past attempts to carry over the peculiarities of the natural scientific method of investigation uncritically into economics have led to most serious methodological errors, and to idle play with external analogies between the phenomena of economics and those of nature. Bacon said of scholars of this description: 'Magna cum vanitate et despientia inanes similitudes et sympathias rerum describunt atque etiam quandoque affingunt', a statement which strangely enough, is still true today of precisely those writers on economic subjects who continue to call themselves disciples of Bacon while completely misunderstanding the spirit of his method."[80]

III. According to Menger, any satisfactory economic theory in general, and a unified price theory in particular, has to be developed as a relational behavioural theory within a framework that combines the principles of methodological individualism and a theory of subjective evaluations. He maintains that such a theory has to be grounded on an empirical basis which is constituted by singular statements describing observations and personal experiences or introspection. Apart from solving the open price theoretical problems his main concern in the *Grundsätze* is to show that any essentialist approach to social science is most

---

[78] Menger (1981, p. 47).
[79] Menger (1981, p. 47).
[80] Menger (1981, p. 47).

unfruitful and that its adequate empirical basis is based on observation and not on history. That Menger discusses these methodological problems in the *Grundsätze* results from the elements that constituted the special historical problem situation in which he happened to find himself. Although the German economists formed some elements of a relational behavioural theory in order to explain relative prices and exchange they rejected methodological individualism and replaced it by methodological essentialist inductivism. But according to Menger all kinds of essentialism have to be discarded in order to establish a successful economic theory.

By describing this project in the preface of his *Grundsätze* and by carrying it out in the ensuing chapters of that book, Menger reanimated a position which was developed much earlier, i.e. in 1807 by Hufeland[81]. Like Menger, Hufeland considers the state of contemporary price theory as most unsatisfactory and tries to develop a unified price theory as a behavioural theory on the basis of a frame work of methodological individualism and a theory of subjective evaluations. Hufeland is the first economists to develop such a combination, but unlike the theory of Menger, his price theory can not explain how marginal utilities determine relative prices since his theory lacks the notion of marginal utility and the equimarginal principle. His price theory is a theory of reservation prices which explains the different factors determining the reservational supply and demand prices.

But, although Hufeland can not explain relative prices satisfactorily, his treatise *Neue Grundlegung der Staatswirthschaftskunst durch Prüfung und Berichtigung ihrer Hauptbegriffe, von Gut, Werth, Preis, Geld und Volksvermögen, mit ununterbrochener Rücksicht auf die bisherigen Systeme*[82] is most important for the ensuing development of economics in Germany and Austria. By discarding any essentialist approach and by replacing it by a combination of a radical theory of subjective evaluations and the principles of metho-dological individualism he radically shifts the problem situation and the pro-blems of economic theory. According to him contemporary economic theories are unsatisfactory because they attempt to solve behavioural problems by providing answers that explain the origin of goods and thus subconsciously remain within an essentialist framework. He maintains that Smith's economic theory like that of the physiocrats asserts that the essence of a good is its nature of being a product of labour or of land and not the result of the evaluating behaviour of individuals under different conditions. Accordingly these theories attempt to establish the origin or source of physical objects but do not provide an explanation of the evaluating behaviour of humans. In contrast Hufeland emphasises that a satisfactory economic theory which attempts to explain the economic behaviour of humans has to be established on the basis of a theory of evaluations which ex-

[81] Hufeland (1807).
[82] Hufeland (1807); quoted as *Grundlegung*.

plains their evaluating behaviour since that evaluating behaviour transforms physical objects into goods.

Since both, Hufeland and Menger reject an essentialist approach to social theory by combining the principles of methodological individualism and a subjective value theory it is not surprising that the structure of Hufeland's *Grundlegung* closely resembles that of Menger's *Grundsätze*. After developing a radical theory of subjective evaluations in the chapter entitled 'Goods in general', he proceeds to explain exchange in a chapter on 'Goods for many' and then continues his analysis with a chapter on the 'Theory of prices' where he develops his price theoretical considerations. In the second edition of his *Grundlegung* Hufeland complements that analysis by adding a chapter on 'The theory of money'.[83]

The structural similarities of Hufeland's and Menger's works result of course from their similar approach of developing a non-essentialist behavioural economic theory based on a framework of methodological individualism and subjective value theory. But unlike Menger in the *Grundsätze*, Hufeland is not concerned about the empirical basis of economics and in fact develops an anti-inductivist approach. Many 19th century German economists believe that the incompetence and failure of contemporary economic theories, especially those of Smith result from having been based on an uncertain and unproven empirical basis. Accordingly it was held that even valid inductive inferences necessarily yield false theories and that economics was in need of a new and proven empirical basis.

In contrast to other German economists Hufeland believes that economic theory needs not to be established on such a new basis. He rather regards economic facts as explanatory problems and not as evidence supporting and verifying theories. He certainly concedes that the facts provided by statistics and history frequently support economic theories;[84] but he proceeds by emphasizing that the seemingly certain facts established by statistics and history are frequently quite uncertain and that science is interested in facts because it primarily considers them to be explanatory problems. He writes as follows:

> „... abgerechnet, daß so viele der durch sie [Statistik, Geschichte] verbreiteten Thatsachen *ungewiß* und *unbestimmt sind*; so sind doch *alle* solche Thatsachen nur dann etwas für die Staatswirthschaftslehre werth, wenn man sie in ihren Ursachen hinauf verfolgen und in ihre Bestandtheile auflösen kann, *weil es gar keinen anderen Weg gibt*, um sie mit staatswirthschaftlichen Lehren in Verbindung zu setzen."[85]

[83] Hufeland (1815).

[84] Statistik und Geschichte [sind] ganz vorzügliche Hilfsmittel für die Staatswirthschaftslehre; sie entfalten in ihren ungeheuren Schätzen Belege für die einzelnen Lehren derselben, und fordern sie gleichsam zu immerwährenden Beziehungen und Anwendungen auf. (Hufeland 1807, Vorrede p. 21).

[85] Hufeland (1807, Vorrede, p. 22).

From such considerations Hufeland infers that the aim of establishing an absolutely certain empirical basis ought to be discarded since it cannot be achieved. According to him so called 'naked' facts, i.e. facts that bear no relation to a theory whatsoever, are completely uninteresting for science. In his view the importance of facts for science rather results from the circumstance that they constitute explanatory problems for scientific investigations. He emphasises that if facts are uncertain it is quite sufficient:

> „... allen nur zur Hälfte bekannten Thatsachen ihre Brauchbarkeit zu sicheren Belehrung abzuleugnen, wenn *gleich sie immer bey der Untersuchung und Anwendung als aufzulösende Probleme ihren großen Werth haben können.* Wie wenig ohnehin Zahlen und Maaße *für sich* und ohne genaueste Kenntniß aller Nebenbeziehungen hier brauchbar sind, wird die Folge der Betrachtungen noch mehr ergeben.“[86]

Presumably Hufeland thought that such insights may be quite surprising for his readers. He probably expected that his readers share the traditional view that empricism is necessarily linked to induction and that empirical science is characterised by inductive methods. Accordingly he warns them not to expect the constitution of a new empirical basis by amassing new and seemingly certain data. He writes as follows:

> „Vielleicht erwartet man auch eine große Menge neuer Thatsachen in diesem Buche. Man wird bey einiger Aufmerksamkeit finden, daß es auch an solchen nicht mangelt ... aber bey weitem der größte Theil meiner Belege ist aus schon bekannten staatswirthschaftlichen Büchern genommen und nur zu meinem Zweck bearbeitet.“[87]

According to Hufeland facts are interesting for science because they constitute explanatory problems and not a certain empirical basis. But in his view the importance of facts for science not only results from their role as explanatory problems. He also emphasises that facts constitute the critical standard of which scientific theories may fall short. And in contrast to the general contemporary philosophical views according to which facts serve primarily as absolutely certain empirical basis and as verifying instances, Hufeland proposes that the importance of facts lies in their function to examine theories. He opines that empirical critique of theories is the motor of scientific progress and that it is

> „... merkwürdig und ergötzend ... nun ferner zu verfolgen, wie in allen folgenden Zeiten immer jedes spätere System dieser Wissenschaft [Staatswirthschaft] aus der Aufdeckung der Fehler der früheren herausgegangen ist.“[88]

---

[86] Hufeland (1807, Vorrede, p. 22).
[87] Hufeland (1807, Vorrede, P. 21).
[88] Hufeland (1807, Vorrede, p. 5).

Accordingly he states that the general task of science is to propose better theories, that is, theories that have more explanatory power than other ones; and he believes that his economic theory meets that methodological requirement.[89] However, although he in effect radically alters the problem situation of economic theory and shifts economic theory onto completely new rails, his intentions are by no means to develop a new and incommensurable theory that disregards available findings. In his view economic thought progresses continuously but he also believes that theories that are unsatisfactory with respect to the solution of the problems which they were designed for have to be improved or given up in that process. According to him theories may founder because they are logically or empirically inconsistent but otherwise have to be integrated into the new theoretical system.

However, he maintains that in order to qualify as better theories, new theories have to meet particular methodological requirements. He states that the new theories have to provide new explanations which are based on principally different ideas as compared to the prevailing ones in that science[90]. In addition he demands that the new theory not only explains the facts explained by the old one, but that those explanations are better. In his view better explanations provide new and better arguments which on the basis of his new ideas provide new interpretations of well known old contentions and processes.[91]

Hufeland, however, maintains that the methodological requirements of "novelty" and "better explanation" are not sufficient for a new theory to be accepted. He also emphasises that such a theory must be capable of providing new and satisfactory explanations of new facts and processes. Such a theory he demands must be capable of triggering the development of other new theories.[92]

To put it in a nutshell, Hufeland develops a *behavioural* and *non-essentialist* economic theory that consists of two elements: a behavioural theory explaining the evaluating behaviour of humans and a methodological theory saying that a

[89] „Denn ich gestehe es frey, daß ich eine durchaus veränderte Hauptansicht dieser Wissenschaft darzustellen vorhabe, unter der sich, wie mir scheint, vieles bisher schon behauptete fester begründen, und manch neue Lehre hervorgehen wird. Ohne diese Veränderung würde mir mein ganzes Vorhaben kaum der Mühe werth scheinen." (Hufeland 1807, p. 18, Vorrede).

[90] Cf. the quotation in ftn. 28 where it says " … wie es nun scheint, vieles bisher schon behauptete fester begründen, und manch neue Lehre hervorgehen wird ..." (Hufeland 1807, Vorrede, p. 18).

[91] „Immer hoffe ich, Unpartheyische werden es mir zugestehen, es sey nicht alles, besonders nicht die Hauptansicht entlehnt; und wenn sie daneben noch überzeugt würden, daß selbst bekannte Behauptungen und Entwicklungen durch die Verbindung mit anderen allgemeinen von mir behaupteten zuweilen ein neues Licht erhalten hätten;" (Hufeland 1807, p. 19 Vorrede).

[92] cf. the second part of the quotation given in ftn. 1 where Hufeland says " ... und manch neue Lehre hervorgehen wird." (Hufeland 1807, p. 18, Vorrede).

satisfactory behavioural economic theory must correspond to the methodological principles of methodological individualism. As a behavioural theory economic theory requires that social regularities are explained as unintended man made products which are derived from the interplay of individual human behaviour. Accordingly social and economic theories have to be based on a theory that explains the evaluating behaviour of individuals: a behavioural economic theory that states social and economic laws implies methodological individualism.

Since any economic theory having explanatory power must be based on a behavioural theory explaining the evaluating behaviour of individuals Hufeland first examines contemporary economic theories explaining the evaluating behaviour of individuals. Writing in 1807 he not unreasonably believes that Smith's explanation of that behaviour as well as his economic theories based on that explanation are the most advanced ones. Accordingly he starts with a critical investigation of Smith labour theory and develops 8 different arguments against his theory which are still relevant and defended in present histories of economic ideas.[93] Hufeland discusses Smith's explanations of exchange and relative prices in considerable detail. He not only emphasises the different versions of that theory Smith provides in his writings but also considers the difficulties labour theoretical explanations meet when capital goods are introduced. He also emphasises that the value of goods cannot be measured by the disutility of labour, pointing out that many goods simply are not labour products. According to Hufeland Smith labour theoretical approach is logically inconsistent as well as falsified by experience and therefore has to be rejected.

However, Hufeland maintains that his critique of Smith's labour theory also provides results which are most important with respect to the general research programme of economics. According to him the basic reason for the failure of his theories results from trying to answer behavioural questions by developing not a behavioural theory but by stating a theory that explains the origin of physical objects. He points out that Smith explains that labour is the cause of a commodity's value and therefore falsely investigates the role labour has as a causal factor in the production process of physical objects. Likewise he emphasises that the economic theories of physiocracy suffer from similar mistakes by explaining that the source of value is land or nature. According to Hufeland this pattern of argument can be found in all contemporary economic theories; they all attempt to answer questions of behaviour by trying to find satisfactory answers to questions of origin and therefore are doomed to fail.[94] He states that:

---

[93] cf. Blaug (1985).

[94] Hufeland resumes: „Die gesammten bisherigen Systeme über den Ursprung des Volksvermögens glaubten alles erschöpft zu haben, wenn sie die Entstehung der Gegenstände die Güter sein könnten, entwickelten;“. (Hufeland 1807, p. 40).

> "... all available systems accounting for the origin of the wealth of a nation believed to have provided exhaustive explanations by referring to the origin of objects, which eventually may become commodities."[95]

However, against that approach Hufeland objects that the theories that explain goods by referring to their origin are refuted by experience. Labour, nature and psychological motivations are probable preconditions for producing goods; but by producing physical objects these objects do not become goods. He emphasises that many physical objects that human evaluate as goods are created without using labour or psychological motivations and that by referring to the possible sources of their origin one cannot explain in principle why individuals evaluate them as goods.

However, Hufeland does not only emphasise that theories that explain goods (and services) by referring to their origins are inconsistent and empirically refuted. He also tries to explain the origin of that fundamental mistake which triggered a most unsuccessful research programme for economics. According to him the theories based on that mistaken research programme result from confounding two central points any satisfactory theory explaining goods has to observe. Theories that explain goods necessarily have to presuppose the existence of the physical objects which are evaluated as goods by humans; and they also have to regard the aims which individuals seek to achieve by using those physical objects as means. He therefore emphasises that economic theories need to presuppose the existence of physical objects and the existence of human wants in order to explain the evaluating behaviour of individuals. However, according to Hufeland the presupposition of physical objects by any economic theory is quite unimportant compared to an analysis of the different aims individuals want to achieve. In order to explain the evaluating behaviour of individuals and on that basis social regularities and institutions only their preferences, their aims and their consideration regarding the capability of physical objects to satisfy wants are important. The unsuccessful contemporary research programme of economics originated simply from having confounded the issues that have to be analysed. Hufeland writes as follows:

> "The proper characteristic of the concepts 'good' and 'value' [refers] not to something previous ... Rather it is determined by that what emerges and what can be produced from them – in any case by something whose present existence needs to be assumed: they ought to have an effect on an aim; and thereby their origin has not to be taken into account. Immediately this is a point which cannot be emphasised early enough; because precisely the point that all goods relate to something in the future was not sufficiently observed and seems to me to be the major cause for the deficiency of some of the new economic systems. They all based their doc-

[95] translation of ftn. 33.

> trines on the origin of objects, which may become goods; but just their quality as goods, which is decisive in this science, is independent of their origin."[96]

According to Hufeland the value and price theories that ascertain questions of origin of objects must therefore fail in principle. The basic questions of "How are goods possible? [and] How can physical objects become goods?",[97] those questions await new solutions. In his view, however, these new solutions can only be found by posing a new research question which refers to the evaluating behaviour of humans and not to the origin of physical objects. Questions of origin have to be substituted by questions of behaviour.

On the basis of those considerations Hufeland develops a radical theory of subjective evaluations. Whether humans regard physical objects or actions as goods and services depends according to that theory on the aims which they try to achieve. He explains that human aims primarily originate in human ideas and opinions and that knowledge, ideas and fantasy are the prime movers of economic development and not for instance land or mineral resources. And although he admits of course the biological nature of human wants he regards them as negligible factors for explaining the diversity, historicity and complexity of the social world and in particular emphasises that humans are rather indetermined with respect to their choice of aims and means of achieving them. He maintains that different individuals have different knowledge and that their different knowledge as well as the uncovering of new aims and new means for achieving them is decisive for economic development. According to Hufeland, one may say that:

> "... goods are goods only because of the ideas humans (one or more) have about them. They never would be and could not be [goods] without that relation between them and the human ideas on them."[98]

And he also states the following:

> "Perhaps not one good can be found which to all humans appears as a good on the basis of a necessary idea which is equal to all of them – let alone one which is equally evaluated by them. Hence the designation of *good* and *value* depends only on accidental, different and changing ideas, i.e. on *opinions*."[99]

This radical theory of subjective evaluations is the foundation upon which Hufeland explains market prices. He develops a kind of reservational price theory

[96] Hufeland (1807, pp. 19, 20).
[97] Hufeland (1807, p. 20).
[98] Hufeland (1807, p. 21).
[99] Hufeland (1807, pp. 22 – 23).

and ascertains the factors that determine the reservation prices of buyers and sellers. According to him any satisfactory explanation of exchange has to run in terms of an analysis that describes social situations in which humans act as evaluating individuals. In such situations buyers as well as sellers evaluate goods according to their preferences and compare the exchange values of supplied and demanded goods. Hufeland calls that comparison of exchange values price and emphasises that all values of exchange result from subjective evaluations of individuals.

However, according to him, individuals first determine their own reservation prices which are different from that price according to which goods exchange on the market. The individual reservation prices of buyers and sellers he calls unilateral prices; those at which exchange takes place bilateral prices. According to the factors determining the unilateral prices he distinguishes between internal unilateral prices and external unilateral prices. Whereas the former is determined by factors influencing the sellers' reservation price, the latter is determined by factors influencing the buyers' considerations. However, according to Hufeland the factors determining the internal as well as the external unilateral prices can be classified into two broad categories. One set concerns the costs of production of a good and one the preferences of humans. If an internal or external reservation price is primarily determined by cost considerations Hufeland calls that price real internal price if it relates to the seller's considerations; if it concerns the buyer's decision he calls it real external unilateral price; if it is primarily determined by the preferences of individuals he calls it voluntary internal or voluntary external price.

Hufeland's analysis of the different factors determining the reservational prices of buyers and sellers provides the basis for his price theory. He claims that his theory is more general and has greater explanatory power than other contemporary theories because it integrates cost theoretical considerations as factors that determine prices in special situations only. However, basically his price theory explains relative prices mainly by referring to the factors determining the internal and external prices of buyers and sellers. Since internal and external prices are reservational prices he explains market prices as an outcome of the interplay of individual intentions. However, his price theoretical considerations remain unsuccessful since his theory lacks the notions of marginal utility and the equimargnial principle, and thus can not explain how relative prices are determined on the basis of the evaluating behaviour of individuals. Although he tried to explain prices as an unintended outcome of the interplay of intended actions by referring to the role of preferences, knowledge, information and opinions and their unequal distribution among individuals the price theoretical problem remains open.

Hufeland combines this radical subjective value theory according to which individuals evaluate physical objects as goods primarily on the basis of their preferences, subjective knowledge and opinions with the principles of methodological individualism since he believes that otherwise a satisfactory behavioural economic theory can not be established. In order to show the necessity of combining his theory of subjective evaluations with the principles of methodological inidividualism he contrasts his considerations with an essentialist and collectivist explanation of societies and social institutions. Actually his non-essentialist approach to economics is already exemplified by the structure of his *Grundlegung* and the manner he carries out his project of establishing a behavioural economic theory. However, in order to support his claim Hufeland explicitly discards any essentialist and collectivist approach by criticising the so called organic theory of the state and other collectivist or essentialist ideas.

An essentialist theory of the state or of society regards the state or society not as structures which are the outcome of individual actions but as entities which are characterized by their own essence or nature and determined by specific regularities. Since according to that theory the society or the state can act like individuals, Hufeland scrutinises the problem whether societies, social institutions, the state or nations are capable of setting and achieving aims like individuals. According to him they can not. If the state or other social institutions were endowed with essences such that they were able to act like individuals they were also capable of evaluating physical things as goods. But according to Hufeland states neither have preferences, nor subjective knowledge nor fantasy. The state can not create goods, although it may perhaps produce physical things which through the preferences and evaluations of individuals may become goods. He resumes that as follows:

> „Die Wirksamkeit des Staates ist wieder nur eine Wirksamkeit von Menschen; und auch diese, die im Namen des Staates wirken, können auf andere nur wirken, wie andere Menschen; sie wirken auf die Natur, und dadurch auf die Menschen.“[100]

According to Hufeland social institutions, structures or regularities can only be explained by a relational behavioural theory which explains them as the unintended result of the interplay of intended individual actions, or as he says with respect to economic phenomena as a result of the "... busy and often unconscious concurring activities of many"[101] He maintains that the task of social science is to explain social processes or institutions not as a designed result of some contractual agreement or as the result of a single conscious and individual voluntary decision but as the unintended feed back of the concurrence of many individual intended actions. He states the following:

---

[100] Hufeland (1807, p 114).
[101] Hufeland (1807, Vorrede p. 26).

> "One admires the effects great souls exert on humans, and I am not in the least inclined to impair that object of admiration with petty psychological assessments or to drag it down to something ordinary. [...] But with respect to the human race admiration is called by the consideration of the products and the sum of products which originated slowly and unnoticed from the busy and unconscious concurring activities of many."[102]

As a consequence of his rigorous adherence to the principles of methodological individualism he also rejects the concept of 'Volkswirtschaft' or 'national economy' stating the following:

> "With economy one always associates a leading manager, who, however, is absent according to the correct view of a national economy, where many thousand manage their affairs and where precisely the amalgamation of their views and intentions is quite arbitrary."[103]

IV. Hufeland's rejection of any kind of essentialist approach to the theoretical social sciences of which only a brief outline was given here is very detailed. He even tries to support his individualistic behavioural approach by developing a philosophical doctrine according to which one can distinguish different autonomous spheres and among them a social universe. However, the history of economic ideas in Germany shows that Hufeland's anti-essentialist relational behavioural approach did not succeed. The main authors publishing after him such as Rau or Hermann accept only a much less radical version of his subjective value theory as a basis for explaining (relative) prices. In doing so they impli-citly also accepted a behavioural approach to economics. But the importance of Hufeland's combination of subjective value theory and methodological individualism seems to have gone unnoticed by them.

Hufeland's ideas of an autonomous social universe which is governed by social regularities that are the unintended results of the interplay of intended actions and which have to be explained on the basis of a relational behavioural theory seems not to have inspired their works. Unlike Hufeland, Rau for instance, believes that the social universe is not an autonomous and unintended product of man. In his view the social regularities derive from the regularities of the natural universe which also entails the laws that regulate the psychology of humans. According to him these regularities or laws can be uncovered by the method of induction and it seems that he, although before Mill, develops ideas not quite unlike to those of Mill, although perhaps for different reasons. Other authors, such as Hermann, primarily discuss economic problems and rather refrain from considering epistemological and methodological problems. With the

---

102 Hufeland (1807, Vorrede p. 26).
103 Hufeland (1807, Vorrede p. 14).

publications of Roscher, the founder of the so called German historical school of economics this development in German economics comes to an end.

A major problem considered in the methodological debates in the 19th century was the structure of a theoretical explanation in the theoretical social sciences. In contrast to the 18th century positions social and cultural institutions were regarded as man made products which though unplanned require a special kind of explanation. Basically two types of explanations were considered here: individualistic and collectivistic ones.

However, for many 19th century social scientists individualistic explanations are inadequate and unacceptable. A standard argument put forward against individualistic explanations is that they can not explain the coherence of social institutions or society unless a special psychological hypothesis about the nature of man is introduced. Other objections emphasise that individuals act within a framework of social and cultural institutions and that any individualistic explanation of that framework again requires the presupposition of a different framework. It is argued that this procedure necessarily leads into an infinite regress of explanations which can not be accepted according to scientific standards. In order to be accepted these standards require that genuine scientific explanations are ultimate explanations which means that they provide absolutely certain and proven true knowledge. Accordingly it is reasoned that other than individualistic methods are needed in order to provide satisfactory explanations of the cultural and social framework in which individuals act.

In order to solve that problem Roscher developed an essentialist and inductivist method which became the basis of the German historical school's research programme. In his *Leben, Werk und Zeitalter des Thukydides*, published in 1842, Roscher transforms Rankes essentialist philosophy of history into an inductivist approach. According to that approach history is the empirical basis of theoretical social sciences and the theoretical social sciences are the theory of history. According to that view the task of social science is to establish the laws of historical development.

Ranke, like Hegel and many other representatives of German idealism and historism reanimated some Aristotelian essentialist ideas in his philosophy of history.[104] According to Ranke social and cultural institutions are concrete emanations of the essence of a people or a nation. Similar to Aristoteles' essentialist philosophy he explains that the essence of a thing resides within that thing as potentiality, and may come to existence in concrete historical situations. Thus the essence of a thing becomes at least partly observable and by studying its historical development may finally be described by some historical law. Accordingly true scientific knowledge of a people, a nation or of social institutions or economic systems can be acquired by describing that nation's, or people's, or social institution's historical development by some kind of historical law.

[104] Cf. G. Iggers (1997).

However, although much influenced by Ranke's essentialist philosophy of history, Roscher is much more interested in its empirical and inductivist transformation.[105] In his *Leben, Werk und Zeitalter des Thukydides*, Roscher tries to carry out that transformation by developing a philosophy of history and of the social sciences which explains how such laws of historical development can be uncovered and established. This philosophy, however, Roscher formulates in 'naturalistic' terms, that is, as a sociological description of the historian's behaviour when they research. Basically Roscher develops here a theory which corresponds closely to an inductivist picture of science. Accordingly he describes the activities of historians when establishing the empirical basis as collecting historical data and facts which form the basis upon which the historical (and social) theories are grounded. However, he emphasises that, although science is capable of establishing laws of historical development, it can not explain them. In his view trying to explain the historical and natural laws means to uncover God's plans which possibly may be achieved by other divine creatures, but never by humble humans.

V. In his *Grundriß zu Vorlesungen über Staatswirthschaft*, published in 1843 Roscher transfers this methodological essentialist inductivism to economics and to politics. In his economic works, however, he also retains a theory of subjective evaluations upon which he establishes a reservational price theory. Basically this combination became characteristic for the representatives of the so called older and younger German historical school of economics, although the different authors of those schools placed much different emphasis on either of the elements of that combination. Schmoller, the major representative of the so called younger German historical school of economics placed much emphasis on the issue of constituting an absolute certain empirical basis for economic theory and publishes very detailed historical studies in economic history. Other authors such as Hildebrand and Knies who are representatives of the younger German historical school of economics are much influenced by the general tenets of historism such as relativism, and antinormativity. They believe that the idea of strictly universal social laws that are empirical, of social laws that are independent of time and place, has to be discarded altogether since social regularities are restricted to certain domains and historical periods only. And they also believe that historical periods can only be appraised and evaluated according to the standards existing in those periods.

In his *Grundsätze* Menger primarily reacts to the German's substitution of methodological essentialist inductivism for any kind of individualistic approach. According to him this substitution caused a disastrous problem shift in economic theory. He is well aware of the fruitful contributions of the authors of the Ger-

---

[105] For a detailed analysis of that transformation, cf. for instance Weber (1988) and Milford (1995).

man Gebrauchswertschule and their different subjective value theories as basis for explaining prices. This is not only shown by a general statement in the preface of his *Grundsätze* but also by his rather long digressions in the text regarding their different positions with respect to value and price theory.[106]

However, Menger not only rejects Roscher's methodological essentialist inductivism by developing a price theory on the basis of methodological individualism. The anti-essentialist position which he defends in the *Grundsätze* shows itself more explicitly in his theory of good and the theory of exchange. There Menger argues that Smith's failure to provide a satisfactory explanation of relative prices or exchange is basically due to the essentialist roots of labour theoretical explanations; and he also shows that as a consequence of that explanation Smith is forced to abandon methodological individualism, in contrast to his own intentions.

An essentialist theory of the good requires uncovering its essence that is a special characteristic that is constitutive for a physical object to be a good. If essences reside within things the essence of goods may be uncovered by observing the historical development of physical objects, either by intuition or by inductivist procedures. However, any historical study required to trace the essence of a good will try to ascertain its historical origin because only by having studied its complete course of historical development certain knowledge of its essence can be acquired. Essentialist doctrines typically pose questions of origin and not questions that ask for answers that explain the relational behaviour of some kind of entity or object under different conditions.

In contrast to such an essentialist approach in order to explain goods Menger develops a completely different theory in his *Grundsätze*. He develops a behavioural theory that scrutinises the conditions under which individuals regard physical objects and actions as goods and services and which emphasises the individuals' evaluative behaviour. According to that theory the wants, the preferences and the subjective evaluations determine whether they regard physical objects or actions as goods and services. Menger emphasises that the individual's preferences and evaluations may change under different conditions and that physical objects which once were evaluated as goods may again be regarded as such. After having explained the conditions under which individuals regard physical objects and services as goods he resumes his theory as follows:

> "From this it is evident that [the] goods-character is nothing inherent in goods and not a property of goods, but merely a relationship between certain things and men, the things obviously ceasing to be goods with the disappearance of this relationship."[107]

---

[106] cf. for instance appendix D of (Menger 1981) and Menger (1871, ftn. starting on p. 78).

[107] Menger (1981, p. 52).

Menger emphasises that anti-essentialist approach of explaining goods fairly frequently. For instance in a passage where he explains the distinction between economic and non-economic goods he opines that an essentialist theory can not establish such a demarcation. According to him such a demarcation can only be established with respect to the idea of scarcity, which, however, depends largely on the individualistic subjectivist evaluations of humans with respect to goods and wants. He maintains that

> "... if this has been established, it is also evident that the economic or non economic character of goods is nothing inherent in them not any property of them, and that therefore every good, without regard to its internal properties or its external attributes, attains economic character when it enters into the quantitative relationship explained above, and looses it when this relationship is reversed."[108]

Other passages in which he criticises an essentialist theory of the good can be found in his discussion of value theory. He summarises that discussion as follows:

> "Value is nothing inherent in goods, no property of them, nor an independent thing existing by itself. It is a judgment economizing men make about the importance of the goods at their disposal for the maintenance of their lives and well-being. Hence value does not exist outside the consciousness of men. It is, therefore, also quite erroneous to call a good that has value to economizing individuals a 'value' or for economists to speak of 'values' as of independent real things, and to objectify value in this way. For the entities that exist objectively are always only particular things, and their value is something fundamentally different from the things themselves; it is a judgment made by ... individuals ... Objectification of the value of goods, which is entirely *subjective* in nature, has nevertheless contributed very greatly to confusion about the basic principles of our science."[109]

According to Menger the disastrous consequences of an essentialist doctrine of goods are clearly exemplified by Smith's explanation of exchange. He explains that according to Smith individuals exchange equivalents when exchanging goods. However, he emphasises that such an explanation completely fails since it neither explains the end of that process nor its irreversibility. It is simply falsified by experience. In Mengers view this situation forces Smith to introduce a special psychological assumption about the nature of men which asserts a special propensity to truck and barter. However, according to Menger the introduc-

[108] Menger (1981, p. 101). and (1871, pp.60, 61); cf also the lengthy footnote on p. 61 of Menger (1871) which is included in the text of Menger (1981).
[109] Menger (1981, p. 121).

tion of that hypothesis worsens the theoretical situation for Smith even more because it completely drains the explanatory power of his theory. For,

> "[i]f trading were a pleasure itself, hence an end in itself ... there would ... be no reason ... why [men] should not trade back and forth an unlimited number of times."[110]

However, Menger not only shows that Smith's theory of exchange fails for logical and for empirical reasons. He also tries to explain that failure; and according to him this failure is basically due to the essentialist roots of any labour theory of goods. He explains that labour theoretical explanations of goods regard a good's essence in its being a labour product. In his view this may have triggered the idea that in an exchange process individuals actually exchange labour, because labour is the essence of goods. However, he reasons that since prices are the observable outcome of an exchange process, they may have been regarded as observable manifestations of the essence involved in that process, that is, labour. Accordingly he suggests that the magnitude of a price may also have been regarded as an observable measure of that essence and that goods are actually equivalents because they exchange at one observable price. He states:

> "But since prices are the only phenomena of the process that are directly perceptible, since their magnitudes can be measured exactly, and since daily living brings them unceasingly before our eyes, it was easy to commit the error of regarding the magnitude of price as the essential feature of an exchange, and as result of this mistake, to commit the further error of regarding the quantities of goods in an exchange as equivalents."[111]

Menger emphasises that there exist other unwanted consequences of essentialist doctrines in economics as well. In particular he believes that the essentialist elements in Smith's and in the German's authors theories become manifest in their explanations regarding the coherence of social institutions. According to him both, Smith and the German authors, especially Roscher, need to introduce special psychological assumptions in order to explain the coherence of social instiutions. In his view Smith explains the coherence of markets basically by introducing a special human propensity to truck and barter; and Roscher likewise introduces a psychological assumption which proposes a special 'Gemeinsinn' in individuals in order to explain their coherence. Both, Smith and Roscher reject thereby the principles of methodological individualism.

VI. That Smith and Roscher have to discard methodological individualism is in Menger's view a consequence of the essentialist roots of their theories. In contrast he maintains that explanations in the theoretical social sciences that are

---

[110] Menger (1981, p. 177).
[111] Menger (1981, p. 192).

structured according to the methodological requirements of methodological individualism do not require such additional assumptions in order to explain the coherence of social institutions. Individualistic explanations explain social coherence as unintended result of the interplay of intended actions. However, whereas Menger demonstrates that anti-essentialist approach of explaining social institutions by exemplifying it in the *Grundsätze* he develops a much more detailed and sophisticated analysis of that approach in the third book of his *Untersuchungen*. Similarly he provides a much deeper analysis of the role of inductive methods in the social sciences in that book. Whereas in the *Grundsätze* his considerations with respect to induction primarily concern the problem of an adequate empirical basis his analysis in the *Untersuchungen* focuses on the so called problem of induction and its epistemological consequences for the epistemological justification of social sciences as scientific disciplines.

It seems that both investigations were triggered by the reactions that followed the publication of the *Grundsätze*. Considering these reactions it seems that Menger's main point that any successful explanation of relative prices must be developed as a relational behavioural theory within a framework that combines subjective value theory and methodological individualism fell dead born from the press. Among the first reviews that appeared after the publication of the *Grundsätze* only one conveys a vague appreciation of the importance of Menger's work. But even that fairly brief review, authored by a certain Hack misses Menger's emphasis on that combination as well.[112] According to Hack Menger's *Grundsätze* " [...] is one of the best works on economics that appeared recently". Yet it is interesting to note that instead of considering Menger's new explanation of relative prices on the basis of the notions of marginal utilities and the equimarginal principle, Hack only refers to some unimportant points regarding the empirical basis of the social sciences and the possibility of establishing strictly universal social laws in view of the notion of free will. Whereas he accepts Menger's views on the empirical basis of the theoretical social sciences he rejects his views regarding the possibility of strictly universal social laws, however, without providing any argument. Hack certainly does not see Menger's point of a combination of subjective value theory and methodological individualism. Menger structured his Grundsätze rigorously and quite systematically according to the fundamental principles of methodological individualism in order to argue against essentialist economic theories of whatever kind. Hack, however, simply states that in the *Grundsätze* " ... without a rigorous and systematic method, good, economy, value, exchange, price, commodity [and] money are discussed".

Neither of the main problems discussed by Menger in the *Grundsätze* are mentioned by Hack; in fact his review is one of those brief industrial book reviewes that have no informative content whatsoever. Other reviews or com-

---

[112] Hack (1872).

ments on Menger's *Grundsätze* are certainly not better. Roscher, the doyen of economics in the German speaking world and to whom Menger like other authors dedicated his work mentions him in the last section on the German historical school of economics in his *History of economic ideas*, published in 1874. Like Hack he misses Menger's main points to develop a unified price theory on the basis of a non-essentialist relational behavioural economic theory. He neither mentions Menger's contribution of applying systematically the notions of marginal utilities and the equimarginal principle for explaining prices. Patronizing Menger he simply states that Menger provides a rigorous and rather abstract analysis of different concepts based on a thorough analysis of the history of economic ideas, without, however, indicating what concepts Menger investigates. Roscher mentions that Menger explains prices first by analysing a bilateral monopoly and only then atomistic competition, however, without explaining the improvements Menger achieved by introducing the notions of marginal utility and the equimarginal principle systematically into price theory. He also seems not to have been aware that Menger's non-essentialist approach is a radical attack on his essentialist inductivism.

In view of those reviews it is not surprising that Menger again tried to clarify the main points of his *Grundsätze*. Unlike Hufeland, he is an inductivist who believes that the social laws are inferred from singular statements describing observations and personal experiences. In view of the German authors' substitution of methodological essentialist inductivism for methodological individualism he considers a discussion of inductive methods in the theoretical social sciences as most important. First, because he believes that this substitution impeded the progress of economic theories seriously since it basically discards the idea of a rigorous behavioural economic theory which, however, is needed in order to develop a successful price theory; and secondly because it seems to him that the research programme of the German historical school of economics has to be discarded on logical and epistemological grounds. However, apart from showing that the methodological essentialist inductivist approach of the German historical school has to be rejected on logical and epistemological grounds he also tries to support his view that it has to be substituted by a rigorous methodological individualism in order to develop a successful price theory. But in contrast to the *Grundsätze* where he tried to show this necessary substitution by actually carrying it out, he develops a detailed analysis of that method in the third book of his *Untersuchungen*. Hence he structures the *Untersuchungen* accordingly. After discussing induction in the first two books he turns to analyse the principles of methodological individualism in the third book, which is followed by a historical account of the rise of essentialist methods in the social sciences in the fourth one. 10 appendici explicate several points stated in the four books previously.

According to the method of induction science starts from an empirical basis which consists of absolutely certain and proven true singular statements. From that basis science infers by content enlarging and truth preserving inferences strictly universal statements that are empirical, so called "laws". In order to show that the German historical school's idea, that history is the empirical basis of the theoretical social sciences has to be discarded, Menger is much concerned with the problem of an adequate empirical basis for the theoretical social sciences in the *Grundsätze*. However, Hume and before him, Sextus Empiricus, have shown that content enlarging and truth preserving inferences have to be rejected on logical grounds: strictly universal statements which are empirical and claim to be independent of time and place can not be established by inductive methods. This so called problem of induction results from the logical invalidity of inductive inferences but it seems that Menger in his *Grundsätze* was not troubled by this logical objection. In fact he opens his analysis in the *Grundsätze* with an argument that Mill used in order to support a principle of induction which he introduces in order to justify inductive inferences. According to Mill the principle of causality can be introduced as a principle of induction which justifies inductive inferences, because any verification of a special causal law on the basis of the rules of causal induction verifies that principle as well. Thus in Mill's view the domain of the principle of causality increases with every verification of a special causal law; it is most general, strictly universal and due to its verification by experience, empirical.[113] Likewise Menger states in the *Grundsätze:*

> "All things are subject to the law of cause and effect. This great principle knows no exception, and we would search in vain in the realm of experience for an example to the contrary. Human progress has no tendency to cast it in doubt, but rather the effect of confirming it and of always further widening knowledge of the scope of its validity."[114]

But whereas Menger focuses on the problem of an adequate empirical basis for social sciences in his *Grundsätze* and not on the problem of justifying inductive inferences, the problem situation in the *Untersuchungen* is quite different. In that book Menger primarily discusses the so called problem of induction and its epistemological consequences in order to provide an epistemological justification of the theoretical social sciences, thereby trying to solve the problem of the possibility of the theoretical social sciences as empirical disciplines.[115]

However, before trying to establish the social sciences on a correct epistemological basis, he attempts to show that the research programme of the German historical school has to be discarded on logical and methodological

---

[113] Cf. Mill (1843/1974 book 3, chap. XXI, §3).

[114] Menger (1981, p.51).

[115] for a detailed analysis cf. Milford (1989), (1990).

grounds. In order to do so he first analysis the structure of theoretical explanations in the social sciences and contrasts this explication with an analysis of the structure of a historical explanation, emphasising that it is the specific interest of the historian and the theoretician which really accounts for the difference of the two types of explanations. Whereas the historian typically is interested in the description of the initial conditions of the explanation in order to describe historical situations and only applies given strictly universal statements or social laws, the theoretician is primarily interested in uncovering new and interesting social laws and not in initial conditions. Menger regards both types of investigations as sound but rejects the so called pseudo-historical positions which either try to establish laws of historical development or object to the possibility of strictly universal social laws by favouring relativism and anti-normative positions according to which the validity of social regularities is restricted to certain historical and cultural periods only.

According to Menger, the authors of the German historical school explain the falsification of classical price theory by referring to its seemingly false empirical basis. According to them, the representatives of classical price theory not only induced their theories from an uncertain and false empirical basis but committed the errors of 'absolutism' and 'cosmopolitism' as well, by not observing the principle methodological requirements of historism, that is, relativism and anti-normativism. Accordingly they suggest the necessity of a new and proven empirical basis as an absolute precondition for inducing true economic theories by content enlarging and truth preserving inferences on the basis of that foundation. In Menger's view, however, the German historical schools' representatives try to establish that basis by trying to avoid any kind of abstraction from reality because in their view this involves the danger of false descriptions of reality.

Against that view Menger objects that it can not be defended. He refers to the so called argument of the transcendence of first order and points out that the singular observational statements require universals in order to be able to describe observations. Even singular observational statements presuppose some kind of abstraction. But according to Menger the Historical schools' research programme cannot be carried out even if the transcendence of first order is conceded. In his view the authors of the German historical school especially Roscher defend a position of Naive Inductivism which disregards the logical objection against inductive inferences and its basic epistemological consequences. Empirical science is defined by two methodological requirements, namely empiricism and strict universalitiy; the requirement of empricism states that the truth value of all empirical statements has to be decided by experience; and the requirement of strict universality states that the laws which science proposes are independent of time and place. The method of induction seems to be capable of fulfilling those two requirements simultaneously, since according to that method the strictly universal statements are inferred from singular observational statements by content enlarging and truth preserving inferences.

But according to Menger the logical objection against induction can not be disregarded for logical reasons. And he points out that one of the primary consequences of that logical objection is that the two requirements defining empirical science can not be met anymore. Regarding that logical objection implies that one has to reject either of the two requirements. Either one rejects the requirement of empricism and retains that of strict universality; or one discards that of strict universality and retains empiricism. Accordingly Menger distinguishes between an empirical realistic orientation of theoretical research on the one hand and an exact orientation of theoretical research on the other. The foundation of the truth values of the statements of the realistic empirical orientation of theoretical research is experience; in contrast the statements of the exact orientation of theoretical research do not find their critical standard in experience and can not be tested by experience. However, Menger believes from a pragmatic point of view that both orientations of theoretical research are required for social and economic analysis; but logically and epistemologically there is no solution to the problem of induction.

In order to support this argument Menger first considers the consequences of the logical objection against inductive inferences. He writes:

> "If the world of phenomena is considered in a strictly realistic way, then laws of the latter signify merely the actual regularities, determined by way of observation, in the succession and in the coexistence of real phenomena which belong to certain empirical forms. A 'law' obtained from the above point of view can in truth only state that in reality, regularly or without exception, phenomena belonging to the empirical form C have followed the concrete phenomena belonging to the empirical forms A and B or that they were observed coexistent with them. The conclusion that the phenomenon C follows the phenomena A and B *in general* (that is, in all cases, even those not observed!), or that the phenomena under discussion here are *in general* coexistent, transcends experience, the point of view of strict empiricism. From the standpoint of the above manner of consideration it is *not strictly* warranted."[116]

Since inductive inferences can only justify empirical or numerically but not strictly universal statements the idea of inferring strictly universal statements by simple inductive methods has to be given up. Accordingly Menger emphasises

> *"The realistic orientation of theoretical research excludes in principle, rather, in all realm of the world of phenomena the possibility of arriving at strict (exact) theoretical knowledge."*[117]

[116] Menger (1985, p. 57).
[117] Menger (1985, p. 58). Italics are ours.

However, in his analysis of the structure of historical and theoretical explanations, Menger shows that strictly universal statements, or as Menger says, exact statements are required and proposed. Thus the question regarding the possibility of such statements arises in order to provide a valid epistemological foundation of the theoretical social sciences. According to Menger, however, a solution of that problem is possible only if one rejects the requirement of empiricism and introduces and induction principle that justifies inductive inferences. Accordingly he introduces such an induction principle or rule of research, emphasising however, that the statements justified by that principle cannot find the foundation of their truth value in experience. He writes:

> "The only rule of cognition for the investigation of theoretical truth, which as far as possible is verified beyond doubt not only by experience but simply by our laws of thinking, and which is of utmost fundamental importance for the *exact* orientation of research, is the statement that *whatever was observed in even only one case must always put in an appearance again under exactly the same actual conditions*; or, what is in essence the same thing, that strictly typical phenomena of a definite kind must always , under the same conditions, and, indeed inconsideration of our laws of thinking, simply of *necessity*, be followed by strictly typical phenomena of just a definite and different a type."[118]

Although saying that this rule is based on experience as well as on our laws of thinking, Menger provides no justification of it. However, such a justification is required if Menger wants to establish the theoretical social sciences on valid epistemological grounds.

Yet Menger does not provide such a justification perhaps because his intentions are primarily to reject the Naive inductivist views of some of the authors of the German historical school. But he seems to have defended a kind of aprioristic position according to which one has to reject empiricism if one attempts to establish exact or strictly universal laws. Accordingly, with respect to the exact orientation of theoretical research:

> "... testing the exact theory of economy by the full empirical method is simply a methodolgical absurdity, a failure to recognize the basis and presuppositions of exact research."[119]

VII. Having shown that the German historical schools' position of Naive Inductivism, has to be rejected on logical and epistemolgical grounds, Menger proceeds by analysing the importance of methodological individualism with respect to developing a successful behavioural economic theory. Menger explicates the

---

[118] Menger (1985, p. 60; my translation).
[119] Menger (1985 p. 69).

principles of methodological individualism with similar arguments as Hufeland had done previously. Like him he formulates this explication by contrasting it with the so called organic theory of the state and also explains the difference between pyshological and pragmatic explanations on the one hand and individualistic explanations on the other.

The furious and patronising reactions of Schmoller and Roscher with respect to Menger's *Untersuchungen* are well known. However, after having published a very polemical response to Roscher and especially Schmoller[120] Menger abstained from participitating in the ensuing debate and returned to work on economic problems. But the debate raged on well into the 20th century though with different opponents. His and Hufeland's main point, however, that economic theory needs to reject all essentialist notions and has to be developed on the basis of a behavioural theory that runs in terms of a theory of subjective evaluations and methodological individualism and which analysis the conditions of economic behaviour has become the basis of modern economic theory as partial sociology.

[120] Menger (1884).

Zu Carl Menger im Hinblick auf die Ökonomik des Aristoteles

Stephan Haltmayer

> Als man Ghandi nach der Unabhängigkeit Indiens fragte, ob Indien nun ein ähnliches Wohlstandsniveau wie England erreichen werde, antwortete er: „England hat die Ressourcen der halben Welt für seinen Wohlstand benötigt. Wie vieler Planeten bedarf wohl ein Land wie Indien?“ (Siehe Felber [2006] S. 282.)

1. V o r b e m e r k u n g: Als Herr Kollege Gilles Campagnolo vor nun wohl schon 5 oder nahezu 6 Jahren mir seinen in mancher Hinsicht ungewöhnlichen ursprünglichen Plan der Herausgabe eines Sammelbandes von Arbeiten über Carl Menger vorlegte, die teils in den Vereinigten Staaten und zum größeren Teil in Japan befindliche kaum oder noch nicht bekannte Mengersche Texte präsentieren bzw. interpretieren sollten, da erklärte ich mich dazu mit der Einschränkung, dass das Werk – als Band in der Reihe „Wiener Arbeiten zur Philosophie“ – in Teilen auch philosophischen Inhalts sein müsste, sehr gerne bereit. Denn es geht mit solch einer Herausgabe ja zugleich auch darum, den bisher vielleicht bedeutendsten, aber wohl noch nicht wirklich gebührend geschätzten österreichischen (und so auch einen bedeutenden europäischen) Ökonomen nicht nur in die ja ohnedies ständig in Gang befindliche wirtschaftshistorische und -wissenschaftliche Debatte ganz allgemein, sondern ihn in diese Debatte als eine inzwischen weitgehend schon in sich verschlossene solche Auseinandersetzung so einzubringen, dass dabei die bzw. eine besonders in jüngerer und jüngster Zeit gewiss allzu sehr auf Nutzen- und Gewinnmaximierung hin orientierte, auch technizistisch hochgejagte finanztheoretisch-wirtschaftliche Umtriebigkeit, ja Hektik zumindest in Teilen nachdrücklicher in Frage gestellt wird – eine Debatte bzw. eine Hektik, die ja allzu sehr auf einen solchen Nutzen bzw. Gewinn bzw. Profit hin orientiert sind, dass diese letzteren der Intention nach zu einem Instrument für nahezu beliebig zu definierende und verwendbare wirtschaftlich-politische Macht oder, und dies wohl noch als bessere der zwei Varianten, zum rein kommerziellen Selbstzweck (wenngleich dabei vielleicht auch eigengesetzlicher Struktur) zu werden drohen. Die Hoffnung auf Mitanregung bzw. Unterstützung einer daher verstärkt ethisch-politisch offenen Debatte und Auseinandersetzung gründet dabei bereits darin, dass sich Menger (allein schon den von Emil Kauder angestellten Ermittlungen in Japan zufolge) auch mit philosophischen Texten – jedenfalls mit solchen von Aristoteles und Hegel – explizit befasst hat.

So bin ich denn froh nicht nur darüber, selbst die hier folgenden wenn auch nur kurzen Ausführungen zu diesem Sammelband beitragen zu können, sondern auch über den Umstand, dass ich einerseits zwei Wiener Mitarbeiter für die Beteiligung am vorliegenden Unternehmen gewinnen konnte, nämlich Herrn Dr. Dr. Werner Wilke, dessen von der Wiener Wirtschaftsuniversität approbierte sozial- und wirtschaftswissenschaftliche vortreffliche Dissertation ich mit begutachten konnte (und dem ich für seinen freundlichen Literaturverweis Bertram Schefold betreffend herzlich danke) sowie Frau Dr. Herta Mayerhofer, die mit mir auch insofern in Zusammenarbeit steht, als sie für mich Kollegen Campagnolos unten in der „Bibliographie" angeführten Aufsatz (2002) dem Inhalt nach sehr dankenswerter Weise so genau ins Deutsche transformierte, wie ich selbst es bei weitem nicht vermocht hätte[121]; und sehr froh bin ich andererseits auch darüber, dass ich die von Kollegen Campagnolo in relativ fortgeschrittenem Stadium unseres Vorhabens erbetene Zusammenführung mit Kollegen Milford initiieren konnte, mit dem ich seit einer gemeinsamen Reise zu beiderseits einem Vortrag im Rahmen eines Seminars an der Universität Istanbul in bester Verbindung bin und dem ich für sehr wertvolle wirtschaftswissenschaftliche Informationen zu meinem vorliegenden Beitrag herzlich danke.

2. Konzentriert man sich darauf festzustellen, wo in Carl Mengers Werk „*Grundsätze der Volkswirthschaftslehre*" explizit bzw. unter Nennung seines Namens A r i s t o t e l e s aufscheint, so sind es, soweit ich sehe, jeweils Anmerkungen auf den Seiten 2, 4, 108, 173, 215, 256–258 und 277, d.h. dort, wo sich Kapitelanfänge von Lehrstücken befinden, bei denen Aristoteles traditionell eine historisch besondere Bedeutung zugesprochen ist. In solchem Sinne beginnt auch auf Seite 172 die „Lehre vom Preise", dies freilich, wenn auch das einzige Mal an den besagten Stellen, sogar so, dass dabei (meines Erachtens aber zu Unrecht) Aristoteles der Vorwurf des Sich-Irrens gemacht wird. Das Kapitel setzt ein bzw. fährt nach von mir vorgenommenen Weglassungen fort wie folgt:

> „Die Preise, oder mit andern Worten, die im Tausche zur Erscheinung gelangenden Güterquantitäten [!], so sehr sie sich auch unseren Sinnen aufdrängen und desshalb den gewöhnlichsten Gegenstand der wissenschaftlichen Beobachtung bilden, sind doch nichts weniger als das Wesentliche der ökonomischen Erscheinung des Tausches. ... Die Preise sind hiebei

---

[121] Unter nicht näher konkretisierter Bezugnahme auf Streissler (1990) sei, wie Gilles Campagnolo auf S. 16 seines Aufsatzes schreibt, Carl Menger im Zusammenhang mit seiner Funktion als Hauslehrer des „jungen Prinzen Habsbourg" (d.i. des später unter nicht restlos geklärten wohl tragischen Umständen zu Tode gekommenen Kronprinzen Rudolf) der mangelnden Pietät (d'impiété) beschuldigt worden, weil er die bei der Lehre herangezogenen Autoritäten Aristoteles und Thomas von Aquin zu frei und wenig konform (trop libérales et peu conformes) verwendet habe. Aus anderen Passagen von Streisslers Buch ergibt sich demgegenüber jedoch eine besondere Schätzung des Wiener Hofes für Menger sei es im allgemeinen oder sei es für dessen Privatlehrertätigkeit.

aber lediglich accidentielle Erscheinungen, Symptome des ökonomischen Ausgleiches zwischen den menschlichen Wirthschaften. ...

Weil aber die Preise die einzigen sinnlich wahrnehmbaren Erscheinungen des ganzen Processes sind, ihre Höhe sich genau messen lässt und das tägliche Leben uns dieselben ohne Unterlass vor Augen führt, so war der Irrthum naheliegend, die Grösse derselben als das Wesentliche am Tausche, und, in weiterer Consequenz dieses Irrthums, die im Austausch erscheinenden Güterquantitäten als A e q u i v a l e n t e zu betrachten. Hierdurch wurde aber der unberechenbare Nachtheil für unsere Wissenschaft herbeigeführt, dass sich die Forscher auf dem Gebiete der Preiserscheinungen auf die Lösung des Problems verlegten, die angebliche [!] G l e i c h h e i t zwischen zwei Güterquantitäten auf ihre Ursachen zurückzuführen und die einen dieselben in gleichen auf diese Güter verwandten Arbeitsquantitäten, die andern in gleichen Productionskosten suchten, ja sogar darüber Streit entstand, ob die Güter gegen einander hingegeben werden, weil sie Aequivalente sind, oder ob die Güter Aequivalente sind, weil sie im Austausche gegen einander hingegeben werden, während eine solche Gleichheit des Werthes zweier Güterquantitäten (eine Gleichheit im objectiven Sinne) in Wahrheit nirgends besteht." [Menger (1871), S. 173 f.]

In der Anmerkung zu diesem Text – und zwar in direktem Anschluss an das gesperrt gedruckte „G l e i c h h e i t" – führt Menger an erster Stelle Aristoteles an, und zwar mit folgenden zwei Zitaten:

„Schon A r i s t o t e l e s (Eth. Nicom. V. 7) verfällt in diesen Irrthum: `Wenn Jemand mehr erhält, als er ursprünglich hatte, so sagt man, er sei im Vortheil; wenn er weniger erhält, so ist er im Nachtheil; so beim Kaufen und Verkaufen. Wenn aber der ursprüngliche Besitz weder grösser noch kleiner geworden, sondern im Verkehre gleichgeblieben, so heisst es, man habe das seinige, und sei weder im Vortheil noch im Nachtheil.´ Derselbe sagt (ibid. V. 8): `Wenn vorerst die verhältnissmässige Gleichheit bestimmt ist und demgemäss die Vergeltung oder Ausgleichung stattfindet, so ist dies das, was wir meinen. ... Denn ein Austausch ist unmöglich ohne Gleichheit.´"

Der hier in Frage stehende Austausch ist in der Tat zwar „unmöglich ohne Gleichheit", aber es handelt sich bei diesem bzw. bei solchem Austausch eben durchwegs um verhältnismäßige Gleichheit, um Gleichheit irgendwie, um gewissermaßen Gleichheit – d.i. um Gleichheit πώς; um Gleichheit außerdem nicht nur der Quantität, sondern auch der Qualität nach, zumal ja auch der ganze Kontext in die Interpretation mit einbezogen werden muss.

Oder etwas ausführlicher mit anderen Worten gesagt: Einerseits sagt Menger ja ohnehin dasselbe wie Aristoteles; denn er sagt genau besehen wie letzterer, dass „Gleichheit“ der Tauschgegenstände – „in Wahrheit“ – nicht besteht; sondern was allein gleich ist „in Wahrheit“, so Aristoteles, das sind die Bedürfnisse derer, die tauschen: „So muss [beim Tausch] denn für alles ein Eines als Maß bestehen, wie vorhin bemerkt worden ist. Dieses Eine ist in Wahrheit das *Bedürfnis*, das alles zusammenhält“ (EN V 8, 1133 a 25–27) – zusammenhält sozusagen bis hin zu Shakespeares Richard III., der, wie bestens bekannt, gegen Ende der gleichnamigen Tragödie (V. Akt, 4. Szene) ausruft: „Ein Pferd, ein Pferd! Mein Königreich für ein Pferd!“ Die Entscheidungsschlacht ist zu diesem Zeitpunkt aber schon so gut wie verloren und passend zu dieser Situation ein brauchbares Pferd selbst durch Zufall so gut wie nicht auftreibbar. Trotzdem kritisiert Menger den Stagiriten andererseits, wie ausgeführt; das freilich zu Unrecht.

3. Die sehr wichtige Erörterung zur M e t h o d e , soweit zu ihrer wenigstens gerafften Betrachtung hier Platz und Zeit ist – Menger selbst kommt ja schon in der Vorrede zu seinen „Grundsätzen“ darauf zu sprechen –, hätte zuerst die diesbezüglich (hier) relevante reiche Literatur einzuarbeiten und zu würdigen (siehe diesbezüglich gleich unten unter Karl Milford, 1989). Da dies – auch wenn der vorliegende Ort dazu durchaus passend wäre – aber nicht mehr möglich ist, soll (denn aus Sicht des Aristotelischen Organons bzw. der Aristotelischen Philosophie erscheint dies unerlässlich) an hier gegebener Stelle daran sozusagen erinnert werden, dass eigentlich niemandem eine so geartete erkenntnistheoretisch-logische Position zuzusprechen ist, die – im Anschluss an Karl R. Poppers Buch „*Objektive Erkenntnis. Ein evolutionärer Entwurf*“ (^{2}1974) – als „Kübeltheorie-Scheinwerfertheorie“-Spaltung bzw. als einseitig „kübeltheoretische“ anzusprechen wäre, also als ein um Erkenntnis bemühtes Ausgehen einseitig von vor allem materiellen (Einzel-)Gegenständen in Raum und Zeit her. Bei Aristoteles jedenfalls ist die „scheinwerfertheoretische“ Position – wenn wir diese Bezeichnungsweisen hier benützen wollen – freilich von Anfang an wenn auch in unterschiedlicher Deutlichkeit mit im Spiel. Vgl. dazu insbesondere sein Werk „*Über die Seele*“. In III.5, also am Kulminationspunkt der berühmten, überknappen Ausführungen dieses Kapitels 5 wird (im Wege einer Zweiseitigkeit, siehe insgesamt unten die Übersetzung von Theiler) der Geist wie folgt mit dem Licht verglichen: Denn wie es „im ganzen Naturbereich einmal [=einerseits] Materie gibt ... und dann [=andererseits] das Ursächliche und Wirkende“, so müssen „auch in der (Denk)Seele diese unterschiedlichen Dinge vorhanden sein“, so dass „es einen Geist (νοῦς) von solcher Art gibt, dass er zu allem wird, und einen andern von solcher, dass er alles wirkt (macht) als eine Art Kraft wie die Helligkeit (φῶς) ...“

Der Weg „hinauf“ und „hinab“ ist – schon mit Heraklit zu sprechen – in Umkehrung eben ein und derselbe. Welche richtungsmäßige Gegenläufigkeit nur bedingt bzw. nur in einer gewissen neuzeitlichen Vereinfachung als Deduktion und Induktion aufzufassen ist; letztere, die Epagogé nämlich, ist jedenfalls weit besser als „Hinführung“ zu charakterisieren; erstere, (vereinfachend) der Syllogismus, hat (gleichfalls schon) von vornherein beide Richtungen – in umgekehrter Hervorhebung – in sich und er ist es, aber nicht die Epagogé, der von beiden Begriffen in dem Maße einen Vorrang hat, in welchem man bei der in Rede stehenden stets mitgemeinten Zweiseitigkeit von einem solchen gleichwohl sprechen kann.

Was den Syllogismus oder Schluss angeht, heißt es (teils in etwas veralteter, der Scholastik zu naher Übersetzung von Rolfes, die hier aus Zeitknappheit trotzdem unverändert übernommen sei) daher schon in Kapitel 30 des ersten Buchs der Ersten Analytik – und zwar im Prinzip auch in Hinsicht auf die Ökonomie:

> „Der Weg ist mithin überall derselbe, in der Philosophie und in jeder beliebigen Kunst und Wissenschaft: bei jedem Problem muß man sehen, was einem [Gegenstand im engeren oder auch weiteren Sinne gefasst] beiwohnt und wem es beiwohnt, und dessen möglichst viel zur Verfügung haben und es an Hand der drei [!] Begriffe mustern, bei der Widerlegung auf diese, bei der Erhärtung auf jene Weise, und muß, wenn es die Wahrheit gilt, aus solchem schließen, was nach der Wahrheit als tatsächlich vorgemerkt ist, wenn aber einen dialektischen Schluß, [dann] aus bloß wahrscheinlichen Prämissen.“

Und in der an vorliegender Stelle gleichfalls brauchbaren generelleren Perspektive der Zweiten Analytik heißt es auch gleich in deren Kapitel 2 des ersten Buches:

> „Früher und bekannter ist etwas aber in zweifachem Sinne. Denn nicht dasselbe ist von Natur früher und für uns, und von Natur bekannter und für uns. Ich nenne für uns früher und bekannter was der sinnlichen Wahrnehmung näher liegt, schlechthin früher und bekannter was ihr ferner liegt. Ihr am fernsten ist das Allgemeinste, am nächsten das Einzelne. Und dieses beide ist sich entgegengesetzt.“

(À propos Scholastik und ihren „Essentialismus“, soweit und sofern letzterer Begriff als Vorwurf bzw. als Kritik an Menger verwendet wird: Ein solcher Vorwurf gegen letzteren ist wohl ebenso wenig angebracht, wie er es je in bezug auf Aristoteles sein könnte. Unser neuzeitlicher deutschsprachiger Terminus Verkehrswesen beispielsweise bzw. der Begriff Wesen darin besagt wohl nicht einmal etwas von dem, was auch „nur“ in der Scholastik als essentia in Rede stand; vgl. diesbezüglich unten S. 212 im Beitrag 10 das englische essence. Doch wäre diese Schwierigkeit an relevanten Textstellen selbst des näheren zu diskutieren und erst so als unzutreffend konkret abzuweisen.)

Wenn auch, wie oben gesagt, hier leider nicht auf die „Frage der erkenntnistheoretischen Methode“ Menger betreffend gebührend eingegangen werden kann, soll an dieser Stelle im Anschluss an die „Problemstellung" der „Einleitung" bei Karl Milford (1989, S. 9 ff.) doch kurz folgende zentrale Überlegung eingeschoben werden. Hier lesen wir gleich eingangs:

> „Als erfahrungswissenschaftliche Erkenntnis pflegt man solche Erkenntnis zu bezeichnen, die zwei Anforderungen gerecht wird: `Strenge Allgemeinheit´ und `Empirismus`. Die erste dieser beiden Forderungen, nämlich die der `Strengen Allgemeinheit´, wird aus den Aufgaben und aus den Zielsetzungen der Erfahrungswissenschaften abgeleitet."

Dieser Satz wie die (bei Karl Milford) an ihn anschließenden betreffen also – im Unterschied zu den anderen bisherigen Sätzen des Punktes 3, die allgemeinphilosophischen (oder, mit Karl Milford zu sprechen: die erkenntnislogischen) Charakter haben – die Erfahrungswissenschaften. Speziell auf Menger bezogen fährt Milford (auf S. 15 f.) sehr schön pointierend so fort:

> „Mengers zentrales erkenntnislogisches Problem seiner Untersuchungen besteht darin, die theoretischen Sozialwissenschaften und hier insbesondere die theoretische Ökonomie als Wissenschaft einwandfrei erkenntnistheoretisch zu begründen. Menger versucht nicht, die Wirklichkeit oder die Existenz der theoretischen Sozialwissenschaften zu erklären, sondern die Möglichkeit einer solchen Wissenschaft, ihre formalen Voraussetzungen und die `formale´ Natur ihrer Sätze sowie die zur Begründung ihrer Erkenntnisse angewendeten Verfahren aufzuklären. Der Versuch, die theoretische Ökonomie als Wissenschaft zu begründen, führt Menger zwangsläufig zur Frage der Rechtfertigung von streng allgemeinen Wirklichkeitsaussagen und damit zu einer Erörterung des Induktionsproblems. Die Diskussion des Gegensatzes zwischen `Empirismus´ und `Strenger Allgemeinheit´ findet ihren sichtbaren Ausdruck in seiner Unterscheidung zwischen einer `empirisch realistischen Forschungsrichtung´ einerseits und einer `exacten Richtung der theoretischen Forschung´ andererseits. Die gesamte Analyse dieser Fragen ist dabei in eine Auseinandersetzung mit anderen Auffassungen zur Frage von streng allgemeinen Wirklichkeitsaussagen, insbesondere aber mit den Auffassungen der Vertreter der älteren und jüngeren Historischen Schule der Deutschen Nationalökonomie eingebettet. [Aus Mengers Kritik insbesondere an deren „unzulänglichem" Lösungsversuch des Induktionsproblems] ... erwächst Mengers eigener Versuch einer Lösung des Induktionsproblems. Diese ist aprioristisch."

Letztere beide Zitate bestätigen, dass eine nähere Erörterung des hier angesprochenen Methodenproblems den vorliegenden Rahmen sprengen würde. Sie würde – außer der adäquaten Beachtung des schon bisher Angeführten und außer einem Rückgriff zumindest gewiss auf Humes (aber auch schon auf Platons, siehe dazu auch unter Haltmayer [1976] und auch [1987]) und auf Poppers [^{6}1976]

Auseinandersetzung mit dem Induktionsproblem – auch Aristoteles und wohl auch Kant einbeziehen müssen. Was Aristoteles und die erkenntnislogische Hinsicht dieses Problems, aber auch schon was Platon angeht, muss besonders beachtet werden, dass die Epagogé eben nicht einfachhin Induktion ist bzw. dass ein bloß Einzelnes – ein nichts als Einzelnes, wie man auch sagen kann – weder sein noch erkannt werden kann (wie der Wiener Philosoph Erich Heintel zu sagen pflegte), sondern dass es ein bloß Einzelnes nur vermeintlich ist: es ist hingegen richtig gesagt vielmehr ein Einzelwesen, nämlich etwas, das als etwas Individuelles einem Allgemeinen zugehört, in welchem es aufgehoben ist. [Bzw. generell gesagt: Karl R. Popper steht mit seinem Gedanken der – m. E. auch selbst aprioristischen – „Theoriegetränktheit" aller Erkenntnis, auch der Beobachtungen, Aristoteles letztlich wohl sehr nahe; vgl. dazu im Buch „Objektive Erkenntnis" auf S. 121 den Satz: „Selbst unsere Sinnesorgane (nicht zu reden von der Deutung ihrer Meldungen) sind theoriegetränkt und fehlbar, wenn auch bei gesunden Organismen nur gelegentlich."]

Ob auch Menger selbst auf diese Weise zu verstehen und auf dieser Basis zu entwickeln ist, müsste die hier angesprochene nähere Erörterung (unter Heranziehung wohl auch von Notizen bzw. Quellen, die bisher nicht ausgewertet worden sind und um die sich Herr Kollege Campagnolo bemüht) zeigen. In diese Erörterung kann auch Mengers Beziehung zu Franz Brentano hereinspielen, der Frau Andrea Reimherr [2005] neuerdings nachgegangen ist bzw. vielleicht weiterhin nachzugehen bemüht ist.

4. Wendet man sich der A r i s t o t e l i s c h e n Ö k o n o m i k im engeren Sinne zu, dann ist man gewiss gut beraten, wenn man sich des kleinen Bandes „Klassiker der Nationalökonomie" bedient, den als „Geschäftsführender Editor" Bertram Schefold herausgegeben hat. Er selbst, H. Flashar, O. Issing und S. T. Lowry schreiben darin je einen Beitrag (siehe diesbezüglich unten in der Bibliographie). Man müsste auf alle diese Beiträge hier im Einzelnen eingehen, so instruktiv sind sie. Da dies nicht möglich ist, dürften einige Zitate genügen.

Eine besonders schöne Passage aus dem einleitenden Abschnitt „Epigrammatisches zu Aristoteles" – sie stammt von P. Koslowski – lautet übrigens: „Die aristotelischen Ausführungen zur Wirtschaft sind nur knapp und über mehrere Werke, hauptsächlich über die *Nikomachische Ethik* und die *Politik*, zerstreut ... Die Wirtschaft ist kein von der Politik und der Ethik unabhängiger Bereich, der eigenen Gesetzen folgt ... Die Ökonomik ist in der *Politik* Wirtschaftslehre der Institution Familie (oikía) und [!] der Institution Staat, d.h. Finanzwissenschaft." (Siehe S. 8 f.) Und eine zweite: Mengers „vielverherrlichte empirische oder induktive Methode ist ... keine einseitige", so A. Oncken auf S. 10.

Der erste der vier Beiträger also, Schefold, schreibt u.a.:

„Die moderne Theorie ist dagegen nicht mehr primär ethisch, sondern an der Wahrheitsfrage orientiert: Ob von Eigeninteresse geleitetes Handeln zu einer bei gegebenem Aufwand bestmöglichen Güterversorgung führt." (S. 28.) Dann auch: „Es geht dabei um die Frage, ob das aristotelische Bild des Vorwiegens landwirtschaftlicher Produktion mit wenig entwickelten Gütermärkten, eingeschränkten Märkten für Land, mäßigem Sklavenbestand, wenig Fernhandel, kaum bestehenden Kreditbeziehungen der Wirklichkeit Athens im ausgehenden 4. Jahrhundert entsprach oder ob nicht in jener Zeit schon ein Entwicklungsstand erreicht war, der sich dem der frühen Neuzeit vergleichen ließe." (S. 49.) Sowie zum attischen Nationalvermögen: „Doch fand er [R. W. Goldsmith] zu seinem Erstaunen, daß, in dem auf die freie Marktentfaltung gerichteten, sich von den als despotisch empfundenen orientalischen Reichen absetzenden Athen, über die Hälfte des Gesamtvermögens in öffentlicher Hand war, und zwar nicht als Ausdruck der Zentralisierung wirtschaftlicher Funktionen in einem anonymen Staatsapparat, sondern als Mittel einer partizipatorischen Demokratie, in der die Bürger bedeutende Einkünfte, wie die aus dem Seebund und den Silberminen, gemeinsam verwalteten." (S. 51.) Und Menger aus den Anfangspassagen von dessen „Grundsätzen" zitierend: „Der vorwiegend ethische Standpunkt, von welchem [her] das Altertum die Lebensverhältnisse betrachtet, macht sich ... in den Anschauungen der meisten Alten über das Wesen der Nützlichkeit, bzw. der Güter geltend ..." (S. 54.) Und schließlich: „Es handelt sich bei diesem [Aristotelischen] `Guten´ selbst aber nicht um Genußgegenstände, schon gar nicht um die technischen Hilfsmittel wie Güter zweiter und höherer Ordnung bei Menger, sondern um die geistige Grundlage einer Lebensform, von der ein Lebensglück, eine Eudaimonia, erhofft wird [– die Eudaimonia allein erwartet werden könne, müsste man hier wohl etwas treffender sagen]. (S. 55.) Und „obwohl sich Aristoteles so gewissermaßen als Gegner dessen darstellt, was die ökonomische Theorie schließlich entwickelte, wurde er zu einem ihrer wichtigsten Begründer ..." (S. 67) – „als Stammvater moderner [ökonomischer] Theorie". (S. 69).

Als zweiter führt H. Flashar u.a. aus:

„Nur aus den besonderen Voraussetzungen des aristotelischen Ökonomie-Begriffes wird verständlich, warum der Kapital- und Handelsverkehr mittels des Geldes nicht zur Ökonomik gehört." (S. 81.) „Denn die Ökonomie des Aristoteles bezieht sich weniger auf den leblosen Besitz als auf den Menschen (Pol., I 13, 1159 b 18–20)." (S. 83.)

O. Issing schreibt als dritter u.a.:

„In der Erwerbskunst unterscheidet Aristoteles zwischen verschiedenen Arten. Die eine (Oikonomia) als Teil der Haushaltskunst ist lobenswert und notwendig, dient zur Ergänzung und Vervollständigung des Selbstgenügens und ist damit – das wichtigste Kriterium in der Philosophie des Aristoteles – im Einklang mit der Natur. Die andere (die Chrematistik) dagegen ist auf Anhäufung (eines möglichst großen) Vermögens gerichtet, kennt kein Ende und keine Grenze und ist daher gegen die Natur. Dieses Verdikt gilt im besonderen Maß für eine dritte Form, den Wucher, das Verleihen von Geld gegen Zinsen." (S. 98.) „Das Interesse des Aristoteles gilt vorrangig dem summum bonum und der Verfassung des besten Staates; die Wirtschaft hat eindeutig eine untergeordnete, eine dienende Funktion." (S. 104.) „Gemessen an der Resonanz in den folgenden Generationen hat der Beitrag des Aristoteles zur Werttheorie wohl die größte Beachtung gefunden." (S. 109.)

Und unter Bezugnahme auf S. T. Lowry folgen auf S. 110 ff. dann Ausführungen zum „Prinzip des Grenznutzens", und in einer Anmerkung der Seite 120 steht der interessante, aber nicht ganz eindeutige Satz:

„Jede Zeit hat mit der Weiterentwicklung der Theorie [wohl auch der Nationalökonomie oder Politischen Ökonomie] neue Ansätze und Aussagen im Werk des Aristoteles entdeckt; dies lässt auch für die Zukunft noch manche überraschende Interpretation erwarten."

Und auch aus dem vierten Beitrag, aus dem aus dem Amerikanischen übersetzten Beitrag von S. T. Lowry, sei nur Weniges als Zitat ausgewählt:

„Was Aristoteles beunruhigte war, daß die Anhäufung von Geld zum Selbstzweck wurde, berufsmäßige Zwischenhändler, sogenannte Chrematisten, damit begannen, am Handel teilzunehmen – denn sie benutzten Geld zum Ankauf von Waren, die sie später gegen Geld wieder verkauften –, und daß dem Bedürfnis oder dem Wunsch nach Geld keine natürliche Grenze gesetzt war [d.h. ist]." (S. 139 f.) Andererseits: „Mit Hilfe dieser Theorie eines Haushaltsvorstandes als einem effizient arbeitenden Verwalter der Gaben der Natur (als der eigentlichen Quelle des Unterhalts des Menschen) deutet er die Tradition des Menschen als Verwalter der Natur mit der Verpflichtung zur `weisen Nutzung´ im Namen der Menschheit an – eine Tradition, die viele moderne Umweltschützer aufgreifen." (S. 142.) Und schließlich: „Darüber hinaus ist das Individuum so mit dem Staat verbunden, daß das höchste Niveau der individuellen Vollendung mit dem Erfolg des ganzen Staates einherzugehen scheint" [oder im Blick auf Buch X der Nikomachischen Ethik passender gesagt: mit dem „Erfolg" – d.i. in Fortführung der Wohlstrukturiertheit – des ganzen Staates am besten umzusetzen ist]." (S. 148 f.)

5. Womit wir zu demjenigen Zusammenhang unserer Überlegungen gekommen sind, den P. Koslowski in seinen in der Bibliographie angeführten zwei Büchern beschreibt. Er tut dies u.a. so:

> „Das Verhältnis von Polis und Oikos, von Politik und Ökonomie, das bei Aristoteles zum ersten Mal thematisiert wird, bildet den Anfang der für die europäische Geschichte zentralen und wohl nur in ihr ausgebildeten Unterscheidung von politischer Gemeinschaft oder Staat einerseits und bürgerlicher Gesellschaft, Wirtschaftsgesellschaft sowie Privatsphäre des Bürgers andererseits." [Koslowski (^{3}1993) S. 7.]

Diesen besonders wichtigen Zusammenhang und diese Entwicklung bzw. diese Entwicklungsmöglichkeit bis zu dem hin, was heute Z i v i l g e s e l l s c h a f t genannt wird, gälte es hier nun genauer nachzuzeichnen. Doch teilweise ist davon im oben Ausgeführten schon viel gesagt und andererseits reicht die Zeit hiefür leider ebenfalls nicht. Abschließend sei hier daher nur noch ein letztes, wenn auch längeres Zitat aus Koslowskis Buch wiedergegeben:

> „Sehr schön sichtbar wird die Einbettung der politischen Verfassungs- und der ökonomischen Ordnungstheorie in den ethischen Diskurs bei Aristoteles an seiner Behandlung des Pleonexie-Problems. Das maßlose Sich-Bereichern-Wollen und der Mißbrauch der Amtsgewalt zum eigenen Vorteil ist ein Problem, das nach Aristoteles in allen Verfassungsformen und Wirtschaftsordnungen auftritt und das durch organisatorische und institutionelle Vorkehrungen nicht vollständig beseitigt oder vermieden werden kann. Es bleibt vielmehr das Problem der *intentio recta*, der richtigen Intention der Handelnden, in allen Verfassungs- und Wirtschaftsordnungen unauflöslich bestehen. Auch in der Demokratie ist die gute politische Ordnung darauf angewiesen, daß die in ihr Handelnden das Gute oder allgemeine Wohl auch zu ihrem individuellen Gut und Interesse machen. Die Pleonexie, die Habsucht [das Immer-noch- und Immer-wieder-mehr-haben-Wollen], ist nur durch die richtige politische Verfassung und Wirtschaftsordnung und durch die *intentio recta* der Akteure in ihr [so weit wie möglich] zu vermeiden." (Ebd. S. 89 f.)

(Im Hintergrund steht hier auch das Problem einer Weltwirtschaftsordnung, mit dem sich Peter M. Schmidhuber in interessanter Weise befasst hat. Ihm zufolge müssten „die Vorschläge für eine Verbesserung der Weltwirtschaftsordnung ... in die anstehende, aber noch nicht terminisierte Reform des UN-Systems eingebracht und zu einem Gesamtsystem verbunden werden. Ob ein solches ambitioniertes Programm gelingen kann, ist allerdings eine offene Frage – aber es wäre größter Anstrengungen wert." [Schmidhuber (2007), S. 50].)

6. In der Weise eines E x k u r s e s, und dies als Anregung zur Überprüfung mit Bezug auch auf Carl Mengers U n t e r s c h e i d u n g bzw. Differenzierung

zwischen G u t und W e r t schon in seiner Vorrede zu den „Grundsätzen" verstanden, sei hier H. Kuhn zitiert (siehe Bibliographie) – verkürzend freilich und unter Beiseitelassung von Descartes und damit auch der insbesondere neuzeitlichen transzendentalphilosophischen Tradition:

> „Das Gute erweist sich in der Metaphysik als ein Begriff von höchster systematisierender Kraft. Diese Konstruktivität ergibt sich aus seiner innigen Verbindung mit dem Begriff des Seins. Mit der Zersetzung des metaphysischen Seinsbegriffes zerfällt auch der Begriff des Guten, und jeder seiner Bestandteile entwickelt die Tendenz, das ganze Gute darstellen zu wollen. In dieser Parzellierung verliert das Begriffswort seinen Rang. Teils wird es als Terminus in eine sich als selbständige Disziplin begreifende Ethik eingeschlossen, teils wird es in die Freiheit der Umgangssprache entlassen und damit dem dichterischen und praktischen Gebrauch überantwortet. Der Statusverlust, den das Gute erleidet, führt schließlich dazu, daß ein Ersatzwort seine Stelle einzunehmen versucht. Der aus der Nationalökonomie importierte „Wert" ist das *caput mortuum* des einst lebendigen Begriffes. Das Gute, losgerissen vom Sein, ontologisch entwurzelt, nicht mehr über-seiend wie bei den Platonikern, sondern eher unterseiend, nur noch „geltend" (wie wir auch vom Dollar oder der Mark sagen, daß sie soundsoviel gelten) – das ist der zu kurzlebigen philosophischen Ehren aufgestiegene Wertbegriff."

Zu diesem interessanten Zitat und besonders zur abschließenden Wendung muss aber wohl bemerkt werden, dass der Wertbegriff nicht erst seit kurzem und nur für kurze Zeit zu „philosophischen Ehren aufgestiegen" ist, sondern er ist dies vielmehr schon mit Aristoteles, und das in eben dem Maße, wie es durch letzteren selbst und damit für welche künftige Zeit auch immer jetzt schon gelten mag. Als Beleg hiefür darf der Begriff ἀξία angesehen werden, der in der Bedeutung von Wert jedenfalls auch in der „Nikomachischen Ethik" und der „Politik" vorkommt. So heißt es in ersterer in Buch IV, Kap. 1 1119 b 26 f.: „Mit dem Begriff `Geldeswert´ bezeichnen wir alles, dessen Wert durch Geld gemessen wird" (Übersetzung Dirlmeier) bzw. „Vermögensobjekt ist uns alles, dessen Wert nach Geld bemessen wird" (Übersetzung Rolfes; χρήματα λέγομεν ὅσων ἡ ἀξία νομίσματι μετρεῖται). (Vgl. den Begriff ἀξία auch schon bei Platon unter Astius unten in der Bibliographie.)

Auch Menger selbst jedenfalls unterscheidet, wie bekannt, schon in der Vorrede (S. IX) seiner „Grundsätze der [„theoretischen"] Volkswirthschaftslehre" ausdrücklich zwischen „nützlich", „Gut", „wirthschaftlichem Gut" und „Werth" – und zwar dezidiert im Blick auf die „eigentümlichen Gesetze", die es in Konstituierung dieser Lehre herauszustellen gelte.

Was dabei den Gesetzesbegriff selbst anlangt, der Menger zufolge die Ökonomik charakterisiert, so ist er seiner Auffassung nach offensichtlich nicht als der Dimension des konsenstheoretischen, sondern (dem traditionellen Verständnis entsprechend fundamental gefasst) als der des zugleich adäquations- und konsenstheoretischen Wahrheitsbegriffs so zugehörig anzusehen, dass er zusammen- und (der Intention nach) übereinstimmend (bzw. übereinzustimmend) als „subjektiver", d. i. als vom Subjekt erfasster Gehalt einerseits und als objektive, d. i. als der Sache nach vorliegende Gegenständlichkeit andererseits verstanden wird. Ob der Gegenstand – zuletzt der Gegenstand Ökonomik – dabei tatsächlich in dieser doppelten Hinsicht als Übereinstimmung zum Ausdruck gebracht und gegen die „schlechte Unendlichkeit" quantifizierender Sisyphusarbeit (siehe dazu auch den folgenden Punkt) gefeit ist, braucht in der besagten Vorrede natürlich nur Ankündigung zu sein; deren Einlösung aber muss dann die durchgeführte Ausarbeitung der „Grundzüge" selbst darstellen.

(Besonders an dieser Stelle ist auf [Reimherr (2005)] zu verweisen.)

7. Zusammenfassung und Ausblick: Wesentlicher noch als erkenntnistheoretisch-logische Probleme (siehe Punkt 3) ist für unsere hier vorliegende Aufgabe die Frage nach dem Zusammenhang von – sagen wir – Ökonomik hier und von und zu philosophischer Wissenschaft bzw. Systematik dort, oder, in etwas anderer Formulierung, die Frage nach dem Zusammenhang der Wissenschaft, in der die – mit Platon oder auch mit Hegel zu sprechen – „schlechte Unendlichkeit" zu bewältigen ist hier, und derjenigen Wissenschaft, die Status und Ziel der praktisch-theoretischen Gesamtwirklichkeit[122] des nähe-

[122] Nach Aristoteles stellt sich die Systematik der Wissenschaft – der Wissenschaften – grob gesprochen wie folgt dar (vgl. dazu eventuell die einschlägigen Standardwerke von Friedrich Ueberweg – in diesem Fall in der Herausgabe von Hellmut Flashar – und von Eduard Zeller):

1. Organon (das die logisch-erkenntnistheoretischen Grundlagen erörtert).
2. "Theoretische Philosophie" ("theoretische Wissenschaft"):
   a) "Physik"
   b) Mathematik
   c) "Erste Philosophie" (auch "Theologie").
3. "Praktische Wissenschaft" ("praktische Philosophie"):
   a) Ethik
   b) Politik.
   Die ergänzenden – oder vielmehr die vervollständigenden – Disziplinen der letzteren sind Strategik, Ökonomik und Rhetorik.
4. "Poietische Wissenschaft".

Zu dieser Übersicht kann man anmerken: Weisheit (σοφία) und Philosophie bzw. erste Philosophie werden weithin oder überhaupt synonym gebraucht.

In diesem Sinne liest man in der Nikomachischen Ethik VI 7 (sehr weitgehend in Übernahme der Übersetzung von Olof Gigon): "So wird denn die Weisheit die genaueste der Wissenschaften sein. Der Weise muß also nicht bloß wissen, was sich aus den Prinzipien ergibt, sondern er muß auch hinsichtlich der Prinzipien selbst die Wahrheit kennen. So wird also die Weisheit Geist (νοῦς) und Wissenschaft sein und als Haupt der Wissenschaften die erhabensten Gegenstände haben."

ren zu lösen die Aufgabe hat dort. Auf diese Formel lässt sich, stark vergröbert ausgedrückt, alles Bisherig wohl mit Recht bringen. Doch insgesamt gesehen geht es für den Menschen als solchen um das εὖ ζῆν oder die Eudaimonie – dies natürlich keineswegs im Sinne einer psychologischen Kategorie gefasst. Und wenn man dabei die Ökonomie als Weg oder Mittel anzusehen hat – als der Möglichkeit nach Mittel sowohl zum „Guten" wie zum „Schlechten" –, dann ist besonders heute, wo die Wirtschaft unwiderruflich in die Dimension der Weltwirtschaft eintritt bzw. eingetreten ist, (ähnlich geradezu wie bei der Frage nach Krieg und Frieden) durchgängig höchste Aufmerksamkeit und höchste philosophische Bemühung geboten.

Doch genauer besehen ist die im Unterschied zur bloßen Chrematistik – zur „Gelderwerbswirtschaft" [Koslowski (1993), S. 65] – und zu der damit eo ipso verbundenen Machtakkumulierung verstandene Ökonomie bei allem individuellen und weltweiten Verbesserungsbemühen der staatlichen und zivilen, in ständigem Umbruch befindlichen wirtschaftlichen und sozialen bzw. humanitären Gesamtsituation nicht nur Weg und Mittel, sondern vielmehr wesentlich zugleich konstitutives und integratives Lebensgestaltungsmoment – und zwar schon, wenn man bis hierher Angesprochenes aufnimmt. Dies kann man in Entsprechung zu Aristoteles` eigenen Ausführungen mit Koslowski – anderweitig von letzterem Gesagtes mit voraussetzend und einbeziehend – abschließend durchaus wohl so formulieren:

> „Die aristotelische Ökonomik und Politik bilden eine Einheit und erinnern so daran, dass in der Politischen Ökonomie die politisch-sozialen Voraussetzungen des Wirtschaftens ebenso bearbeitet werden müssen wie in der Politischen Philosophie die ökonomischen Bedingungen einer optimalen politischen Verfassung und Gesellschaftsordnung. Weder kann die politische Theorie ohne Ökonomie noch die ökonomische Theorie ohne die politische und soziologische Theorie betrieben werden, weil die Erhaltungsbedingungen der `bürgerlichen Gesellschaft´ und gemischten Verfassung der Politie durch die `Interdependenz der Ordnungen´ bestimmt ist.
>
> [...] Die Einheit der praktischen Philosophie bei Aristoteles führt zu einem Verständnis von Sozialwissenschaft, in dem deren Einheit betont wird und die Ökonomie selbst als Sozialwissenschaft verstanden wird, die über die Theorie der Preisbildung hinausgeht zu einer Theorie der Wirt-

Was dabei die Aristotelische sogenannte Psychologie angeht – d.i. De anima und „Eudemus", siehe hierzu Hellmut Flashar (im Band 3 von „Grundriss der Geschichte der Philosophie", begründet von Friedrich Ueberweg, [Basel/Stuttgart 1983] S. 411 ff.) –, so hat man sie in obiger Systematik wohl zwischen „Physik" und „Erster Philosophie" zu positionieren, mit anderen Worten in dem Forschungsbereich bzw. Wissenschaftsbereich, der zu den wissenschaftlich genauesten (akribischesten) gehört (vgl. De an. I 1, 402 a 1–7). Sie hat mit dem sogenannten Psychologismus neuerer und neuester Zeit und Modifizierung also nichts zu tun.

> schaftsverfassung und Wirtschaftskultur als Teil der Ordnung und Kultur einer Gesellschaft." (Ebd., S. 88.)

Auf das politisch-praktische Ganze gesehen ist es dabei sehr wichtig, ständig mit zu bedenken:

> „Aristoteles' Theorie von der Möglichkeit der Dekadenz *jeder* Gesellschafts- und Verfassungsform und sein Beharren darauf, dass die Theorie der Verfassung nicht nur die Optimalformen Monarchie, Aristokratie und Demokratie, sondern auch deren Defizienzformen Tyrannis, Oligarchie und Ochlokratie genau analysieren muß, folgt aus seiner Betonung des ethischen Elements in der Staats- und Wirtschaftsordnung." (Ebd., S. 89.)

Die Defizienzbedrohungen, die in der Gegenwart gegeben sind, weisen verstärkt in den Bereich der (Politischen) Ökonomie. Sie sind einerseits aus der Geschichte her im allgemeinen wohlbekannt. Und sie sind andererseits – besonders was ihre konkrete Erscheinungsform angeht – auch gegenwartsspezifisch. Zu letzteren sind gewiss die Gehalte der Bedürfnisse (vgl. im Singular ἡ χρεία [πάντα μετρεῖ, alles misst das Bedürfnis, EN V 8, 1133 a 27]) zu rechnen, die als subjektiv-individuelle oder -individualistische Erfüllung der – sagen wir – „Lust bzw. Freude des Lebens bzw. am Leben" gelten. (Die Richtung und Möglichkeit dazu hat Aristoteles schon am Beginn der Metaphysik – in Kapitel 1 des ersten Buchs, vgl. πρὸς τἀναγκαῖα, „für die notwendigen Bedürfnisse" in Zeile 981 b 18 – in grundsätzlicher Weise angegeben.) Zu jenen gehört in erster Linie die Differenz Arm (arm als die Grenze des Existenzminimums nicht überschreitend verstanden) bzw. Mittelständisch auf der einen und Reich und damit Mächtig auf der anderen Seite. Diese wird heute weniger (wie schon in alter Zeit) durch den Adel und den Großgrundbesitz verkörpert, sondern, und das besonders international und allmählich global, mehr durch die verschiedenen Formen des Finanzkapitals, also – aristotelisch gesprochen – durch die Chrematistik. (Siehe dazu auch Koslowski [1993] S. 67 f.) Abhilfen, welche sich gegen eine solche Entwicklung empfehlen, zu finden kann eine vertiefte Lektüre der Aristotelischen „Politik" bzw. schon der Nikomachischen Ethik wesentlich mithelfen. In letzterer wird der Reichtum [πλοῦτος] als adäquates Prinzip bzw. als zentraler Inhalt des Eudaimoniebegriffs wie bekannt entschieden zurückgewiesen[123].

---

[123] Siehe dazu in Kap. 3 des 1. Buches der Nikomachischen Ethik die bekannte Stelle (in der Übersetzung von Dirlmeier): „Das Leben des Geldmenschen hat etwas Forciertes an sich und der Reichtum ist gewiß nicht das gesuchte oberste Gut. Er ist nur ein Nutzwert: Mittel für andere Zwecke. Daher kann man eher die vorher genannten Dinge (Lust und Ehre) als Endziele auffassen, denn sie werden um ihrer selbst willen geschätzt. Und doch sieht es so aus, als seien auch dies keine echten Ziele, obgleich viele Argumente zu ihren Gunsten Gemeingut geworden sind."

Und in Rhet. II 16 lesen wir u.a.: „Der Reichtum nämlich ist wie ein Maß für den Wert der anderen Dinge; deswegen scheint alles damit käuflich zu sein. … Auch zu meinen, man

Dieser Umstand ist zweifellos als fest bleibende Kennzeichnung des Charakters der Aristotelischen Anthropologie zu begreifen. Er sollte auch heute – ja sogar heute mehr denn je – von uneingeschränktem allgemeinem Interesse sein. Im fortdauernd gegebenen und aufgegebenen Bemühtsein um die Eudaimonie gebührt dabei dem Geld – dem Finanzkapital – keine bestimmendere Funktion als diejenige eines Mittels –, welcher Funktion von Mittel ja eo ipso stets nur eine dienende Rolle zusteht, aber keine solche von Vorrang oder von Dominanz bzw. von Vormacht (sei dies nun im kleineren bzw. nationalen Bezug oder sei es im globalen Umfang) – keine Rolle von Führungsfunktion oder Leitmaßstab. Zwar ist

> „… strittig, ob sich die Einteilung der Trias Ethik, Politik, Ökonomik der Praktischen Philosophie als Trias von Ethik, Politik und Wirtschaftswissenschaft interpretieren läßt. ... Die aristotelische Unterscheidung von Ö-

---

verdiene zu herrschen (gehört zum Charakter der Reichen); denn sie meinen, dass sie das besitzen, was würdig zum Herrschen macht."

Besonders scharf schließlich äußert sich Aristoteles zu den Begriffen Reichtum und Geld in seiner „Politik" u.a. so:

Der Reichtum – und zwar „der wahre Reichtum" (Aristoteles, Pol. I 8, 1256 b 30 ff.) „ist nichts anderes als eine Menge von Werkzeugen [Hilfsmitteln] für die Haus- oder [/und!] Staatsverwaltung". Er ist als solcher nicht unbegrenzt (ἄπειρος), sondern hat „wie alle übrigen Künste (τέχναις)" eine Grenze (τέρμα); er ist damit „so etwas wie eine der Natur folgende Erwerbskunst (ἔστι τις κτητικὴ κατὰ φύσιν, ebd. b 37 f.)", die als solche notwendig ist.

Eine zweite – der Natur jedoch nicht zugehörige und in diesem Sinne nicht notwendige – Erwerbskunst erstreckt sich vom Tauschhandel (der notwendig, aber „weder gegen die Natur, noch ... eine Art des Gelderwerbs [χρηματιστικῆς]" ist, ebd. 9, 1257 a 29, und der sich in „immer fernere Länder" ausdehnte und die Schaffung des Geldes notwendig nach sich zog) über das Händlergewerbe (das „nicht von Natur zur Kunst des Gelderwerbs gehört", das sich aber jedenfalls „bei zunehmender Routine ... mit steigendem Raffinement", vgl. ebd. b 3 f., abspielt, dabei sich auf Gelderwerb konzentriert und aus allem – siehe Wohl- bzw. Genussleben u.a. – möglichst grossen Geldgewinn ziehen will) bis hin zur Erwerbskunst – der dritten? – des Wuchers. (Ebd. 10, 1258 b 2 f., ὀβολοστατική.) An dieser Stelle übersetzt Eugen Rolfes teils bezogen auf die zweite und teils gegebenenfalls auf die dritte Erwerbskunst u.a. so: Sie ist eine „auf dem Umsatz beruhende", die „gerechten Tadel erfährt, weil sie nicht bei der Natur bleibt, sondern den einen Menschen vom anderen sich bereichern lässt"; als Wucher ist sie „mit vollstem Rechte eigentlich verhasst", weil sie „aus dem Gelde selbst Gewinn zieht und nicht aus dem, wofür das Geld doch allein erfunden ist".

Die besondere Schwierigkeit für die Analyse der letzteren Erwerbskünste ist, dass diese – als chrematistische, die dasselbe Anliegen haben – sehr nahe beisammen liegen, ja dass sie ineinander übergehen. (Ebd. 9, 1257 b 35.) Größer freilich noch ist die Schwierigkeit in betreff des Begriffes Bedürfnis, der offensichtlich ja auch schon die erste Erwerbskunst mitbetrifft.

(Siehe zu dieser Anmerkung auch schon oben S. 95 unter Pkt. 4 Isser.)

(Leider übrigens scheint Jaques Le Goff in seinem Buch „Wucherzins und Höllenqualen. Ökonomie und Religion im Mittelalter", Klett-Cotta, Stuttgart 1988 auf Aristoteles nicht ausreichend bzw. nicht wirklich gebührenden Bezug genommen zu haben.)

konomik und Chrematistik klärt [aber] auch die wirtschaftlichen Grundlagen der Politie. ... Eine Gesellschaft wie die Politie, die das Maß und den Ausgleich zu ihren Grundvoraussetzungen zählt, wird durch maßlose Anhäufung von Finanzkapital und Geld in ihren Grundlagen in Frage gestellt." [Koslowski (^{3}1993) S. 63.]

„Die [Einkommen bzw. die] Gewinne entwickeln sich [jedenfalls] rascher als die Löhne", sagte in diesen Tagen offenbar im selben Sinne auch der Chef einer der beiden größeren österreichischen Parteien – welcher Partei, dies bleibe hier dahingestellt; denn damit entstehe „gesellschaftlicher Sprengstoff". Eine Lösung des so angesprochenen Problems kann sich heutzutage, wie schon gesagt, aber immer schwerer nur auf den nationalen Rahmen beschränken; dies wohl umso weniger, wo Zeitungsmeldungen zufolge international Einzelfälle von (durch geglückte Geschäftoperationen zustandegekommenen) Verdienstspannen einzelner Personen bis über die Eine-Milliarde-Dollar-Jahresverdienst-Grenze hinaus vorkommen; und vor allem wo das Großkapital in Gestalt von Unternehmenszusammenschlüssen und Konzernen bald schon kleinere und sogar mittelgroße Staaten finanziell bedrängen, bedrohen und sogar vernichten kann, sofern keine einschränkenden Regelungen gefunden werden.[124]

Doch die angesprochene internationale bzw. globale Lösung oder zumindest adäquate Behandlung findet das im vorigen Absatz angesprochene Problem aber wohl erst dort, wo es um Krieg und (gerechten) Frieden im engeren und weiteren Rahmen der regionalen und nationalen bzw. staatlichen Geschichte bzw. der Weltgeschichte insgesamt geht. Siehe dazu auch in der Bibliographie unter Haltmayer [2004].)

8. Das vorliegende P o s t s k r i p t u m als Zusatz zu dem im vorhergehenden Punkt zur Sprache gebrachten zentralen Anliegen dieses Aufsatzes (und analog wohl auch der Aristotelischen Systematik und im relevanten Zusammenhang wohl auch Carl Mengers) erklärt sich daraus, dass ich die unten angeführte sehr wichtige Arbeit von J. Huerta de Soto erst nachträglich (in einer Buchhandlung) entdeckte und dass diese Arbeit darüber hinaus teils unter vervollständigender Perspektive den vorhergehenden Punkt 7 in seinem Doppelaspekt Zusammenfassung-Ausblick (wenn hier zumeist auch nur im Zitat) fortführt.

---

[124] Siehe dazu auch schon in Kants berühmtem Werk „Zum ewigen Frieden. Ein philosophischer Entwurf" im ersten Abschnitt die Präliminarartikel 2 und 4. Dem Artikel 2 zufolge „soll kein für sich bestehender Staat ... von einem andern ... [z.B.] durch ... Kauf ... erworben werden können". Und zufolge von Artikel 4 „sollen keine Staatsschulden in Beziehung auf äußere Staatshändel gemacht werden". Solche Schulden können eine „gefährliche Geldmacht" darstellen, „einen Schatz zum Kriegführen" u.a.

Huerta de Soto beginnt seinen 3. Abschnitt („Carl Menger und die Vorläufer der Österreichischen Schule") besonders auch mit der Behauptung, dass das größte Verdienst Mengers darin bestehe,

> „eine Denktradition katholischen und kontinental-europäischen Ursprungs wieder aufgenommen und vorangetrieben zu haben, die sich bis zu den Anfängen des philosophischen Denkens in Griechenland und – noch deutlicher – bis zur Tradition des juristischen, philosophischen und politischen Denkens des alten Roms zurückverfolgen lässt." [Huerta de Soto (2007), S. 43].

Diese Behauptung ist, soweit ich sehe, eine gewiss ungewöhnliche Perspektive. Sie wird in der Folge – auch hinsichtlich des hier besonders interessierenden antiken Griechenland, siehe auch weiter unten – zunächst vor allem durch mehrfache sehr interessante Hinweise und Belege aus der spanischen scholastischen Tradition konkretisiert. Denn es könne „kein Zweifel daran bestehen, dass die spanischen Scholastiker als die eigentlichen Vorgänger der Österreichischen Schule angesehen werden müssen." (Ebd., S. 44.) Und auf S. 53 schreibt Huerta de Soto:

> „Das wichtigste und originellste Unterscheidungsmerkmal des Beitrags Mengers lag ... in dem Versuch, die Wirtschaft in ihrer Gesamtheit vom Menschen ausgehend zu konstruieren und ihm die Vorreiterrolle eines kreativen Akteurs in allen sozialen Prozessen zuzuweisen. Menger betrachtete es als unbedingt erforderlich, den sterilen \`Objektivismus´ der klassischen englischen Schule zu verlassen. Im Gegensatz zu dieser Schule, die besessen war von der angeblichen Existenz objektiver Gegebenheiten (sozialer *Klassen, Aggregaten, materiellen* Produktionsfaktoren), sollte der Wissenschaftler stets die subjektive Perspektive des handelnden Menschen einnehmen, um auf diese Weise und durch diese Perspektive über das entscheidende Kriterium bei der Ausarbeitung seiner Theorie zu verfügen. Hayek, der diese neue subjektive Konzeption Mengers kommentierte, meinte hierzu: \`Es ist wahrscheinlich keine Übertreibung zu sagen, dass in den letzten hundert Jahren jeder bedeutende Fortschritt in der Wirtschaftstheorie ein weiterer Schritt in der konsequenten Anwendung des Subjektivismus war.´"
>
> „Somit ist der wichtigste und originellste Beitrag, den wir Menger verdanken, nicht, wie bisher angenommen wurde, die Entdeckung des Konzeptes des Grenznutzens (welches er unabhängig und parallel zu Jevons und Walras entwickelte), sondern die subjektivistische Konzeption menschlichen Handelns." (Huerta de Soto ebd., S. 55.)

Auf S. 56 f. dann befindet sich der Abschnitt, der die Thematik „Menger und die ökonomische Theorie sozialer Institutionen" behandelt, welch letztere in dessen „Grundsätzen der Volkswirtschaftslehre" auch hinsichtlich ihres Ursprungs und ihrer Entwicklung erörtert, „später von Hayek wieder aufgegriffen und bis zur letzten Konsequenz entwickelt wird“, so Huerta de Soto. Diese „für das Leben in einer Gesellschaft wichtigsten und wesentlichsten [sozialen] Institutionen für den Menschen (sprachlicher, ökonomischer, rechtlicher und moralischer Natur)“, die eine als solche „`nicht beabsichtige Konsequenz menschlichen Handelns sind´“, „entstanden ... in einem spontanen und evolutiven Prozess ... [„subjektivistisch“ gefasster] menschlicher Interaktionen, welcher für Menger und die Österreichische Schule das wichtigste Forschungsfeld im Bereich der Wirtschaftswissenschaften darstellen sollte“. Diese Institutionen (Verhaltensmuster) werden, so Huerta de Soto, nach Menger im Zuge „eines dezentralen trial and error Prozesses“ so gefunden, dass „aufgrund dieses unbewussten Prozesses des Lernens und der Nachahmung die Handlungsmuster der kreativsten und erfolgreichsten Personen sich ausbreiten und von den restlichen Mitgliedern der Gesellschaft befolgt werden“.

Zum Abschluss des Menger-Kapitels charakterisiert unser Autor auf S. 57 f. schließlich den „Methodenstreit“, und das so, dass dabei dezidiert und ausführlich auf Aristoteles Bezug genommen ist. Diese und andere – indirekte bzw. unausgesprochene – Bezugnahmen können hier leider nicht mehr interpretiert und vertieft werden. Sie passen aber gut zu den zentralen Aristoteles-Zitaten oben in Pkt. 3. Ja sogar Karl R. Poppers deduktivistischem Ansatz wird damit m.E. insofern Genüge getan, als – siehe die hier folgenden Ausführungen – die Ökonomie-relevante „Geschichte nur interpretiert, strukturiert und verständlich gemacht werden kann, wenn man vorher über eine ökonomische Theorie verfügt“.

> „Es kam für Menger einer großen Enttäuschung gleich, dass sein Beitrag nicht nur nicht von den Vertretern der historischen Schule verstanden wurde, sondern dass diese Vertreter meinten, Mengers Beitrag fordere den Historizismus heraus. Statt zu erkennen, dass Mengers Beitrag die theoretische Unterstützung war, welche die evolutorische Konzeption der sozialen Prozesse benötigte, betrachteten sie seine abstrakte und theoretische Analyse als unvereinbar mit dem von ihnen verfochtenen engen Verständnis des Historizismus. Auf diese Weise entstand die erste, und vielleicht berühmteste Polemik, in welche sich die Österreichische Schule verwickelt sah, der so genannte *Methodenstreit*, der die intellektuelle Energie Mengers über mehrere Jahrzehnte hinweg beanspruchen sollte. ... Gegen diese Auffassung publiziert Menger im Jahre 1883 sein zweites wichtiges Buch mit dem Titel *Untersuchungen über die Methode der Sozialwissenschaften und der politischen Ökonomie insbesondere* (Menger, 1969); von Aristoteles ausgehend vertritt er darin die Auffassung, dass das Wissen der sozialen Wirklichkeit zwei gleich wichtige Disziplinen verlangt, die jedoch, trotz ihres komplementären Charakters, radikal und epistemologisch verschieden sind. Auf der einen Seite die *Theorie,* wel-

che in einer bestimmten Weise die „Form" ist (in ihrem aristotelischen Sinne) und welche die Essenz [!] der ökonomischen Phänomene aufnimmt. Diese theoretische Form entdeckt man mit Hilfe der Introspektion, d.h. durch die innere Reflexion des Wissenschaftlers, die durch die Tatsache ermöglicht wird, dass die Ökonomie die einzige Wissenschaft ist, in welcher der Forscher das Privileg hat, über dieselbe Natur zu verfügen wie der zu untersuchende Gegenstand, was ihm ein wertvolles Wissen aus erster Hand verschafft. Außerdem wird die Theorie in einer logisch-deduktiven [!] Art aufgrund von offensichtlichem Wissen axiomatischen Typs ausgearbeitet. Von der Theorie verschieden ist die *Geschichte*, welche in einer bestimmten Art und Weise die „Materie" bildet (in ihrem aristotelischen Sinne) und die sich in empirischen Tatsachen historischer Ereignisse konkretisiert. Für Menger sind beide Disziplinen, Theorie und Geschichte, gleich wichtig, um die Realität zu erkennen. Aber er lehnt nachdrücklich in jedem Fall die Auffassung ab, eine Theorie aus der Geschichte gewinnen zu können. Die Beziehung zwischen beiden ist eher in dem Sinne umgekehrt, als dass die Geschichte nur interpretiert, strukturiert und verständlich gemacht werden kann, wenn man vorher über eine ökonomische Theorie verfügt. Auf diese Weise formuliert Menger, sich dabei auf die bereits von J.B. Say im Großen und Ganzen intuitiv erkannten methodologischen Positionen stützend, die Fundamente, die später die „offizielle" Methodologie der Österreichischen Schule der Nationalökonomie sein sollten."

Und Huerta de Soto beschließt seinen Menger-Abschnitt bemerkenswerter Weise wie folgt:

„Jedenfalls, und im Gegensatz zu der Standardversion der Lehrbücher, die den Methodenstreit als eine vergebliche Mühe qualifizieren, meinen wir, dass sich in diesem Streit die konzeptionell unvermeidlichen Unterschiede zwischen der Wissenschaft vom menschlichen Handeln (Human Action) und den Naturwissenschaften läuterten und abzeichneten, so dass die anhaltende Konfusion auf diesem Gebiet zweifellos darauf zurückzuführen ist, dass die Ökonomen dem von Menger gemachten Beitrag nicht die notwendige Aufmerksamkeit in der Auseinandersetzung mit der historischen Schule geschenkt haben." (Huerta de Soto, 1982).

II.
Menger als Denker in der Tradition des Liberalismus?
A thinker in the “true” Tradition of Liberal economics?

Menger und die Tradition des Liberalismus

Herta Mayerhofer

Der Liberalismus setzt sich aus drei Komponenten zusammen, er umfasst eine Staats-, eine Wirtschafts- und eine Gesellschaftslehre. Alle drei Elemente des Liberalismus gehen von der Voraussetzung aus, dass sich bei freier Entfaltung der Anlagen und Bestrebungen des einzelnen Individuums eine kontinuierliche positive Entwicklung für den Staat, die Wirtschaft und die Gesellschaft ergeben werde. Der Liberalismus wurde durch das Bürgertum repräsentiert, das in seinem Kampf gegen Absolutismus, Feudalismus und Klerikalismus seine eigenständige Position zu behaupten suchte. Der wirtschaftliche Liberalismus, mit dem sich dieser Beitrag beschäftigen wird, fand von England ausgehend in der klassischen Schule der Nationalökonomie seinen Ausdruck und verbreitete seine Ideen in den westeuropäischen Ländern und den Vereinigten Staaten von Amerika, die 1776 ihre Unabhängigkeit erlangt hatten. Vom philosophischen Standpunkt aus gesehen vertritt die klassische Nationalökonomie kein einheitliches System, ihre einzelnen Vertreter hingen unterschiedlichen philosophischen bzw. weltanschaulichen Ideen an, gemeinsam ist ihnen die Forderung nach wirtschaftlicher Unabhängigkeit gegenüber übergeordneten Institutionen. In der Folge soll die Lehre der drei bedeutendsten Repräsentanten der Politischen Ökonomie, als die sich die klassische Nationalökonomie versteht, kurz vorgestellt werden, um dann mit den Grundsätzen Carl Mengers, des Begründers der „Österreichischen Schule der Nationalökonomie“, oder der „Wiener Schule der Nationalökonomie“, wie diese Richtung der Volkswirtschaftslehre auch genannt wird, verglichen zu werden.

1. Adam Smith

Adam Smith, der Begründer der Politischen Ökonomie, geht von der Annahme aus, dass der Mensch von Natur aus über positive Anlagen verfüge, auf deren Fundament eine dauerhafte gesellschaftliche Ordnung errichtet werden könne. Im Jahr 1759 veröffentlichte er seine moralphilosophische Schrift „The Theory of Moral Sentiments“, in der er die gegen die Erbsündenlehre des Christentums und den Pessimismus Hobbes' gerichtete These vertritt, Moralität sei von den Naturtrieben des Menschen nicht loszulösen. Nach der Veröffentlichung seiner Ethik konzentrierte sich Smith auf die Jurisprudenz und die Politische Ökonomie, die Inhalte seiner Vorlesungen wurden später im „Wohlstand“ veröffentlicht. Sein Denken steht unter dem Einfluss von Hume, Rousseau, Holbach, Voltaire und den Physiokraten[125]. 1776 erschien sein Hauptwerk „An Inquiry into

[125] Bei den Physiokraten handelt es sich um eine Gruppe französischer Wirtschaftswissenschafter, die in der zweiten Hälfte des 18. Jahrhunderts die erste nationalökonomische Schule

the Nature and Causes of the Wealth of Nations“ („Der Wohlstand der Nationen. Eine Untersuchung seiner Natur und seiner Ursachen“), welches fünf Bücher umfasst. In den Büchern eins und zwei erarbeitet Smith die Grundbegriffe der Politischen Ökonomie (Arbeitsteilung, Werttheorie, Lohn, Gewinn, Rente). Am berühmt gewordenen Stecknadelbeispiel illustriert er, wie Arbeitsteilung die Geschicklichkeit des Handwerkers oder Arbeiters fördert, Zeit spart, den Einsatz moderner Maschinen optimiert und das Erfinden neuer Techniken anregt. An der Größe des bestehenden Marktes findet eine eventuelle weitere Arbeitsteilung ihre Grenze. Wird der Markt aber ausgeweitet, können Güter, die nicht konsumiert werden, gegen andere Güter getauscht werden. Beim gegenseitigen Austausch von Gütern erhebt sich die Frage nach dem Tauschwert bzw. dem Preis des auszutauschenden Gutes. Da der Wert von Gold und Silber schwankt, sucht Smith nach einem Wertmaßstab, der seiner Meinung nach für alle Zeiten und an allen Orten seine Gültigkeit bewahren wird. Er findet ihn in den Arbeitskosten, die bei der Produktion eines Gutes aufgewendet wurden. Obwohl Smith anerkennt, dass im Wert oder Preis einer Ware auch andere Faktoren wie Boden und Kapital beteiligt sind, misst er sie alle mit dem Maß der „Arbeitsmenge“. Die Erträge, die sich auf Lohn, Rente und Gewinn verteilen, werden ebenfalls nach diesem Maßstab gemessen. Bei den Preisen unterscheidet Smith zwischen dem „natürlichen“ Preis, der dem Aufwand an Arbeit, Kapital und Boden und den in der jeweiligen Gesellschaft üblichen Durchschnittssätzen entspricht, vom Marktpreis, der durch Angebot und Nachfrage größeren Schwankungen ausgesetzt ist. Der freie Wettbewerb zwischen den Konkurrenten bildet den Garant dafür, dass sich der Marktpreis immer wieder auf den natürlichen Preis hin bewegt. Wenn beide Preise – natürlich langfristig gesehen – zusammenfallen, wird ein Gleichgewichtspreis erzielt, der die gerechte Verteilung von Lohn, Rente und Gewinn an die Inhaber der Produktionsfaktoren Arbeit, Boden und Kapital regelt. In seiner Wachstumstheorie führt Smith aus, dass die Nettoersparnisse eines Jahres für die Kapitalbildung und damit für den Wachstumsprozess von entscheidender Bedeutung sind. Was jemand von seinem Einkommen spart und nicht für Dienstpersonal und Vergnügungen ausgibt, fügt er seinem Kapital hinzu. Mit dem ersparten Kapital können entweder neue Arbeitskräfte beschäftigt oder es kann gegen einen Zins einem anderen geliehen werden, der es für die Entlohnung neuer Arbeitskräfte verwendet.

---

entwickelte (Quesnay, Riqueti, Mirabeau, Turgot). Sie unterscheiden zwischen einer unveränderlichen und vollkommenen Ordnung, „ordre naturel“ und einer zeitbedingten Ordnung „ordre positif“, die durch Gesetze der ersten Ordnung möglichst angenähert werden soll. Die Physiokraten haben eine alle Stände des Landes umfassende Wirtschaftstheorie entwickelt; wertschöpfend ist nur die Landwirtschaft, der „classe productive“ gehören Bauern und Pächter an, die Grundeigentümer, der König, der Adel und die Kirche gelten als „classe propriétaire“ und setzen die an sie abgeführte Grundrente in Umlauf, womit sie den volkswirtschaftlichen Reinertrag vermehren. Arbeiter, Kaufleute und Handwerker gelten als „classe stérile“, sie fügen den Gütern im Wirtschaftsprozess nur die eigene Arbeit hinzu.

Die von ihm entwickelte Theorie und die Umsetzung dieser Theorie in die Wirtschaftspolitik sind bei Smith eng miteinander verknüpft. So zieht er aus der in Buch drei entfalteten, durch die Lektüre von Montesquieu und Voltaire inspirierten Entwicklungstheorie die Folgerungen und wendet sie im Buch vier gegen den Merkantilismus und die Lehre der Physiokraten. Schließlich behandelt er in Buch fünf die Funktion des Staates, die dieser zu erfüllen hat, um das gesellschaftliche und wirtschaftliche Wohl eines Staates zu fördern. Um dem Volk die Ausübung seiner „natürlichen" Freiheit zu ermöglichen und den freien Wettbewerb nicht zu behindern, muss der Staat diese Freiheiten durch eine geeignete Rechtsordnung schützen und fördern. In diesem Sinne müsse der Staat Gesetze, die Vererbung, Schenkung, Kauf und Tausch von Eigentum beschränken, aufheben, Monopole und Zunftzwang beseitigen. Die Koalitionsfreiheit der Arbeiter ist zu fördern, die Abschaffung von Handelsschranken im In- und Ausland habe dem freien Wettbewerb und der Erweiterung der Märkte zu dienen, jede einseitige Förderung durch Ausfuhrprämien und Einfuhrzölle sei im Sinne des Wirtschaftswachstums zu unterlassen. In die Kompetenz des Staates fällt die Aufrechterhaltung der inneren und äußeren Sicherheit; weiters habe der Staat solche Einrichtungen zu gründen und zu finanzieren, deren Bestehen im öffentlichen Interesse liegt, aber die finanziellen Möglichkeiten des Einzelnen übersteigt. Der Ausbau des Verkehrsnetzes, die Errichtung von Botschaften und das Schulwesen werden dem Staat überantwortet.

Nachdem Adam Smith das Fundament der Volkswirtschaftslehre errichtet hatte, haben andere Nationalökonomen, die der Klassik zugerechnet werden, versucht, seine Lehre durch erweiterte Darstellungen zu erklären oder durch eigene, neue Überlegungen zu ergänzen. Als nächster „Klassiker" soll David Ricardo kurz vorgestellt werden.

2. David Ricardo

schließt sich den grundsätzlichen Überlegungen Smiths an und unterwirft einige Thesen einer detaillierten Darstellung. 1817 erschien sein Hauptwerk „On the principles of political economy and taxation" („Die Grundsätze der Politischen Ökonomie oder die Staatswirtschaft und die Besteuerung"). Dieses Werk enthält eine Werttheorie, eine Arbeitswertlehre, eine Theorie der Bodenrente, das Entwicklungsgesetz der Einkommensverteilung, eine Preis- und Geldtheorie und die Theorie der komparativen Kosten.

Smith sieht im Tauschwert eines Gutes eine objektive Kategorie, da dieser die Menge anderer Güter angibt, gegen die man dieses Gut austauschen kann. Die Menge kann sowohl in anderen Waren als auch in Geld bestehen, wodurch sich der Tauschwert dem Preis nähert, der erfahrungsgemäß schwankt. Um einen Wertmaßstab zu finden, der dem Kriterium der Unveränderlichkeit in höherem Maß entspricht als der in Geld ausgedrückte Tauschwert, entwickelt Ricardo eine eigene Arbeitswerttheorie, der zufolge der Wert aller Güter durch die Menge der zu ihrer Herstellung aufgewendeten Arbeit bestimmt wird. Der Wert eines Gutes oder die Menge irgend eines anderen, für die es sich austauschen lässt, hängt demnach von der verhältnismäßigen Menge der zur Herstellung erforderlichen Arbeit ab und nicht von der größeren oder geringeren Vergütung, die für die Arbeit bezahlt wird. Damit erweitert Ricardo Smiths Lehre, für den der Wert (Preis) eines Produktes von den darauf verwendeten Produktionskosten abhängig ist. Die reinen (unmittelbaren) Produktionskosten werden nach Ricardos Auffassung um diejenigen in Zeit gemessenen Arbeitsmengen erweitert, die zur Hervorbringung von Rohstoffen bzw. von Hilfsmitteln für die Erzeugung notwendig sind. Durch Ricardos Theorie werden alle Produktionsmittel in eine Relation zur Arbeit gebracht. Sie haben nur so viel Wert, wie in ihnen Arbeit vorhanden ist. Das zur Produktion benötigte Kapital und die zur Produktion eingesetzten Maschinen sind nach Ricardo als „vorgetane Arbeit" zu verstehen und mit der zu ihrer Entstehung benötigten Arbeitsmenge zu bewerten. Als der einzige wertbildende Faktor hat Arbeit auch für die Landwirtschaft und damit für die Grundrente Gültigkeit.

Wie Smith vertritt Ricardo die Auffassung, dass der Preis eines Gutes dafür entscheidend ist, was an Lohn, Kapitalzins und Grundrente aus dem Sozialprodukt zurückfließt. Im Gegensatz zu Smith, der vor allem ein Mittel an die Hand zu geben versucht, um zu Wohlstand zu kommen, beschäftigt sich Ricardo mit dem Problem der Einkommensverteilung. Er sucht nach Gesetzen, die für die Verteilung maßgeblich sind. Sorge bereiten ihm die Bevölkerungsvermehrung und die damit einhergehende Ressourcen-verknappung: die Produktivität des Bodens falle stärker als die der Arbeit und des Kapitals. Die Grundrente ist die Vergütung, die für die Benützung der „unzerstörbaren Kräfte der Natur", in diesem Fall des Bodens, zu entrichten ist. Ricardo geht davon aus, dass die jeweilige Bodenbeschaffenheit konstant bleibt, wodurch nur die von Natur aus begünstigten Böden eine Rente abwerfen, die weniger fruchtbaren Böden, insbesondere der „Grenzboden", als derjenige Boden, der zu einer bestimmten Zeit noch bebaut wird, aber ohne Rente bleibt. Die Grundrente entsteht demnach nur auf den von der Natur aus begünstigten Böden, deren Produktionskosten unter denen der Grenzböden liegen. Macht das Bevölkerungswachstum die Produktion einer größeren Menge an Nahrungsmitteln erforderlich, werden die Böden der zweiten Qualität erst dann bearbeitet, wenn sich der gesunkene Grenzertrag der Arbeit auf den Böden der ersten Qualität dem Durchschnittsertrag der Arbeit auf den Böden der zweiten Qualität angeglichen hat. Die Anbieter mit besserer Bodenqualität erzielen den gleichen Preis pro Einheit bei vergleichsweise niedrigeren Kosten für Arbeit und Kapital pro Einheit.

Während sich Smiths Thesen hauptsächlich mit der Produktion von Gütern beschäftigen, richtet Ricardo sein Hauptaugenmerk auf die Vermarktung der Güter. Um den Absatz erzeugter Produkte zu fördern, beschäftigt sich Ricardo intensiv mit dem Freihandel, der das Zentrum seiner Wirtschaftspolitik bildet. Smith hatte den Export eines Gutes dann empfohlen, wenn gegenüber anderen Ländern absolute Kostenvorteile bestehen. Ricardo geht von der Erfahrung aus, dass unterschiedliche Länder aufgrund der dort vorliegenden natürlichen Gegebenheiten und durch den Einsatz verschiedener Technologien einen unterschiedlichen Arbeitseinsatz zur Produktion von Gütern benötigen. Kann nun ein Land ein Produkt mit geringerem Arbeitsaufwand als das andere Land herstellen, wird es dieses Produkt exportieren und solche Güter importieren, deren Erzeugung im eigenen Land einen höheren Arbeitsaufwand erfordern würde. Mit seiner Theorie der komparativen Kosten verbindet Ricardo seine Forderung nach Freihandel, da sich dadurch jedes Land auf die Herstellung von solchen Gütern spezialisieren kann, für die es die wenigsten Kosten aufzuwenden hat. Alle am Freihandel teilnehmenden Länder können an der Kostenersparnis partizipieren und ihren eigenen Wohlstand fördern.

3. John Stuart Mill ...

John Stuart Mill sucht im Gegensatz zum Praktiker Ricardo nach einem Zusammenhang zwischen der geistigen und psychischen Verfasstheit des Menschen und den wirtschaftlichen Phänomenen, wie wir sie in unserer Erfahrung vorfinden. Im Jahr 1848[126] erschien sein Hauptwerk „Principles of Political Economy", welches als das bedeutendste Standardwerk der Nationalökonomie im 19. Jahrhundert gilt. Mill war aber nicht nur Nationalökonom, sondern auch Philosoph; als solcher suchte er den Liberalismus in seiner Gesamtheit zu erfassen. So veröffentlichte er zahlreiche andere Werke, unter anderen „System of Logic" und „On Liberty", in welchem er den engen Zusammenhang der wirtschaftlichen mit der politischen und der geistigen Freiheit aufzeigt.

Das Ziel seines Hauptwerkes besteht darin, das Wissen seiner Zeit über Nationalökonomie zu sammeln und durch Anwendung von Ordnungskriterien überschaubar zu machen. Sein Lehrwerk sucht die Lehre der klassischen Schule zu ergänzen, zu reformieren und zu einem Abschluss zu bringen. Wie seine Vorgänger in der klassischen Nationalökonomie spricht sich Mill für freie Konkurrenz und gegen Monopole aus, da sie den Wettbewerb unterbinden und damit einer Verbesserung in Produktion und Handel hinderlich seien. Preisregulierungen durch den Staat ziehen in seiner Sicht den Wegfall des Gewinns und damit einen Produktionsrückgang nach sich.

Durch die Philosophie hatte Mill eine Welt des Seins und eine Welt des Sollens kennen gelernt, in welcher der Mensch Regeln und Normen zu beachten hat. Diese Gedanken übertrug er auf die Wirtschaft. Während die Güterproduktion natürlichen Bedingungen unterliegt und von Gesetzen abhängig ist, auf die

---

[126] Im selben Jahr erschien noch eine andere wirkmächtige Schrift: das von Marx und Engels verfasste „Kommunistische Manifest".

der Mensch nur wenig Einfluss hat, könne die Güterverteilung im hohen Ausmaß vom Menschen selbst gesteuert werden. Deshalb beschäftigte er sich intensiv mit der Verteilung der Güter und ließ sich bei seinen Vorschlägen zu einer gerechten Verteilung vom Gedankengut englischer und französischer Sozialisten beeinflussen.

Der Staat dürfe keine Gesetze gegen die Koalition von Arbeitern erlassen; der Preis von Gütern dürfe nicht auf Kosten von Löhnen, mit denen die Arbeiter nicht mehr ihr Auslangen finden, niedrig gehalten werden. Allerdings müsse die Freiheit der Arbeiter insofern respektiert werden, dass sie nicht zu einem Beitritt zu einer Arbeitervereinigung gezwungen werden können. Mit seiner positiven Stellung zum Genossenschaftsgedanken bekennt sich Mill zur Wirtschaftsdemokratie. Nur dann, wenn die Freiheit des Einzelnen nicht gefährdet wird, dürfe sich der Staat in die Regelung des Wirtschaftsverlaufs einbringen. So empfiehlt Mill, durch entsprechende Gesetze unverhältnismäßigen, d.h. unverdienten, Bodenwertzuwachs durch Besteuerung zu eliminieren und private Vermögensakkumulation durch Beschränkung des Erbrechts zu limitieren.

In seiner Außenhandelstheorie geht Mill über Ricardo insofern hinaus, dass er erkennt, dass auch die komparativen Produktionskosten für den internationalen Handel nicht den entscheidenden Faktor bilden. Bei seinen Untersuchungen über die Verteilung der Handelsgewinne unter den Güter austauschenden Ländern findet Mill einen Grundsatz, der den Produktionskosten vorangeht und diese bedingt: das Wechselspiel zwischen Angebot und Nachfrage. Dasjenige Land werde aus den internationalen Handelsbeziehungen den größten Vorteil ziehen, nach dessen Erzeugnissen in anderen Ländern die größte Nachfrage herrsche. Aufgrund der gesteigerten Nachfrage sei dieses Land in der Lage, seine Produkte noch billiger anzubieten und durch die Verbilligung des Preises werde die Nachfrage noch weiter steigen.

Somit hängt in Mills Sichtweise der Tauschwert oder Preis neben den Produktionskosten von Angebot und Nachfrage ab, wobei sich der Preis selbst so reguliert, dass die Nachfrage gerade ausreicht, das Angebot abzunehmen. Durch seine Interpretation des Außenhandels als gegenseitigen Ausgleich von Angebot und Nachfrage hat Mill einen wertvollen Beitrag zum Erklärungspotential der Nationalökonomie geleistet.

4. ... und Carl Menger

Carl Menger fand um die Mitte des 19. Jahrhunderts in der klassische Nationalökonomie eine Theorie vor, die den Anspruch vertrat, für alle wesentlichen Probleme auf dem Gebiet der Wirtschafts- und Sozialpolitik einen Lösungsansatz bieten zu können. Allerdings wurde die Fehlerhaftigkeit der auf dem Kostenprinzip beruhenden klassischen Nationalökonomie immer deutlicher: die aus dem Kostenprinzip entwickelten Preistheorien waren sehr unterschiedlich und auf keinen gemeinsamen Nenner zu bringen.

Carl Menger war davon überzeugt, dass eine einheitliche Theorie – wie dies von den Klassikern versucht worden war – nur dann entwickelt werden könne, wenn vorher ein Standpunktwechsel vorgenommen worden ist. Dieser Standpunktwechsel ist für Menger mit einer Erneuerung der bisher als objektiv verstandenen Werttheorie zu verbinden. Den Wert eines Gutes bestimmen nicht die Arbeits- bzw. Produktionskosten, vielmehr ist es der seine Bedürfnisse befriedigende Mensch, der einem Gut nach seinen subjektiven Kriterien einen Wert beilegt. Den zweiten entscheidenden Ausgangspunkt für Mengers Theorie bildet die Auffassung, dass der Mensch zwar nicht Art und Anzahl seiner Bedürfnisse bestimmen, diese aber innerhalb eines von äußeren Umständen gegebenen Rahmens durch kluges Handeln für sich und die Gesellschaft zufrieden stellend befriedigen könne.

In der Folge soll die Frage behandelt werden, ob die Thesen Mengers die klassische Nationalökonomie fortsetzen oder einen Paradigmenwechsel herbeiführen. Dieser Fragenkomplex soll in vier Schwerpunkte unterteilt werden, die zum Ausdruck bringen sollen, dass die klassische Ökonomie durch Mengers Lehre nicht endgültig zu einem Ende kommt, wohl aber in entscheidenden Punkten einer Revision unterworfen wird. Von folgenden Punkten ist dabei auszugehen:

- Weiterhin bilden Kapitalismus und Konkurrenz die Grundlage, auf der wirtschaftliche Prozesse stattfinden. Diese beiden Grundpfeiler werden nicht weiter hinterfragt; der Marktprozess übt weiterhin seine die gesamte Wirtschaft regelnde Kraft aus. Gravierende Veränderungen durch den Staat oder durch eine benachteiligte Bevölkerungsgruppe sind in diesem Konzept nicht vorgesehen. Ricardos Verständnis des Außenhandels als Mittel der Markterweiterung wird übernommen. Aufgrund der Übernahme des von der Klassik gegebenen Menschen- und Gesellschaftsbildes werden die Grenzwertschulen der Neoklassik zugerechnet.
- Beiden Denkrichtungen ist die Auffassung gemeinsam, dass die Preise, wie sie sich auf dem Markt präsentieren, erklärungsbedürftige Phänomene darstellen, die einer Werttheorie als Grundlegung bedürfen. Allerdings nimmt die Erklärungsbasis eine unterschiedliche Gestalt an: die Klassik nimmt dafür die Produktionskosten, die Grenzwerttheorie den individuellen Wert in Anspruch.
- Beide Wirtschaftstheorien stellen den Anspruch, eine umfassende Theorie zu erstellen, aus der Folgerungen für die Praxis ableitbar sind. Sie verneinen deshalb die Notwendigkeit von Zusatztheorien, die sich eventuell aus mangelnder Lösungskompetenz ergeben könnten.
- Neu ist die intensive Beschäftigung mit der Nachfrage, die Mill zwar schon als wichtig für den Preis erkannt, allerdings nicht weiter analysiert

hatte. Es sind nicht mehr die Kosten, die Preis und Nachfrage bestimmen, sondern es liegt im Ermessen des Konsumenten, zu entscheiden, wie nützlich ein Produkt für ihn ist und wie viel er aufgrund der von ihm festgestellten Nützlichkeit für ein Produkt zu zahlen bereit ist.

Die oben angeführten vier Punkte sollen in den folgenden Abschnitten näher behandelt werden.

5. Das Menschenbild und die damit verbundenen wirtschaftlichen Zusammenhänge bei den Klassikern und bei Carl Menger

Vor der Zeit Smiths war man allgemein der Ansicht, dass die soziale Ordnung in einer staatlichen Gemeinschaft nur dann aufrechterhalten werden könne, wenn entweder die Kirche oder der Staat regulierend eingreifen. Erst die Aufklärung, das Naturrecht und die englische Moralphilosophie – und mit ihnen Smith – sind davon überzeugt, dass eine stabile Ordnung ohne Bevormundung durch Autoritäten unter der Voraussetzung möglich ist, dass der Einzelne seinen persönlichen Lebensplan realisieren kann.[127]

Während seines Studiums hatte Smith Vorlesungen des Moralphilosophen Francis Hutcheson, eines Theoretikers des „moral sense", gehört und sich dieses Gedankengut angeeignet. Die Theorie beruht auf der Annahme, dass die Menschen über einen Instinkt verfügen, der sie zum Guten anleitet. Smith wird während seines gesamten Lebens den Überzeugungen seines Lehrers treu bleiben; sein erstes Werk „The Theory of Moral Sentiments" aus dem Jahr 1759 widmet er moralphilosophischen Fragen. Allerdings fordert Smith eine fiktive neutrale Instanz (eine Art Gewissen), die die ursprünglichen Reaktionen und die daraus resultierenden Handlungen kritisch beurteilt.

Da der Mensch seiner Natur gemäß nach moralischer Vervollkommnung strebe, müsse er sich ohne Zwang frei entwickeln können. Aufgrund der Eigenliebe (self-love) – die von Selbstsucht und Egoismus zu unterscheiden ist – ist der Mensch fähig, seine dynamischen Selbstinteressen zu verfolgen, die darin bestehen, seine Existenz durch „Erwerbsfleiß" abzusichern, seine Wohlfahrt zu steigern und seine Position in der Gesellschaft durch die Anerkennung und Wertschätzung seiner Mitmenschen zu verbessern und zu festigen.[128] Eigeninteresse, ein Affekt zwischen Trieb und Vernunft, veranlasst die Menschen, die von ihnen erzeugten, nicht benötigten Produkte gegen andere Güter auszutauschen, die sie selbst nicht herstellen, aber gut gebrauchen können. Alle vom Eigeninter-

---

[127] Die Physiokraten vertraten die aus der Naturrechtslehre stammende These von der „natürlichen Ordnung", der zufolge alle wirtschaftlichen und sozialen Phänomene einer Gesetzmäßigkeit unterliegen, so dass auch von persönlichem Interesse geleitete Handlungen dem Gesamtinteresse dienen.

[128] Vier Kräfte beschränken das dynamische Selbstinteresse des Menschen: a) das Mitgefühl als Gefühl für Gerechtigkeit, b) die Regeln der Ethik, c) positive Gesetze, die mit Sanktionen ausgestattet sind, d) die Konkurrenz (Wohlstand S. XVI, Würdigung durch den Herausgeber).

esse geleiteten Personen ziehen aus einem Kauf oder Tausch Nutzen – sonst würden sie diesen unterlassen – und nützen durch ihre Handlungen ohne Absicht der Gemeinschaft. Hier macht sich die „unsichtbare Hand“[129] bemerkbar. Selbst die Arbeitsteilung, die dem einzelnen Menschen Vorteile gebracht und die Entwicklung der Wirtschaft vorangetrieben hat, stammt nicht aus vernünftigen Überlegungen, sondern aus einer natürlichen Neigung der Menschen“ (Wohlstand S. 16). Die Menschen handeln in wirtschaftlichen Belangen im eigenen Interesse und sind für ihre Handlungen selbst verantwortlich. Durch Arbeitsteilung und Handel wächst der allgemeine Wohlstand, ohne dass der Staat lenkend in den Ablauf der Wirtschaft eingreifen müsste.

Menger entwickelte seine subjektive Werttheorie in einer Zeit wirtschaftlichen Aufschwungs, während der so genannten „Gründerjahre“, als noch keine dirigistischen Maßnahmen zugunsten des Bauerntums und des Kleingewerbes nötig waren. Im Gegensatz zu Smith sieht Menger nicht im natürlichen Hang des Menschen zum Tausch das Movens wirtschaftlicher Aktivität, sondern im Streben nach einer Verbesserung der wirtschaftlichen Situation durch eine möglichst vollständige Befriedigung seiner Bedürfnisse. Der in wirtschaftlicher Hinsicht frei entscheidende Bürger ist in der Lage, durch seinen Fleiß, seine Sparsamkeit und sein planendes Verhalten seinen eigenen Wohlstand zu fördern (1871 S. 29). Menger ist von dem Fortschritt menschlicher Erkenntnis überzeugt, Erkenntnisfortschritt bedeutet für ihn das Erreichen einer höheren Stufe in Kultur und wirtschaftlicher Wohlfahrt. Auf der Grundlage des wirtschaftlichen Wohlstandes seiner Bürger erwachsen dem Staat Macht und Ansehen. Darüber hinaus wird der Staat durch die wirtschaftlich umsichtige Vorgangsweise seiner Bürger entlastet und kann sich auf seine Aufgaben im innen- und außenpolitischen Bereich konzentrieren.

Für Menger ist der Mensch ein nach Befriedigung seiner Bedürfnisse strebendes Wesen. Da aber in unserer Welt die Ressourcen nicht in unbeschränkter Quantität vorliegen, muss das Individuum seinen Verstand einsetzen, um sich in ausreichender Menge mit den nötigen und das Leben angenehm gestaltenden Gütern zu versorgen. Um an die gewünschten Güter heranzukommen, sieht sich der Mensch zu einem zweckmäßigen, d.h. egoistischen, Handeln veranlasst: „Da findet denn der menschliche Egoismus einen Antrieb, sich geltend zu machen, und es wird jedes Individuum bemüht sein, dort wo die verfügbare Quantität nicht für alle ausreicht, seinen eigenen Bedarf mit Ausschluss der anderen möglichst vollständig zu decken“. (1871 S. 55). D.h. der Mensch bedient sich seiner

[129] Wenn der Einzelne nach Gewinn strebt „wird [er] in diesem wie auch in vielen anderen Fällen von einer unsichtbaren Hand geleitet, um einen Zweck zu fördern, den zu erfüllen er in keiner Weise beabsichtigt hat. Auch für das Land selbst ist es keineswegs immer das schlechteste, dass der Einzelne ein solches Ziel nicht bewusst anstrebt, ja, gerade dadurch, dass er das eigene Interesse verfolgt, fördert er häufig das der Gesellschaft nachhaltiger, als wenn er wirklich beabsichtigt, es zu tun“ (Wohlstand S. 370).

Vernunft und trifft Entscheidungen, um aus den vorhandenen Ressourcen den größtmöglichen Nutzen zu ziehen.

Die zweite Auflage der „Grundsätze" enthält ein Kapitel mit der Überschrift „Inwieweit unser unmittelbarer Bedarf und die uns unmittelbar verfügbaren Güterquantitäten determinierte Größen sind" (1923 S. 34f.). Hier legt Menger dar, dass unsere Bedürfnisse ihre Wurzel in unserer menschlichen Natur haben und damit zunächst von unserem Willen unabhängig sind. Allerdings biete uns unser Wille die Möglichkeit, die Befriedigung unserer Bedürfnisse aufzuschieben bzw. durch Gewöhnung einzelne Bedürfnisse zu wecken oder zu modifizieren. Unserer Willensfreiheit wird aber durch die jeweilige wirtschaftliche Sachlage Grenzen gesetzt: unsere Bedürfnisse, die unmittelbar verfügbaren Güter und das Streben des Menschen, seinen Bedarf zu decken, bilden den Rahmen, innerhalb dessen sich der Mensch bewegen kann (Untersuchungen S. 45).

6. Bestimmung des Wertes (Preises) bei den Klassikern und bei Carl Menger

Bei der Suche mach einem allgemeinen Maß, an dem alle verfügbaren Güter gemessen werden können, entscheidet sich Smith für die in die Produktion der Güter investierte Arbeitsmenge: „Arbeit ist demnach ganz offensichtlich das einzige allgemein gültige und auch das einzige exakte Wertmaß oder der alleinige Wertmaßstab, nach dem man die Werte der verschiedenen Waren immer und überall vergleichen kann." (Wohlstand S. 33). Der Mensch „ist arm oder reich, je nach der Menge Arbeit, über die er verfügen oder deren Kauf er sich leisten kann. Arbeit ist demnach das wahre und tatsächliche Maß für den Tauschwert aller Güter" (Wohlstand S. 28). Smith unterscheidet zwischen dem Tauschwert und dem Gebrauchswert von Gütern.[130] Der Gebrauchswert einer Ware korreliert nicht mit deren Tauschwert; so habe Wasser einen hohen Gebrauchswert, aber keinen Tauschwert, weil es ohne Arbeitsleistung erworben worden ist. Da Smiths Lehre den Tausch in den Mittelpunkt wirtschaftlichen Handelns stellt, interessiert ihn lediglich der Tauschwert einer Ware. Der Tauschwert und damit der Preis einer Ware richten sich nach dem Wert der Arbeit, die zu ihrer Produktion aufgewendet worden ist. Smith – und mit ihm die klassische Nationalökonomie, besonders wenn Ricardo in seine Arbeitswertlehre alle Produktionsfaktoren einschließt – geht bei der Bewertung eines Gutes vom Aspekt der dabei aufgewendeten Arbeit aus und sucht dem erbrachten Arbeitsaufwand einen gerechten Wert beizulegen. Dabei wird der Umstand übersehen, dass auch der Ge-

[130] Mill korrigiert Smiths Verwendung von "Gebrauchswert", indem er darunter nicht nur den direkten Gebrauch, sondern auch die Fähigkeit eines Gutes, einen Wunsch zu befriedigen oder einem Zweck zu dienen, versteht. Deswegen sei zwischen Wert und Preis zu unterscheiden, wobei der Wert eines Gutes ein relativer Begriff sei, der die Menge von Gütern zum Ausdruck bringt, welche sich gegen ein bestimmtes Gut eintauschen lassen.

brauchswert der beiden gegeneinander ausgetauschten Waren für die am Tausch beteiligen Personen gleich sein muss, weil diese sonst einen Warenaustausch unterlassen werden.

Für Menger liegt das Motiv, ein Gut gegen ein anderes auszutauschen, in der Tatsache, dass der Mensch bestimmter Güter bedarf, um sein Leben in angenehmer Weise zu gestalten. Darüber hinaus muss der Mensch der Gegebenheit Rechnung tragen, dass die von ihm gebrauchten Güter nur in beschränkter Quantität verfügbar sind. Der Mensch sucht dabei nach einem Maßstab für die Beurteilung der Güter. Die darauf aufgewendeten Produktionskosten, bzw. das dazu benötigte Maß an Arbeit können dem Menschen keine Entscheidungshilfe liefern, ob er ein bestimmtes Gut erwerben soll. Menger drückt diesen Zusammenhang so aus: „Auch die auf ein Gut aufgewendete Arbeit kann demnach nicht das Kriterium des ökonomischen Charakters der Güter sein, es ist vielmehr klar, dass dasselbe ganz ausschließlich in den Verhältnissen zwischen Bedarf und verfügbarer Quantität derselben zu suchen ist." (1871 S. 61 Anmerkung). Um zu einer Entscheidung zu gelangen, muss der Mensch Überlegungen darüber anstellen, welchen Rang er einem Gut bei der Befriedigung seiner Bedürfnisse einräumt. Er wird sich fragen, wieweit ihm ein Gut von Nutzen sein kann, um seiner persönlichen Lebensgestaltung dienlich zu sein. Damit bildet der subjektiv festgesetzte „Grenznutzen" das Kriterium des wirtschaftlichen Wertes eines Konsumgutes: das wirtschaftende Subjekt legt fest, welche Einheit eines teilbaren Gütervorrates als letzte und damit unwichtigste noch nützlich für die Befriedigung eines bestimmten Bedürfnisses ist. Hat der Konsument seine persönliche Situation geklärt, wird er die auf dem Markt herrschenden objektiven Gegebenheiten zur Kenntnis nehmen und einen Plan erstellen, wie er durch wirtschaftliches Handeln seinen persönlichen Bedürfnissen auf optimale Weise Rechnung tragen kann.

7. Theorie und Praxis bei den Klassikern und bei Carl Menger

Sowohl die klassische Volkswirtschaftslehre als auch Carl Menger verstehen die Nationalökonomie als eine Wissenschaft, die ein vollständiges Theoriengebäude zu errichten hat.

John Stuart Mill versteht sich als Vollender der Politischen Ökonomie und sucht deshalb die Erkenntnisse dieser Wissenschaft in ein System einzuordnen. Deshalb soll in diesem Beitrag seine Auffassung von Theorie und Praxis mit den diesbezüglichen Überlegungen Mengers verglichen werden. In Essay 5 seiner 1844 herausgegebenen Schrift „Essays on Some Unsettled Questions of Political Economy" sucht Mill den Gültigkeitsbereich theoretischer ökonomischer Thesen zu bestimmen. Dazu vergleicht er seine eigenen ökonomischen Aussagen mit denen seiner Zeitgenossen, um festzustellen, was unter dem Begriff „Politische Ökonomie" zu verstehen ist. Dabei muss er feststellen, dass weder ein einheitlicher Forschungsansatz noch eine auf einer Definition beruhende Methode vorhanden sind, um ökonomische Phänomene zu untersuchen und nach festgelegten Kriterien zu ordnen. Unter „Definition“ versteht Mill sowohl die Festsetzung des Objektbereichs einer Wissenschaft, als auch die Methoden, die der Bearbeitung des festgelegten Bereichs dienen. Bedauerlicher Weise gehen Ökonomen in der Regel so vor, dass sie zunächst konkrete Fragen zu klären suchen, diese Fragen dann weitere Fragen ergeben, so dass zahlreiche Erkenntnisse zusammengetragen werden, die man durch Abstraktion zu verallgemeinern und zuletzt anhand von allgemeinen Prinzipien zu systematisieren sucht. Mangels einer einheitlichen Definition geht Mill zunächst daran, zu untersuchen, wie es um die „am meisten anerkannten Definitionen dieser Wissenschaft “ bestellt ist (Essays S.148 f.).

Zunächst wendet sich Mill der Definition Adam Smiths zu, die bereits aus dem Titel seines Werkes „An Inquiry into the Nature and Causes of the Wealth of Nations“ hervorzugehen scheint: die Politische Ökonomie ist demnach eine Wissenschaft, „die lehrt, [...] auf welche Weise eine Nation reich gemacht werden kann.“ Trotz dieser Vorgabe muss Mill bei der Lektüre dieses von ihm sehr geschätzten Werkes feststellen, dass hier „Wissenschaft und Kunstlehre“ (science and art), reine und angewandte Wissenschaft oder Theorie und Praxeologie, wie wir heute sagen, nicht nur nicht getrennt, sondern „miteinander verwechselt“ werden. Für Mill hat reine Wissenschaft die Aufgabe, Phänomene unter ein Gesetz zu bringen, während es der angewandten Wissenschaft zukomme, Regeln zu erstellen, wie ein festgesetztes Ziel durch zweckmäßiges Verhalten zu erreichen ist. Regeln, wie man eine Nation reicher machen kann, bilden nicht den Forschungsbereich einer Wissenschaft, sondern können erst als Resultat einer Wissenschaft für die wirtschaftliche Praxis nutzbar gemacht werden. In der Folge untersucht Mill Ricardos bekannte Definition, die die Politische Ökonomie als „die Wissenschaft von den Gesetzen, die die Produktion, die Verteilung und den Konsum des Reichtums regeln“, bezeichnet. Auch dieser Definition kann Mill nicht zustimmen, weil die in der Definition für die Politische Ökonomie verwendeten Begriffe auch in den Natur- und Geisteswissenschaften Verwendung finden und von diesen nicht abgegrenzt werden.

Mill schlägt eine seiner Meinung nach vollständige Definition vor, wobei er eine deutliche Abgrenzung besonders gegenüber der Psychologie vornimmt. Für ihn ist die Politische Ökonomie „die Wissenschaft, die die Gesetze solcher Phänomene aufzeigt, die sich aus dem Zusammenwirken der Menschen bei der Produktion von Reichtum ergeben, soweit diese Erscheinungen nicht durch das Anstreben irgendeines anderen Zieles modifiziert werden“ (Essays S.164).[131]

---

[131] In seinem Hauptwerk "Principles of Political Economy" (S. 21) legt Mill allerdings fest, dass der Gegenstand der Ökonomie die Gesetze der Produktion, der Verteilung und einige daraus praktisch ableitbare Folgerungen zu sein habe.

Sollen die Grundsätze der politischen Ökonomie auf die Praxis, d.h. auf einen speziellen Fall Anwendung finden, müssen alle Umstände dieses speziellen Falles berücksichtigt werden (Essays S. 172f.). Diese Umstände, Mill bezeichnet sie als „Störungsfaktoren", liegen meist in äußeren, unvorhersehbaren Umständen oder in der Psyche und dem daraus resultierenden Verhalten des Menschen. Deshalb könne Theorie niemals eins zu eins in die Praxis umgesetzt werden. Allerdings berücksichtigt Mill nicht ausreichend das Spezifische der gesellschaftlichen Umstände, in denen sich das wirtschaftende Subjekt befindet. Karl Marx wird hier seine Kritik der Politischen Ökonomie ansetzen.

Was bedeutet Theorie und Praxis bei Carl Menger?

Obwohl Mill in seinem oben erwähnten Essay zwischen einer theoretischen und einer praktischen Volkswirtschaftslehre unterschieden hatte, ändert er nichts an den Prinzipien der klassischen Volkswirtschaftslehre. Da Menger überzeugt ist, dass lediglich aus einer auf einem „richtigen" Prinzip basierenden Theorie Handlungsmaximen abgeleitet werden können, verwirft er alle Handlungsanweisungen, die auf einem seiner Meinung nach mangelhaften theoretischen System beruhen. Erst dann, wenn die wirtschaftlichen Gesetzmäßigkeiten erkannt worden sind, werde die reale Welt beherrschbar.

Ähnlich wie Mill unterscheidet Carl Menger zwischen Theorie und Praxis einer Wissenschaft. In der Vorrede seiner 1871 erschienenen „Grundsätze" (1871 S. V) spricht Menger davon, dass „das Bedürfnis nach einer wissenschaftlichen Grundlage des wirthschaftlichen Handelns ein allgemeineres und tiefer gefühltes" sei.

Ebenso wünsche man die „Fähigkeit der Practiker" in Anspruch zu nehmen, um die Errungenschaften der Wissenschaft in die Praxis umzusetzen und damit für die Allgemeinheit nutzbar zu machen. Bedauernd muss Menger feststellen, dass der Entwicklungsstand der Volkswirtschaftslehre noch nicht ausreichend sei, um daraus Handlungsanweisungen für die Praxis zu gewinnen. Bisher sei es notwendig gewesen, bei wirtschaftlichen Tätigkeiten die eigene Lebenserfahrung als Entscheidungsgrundlage in Anspruch zu nehmen, anstatt sich von wissenschaftlichen Erkenntnissen leiten zu lassen.

Die theoretische Volkswirtschaftslehre habe allerdings nicht die Aufgabe, sich mit praktischen Vorschlägen für das wirtschaftliche Handeln zu beschäftigen, sondern, wie Menger präzisiert, „mit den Bedingungen, unter welchen die Menschen die auf die Befriedigung ihrer Bedürfnisse gerichteten vorsorglichen Thätigkeiten entfalten" (1871 S. IX). Der Hinweis auf die Freiheit des menschlichen Willens könne wohl als Einwand gegen die volle Gesetzmäßigkeit wirtschaftlicher Handlungen, niemals aber als Einwand gegen die Gesetzmäßigkeit der von dem menschlichen Willen unabhängigen Erscheinungen gelten, welche den Erfolg wirtschaftlicher Tätigkeit der Menschen bedingen. Die durch wirtschaftliche Gesetze determinierten Bedingungen liegen nicht auf derselben Ebene wie die Willensfreiheit des Menschen, weshalb Determinismus und Willensfreiheit in diesem Fall nicht in Widerspruch geraten können.

Nähere Aussagen darüber, was unter einer „praktischen Volkswirtschaftslehre“ zu verstehen sei, finden sich allerdings erst in den „Untersuchungen“. Menschliche Erkenntnis ist nach Menger immer bestrebt, Vergangenes und Gegenwärtiges zunächst zu beschreiben, um dann durch Reflexion das Unveränderliche herauszufiltern. Die Wirtschaftswissenschaft hat sich nach Menger aus drei Teilbereichen zusammenzusetzen: der historischen, der theoretischen und der praktischen Wirtschaftswissenschaft. Wirtschaftsgeschichte und Statistik bilden den historischen Teilbereich, während die theoretische Volkswirtschaft die allgemeinen Zusammenhänge und damit die Gesetze, die den wirtschaftlichen Phänomenen zugrunde liegen, zu erforschen hat. In den Erscheinungen sind immer wieder auftretende Invarianten, allgemeine Formen, Menger nennt sie „Typen“, aufzusuchen, die sich bei wechselnden Erscheinungen immer wieder manifestieren. Neben der Erforschung des Objektbereiches, der das Sein der Wissenschaft darstellt, fordert Menger die „praktischen Wissenschaften“, die danach zu fragen haben, „was sein soll, damit bestimmte menschliche Zwecke erreicht werden“ (Untersuchungen S. 7). Die „menschlichen Zwecke“, von denen Menger spricht, müssen nicht durch Normen vorgegeben werden, sondern sind durch das Streben des Menschen nach Bedürfnisbefriedigung als Konstanten wirtschaftlichen Handelns vorgegeben. Sie sind damit, wie Menger überzeugt ist, „unserer Willkür entrückt“ (Untersuchungen S. 263). Obwohl wir über die Art und die quantitative Beziehung unserer Bedürfnisse nicht entscheiden können, haben wir einen Entscheidungsspielraum bei der Befriedigung unserer Bedürfnisse. So kann unser Hunger durch den Verzehr unterschiedlicher Nahrungsmittel gestillt werden, gegen Witterungseinflüsse können wir uns mit verschiedenen Kleidungsstücken schützen. Der praktischen Volkswirtschaftslehre kommt die Aufgabe zu, aufzuzeigen, wie unter den von der Natur vorgegebenen Bedingungen unsere Bedürfnisse auf die für die gesamte Volkswirtschaft zuträglichste Weise erfüllt werden können. Theoretisch gibt es nur eine zweckmäßige Form des „wirtschaftlichen“ Handelns, allerdings müssen exakte Gesetze vom oft zutage tretenden „unwirtschaftlichen“ Verhalten der Menschen absehen (Untersuchungen S. 262 ff.). In der Realität weichen Menschen von den rationalen Zwecken wirtschaftlichen Handelns immer wieder ab. Für diese Abweichungen sind sowohl innere, psychische, Faktoren wie Unsicherheit und Irrtum, als auch äußere Einflüsse durch Autoritäten und unvorhergesehene Ereignisse verantwortlich.

Allerdings kam es nie zur Ausarbeitung einer praktischen Volkswirtschaftslehre durch Menger. Wie wir in der zweiten Auflage der „Grundsätze“ aus dem Vorwort des Herausgebers – des Sohnes Mengers – erfahren, hatte Carl Menger die Absicht, seinen 1871 erschienenen „Grundsätzen“, die die Bezeichnung „Erster Allgemeiner Teil“ tragen, noch drei Teile hinzuzufügen, von denen der dritte Teil den Titel „Praktischer Teil" tragen sollte. Dieser Teil sollte sich, wie aus Notizen hervorgeht, mit technischen Anweisungen im Bereich von Produktion und Handel befassen.

8. Makroökonomische versus mikroökonomische Betrachtungsweise

Seit Adam Smith bildet der Wohlstand, genauer präzisiert Volkswohlstand, den Leitfaden für die Gestaltung einer Volkswirtschaft. Diese Auffassung hat sich bis Carl Menger durchgehalten, lediglich die Sichtweise, wem der Wohlstand in erster Linie zukommen soll, hat sich geändert: Ist dabei vom Wohlstand der gesamten Nation oder vom Wohlstand des Einzelnen auszugehen? Die klassische Ökonomie fasst den Wohlstand der gesamten Nation ins Auge, Carl Menger richtet sein Augenmerk auf den Einzelnen.[132]

Bei den Klassikern steht der Produktionsprozess, der den Tauschwert und damit den Preis eines Gutes bestimmt, im Mittelpunkt der Untersuchungen, Mengers Überlegungen sind auf die bestmögliche Versorgung des Einzelnen mit den für ihn nötigen Gütern gerichtet, der Allokationsprozess wird ausschlaggebend.

Während die Klassiker eine makroökonomische Betrachtungsweise für angemessen halten, geht Menger vom einzelnen Menschen aus und von der Beziehung des Menschen zu den Gütern seines Bedarfs. Der Mensch macht die Erfahrung, dass die meisten Güter, die dazu dienen, sein Leben angenehm zu gestalten, nicht in ausreichender Menge vorhanden sind. Deshalb muss der Mensch die Güter nach ihrer Nützlichkeit ordnen und Strategien entwerfen, um an die Güter seines Bedarfs heranzukommen. An erster Stelle stehen die Konsumgüter, da sie der unmittelbaren Bedürfnisbefriedigung dienen, wird ihnen der höchste Wert beigemessen. Der Wert der Produktionsgüter (Arbeit, Nutzung von Boden und Kapital, unternehmerische Tätigkeit) richtet sich nach dem Wert der Konsumgüter. Während die Klassiker das Zustandekommen und die Höhe von Lohn, Profit und Grundrente diskutieren, haben diese Faktoren bei Menger bereits gegebene Größen angenommen und werden ohne weitere Diskussion in die Wertbestimmung aufgenommen. Der Produktionsprozess und das durch diesen realisierte Güterquantum stehen bei den Klassikern im Zentrum des Interesses, rücken aber bei Menger in den Hintergrund, die Produktion ist ausschließlich auf den Konsum ausgerichtet. Die Wert- und damit Preisbestimmung der

---

[132] Die klassische Volkswirtschaftslehre orientiert sich immer an der Steigerung der Wohlfahrt der gesamten Nation. Besonders John Stuart Mill, der dem Verhältnis von Angebot und Nachfrage nachgeht, stellt bei seinen Untersuchungen fest, dass bei erhöhter Nachfrage nach einem Produkt eine Verlagerung des Kapitals von einem Produktionssektor auf einen anderen eintritt, keineswegs aber der gesamten Volkswirtschaft Profit daraus erwachsen könne. Mill unterscheidet bei seinen Ausführungen die Zunahme der Wohlfahrt einzelner Konsumenten vom Nutzen der gesamten Volkswirtschaft, der nur durch einen generellen Anstieg von Produktion und Akkumulation zu erreichen sei.

Güter hängt bei Menger in erster Linie nicht von den Produktionsverhältnissen ab, sondern von ihrem Nutzen für den Konsum. Menger sucht Verteilungsregeln des Einkommens zu erstellen, die zu einer Maximierung des Nutzens führen sollen. Unter Wohlstand ist nicht mehr, wie bei den Klassikern, Kapitalakkumulation zu verstehen, sondern Nutzenmaximierung und damit das, was der Einzelne darunter verstehen will. Den Ausgangspunkt bildet die Präferenz der Konsumenten: die Grenzwerttheorie hat die Frage zu beantworten, wie die Produktionsfaktoren so eingesetzt werden können, dass die Bedürfnisse der Konsumenten möglichst gut befriedigt werden können. Konsumenten und Produzenten treffen ihre auf der Grundlage von Eigennutz und Vernunft beruhenden wirtschaftlichen Entscheidungen. Durch unbeschränkte Konkurrenz stellt sich auf jedem einzelnen Markt ein Gleichgewicht her, Gewinn und Nutzen erreichen ein Maximum. Alle am Wirtschaftsprozess teilnehmenden Individuen sind sowohl Bezieher von Faktoreinkommen als auch Konsumenten; die Themen von Überproduktion und mangelnder Gesamtnachfrage werden in der Grenzwerttheorie nicht behandelt. Mengers Theorie hat eine Vereinheitlichung bzw. Zusammenführung des Preises für alle drei Sektoren, Rente, Lohn und Profit, zustande gebracht. Allerdings fordert diese Vereinheitlichung der Theorie ihren Preis. Die Klassiker stellten ihre Theorie in einen historischen, soziologischen und politischen Kontext, bei Menger kreist sie um das auf die Erfüllung seiner Bedürfnisse bedachte, (meistens) rational wirtschaftende Subjekt. Der Begriff „allgemeine Nützlichkeit" bleibt abstrakt und von der Realität einer breiten Bevölkerungsschicht abgehoben.

Zusammenfassend kann festgestellt werden: Die Klassiker gingen vom objektiven Tauschwert der Dinge aus und richteten ihr Augenmerk auf das Handeln des Kaufmannes, die Grenzwertschule geht vom subjektiven Gebrauchswert der Dinge aus und damit vom Handeln des Konsumenten. Jede der beiden Gruppen errichtet auf der Grundlage ihrer Betrachtungsweise eine Wirtschaftstheorie.

Mit dem Übergang zum Subjektivismus können zwei Probleme gelöst werden, für die die klassische Nationalökonomie keine Lösung gefunden hatte: das Problem des Wertparadoxons und das Problem hinsichtlich der Unterscheidung zwischen wirtschaftlichem und nicht-wirtschaftlichem Handeln.

Die Betonung der Tatsache, dass Marktwert und Nutzen nicht notwendiger Weise miteinander verbunden sind, erklärt das Phänomen, dass der Marktpreis für Wasser deswegen so niedrig ist, weil der Grenznutzen von Wasser aufgrund des reichlichen Vorhandenseins an Wasser niedrig ist, auch wenn der Gesamtnutzen aller verfügbaren Wassermengen größer ist als der Gesamtnutzen aller verfügbaren Diamanten.

Um Preise erklären zu können, macht es keinen Sinn, zwischen wirtschaftlichem und nicht-wirtschaftlichem Handeln zu unterscheiden, da sich die

Preise – aus welchen Motiven auch immer – aus der subjektiven Bewertung des Einzelnen ergeben.

Alfred Marshall suchte die von der Grenznutzenschule entfalteten Thesen mit dem von der klassischen Nationalökonomie entwickelten Kostenprinzip in einen Zusammenhang zu bringen. In seinem 1890 veröffentlichten Buch „Principles of Economics“ sucht er in einem Preis-Mengen-Diagramm die Interessen der Anbieter (Produzenten) und der Nachfrager (Produzenten) darzustellen. Dabei geht er von der Überlegung aus, dass der Anbieter bereit ist, bei steigendem Preis eine größere Menge an Gütern anzubieten, während der Nachfrager, dem Gesetz des Grenznutzens folgend, nach Sättigung eines Bedürfnisses für jede weitere Einheit eines Gutes weniger zu zahlen bereit ist. Im so genannten „Marshall Kreuz“ kreuzen sich die beiden Kurven wie die geöffneten Klingen einer Schere in einem Punkt. Am Kreuzungspunkt werden der Gleichgewichtspreis und damit die Gleichgewichtsmenge ablesbar.

Liberal positions in Carl Menger's writings

Peter Rosner

Amongst economists with a dislike for state interference into the working of a market system – liberals in the European context, libertarians in the parlance dominant in the USA – Carl Menger is a good name. After all, he had been the founder of what later became the Austrian school. Although he was not as combative in favour of a market economy as Mises or Hayek in the 20th century, it would be difficult to depict Menger having been a friend of intensive regulations of the economy. This paper is an attempt to be more precise on Menger's relation to liberal positions.

There is a difficulty. Liberalism is not a set of beliefs and convictions a person has to accept in order to qualify for being liberal. One cannot elucidate Menger's relation to liberalism by controlling his works for the question as whether he would have been expelled from the high church of liberalism by the office of the liberal inquisition or whether he would have been made honorary president of the liberal international.

For Mises and for Hayek developing arguments for a liberal cause was at the centre of their intellectual endeavour. Therefore, in most of their publications arguments against state intervention can be found. It is a straightforward exercise to describe and evaluate their positions concerning markets and the state. This is not the case with Menger as he did not publish any texts on economic policy except those on monetary policy. Particularly there are no publications on what is called *Ordnungspolitik* in Germany: how should the institutions of the state be construed in order to serve the political aims optimally, whatever they are. Therefore working out what is meant when one says that Menger belongs to the liberal camp – that is not to be doubted – needs a different strategy than asking the same question for Mises and Hayek. Besides looking at the remarks and hints concerning policy in his work, I ask how and to what extent his analysis and his arguments can be used for a liberal cause.

In the first part I look at a small essay on Smith in a daily paper. There Menger defends Smith against the claim that he did not care how workers fared in the capitalist society. This claim was expression of a widespread held opinion that liberal economic policies would harm workers. Criticising Smith as the foremost theoretician for such a policy was tantamount to a critique of liberal policies. I show that in Germany mainstream economists – the Historic School – accepted this critique of Smith. Menger's praise of Smith is seen as a defence of a liberal position concerning economic policy.

In the second part the lectures Menger gave to the Crown Prince are discussed. They are of relevance, because Menger was supposed to acquaint his pupil with liberal ideas. It is shown that he supported liberal policies with the argument that they contribute to bigger savings, higher labour supply and therefore to greater wealth. He also discusses activities of the state which may have a positive impact on the economy. Altogether Menger argued in favour of policies which were similar to those described in German economic textbooks, beginning with Rau.

In the third part it is asked what relevance Menger's methodological position in his conflict with the Historic School has for liberal values. The central question was whether the existence of social totalities as there is the society, the nation, or the people can be used as fundamental concept for social sciences. Menger denied that this would be sensible for an economic research programme. Thereby he undermined the assumption of a normative priority of the society over individuals. In the fourth part some conclusions are drawn.

1. Of all of Menger's publications his small essay about Smith written at the occasion of the centenary anniversary of his death comes closest to a text on *Ordnungspolitik*. Published in 1891 in the *Neue Freie Presse*, the leading liberal daily in Vienna, it is not meant being a systematic treatment of the subject. However, its title, *Die Sozialtheorien der klassischen Nationalökonomie und die moderne Wirtschaftspolitik* (Social theories of classical economics and modern economic policy), suggests that Menger's intention was not merely praising a great thinker of the past; rather to discuss his contemporaneous importance.

To understand Menger's interest, one has to take into account that Smith has not been held in high esteem in German mainstream economics for quite some time. After a short period at the beginning of the 19th century, when German economists argued for economic and political reforms according to ideas laid out in the *Wealth of Nations* (Lueder, 1800; Jacob, 1805; Sartorius, 1806; Kraus, 1811), an attack on his theory was started by the so called *Romantic School*. It was part of the broad Romantic Movement in Germany by the generation after the enlightenment period. Smith and the German liberals were criticized for conceptualising society merely as a combination of individuals. They did not accept that the community of persons (*Gemeinschaft*) is of relevance. According to the view of the Romantic School this is wrong. The existence of the society as a whole is of prime importance – the well-being of persons depends on the well-being of the society.

That has implications for the analysis of society. It is an existing entirety. The relation between person and society cannot be reduced to relations between persons. Indeed, persons are bound to each other through families, culture, and language. They have a common fate and a common interest. In many instances the communities stand against other communities – persons form a people, a nation. Thus two questions were intertwined: that of a state as organisation of society and that of a nation as an ethnic unity. This position became prominent at the onset of the 19th century, probably due to Napoleonic wars, and grew all through this century.[133]

In this literature the state has the function to care for the welfare and on-going existence of the society. People live in a state because it can provide welfare. Therefore the state cannot be conceptualised merely as a device for correcting market failures. It is the institutional framework of the community of persons, often compared to a family. It is not a contract of citizens. The first influential author in this tradition was Adam Müller (Müller, 1809; Müller, 1816). His conservative ideas motivated by his religious creed[134] served as a fundament for the attack on Smith's theory.

The basic argument is that no person is able to produce the means for his own subsistence. Everybody needs the products of others' people labour. This could be argued with Smith and his theory of the dynamic effects of the division of labour. Now, differently from Smith and differently from modern mainstream economics, Müller concludes that society is a subjective end of the actions of persons and that society itself is an acting subject. It pursues ends. Persons orient their actions on the ends of the society because they only can live in a society. This assumption became later the main methodological difference between the German Historic School on the one hand and Classical economics as well as modern economics on the other hand.[135] Müller makes use of an argument developed by a French philosopher of the enlightenment, Jean-Jacques Rousseau, namely the distinction between the *volonté de tous* and the *volonté générale* (Müller, 1809, p. 159). Whereas the former is merely a result of voting, the latter is an objectively existing will.[136]

The orientation of people's action towards the society is not presented as an ethical norm, as for example in Kant's Categorical Imperative; it is something really existing.

> „Jeder einzelne Mensch dient dem Ganzen der Menschheit und des Staates und erhält von demselben Gegendienste. Jeder einzelne produziert für

---

[133] Theories of political philosophy were dominant in Germany which gave the state a strong position in relation to the society of citizens as well. Fichte provided the blueprint of an economy planned by the prince without foreign trade (Fichte, 1800). Hegel, though analysing intensively the society of citizens, leaves no doubt that the state as political institution has precedence over society (Priddat, 1990).

[134] He converted from Protestantism to Catholicism and worked for the Chancellor of the Austrian Empire, Prince Metternich.

[135] It can be shown that Marx as well uses in many instances the idea of the society as an acting agent.

[136] The appeal to the general will is common to conservative state-oriented ideas as well as for revolutionary ones. "The general will is always right; however the guiding judgement is not always enlightened. One has to show it the objects, how they are, sometimes how they have to appear; to show him the right way which he looks for; to protect him from the seduction of the will of single persons; ..." (Rousseau, 1762, p. 412, translation by P. R. from the German) This idea cannot find support in liberal sentiments.

> die Gesellschaft; also können wir auch sagen, er produziert die Gesellschaft, wenn er etwas hervorbringt, was der bürgerlichen Gesellschaft nützt oder ihrem Verband, ihren Zusammenhang befördert. Aber die Gesellschaft produziert auch wieder für den einzelnen; sie produziert, was den Wert, die Kräfte oder die Bedeutung des einzelnen erhöhet; also kann man sagen: die Gesellschaft produziere auch wieder den einzelnen Bürger.“ (Müller, 1809, p. 229)[137]

Due to this emphasis of the totality of persons in the society Müller stresses the special role of the state. It does not make sense to ask as to whether the state increases the welfare of its citizens, as this was done by Smith and still is the dominant approach in modern economic theory. To analyse the functions of the state in that way is tantamount to persons having an existence independently from society. But that, according to Müller, is impossible. The state cannot be a founded by a contract of its citizens.[138]

He assumes that people have specific human needs. They do not maximize income; they not only want to consume goods. They want to live with others. Therefore they need the state. It is not a compulsory institution which people accept voluntarily, in order to protect them against the own-interest of others. Concerning the economy, he rejects the market system. He makes use of some ideas of Aristotle; that is the distinction between the provisioning for the needs of persons with goods in a society and gainful economic actions by exchange. Similar as Aristotle Müller rejects the latter, because these actions destroy the community.[139]

He was read for many decades in the German states and his critique of Smith's theory has been accepted by many. In other societies similar conservative criticism of the profit motive, namely stressing its potential for the destruction of the community of people, was of importance as well.[140] But differently from other cultures in Germany it was accepted also by many economists, although they did not accept his total rejection of the profit motive.

---

[137] "Every individual person serves the whole of humanity and of the state and he gets from it services in return. Everybody produces for the society; thus we can say, he produces the society, whenever he procreates something useful for the civil society or its formation, or he is furthering its cohesion. Now, the society produces for the individual as well; it produces that what enlarges the value, the abilities and the importance of the individual; one can say, the society produces the individual." (Translation by P. R.)

[138] Today this problem is discussed in political philosophy between *Liberals* (for example, Rawls, 1993) and *Communitarians* (for example, Walzer, 1983).

[139] Müller even rejects the strict acceptance of private property. „Das strenge Privateigentum zerstört das Gefühl der Gemeinschaft.“ (Müller, 1809, p. 110) („Strict private property destroys the feeling of the community", translation by P. R.)

[140] An example from England: *Mr. Grandgrind* – the main negative character of Dickens' novel *Hard Times* – gave his two sons the names *Adam Smith* resp. *Jeremy Bentham.*

This ethical view was of special importance for the Historic School, the German mainstream in the second part of the 19th century. For example, more than 100 years later Schmoller writes: "Die Arbeitsteilung setzt … eine soziale Gemeinschaft voraus". (Schmoller, 1918, p. 71)[141]

Essential elements of Müller's ideas can be found in many of their writings: all production takes place in a society, and thus people relate to each other in their volitions. These positions can be summarized in the following way. (i) People living in a state relate to each other not only through market transactions, but first of all through common culture. (ii) Culture comprises abilities, needs, knowledge, and ethical attitudes. (iii) Societies differ as they exist under different natural conditions; their histories are different. Peoples of higher culture typically live in organised states. (iv) The economy cannot be analysed without taking account of the structures of the state. There are no economic laws independent of time and the specificity of a nation, as it is the case in physics or in biology.

It is presented as a psychological fact that persons have a positive interest into the nation and its wellbeing. A kind of altruism is ascribed to individuals.[142] The latter point is important as it implies a rejection of Smith's fundamental idea that people serve each other by pursuing their own interest – the argument without which no liberal concept about economic policy can be sustained.[143] On the other hand, a good society presupposes that people not only act according to their own self-interest. Merely pursuing economic interests is unethical. The nation as community has priority over the individuals in a normative sense. In the books of Roscher, of Knies, of Schmoller and others many statements condemning or at least delimiting the motive of self-interest can be found.

> „Der [nach Smith] … in allen Menschen vorhandene…instictive Egoismus konnte und musste wie eine naturgesetzliche Kraft angesehen werden, auf welche man in der Herausstellung der nationalökonomischen Gesetze in derselben Weise, ebenso sicher rechnen und bauen könne, wie auf die Beschaffenheit der Edelmetalle oder auf den Unterschied des fetten und des mageren Bodens. Die Wirksamkeit der Naturgesetze widerstrebt nicht der mathematischen Formulierung. …unschwer kann man sich überzeugen, dass in den nationalökonomischen Darlegungen, welche auf den Egoismus des Menschen, als auf ein naturgesetzliches Fundament gebaut sind, uns nicht der wirkliche Mensch, nicht der Mensch des statistischen Durchschnitts, auch nicht ein ‚hegelscher' allgemeiner Mensch, entgegentritt,

---

[141] "The division of labour presupposes … a social community." (Translation by P.R.)

[142] This of course carried normative implications, namely that a good person has to have positive feelings for his or her compatriots.

[143] "It is not from the benevolence of the butcher, the brewer, or the baker, that we expect our dinner, but from their regard to their own interest. We address ourselves, not to their humanity but to their self-love, and never talk to them of our own necessities but of their advantages." (Smith, 1776, I.ii.2)

sondern eine elementare Naturkraft in Menschengestalt, die Personification eines bloßen Begriffes, des Begriffes des wirtschaftlichen Eigennutzes, dem Anschein nach als Mensch, in der That mit untermenschlichen Berechnungen und übermenschlichen Leistungen.“ (Knies, 1853[1883], p. 353) [144]

The inclusion of ethics is not merely the appeal to act in an ethically responsible way, for example, to pay higher wages, to leave capital in one's home-country, but the stipulation that in many situations people do not act egoistically. That is a specification of Müller's idea that persons relate their actions consciously to the society's needs. This is due to special motives and drives.

„Ihr [der Wirtschaft P. R.] liegen regelmäßig zwei geistige Triebfedern zu Grunde. Zuerst der *Eigennutz*, self interest, welcher sich positive in dem Streben äußert, möglichst viele Güter zu gewinnen, negativ in dem Streben, möglichst wenige Güter zu verlieren. ... Sodann aber die Stimme Gottes in uns, des *Gewissens* ... Durch diese Richtung nun wird der Eigennutz im Zaume gehalten; ja, er wird irdisch zum irdisch verständigen Mittel für einen ewig idealen Zweck verklärt.“ (Roscher, 1854, p. 18, emphasis by Roscher)[145]

This ethical attitude shows itself, for example in the patriotism for one's own state with political implications.

„Wir aber, wir Menschen in der zweiten Hälfte des 19. Jahrhunderts – ‚Bürger und Bauern, ‚Gebildete und Ungebildete', Kopf-Arbeiter und Hand-Arbeiter, haben mit Einschluss selbst der heutigen ‚Freihandelsleute' diese Auffassung der Physiokratisch-Smithischen Lehre ... entschieden nicht mehr, und wir haben sie vorab deshalb nicht mehr, weil neue Lebenserfahrungen, wie sie von Menschen des vorigen Jahrhunderts noch nicht gemacht waren, unser ‚Inneres' beeinflusst haben. Wir haben wirkliche *Volks-*

---

[144] „The instinctive egoism, prevalent in all humans [according to Smith, P. R.], could be seen as force of nature and must be seen so, upon which one could built economic laws as one could make calculations based on the characteristics of precious metals or on the differences between rich and poor soils. The efficacy of laws of nature does not resist mathematical formulation. ...it is easy to convince oneself that in economic expositions which use as scientific fundament the egoism of man we do not see the real man, the man of the statistical average, neither the general man of Hegel; merely an elementary force of nature in human figure, the personification of a concept; namely the concept of the economic self-interest; it is presented as man; however with sub-human calculations and super-human achievements." (Translation by P.R.)

[145] "There are always two mental incentives at the foundation of this economy. There is, first, *self-interest*, the positive manifestation of which is the effort to acquire as much of the world's goods as possible, and the negative expression of which, the effort to lose as little of them as possible. ... Then there is the incentive of the demand of God's voice within us, the voice of *conscience* ... This puts bounds to our self-interest, and transmutes it into an earthly means to enable us to approximate to an eternal ideal." (Roscher, 1878, vol. I, p. 73)

> Kriege mit opferwilligster Teilnahme der ‚großen Masse' erlebt; unsere Zeitgenossen haben hier den freudigsten Jubel, dort die schmerzlichste Trauer der demselben einen Staate Angehörigen mit empfunden." (Knies, 1853[1884], p. 296)[146]

Statements like that one, and there are many similar ones to be found in the writings of Knies, Roscher, or Schmoller, show the above mentioned amalgamation of two functions of the state, namely to be an institution of the society against the self-interested actions of individual persons and being the object of subjective ends of persons.

The regard for ethics has consequences for economic and social policy. Ethical sentiments contribute to the provision of public goods, allow for the redistribution of income and the protection of workers via the state. Such policies and the provision of public services call for sacrifices of those better-off.[147] Each improvement for the lower orders of society is seen as victory of ethical actions over egoism.[148]

---

[146] "We, living in the second half of the 19th century – 'burgher and peasant', 'educated and non-educated', workers of brain and workers of brawn, with inclusions even of the contemporary 'free-trade persons' entertain not any longer this idea of the Physiocratic-Smithian teaching, and we do not do so because new experiences have influenced our 'innermost', in a way unknown to people in the last century. We have seen real people-wars with the most self-sacrificing participation of broad masses; our contemporaries have experienced the most exalting rejoicing as well as deepest sorrow with the compatriots in the state." (Translation by P. R.)

[147] „Überall erweitert sich beim Fortschreiten der Kultur das Gebiet der Staatszwecke. Während die Regierung ursprünglich nur nach Außen zu für die Sicherheit ihrer Angehörigen einstehen musste, sorgt sie allmählich durch Einführung des Landfriedens, Abstellung der Blutrache etc. auch für die innere Sicherheit; weiterhin für den Wohlstand, die Gesundheit, die Bildung, ja die Bequemlichkeit des Volkes." (Roscher, 1854, p. 159) ("Everywhere as civilization advances, the sphere of action of the state grows lager, and the ends it serves grow more numerous. In its origin government was established to preserve only the external security of its subjects. By degrees, it comes to look after their internal legal security, by enforcing internal legal security, prohibiting revenge for bloodshed etc. It next extends its care to the well-being, the culture, and even to the comfort of the people." (Roscher, 1878, vol. I, p. 256). These activities are favourable, as long as they conform to the public spirit. „Die Annäherung an die Gütergemeinschaft soll von der Liebe der Reichen ausgehen, nicht vom Hasse der Armen." (Roscher, 1854, p. 160) ("Every approximation towards a community of goods should be effected by the love of the rich for the poor, not by the hatred of the poor for the rich." Roscher, 1878, vol. I, p. 258)

[148] Before universal suffrage was introduced – in Germany not until 1918 – all spending for social affairs or favouring otherwise the poor were in one way or another a self-taxation of those eligible to vote – mostly people with means.

Smith approval of self-interest made them reject Smithian ideas about economic policy.[149] And because Smith was the founder of the classical school, this rejection was extended to the whole school. The theories of the classical school were considered hostile to a well ordered society, subjecting everything to profits. What was called *Manchester Liberalism* was considered a consequence of this theory.

Menger's defence of Smith against the German mainstream did not rely primarily on the positive arguments against state intervention – the liberal argument. Instead, he vindicated him against the common charge that Smith had been hostile to the protection of the working people against capital; that he had had no sympathy for the cause of the workers. According to Menger this was not true. Whenever there had been a conflict between the strong and the weak, Smith had been on the side of the weak. Particularly he did not have objections against state interference into the working of the labour market due to a non-interference principle; he had rejected such activities of the state only insofar as it had been at the disadvantage for the workers. To demonstrate Smith's stance for the labouring men Menger referred to the wording of Smith's theory of distribution, that profits are a *deduction from the reward of labour*. And he referred also to Smith's polemical phrase, *...the landlords, like all other men, love to reap where they never sowed, and demand a rent even for its natural produce.* (Smith, 1776, I.vi.8)

The point is not whether Menger's interpretation of Smith is correct, but that he considered it a positive trait of Smith to be on the side of the workers in a conflict of distribution with capital and the landlords. The issue under discussion was that the economists of the Historic School claimed that Smith and the classical school were hostile to social policy, thereby taking side with capital. They of course did not suggest that economics should side with the workers as socialist economists did, but considered it essential that the state has to regulate the labour market and enhance the well-being of workers through means of social policy in a well ordered society. After all, Gustav Schmoller was at that time the head of the *Verein für Socialpolitik*, an organization of economists, journalists, politicians and entrepreneurs arguing and lobbying against what was termed *Manchester Liberalism* as well as against socialist ideas.[150] Otherwise workers would be in a bad position.

Menger did not deny that such regulations can be appropriate. Of course, there is an important difference between Menger's idea of good regulations and those envisaged by economists from the *Verein*. He uses what he considered to

---

[149] At the end of the 19th century, a German, namely August Oncken, 'discovered' the so called *Adam Smith Problem*, namely that Smith had a theory about mutual sympathy between people as an important basis for society. See Oncken, 1897.

[150] Today the *Verein für Socialpolitik* is the organisation of the academically working economists in the German speaking countries.

be the essential of Smith's position to describe this difference. Whereas the regulations as envisaged by the German economists should reduce the freedom to enter markets, Smith wanted the state to abolish all demarcations between markets. To put that into other words, Smith, according to Menger, proposed that the state actively reduce the position of incumbents; the German economists, on the other hand, praised the role of the state for social policy by arguing in favour of preserving protected access to markets for special groups. Menger praised Smith for supporting with arguments the outsiders against the privileges of the insiders. He claimed that any policy as proposed by the German social policy school would increase the economic difficulties of those excluded. It is clear that this argument is an important liberal agenda.

2. A special text by Menger on economic policy issues is the written version of his lectures for a very particular audience. By invitation of Elisabeth, the wife of Emperor Franz Josef, Menger taught the young Austrian Crown Prince (born 1858) the essentials of economics during winter and spring of 1876. At that time he was still associate professor at the University of Vienna.[151] It is very unlikely that he was chosen for having contributed to a scientific revolution. Five years after the *Grundsätze* had been published his theory was hardly known outside a small group of people publishing economic texts and it was even less understood. Probably he was chosen because the future emperor should be made familiar with liberal ideas. Though this was unlikely to be in the Emperor's interest, in her conflict with him Elisabeth supported the liberal faction of Austrian so-ciety.[152]

The text, published in 1994, was recovered from Rudolf's notes which he made during the lectures and which were controlled by Menger. One can therefore assume that the notes do not contradict what he had said and what he believed to be true. Nevertheless, one must be cautious when using this text as evidence of his ideas. When teaching the Crown Prince of a major European Power about the state and its functions there are limits to what one can say. It is like tutoring the president-elect of the USA about economic policy. One wants to direct his attention to certain issues, to influence him of what is to be done; but one knows that he has convictions not to be challenged. For example, Menger emphasized the importance of the state for external security. This fits into Adam Smith's enumeration of functions of the state. But Menger could not have taught his pupil otherwise. There are also some aspects of modern liberal ideas he could not have told his pupil, even if he were convinced by them. For example,

[151] He became full professor in 1879 (Streissler, 1994, p. 4).

[152] Rudolf never became Emperor of Austria. He committed suicide in 1889 after having shot his mistress, Baroness Vetschera. Franz Josef remained Emperor until 1916. His grand-nephew Karl became heir to the throne for the remaining two years of the Austro-Hungarian Empire.

the idea that pursuing the question of justice is anathema to economic theory or that the state should be neutral between ends for which its citizens care, could not be told to Rudolf. Furthermore, Menger always uses in all his arguments the assumptions that the government is wise and not captured by special interests. These assumptions were elements of the ideology of the Austrian monarchy.

Be that as it may, it is justified to say that in this lectures Rudolf was fed with liberal ideas. They were of special sort. They are, for example, different from those of J. St. Mill as exposed in 'On Liberty'. For Mill liberty is the right to act according to one's own plan. This right can only be limited by the state if a person's action infringes the liberty of another person to act. There is no societal good involved. As social institution liberty is an end not a means. This is not the case in Menger's lectures to Rudolf. There, the liberty to act and the limitations for the state to interfere into people's actions are a means to a specific end – increasing the wealth of the nation and the state. This can be seen in many instances.

Already in the first and in the second lecture he states his rejection of communism and socialism, then a very important agenda of policy in the Austro-Hungarian Empire. He uses the argument that persons strive for property. This is presented as something evidently good.

> "... The individual cannot provide such protection out of his own means and would therefore be exposed to assaults by anybody stronger than himself; and in that case all efforts to accumulate wealth by work would be in vain." (Menger, 1876, p. 45)[153]

Therefore the state has an important task: he has to protect private property – a Hobbesian argument. The socialist assault on the right of inheritance is rejected with a similar argument. Socialists attack the right of inheritance because it allows a small number of people to live well without having to work. That is an offence for people who by working hard only get meagre earnings. Modern liberal ideas reject this argument that the state further justice because that would be a curtailment of basic liberties. Menger argued differently.

> "...the institution of inheritance laws provides one of the most important levers to human industry, self-restraint and thrift, as the individual seeks to provide for his family and has a natural desire to found a well-situated family." (l. c., p. 51)

The function of private property is not to serve as a basis for a liberal society; rather for a wealthy society. Liberty increases the wealth of the society and that helps for another end, namely to care for the family. In the case of an original

---

[153] The 1994 edition contains the German text and the translation by Monika Streissler as well.

appropriation of land and of conquests the possession is fully legitimized due to long possession – a Lockean argument. A liberal society was not presented in the lectures as an end, nor did Menger invoke any right to the freedom to act, it was a means.

He develops a similar position when he discusses the importance of savings (l. c., p. 64ff). It is a means to achieve greater wealth for the country. Being thrifty is in this context a virtue, not a preference for a specific time pattern of consumption. People should save, because it furthers economic progress.

> "Individual squandering is an offence against the common good and an outrage considering the exhausting labour of men." (l. .c, p. 71)[154]

It is not a liberal position in the sense of neo-Austrian liberalism that too much consumption is an offence against the state or against the common good. This argument presupposes the existence of a common good separately from the welfare of the individuals comprising the society. The existence of such a common good is anathema for neo-Austrians. Also, Menger does not use the argument of a market failure; that is aggregate welfare of the people could fall short of what is optimal if people save according to individual optimisation. That would be an argument in favour of political intervention for the optimal savings rate in the framework of modern mainstream economics. Without further argument Menger does not rule out the possibility that higher future wealth at the cost of current consumption can be good, even in case the plans of persons would have resulted in lower savings. Explicitly he states that high savings increases the welfare of the state: *The country* is *fortunate and blessed if its inhabitants are economical and thrifty* (l. c., p. 65).[155] One should not put too much weight on such phrases in the lectures. One cannot conclude that Menger really believed that the state (or the country) experiences welfare as Roscher did, or that a people are an existing entirety. But without further assumptions one cannot deduce from these lectures that he had rejected the very idea of a common interest within a society.

Without mentioning him, Menger presents Smith's ideas on accumulation to Rudolf, though the context is slightly different. He is arguing against the idea that consumption, particularly the consumption of luxuries, is necessary for aggregate demand. Menger states, that although it is true that some lines of business may be hurt by increased savings, the stock of capital would be increased. This creates demand for labour as well. He uses words which express similar normative judgements as Smith did in his famous chapter *Of the Accumulation of Capital, or of productive and unproductive Labour* (Smith, 1776, II.iii). For example, the trades which are hurt by thriftiness are "... *concerned with mon-*

---

[154] Actually, the German original has ...*Versündigung an dem Wohle des Staates*... . Though Menger surely did not mean the state as an institution, state is more specific than 'common good'.

[155] Again the original has *Staat* which rather is *state* than *country*.

gering millinery, luxuries and similar trifles intended only for instant pleasure" (Menger, 1876, p. 67). Persons not thrifty, *squander* [their wealth] *at once or quite soon without either increasing its owner's assets or being useful in any way* (l. c., p. 69). The content of such statements probably reflect widely accepted judgements against luxury consumption. It can be found for example in the writings of Roscher, whose moralistic overtones are much stronger than Menger's.[156] Note that the idea that people buy goods which are in no way useful for them is a contradiction to Menger's own theory as laid down in the *Grundsätze*.[157]

Lectures six and seven are explicitly devoted to the benefits and limits of state intervention in the economy. Again, the end of state activity and its limitation is the accumulation of wealth, not liberty or freedom to act according to preferences. Menger underlines the importance of the state's responsibility for the economy – could he have told the Crown Prince otherwise? This responsibility obliges the state to support the citizens in their activities directed at gaining wealth (l. c., p. 109). But he warns against a paternalistic policy, as that could easily turn out to be counterproductive. He uses a psychological argument.

> "Being responsible and caring for the well-being of one's self and family is a powerful incentive to work and industry, and the discharge of these duties becomes the purest and truest pride of the free citizen; now, if the state seizes some of these responsibilities, the individual will feel imposed upon and not free, even in such matters as pertain to his most personal interest. ... if the state relieves him of these, he will feel hurt, and his enjoyment of and incentives to work will disappear along with the responsibility; thus government will achieve the opposite." (l. c., p. 111)

Menger gives a second argument: the state does not have the information necessary to direct people's actions meticulously. It is important to see that people are different, and that the natural tendency of the state's administrative machinery to control all affairs by a unified system can be a hindrance to a good development. This argument later became prominent in modern Austrian economics and is accepted by most *mainstream* economists today as well.

In his presentation of his ideas about state interference Menger makes use of an assumption which shows his affinity to Roscher's ideas. He distinguishes between people in ...*an advanced stage of civilization*... and an uncivilized people (l. c., p. 109). In the latter case the head of the state can be in the position to advance the economy through his initiative. In the former case it is important to grant space for individual action. Menger states that in some cases it may be

[156] Ricardo in his discussion with Malthus was one of the first authors who abstained from all normative judgments when arguing in favour of savings.

[157] Perhaps it was an argument *ad usum Delphini*. Would the heir to the throne really have understood the ideas of Menger's theory of value?

necessary for the state to actively help citizens; they are called *abnormal*. The examples he uses are the cattle plague and the vinelouse.[158] It is beyond the means of any single farmer to protect his livestock against such events (l. c., p. 117). The second example is that of foreign trade. Trade across borders is a relation between states and therefore necessitates treaties between states. As in many other instances, the economic liberty is not presented as something good in itself. It is useful for the end of getting wealthy. It is not a normative position, as for example in the writings of Nozick or Rawls. It is the consequence of a result of the positive science of economics. It has shown a liberal policy being a superior strategy for to increase wealth. Anyway, the good under consideration is wealth not liberty.

The second lecture devoted to the discussion of state interference gives an overview of fields of state interference. He enumerates a few cases of positive effects of state support. First, infrastructure of traffic, etc. *important roads, railways and canals* ..., are mentioned, as they, "...because of their size, are beyond the means of individuals and even private corporations." (l. c., p. 121)

Second, schools, particularly those for agriculture and commerce are alleged. They increase what is now called human capital, and are therefore good for the economy. The establishment of schools does not patronize the citizens. As a general principle Menger states that the state should support industries which are useful for the citizens and "... *surpasses their individual means [...]*, for example ... *prime quality breeding cattle*." (l. c., p.123).

Another reason for state interference is displayed by the cases of exploitation of economic might against the weak.

> "If and when the egoism and greed of a few become an obstacle to the interests of the many, the time has come for the state to defend the equal rights of and, for the benefit of society, to interfere forcibly with the activities of an individual and put his egoism in its legally defined place." (l. c., p. 125)

A few pages are devoted to the conflict between the entrepreneurs and the workers. The state has to protect the weak in the interest of the state and its long term development. Labour contracts should be regulated in one way or the other by the state. Safety measures, maximum working hours, no employment of children are the means to protect the workers.[159] The chapter ends with remarks of the necessity to protect woods against the short-sighted interest of the owners.

Menger follows in these remarks the German tradition of state regulation prevalent at least since the Kameralist Joseph von Sonnenfels at the end of the 18th century (Rosner, 2006). Self-interest of people is accepted as being a useful motive; however, there are many instances wherein state support or state regula-

[158] The existence of the Phylloxera in Austria was proved the first time in 1869.
[159] Menger defends the right to strike in his article on Smith.

tion is favourable. Unlike in the fifth book of Adam Smith's *Principles*, infrastructure for traffic and communication, schools and the common resource of woods were always mentioned as good examples of state support and state regulation. Menger probably follows Rau, whose three volume textbook was widely read for more than 40 years. Rau gives a detailed description of instances of state interference furthering welfare. Most of them would find support in modern economic theory as instances of a market failure (Rau, 1826–1837; Rosner, 2000).

The final chapters of this economic course are devoted to several topics – money, wages, interest, famines, and taxes. With the exception of money, none of them was of relevance in his scientific writings. The general approach concerning the functions of the state is eclectic as in the earlier lectures. For example, when discussing wages, he emphasis justice as a principle the state has to keep in mind when fixing the schedule of incomes for state employees (l. c., p. 155). Justice is, of course, not an agenda for neo-Austrian economists. However, for Menger, justice is not a question of the income distribution. Rather, wages have to conform to economic laws which determine wages in a market society. When paying its employees the state should mimic the schedule of payments the market would deliver for similar jobs. In one aspect the state should, according to Menger, care for justice in the modern sense: he should further the possibilities of its citizens to advance in a career. The possibility to use all options in a market system according to one's skills and dexterity needs an appropriate policy. It is a kind of equal opportunity argument, a traditional liberal idea. After all, Menger was lecturing the heir to a throne to a state, where many positions in the bureaucracy were filled according to rank or by favouritism.

3. Since Adam Smith mainstream economic reasoning and economic theory proceeds by analysing actions of individuals and their aggregate result. It is assumed that persons have no direct interest in that aggregate result. When choosing actions people do not care for the overall good; rather for private ends. In the narrow field of economic questions it is assumed that persons are only interested in their own well-being.

It was shown in the first part that the German mainstream in the second half of the 19th century supported the idea that society was an existing entirety which cannot be reduced to a contract of citizens. However, it is not clear what was meant by this idea and what were the implications of such a position. It comprises positive-substantive statements, methodological positions, and normative consequences. The first aspect, the positive-substantive one, concerns the ontological assumption that societies are existing entities subjected to a historic development and that persons relate consciously in their actions to the society they belong to. They have the aggregate result in mind when making decisions and they are able to act ethically. For example, it is not necessarily true that an employer pays the lowest wage (Hildebrand, 1863, p. 19); rich people leave their capital in their state due to devotion to their homeland, even if the rate of interest somewhere else is higher (Roscher, 1854, p. 391).[160]

The second aspect, the methodological position can be understood to be a consequence of the first one. If society is an existing entity and if people relate to the society, economics has to take account of it. One cannot speak about economic laws similar to laws of nature because persons have consciousness and self-consciousness. Economics has to ask as what the real motives of acting people are and it must analyse persons in their specific historic and social situations. That's why there can be no economic analysis without taking heed of history. However, propositions about the historic development cannot be merely the result of the economic analysis, as for example in Marx' theory. The development of societies in turn is in itself a fundamental aspect of their existence.

From these two characteristics no normative positions can be derived without having made further assumptions. Nor do they unequivocally call for a specific policy. But it is quite clear that the authors of the Historic School uttered normative judgements and wanted to do so. Their propositions concerning the empirics of ethical actions included the proposition that persons acting otherwise are to be judged as of low morals. By describing the favourable effects of people taking care of the society in their actions, they are presented as being laudable. People *ought* to take care of the needs of a society. Indeed, in the writings of the Historic School one finds praising words for activities strengthening the society and condemning ones for actions which were believed to further a private interest at the cost of the community. For example, Roscher often refers to a *healthy* state of society if a common interest seems to prevail; he uses the expression *disease* if self-interested actions have a tendency to weaken the common interest.

The underlying ethical theory is a kind of perfectionism. In the writings of the Historic School acting in regard to the society appears being a virtue. The state has the duty to encourage it. Such a position is difficult to reconcile with some brands of modern liberalism, for example with Rawls' concept of a just society as well as with Nozick's libertarian ideals (Rawls, 1971; Nozick, 1974). There it is posted that the state should be indifferent between different ends people pursue. Being primarily interested in one's own profit should not necessarily be condemned by public authorities, being altruistic not be praised (Pauer-Studer, 2001). The doctrines of the Historic School are clearly at odds with this idea. Patriotism and altruism are good and therefore a good the state should encourage. Self-interest, though necessary for developing production, can be dangerous and must be restrained as motive for action by the state. Smith's position is rejected, namely that being interested in one's own well-being and being dis-

[160] Note that Smith also describes a tendency not to invest abroad. Differently from Roscher that is not due to patriotic sentiments but due to risk aversion.

interested into the well-being of others suffices to achieve a high welfare for all. On the contrary, it is assumed that the state as an institutionalised society has the right and the duty to set limits to actions of individuals to further a common good.

Note that this is different from the harm principle which postulates that the state has the duty to protect people against harm done by third persons. This principle is at the heart of many liberal creeds. Everybody has the right to be unharmed in her person and her belongings. It is not the task of the state to further a particular good; it should only protect its citizens against harm done by others. This position does not use the idea of the society being a moral entity.

Nowhere in his writings published by himself did Menger argue against the normative consequences of believing the society to be a moral entity. It was shown above that in his lectures to the Crown Prince he actually confirmed this position: In order for the economy to become rich good working and moderation in consumption should be encouraged. The state is legitimised to pursue this end.[161]

Be that as it may, Menger attacked the idea of a society being an existing entity in his methodological writings against Schmoller. He insisted that analysing the actions of persons is the only legitimate method for economics. One cannot simple assume that when people act they take account of the effects for the society's well-being. This of course does not imply that the state as institutional set-up for the society not direct actions of its citizens by political means. But it takes away the theoretical fundament the Historic School believed to have found for such a conclusion. Indeed, theories postulating a conceptual primacy of the individual over the society can only with difficulties be used to defend policies which curtail liberties for the sake of the well-being of the overall society, the nation, the state or any other societal entirety. Therefore it makes sense to take account of the methodological discussion between Menger and Schmoller for to evaluate his position in relation to liberalism.

In the third part of his *Untersuchungen über die Methode der Socialwissenschaften, und der Politischen Ökonomie*, his first publication against Gustav Schmoller, he argues at length against the holistic position of the German historic school. This part comprises two chapters. In the first one he criticizes the use of the analogy with organism from nature for the analysis of societies. In the second he sketches a scientific programme; namely, how economics has to proceed when analysing social phenomena which although they are social totalities are not an outcome of an agreement between persons.

Analogies with living organisms can be found in many places in the writings of the Historic School. They have two aspects. First, an organism like a plant or a body is an entirety wherein each part has a special function. It does

---

[161] Menger could not have told his pupil differently. However, there is no reason to assume that he did not believe in it.

not make sense to analyse a part's being for itself. Second, organisms have a natural development. The plant exists first as a seed, then it flowers and finally it fades. A person's life has different stages – youth, maturity, old age.

The first aspect was important for all authors of the Historic School. The analysis proceeds by showing what functions the social institutions have. From that it is derived how persons act and should act. This type of reasoning must be seen as an unsophisticated form of functionalism. The second aspect was of special importance for Roscher. He used it for rationalizing his belief into the rise and decline of peoples. Like persons and flowers nations and their economies experience a development of growth, maturity and decline.[162]

Menger concedes that there is a similarity between organisms in nature and some social phenomena. There are entireties the existence of which makes the functioning of parts necessary.[163] This similarity has limits. First, one has to distinguish between entireties which are set up by agreement, either by contract or by law, and those which are the result of a historic development. Only the latter qualify for the analogy with a organism; the first ones should rather be compared with a mechanism (1883a, p. 143; 1883b; p. 132).

Second, whereas an organism of nature can be analysed by describing the functions of its parts for the existence of the organism, one cannot overlook that

> „..sie [the social organisms P.R] sind vielmehr das Ergebniss menschlicher Bestrebungen, der Bestrebungen denkender, fühlender, handelnder Menschen." (1883a, p. 145)[164]

[162] For example, „Die Volkswirthschaft entsteht zu gleich mit dem Volke. Sie ist weder vom Menschen erfunden, noch von Gott übernatürlich gelehrt, sondern ein natürliches Product der Anlagen und Triebe, welche den Menschen zum Menschen machen. ... Mit ihrem Volke zugleich wächst auch die Volkswirthschaft heran und kommt zur Blüthe und Reife. Diese Blüthen- und Reifezeit charakterisiert sich durch höchste Kraft und zugleich vollkommene Harmonie aller wichtigen Organe. ... Endlich sinkt auch die Volkswirthschaft mit ihrem Volke." (Roscher, 1854, p. 27) ("The public economy of a people has its origin with the people. It is neither the invention of man nor the revelation of God. It is the natural product of the faculties and propensities which make man man. ... The public economy rises of a nation grows with the nation. With the nation, it blooms and ripens. Its season of blossoming and of maturity is the period of its greatest strength, and, at the same time, of the most perfect development of all its more important organs. ... Finally, the public economy of a nation declines with the people". 1878, vol. I, p 84.)

[163] "Es liegt auf der Hand, dass hier eine gewisse Analogie zwischen dem Wesen und der Function der natürlichen Organismen einerseits und den socialen Gebilden andererseits vorhanden ist." (Menger, 1883a, p. 140) ("It is obvious that we have here a certain analogy between the nature and the function of natural organisms on the one hand and social structures on the other." Menger, 1883b, p. 130)

[164] „They [social organisms] are, rather, the result of human efforts, the effort of thinking, feeling, acting human beings." (1883b, p. 133)

Note that in sentences like that one Menger transgresses the limits of a pure methodological inquiry: Economics has to accept that social entireties are the outcome of people's effort. This is a substantive proposition from which methodological rules are derived in the second chapter of part three.

Menger is primarily interested in an understanding of social collectives by exact theoretical research; that are explanations based upon an understanding of the simplest elements of reality (1883a, p. 41; 1883b, p. 60). They are described in the following way:

> „Die ursprünglichsten Factoren der menschlichen Wirthschaft sind die Bedürfnisse, die den Menschen unmittelbar von der Natur dargebotenen Güter … und das Streben nach möglichst vollständiger Befriedigung der Bedürfnisse." (1883, p. 45)[165]

Thus, social 'organisms' cannot be understood by analysing the functions of parts as if a common reason prevailed. That is only legitimate in those cases where the entity under consideration was set up by a common plan – for example, a national bank, a specific exchange rate regime. Such an assumption is completely inappropriate when the entity to be analysed is of different character, namely the result of a historic development – for example, prices, money or a language. No common will was ever consulted to decide what should be done to set up a means of communication or a means to facilitate exchange. Therefore economics has to ask:

> „Wieso vermögen dem Gemeinwohl dienende und für dessen Entwicklung höchst bedeutsame Institutionen ohne einen auf ihre Begründung gerichteten Gemeinwillen zu entstehen?" (1883a, p. 163)[166]

Menger does not provide a general answer. He sketches a method of inquiry by giving an example: How did money come into existence? The starting point of such an inquiry must be the desire of actors to better their situation through their actions as individual persons. To do so they offer goods to get other ones. By doing so, they discover and learn that certain goods are in higher demand than others. That leads them to keep goods which they do not want for satisfaction of specific needs, but can easily be exchanged against other goods at a later date.[167] The important point is that at each step he makes use of the argument of 'the most original factors of human economy' – people act in order to better their

[165] "The most original factors of human economy are the needs, the goods offered directly to humans by nature … , and the desire for the most complete satisfaction of needs possible." (1883, p. 63)

[166] "How can it be that institutions which serve the common welfare and are extremely significant for its development come into being without a common will directed toward establishing them?" (1883b, p. 145)

[167] A few years later Menger published a longish article about money which made intensive use of this type of argumentation (Menger, 1892).

situation. Only that one is used. At no instance the existence of a common will which has contributed to the emergence of money as an institution is presupposed. The famous words of *unintended consequences* apply fully.

These methodological deliberations carry no normative implications without further assumptions. Therefore they cannot be used directly for defending liberal ideas. But they destroy the basis for the assumption of a conceptual priority of the society over the individuals forming the society. This assumption was made by authors of the Historic School and probably was taken for granted by a wider public. Menger's arguments against this holistic approach served a liberal purpose. Whether he intended to so, we do not know.

4. In part II it was said that Menger was chosen to teach the Crown Prince the basics of economics because he was believed to be liberal. At his times that comprised several positions in the political ideologies in the Austro-Hungarian Empire. To mention a few: (i) The Catholic Church should not have a big influence on politics. (ii) The social hierarchies between different grades of nobility and the rest of the population must be overcome. (iii) Workers must have some rights for political organization and representation. (iv) The state is experiencing a change of its economic base; industry is of growing importance whereas that of small-scale production will diminish. The state cannot inhibit this development without curtailing economic growth, and should not do so. It can be said that the Empire developed according to these positions in the last decades of its existence.

There are some remarks in Menger's work, first of all in his lectures to the Crown Prince, showing that he was convinced of the last three of these positions. That was of relevance for the scope of his lectures. But they have not much relevance for a systematic evaluation of his relation with liberalism. For that his debate with the Historic School must be looked at. Two points turn out to be important. One being the relevance of self-interest and the profit motive for actions of persons, the other one the implications of the use of concepts such as society, nation, or a people.

The relevance of these two points for liberal ideas is the following. The power of arguments in favour of liberal economic policies is greatly reduced if it can be shown that self-interested actions of persons have a tendency to weaken the coherence of a society. That was obviously assumed by the Historic School. This does not imply that they were in favour of a strong state – a *Leviathan.* Quite the contrary, as they also had assumed that people have a tendency to act ethically, namely with regard to society, they saw no need for such a state. Indeed, when one looks at the ideas of economic policies proposed by the authors of the Historic School, they can be characterised as being eclectic. There is a strong faith into the incentives markets provide for efficient production and also into policies to further or to curtail a specific industry. There is no systematic theory for that. Most cases presented could be argued within modern economic theory by using the concept of a market failure (Rosner, 2000). As was shown in part II, Menger is not much different in this respect.

Concerning the second point there is a fundamental difference between Menger's works and that of the Historic School. That is due to a further methodological difference between them. In all of Menger's writings the concept of a person is a very abstract one. He assumes that persons have needs and desires which they want to satisfy as good as possible. They have the capacity to make choices consistently and they are able to learn. They are neither moral nor immoral; rather they are disinterested. Nothing is specified. The authors of the Historic School are more specific. Because they look at persons as living in a specific country at a specific period, they take them to have specific needs and wants. This specificity gives a much richer image of a person. However, there is a strong tendency in their writings to use the characteristics ascribed to persons in a prescriptive way. Nouns and adjectives carrying normative valuations are used frequently. The characteristics are ascribed to peoples as well. A nation can be prodigious or frugal, assiduous or lazy. A people can have a low or a high culture. A need can be natural or artificial. These characteristics have direct consequences for the economy.

Others may have had similar opinions. But in the analysis of the Historic School such propositions are not mere opinions. Putting the emphasis on peoples and nations which have psychological characteristics formed by history, climate, and natural conditions, such descriptions are backed by the methodology used in the analysis. Menger's critique of this method destroys the basis for such arguments. An economist bound in his work to use the methods sketched by Menger can have the same opinions concerning characteristics of people and peoples as the authors of the Historic School. But it would be impossible to claim that these opinions are the result of theoretical economic research.

Be that as it may, the importance the Historic School attached to the concept of social entireties and attributing psychological, social and cultural traits to them were of relevance for the founding of economic policy. It has to care for the well-being of the entirety under consideration. This does not imply that the state has to control or guide the economy meticulously. Economic liberalism can be advisable if the characteristics of a nation are such that it serves its wellbeing. Germany is now in such a situation, fortunately! It could be otherwise.

Furthermore, often nations stand against each other in the pursuit of their welfare. A people's gain may be at the costs of another one's. The authors of the Historic School supported Germany.[168] According to their theory such a support

---

[168] In many instances the authors from the Historic School plead for a nationalistic or imperialistic policy, often using racist arguments; for example: „Wollen deshalb europäische Kaufleute mit den ganz wilden Völkern einen Handel anknüpfen, so müssen sie regelmäßig damit beginnen, ihre Nägel, Beile, Spiegel, ihren Branntwein etc. diesen Menschen zum Geschenk

of one nation against others is not merely a normative or a political question. A rising nation is justified in following a course against others because the forces of history cannot be stopped. Economic analysis, according to the Historic School, has shown that nations strive for their well-being as nations. Whatever Menger may have thought about that, his methodological approach does not allow such conclusions. He served the liberal argument against nationalistic policies.

zu machen. Erst wenn der Wilde durch den neuen Genuß ein Bedürfnis nach dessen Fortsetzung empfinden lernt, ist er bereit, für den Handel zu producieren. Bei normaler Entwicklung sollte das vollständige Befriedigtsein der gröberen Bedürfnisse die Grundlage sein, worauf die jeweils feineren sich bilden.“ (Roscher, 1854, p. 452). (“Therefore, when European merchants desire to engage in trade with a savage nation they have uniformly to begin by sending them their nails, axes, looking-glasses, brandy etc., as gifts. Not until the savage has experienced a new enjoyment does the want of continuing it make itself felt; of is prepared to produce for purposes of commerce. In a state of normal development, the complete and continuing satisfaction of the coarser wants should constitute the foundation of the higher.” (Roscher, 1878, vol. II, p. 198) Schmoller’s utterances are stronger; he speaks of higher and lower races.

Carl Menger in der Nachfolge von Adam Smith

Werner Wilke

Versuch eines exemplarischen Aufweises ideengeschichtlicher Verbindungslinien subjekttheoretischer Forschung bzw. sozial- und wirtschaftspolitischer Überlegungen

1. Aristoteles hat im 4. Jahrhundert v.Chr. seinen berühmten Untersuchungen zu Staat und Gesellschaft eine, nach neuerer Terminologie, gewissermaßen politikwissenschaftliche Analyse der zeitgenössischen Polis sowie ihrer verschiedenen historisch hervorgetretenen Verfassungsformen vorangestellt und damit in Ansätzen die Basis für eine wesentliche Distinktion gelegt, die geistesgeschichtlich von großer Bedeutung ist. Der entscheidende Schritt in die Richtung der so angesprochenen Differenzierung von deskriptiven und präskriptiven Elementen in der späteren sozial- und wirtschaftswissenschaftlichen Forschung erfolgt dann bei den englischen und schottischen Denkern des 17. und 18. Jahrhunderts, d.i. bei Thomas Hobbes, Bernard Mandeville, John Locke, David Hume und – im Bereich ökonomischer Erörterungen – vor allem bei Adam Smith.

Wenngleich den erwähnten Autoren eine saubere Trennung von wertenden und sozialtheoretisch erklärenden Aussagen noch kein explizites wissenschaftliches Anliegen ist, so ergibt sich dennoch ab nun grundsätzlich die Möglichkeit einer derartigen Differenzierung, die sich insofern als notwendig erweist, um so elementaren Missverständnissen und -deutungen angemessen begegnen zu können bzw. diese überhaupt zu vermeiden. Letztere entstehen etwa, wenn theoretische Modelle oder Ansätze, die naturgemäß auf ihre Tauglichkeit zur Erklärung ökonomischer oder sozialer Realität zu befragen sind, zu Objekten einer normativen Beurteilung gemacht werden, wobei dieses Vorgehen bis in die Gegenwart reicht und – vor allem im spezifischen Zusammenhang mit individualistischen Konzepten – mitunter nach wie vor zu erstaunlichen Fehlinterpretationen führt.

Carl Menger, der ebenfalls in der Tradition dieser ideengeschichtlichen Entwicklung steht, ist zweifellos nicht der Vorwurf zu machen, mit seinen Ausführungen zu Konfusionen dieser Art beigetragen zu haben, – vielmehr finden sich in seinen Schriften zahlreiche Belege, die eine bewusste und sorgfältige Bedachtnahme auf die Problematik einer mangelhaften Trennung von moralischen und theoretischen Aussagen und den sich hieraus ergebenden negativen Auswirkungen dokumentieren. In seinem Aufsatz 'Über die sogenannte ethische Richtung der Politischen Ökonomie' etwa plädiert er nachdrücklich dafür, „exakte Theorien“, deren Aufgabe es grundsätzlich ist, „einzelne Seiten der realen Welt … zum theoretischen Verständnisse zu bringen“[169], tunlichst nicht mit mo-

[169] Menger (1883), 604.

ralischen Betrachtungen desselben Gegenstandsbereichs zu verbinden, da dies die Untersuchung der jeweils für eine Wissenschaft spezifischen Gesetzmäßigkeiten erschwert. Bei der Nationalökonomie in concreto – wenn sie a priori undifferenziert von einem normativen Standpunkt aus betrachtet wird – resultiert, seiner Auffassung nach, nicht nur eine Verkennung ihrer Natur und der ihr eigentümlichen Aufgabe, sondern damit verbunden auch eine „Unterschätzung der wirtschaftlichen Seite des Volkslebens“[170]. Bestrebungen um eine ethische Fundierung der Volkswirtschaft sind, so die kritische Einschätzung Mengers, „zum Teil ein Überrest antiker und, in einem gewissen anderen Sinne, ein solcher mittelalterlich-asketischer Weltanschauung, zum guten Teil … jedoch eine klägliche Krücke wissenschaftlicher Unzulänglichkeit“[171].

Die ethische Disposition der einzelnen Subjekte bei jeglicher Art von praktischer Handlung, insbesondere auch bei einer ökonomisch motivierten, wird keineswegs in Frage gestellt, vielmehr hebt Carl Menger hervor, dass „jedermann auch in seiner wirtschaftlichen Tätigkeit welcher Art immer dieselbe gedacht werden mag, unter dem Moralgesetze (steht)“[172]. Die – höhere – Sphäre der Ethik wird von ihm somit expressis verbis anerkannt, doch wendet er sich eben deutlich gegen ein „moralisches Urteil über einzelne Erscheinungen der Volkswirtschaft, welches die Ergebnisse der theoretischen Forschung auf dem Gebiete der Volkswirtschaft in keiner Weise zu tangieren vermag“[173]. Seine wesentliche Forderung lautet also, dass die Ökonomie zunächst ihr eigenes spezifisches Untersuchungsfeld zu bestimmen und wissenschaftlich ′exakt′ zu bearbeiten hat und erst dann mit moralischen bzw. damit im weiteren auch mit sozial- und wirtschaftspolitischen Aspekten in Zusammenhang gebracht werden darf[174].

Auf diesem, hier kurz skizzierten Hintergrund erscheint es nun, – wie im Untertitel zum Ausdruck gebracht – von Carl Menger ausgehend, prinzipiell möglich, nach Verbindungslinien zu Adam Smith und dessen Schule bzw. nach Bezügen zwischen beiden in zweifacher Weise Ausschau zu halten, nämlich – wie im Folgenden versucht werden soll – zunächst im Hinblick auf das methodische Konzept des Einzelnen als Gegenstands sozialtheoretischer Forschung (2.) und sodann im Hinblick auf die wertende Betrachtung des Individuums in seinem normativ-ethischen Kontext mit dem/den Anderen im Staat sowie in der Wirtschaft und Gesellschaft (3.). Abschließend gilt es noch, die Ergebnisse dieses Unterfangens, nämlich die – selbstverständlich nur exemplarischen – Belege besonderer Naheverhältnisses ebenso wie mögliche Beispiele nicht unwesentlicher Unterschiede zwischen Menger und Smith in einem etwas erweiterten historischen Rahmen zu betrachten (4.).

---

[170] A.a.O., 607.
[171] Menger ebd. f. - Vgl. auch Burkhardt/Priddat (2000), 940.
[172] Menger a.a.O., 606.
[173] A.a.O., 605 (Fußnote 1).
[174] Vgl. Burkhardt/Priddat a.a.O., 942.

2. In enger Verbindung mit der angesprochenen expliziten Grundlegung jener notwendigen Trennung von normativ-bewertenden und analytisch-erklärenden Aspekten bei der Auseinandersetzung mit sozialen und ökonomischen Erscheinungen bei den Denkern im 17. und 18. Jahrhundert in England bzw. Schottland erfolgt bei ihnen mit der erstmaligen Konzeption von 'individualistischen' Sozialtheorien noch ein weiterer essentieller ideengeschichtlicher Entwicklungsschritt[175]. In späterer Terminologie bezeichnet als Ansätze, die auf dem wissenschaftstheoretischen Prinzip des 'methodologischen Individualismus' beruhen, wird bei diesen Modellen allgemein davon ausgegangen, dass sämtliche soziale und wirtschaftliche Ereignisse und Erscheinungen aus dem nicht intendierten Zusammenspiel isolierter Individuen zu konstruieren bzw. zu deuten sind.

Im Bereich der Politischen Philosophie entwirft Thomas Hobbes vor allem in seinem Werk 'Leviathan', in stärkster Abhebung von der bisher gängigen Vorstellung einer naturgegebenen Gemeinschaftsbezogenheit des Menschen, systematisch das Bild des Einzelnen, der sich in seiner Selbständigkeit und Individualität wahrnimmt und der damit als solcher Eingang in die wissenschaftliche Betrachtung zu finden hat. Die Vergesellschaftung wird, in Abkehr zu bisherigen Überzeugungen, nicht mehr als die elementare Voraussetzung für die Selbstverwirklichung des Menschen dargestellt und muss aus diesem Grund nunmehr auf ihre Zweckmäßigkeit hin überprüft werden, wodurch sich bei Hobbes das Verhältnis von Staat und Individuum gegenüber vorherigen Konzeptionen geradezu umkehrt, – der Staat hat dem Individuum zu dienen und ist im Hinblick auf seine Nützlichkeit für den Einzelnen zu legitimieren. Den Gedanken einer selbständig und gleichsam ungewollt sich ergebenden Wohlfahrt der Gesamtheit der in einer Sozietät lebenden Menschen trotz oder gerade wegen des eigeninteressierten Verhaltens der Individuen hat erstmals Bernard Mandeville zum Ausdruck gebracht und anhand zahlreicher, satirisch anmutender, in der Tat jedoch tiefsinnig reflektierter Beispiele aus dem Bereich zwischenmenschlichen Zusammenlebens zu veranschaulichen und zu belegen versucht. Die Grundthese seiner 'Bienenfabel' lautet, dass 'private Laster', bei einer dosierten Zurückhaltung seitens des Staates, in 'öffentliche Vorteile' umgewandelt werden, und dass nicht ein tugendhaftes Verhalten aller, sondern ein rücksichtsloses Befolgen der jeweiligen Einzelinteressen die Prosperität der ganzen Gesellschaft fördert, – womit sich die besondere Nähe zum freien Wettbewerbsspiel in der Wirtschaft und zur berühmten Idee der *'invisible hand'* bei Adam Smith als offensichtlich ergibt. Das von Hobbes und Mandeville her bekannte Motiv wird bei ihm nun – konkret als ein wohlverstandenes, dynamisches Selbstinteresse des Menschen – zum tragenden Fundament für eine großartige Konzeption, die auf der Basis empirischer Beobachtung die Möglichkeit und

---

[175] Vgl. Wilke (2000), 263 ff.

den Weg zu allgemeiner Wohlfahrt und zu stabilem ökonomischem Wachstum aufzeigt.[176]

Wie grundsätzlich nicht in Zweifel zu ziehen ist, liegt der theoretische Ausgangspunkt für die Analysen und Reflexionen bei Adam Smith beim einzelnen Subjekt, und für Carl Menger kann dies in gleicher Weise behauptet werden[177]. Die Frage ist jedoch, ob und inwieweit die beiden neben einer vordergründigen Übereinstimmung in der methodologischen Position auch in ihren individualistischen Sozialtheorien im Hinblick auf den Versuch, das Verhalten der Menschen zu erklären, konform gehen.

Tatsächlich gibt es hier – um dies vorwegzunehmen – eine nicht ganz unerhebliche Diskrepanz, die Carl Menger selbst kritisch anspricht und mehrfach heraushebt. Im Wesentlichen geht es hierbei um die elementare Basis jener berühmten Konzeption einer ′subjektiven Wertlehre′, die Menger in seinen ′Grundsätzen der Volkswirthschaftslehre′ entwirft[178]. Seiner Auffassung nach ist die Qualität bzw. der Wert von bestimmten Dingen nichts diesen ′Gütern′[179] „Anhaftendes“ und „keine Eigenschaft derselben“, vielmehr stelle sie sich „lediglich als eine Beziehung“ dar, „in welcher sich gewisse Dinge zu den Menschen befinden, eine Beziehung, mit deren Verschwinden dieselben selbst-

---

[176] Vgl. dazu die oft zitierte Textstelle aus *Wealth of Nations* (Smith 1776, IV. Buch, 2, 9): „Da nun jedermann nach Kräften sucht, sein Kapital in der heimischen Erwerbstätigkeit und diese Erwerbstätigkeit selbst so zu leiten, dass ihr Erzeugnis den größten Wert erhält, so arbeitet auch jeder notwendig dahin, das jährliche Einkommen der Gesellschaft so groß zu machen, als er kann. Allerdings strebt er in der Regel nicht danach, das allgemeine Wohl zu fördern, und weiß auch nicht, um wie viel er es fördert. Indem er die einheimische Erwerbstätigkeit der fremden vorzieht, hat er nur seine eigene Sicherheit im Auge und indem er diese Erwerbstätigkeit so leitet, dass ihr Produkt den größten Wert erhalte, verfolgt er lediglich seinen eigenen Gewinn und wird in diesen wie in vielen anderen Fällen von einer unsichtbaren Hand geleitet, einen Zweck zu fördern, den er in keiner Weise beabsichtigt hatte.“

[177] Carl Menger, sei „mit unter den ersten“ gewesen, „die in neuerer Zeit den methodischen Individualismus des Adam Smith und seiner Schule zu neuem Leben erweckt“ hätten, bemerkt Hayek (1976, 13, Fußnote 3), und er unterscheidet einen ′wahren′ von einem ′falschen′ Individualismus und charakterisiert ersteren im Hinblick auf dessen „grundlegende Behauptung“, die laute, dass „es keinen anderen Weg zum Verständnis der sozialen Erscheinungen gibt als über das Verständnis des Handelns des Einzelnen, das sich nach den Nebenmenschen richtet und von deren zu erwartendem Verhalten bestimmt wird“. Dieses Argument richte sich „vor allem gegen die eigentlichen kollektivistischen Gesellschaftstheorien, die vorgeben, soziale Ganzheiten wie die Gesellschaft oder dergleichen unmittelbar verstehen zu können als Wesenheiten sui generis, die unabhängig von den sie zusammensetzenden Individuen existieren“ (a.a.O., 15 f.).

[178] I. A. an Milford (1997).

[179] Ein ′Gut′ ist, nach Menger (1871, 3, Fußnote) „jede Sache, welche der Mensch zur Befriedigung seiner Bedürfnisse als Mittel anerkennt“. Der ′Güterbesitz′ stellt die „Gesamtheit der einem wirthschaftenden Individuum für die Befriedigung seiner Bedürfnisse verfügbaren Güter“ dar, die „jenen Erfolg herbeiführt“, der „die Deckung des Bedarfs und in weiterer Folge die Sicherung des Lebens und der Wohlfahrt des Menschen“ bezeichnet (a.a.O., 31).

verständlich auch aufhören, Güter zu sein"[180]. Im Gegensatz dazu steht eine Theorie der objektiven Bewertungen, die Menger prinzipiell ablehnt, wobei er betont, es habe „die Objectivierung des seiner Natur nach durchaus subjectiven Güterwerthes"[181] sehr viel zur Verwirrung der Grundlagen der Volkswirtschaftslehre beigetragen.

Adam Smith spricht an einer häufig zitierten Stelle von „einer natürlichen Neigung des Menschen, zu handeln und Dinge gegeneinander zu tauschen" [182], und kennzeichnet dies als das elementare Prinzip, das der Arbeitsteilung zugrunde liege. Die in der Folge aufgeworfene Frage „ob es sich bei dieser Neigung um eine jener angeborenen oder ursprünglichen Eigenschaften der menschlichen Natur handelt, die nicht weiter erklärt werden kann, oder ob sie, was wohl wahrscheinlicher sein dürfte, die notwendige Folge der menschlichen Fähigkeit, denken und sprechen zu können, ist"[183], lässt er unbeantwortet, jedenfalls, so meint er, handle es sich um eine Eigenschaft, die „allen Menschen gemeinsam" sei, in der Tierwelt hingegen nicht existiere. Auf diese Aussage bezieht sich nun Carl Menger und beschäftigt sich in der Folge ausführlich mit dem Phänomen des Tausches.

An der Theorie der objektiven Bewertungen kritisiert er, dass diese dem an sich naheliegenden Irrtum verfallen sei, aufgrund der genauen Messbarkeit der Preise deren Größe als das Wesentliche am Tausch, und in weiterer Konsequenz „die im Austausch erscheinenden Güterquantitäten als Aequivalente zu betrachten"[184]. Bei einer solchen Annahme könne, so argumentiert Menger, nicht einsichtig gemacht werden, warum ein Tauschgeschäft in einer unveränderten ökonomischen Situation nicht nach Belieben wieder rückgängig gemacht werden sollte[185]. Da eben im Rahmen dieses Ansatzes keine Erklärung möglich sei, habe Adam Smith eine andere Position bezogen und eine naturalistische Hypothese über die Natur des Menschen eingeführt, die ihrerseits jedoch gleichermaßen überhaupt keinen befriedigenden Erklärungswert für das Phänomen ´Tausch´ liefern könne[186]

Der „Hang der Menschen zum Tausche" müsse somit einen anderen Grund haben, als die „Lust an dem Tausche selbst", betont Menger[187], und be-

---

[180] A.a.O., 3, Fußnote bzw. 86.
[181] A.a.O., 86.
[182] Smith a.a.O., I. Buch, 2, 1.
[183] Ebd. f.
[184] A.a.O., 173.
[185] Vgl. Milford a.a.O., 111 f.
[186] Vgl a.a.O., 114.
[187] Denn, so fährt er fort (a.a.O., 154), „wäre der Tausch an sich eine Lust, also Selbstzweck, und nicht vielmehr eine, nicht selten mühselige und mit Gefahren und ökonomischen Opfern verbundene Thätigkeit, so wäre in der That nicht abzusehen, warum die Menschen nicht … in tausend … Fällen tauschen, ja den Tausch bis ins Unbegrenzte fortsetzen würden, während wir doch im Leben überall zu beobachten vermögen, dass die wirthschaftenden Menschen

müht sich in der Folge das Wesen und den Ursprung dieses, für die Ökonomie insgesamt sehr weitreichenden und bedeutsamen Phänomens zu begründen. Allgemein, so seine Auffassung, sei das Verhalten jedes einzelnen Menschen abhängig von dessen Situationsbewertung und insofern von dessen Präferenzen und dessen Informationen. Aufgrund der subjektiven Zuerkennung von Güterqualitäten, die bei jedem Individuum in unterschiedlicher Weise erfolge, ergebe sich die besondere Zweckmäßigkeit eines Güteraustausches, wobei im Hintergrund jenes Prinzip stehe „welches die Menschen in ihrer wirthschaftlichen Thätigkeit überhaupt leitet", nämlich „das Bestreben, ihre Bedürfnisse möglichst vollständig zu befriedigen"[188].

Obwohl Carl Menger stets mit Hochachtung und Respekt von Adam Smith spricht und ihn als einen ausgezeichneten Forscher und Denker[189] würdigt, so äußert er im Hinblick auf die geschilderte Implikation jener individualistischen Sozialtheorie seine massiven Vorbehalte. Im Zuge dieser kritischen Analyse expliziert Menger die Vorzüge seiner eigenen Positionierung, die einen methodologischen Individualismus mit einer Theorie der subjektiven Bewertungen kombiniert und in dieser Verbindung eine besonders fruchtbare Konzeption einer theoretischen Sozialwissenschaft darstellt, deren Hauptaufgabe es ist, die gesellschaftliche und ökonomische Wirklichkeit zu erklären[190].

3. Inhaltlich verbunden mit den zentralen Erkenntnissen ihrer sozialtheoretischen Analysen stehen Adam Smith und Carl Menger im Hinblick auf ihre sozial- und wirtschaftspolitische Orientierung gleichermaßen in der Tradition des Liberalismus. Wenn auch in Ansätzen wohl schon bei Thomas Hobbes vorhanden, so geht diese Denkströmung in ihrer ′klassischen′ Form zurück auf John Locke, der eine explizit ′liberale politische Theorie′ begründet als eine Lehre, die den Wert der bürgerlichen Freiheit des Einzelnen hervorhebt und die elementare Aufgabe des Staates darin sieht, eine derart freie Lebensweise des Individuums gegen Übergriffe jeglicher Art zu schützen. Der in der Folge von John

---

sich jeden Tausch vorher wohl überlegen und schließlich für jeden gegebenen Zeitpunkt eine Grenze eintritt, über welche hinaus zwei Individuen nicht weiter tauschen".

188 A.a.O., 158.

189 Vgl. a.a.O., 27 bzw. 153.

190 Vgl. Milford a.a.O., 119. – Priddat (1997) glaubt allerdings, auch Carl Mengers Theorie sei „eine – wenn auch anders begründete – objektive Wertlehre" (ebd. 291). Genau genommen gebe es in seinem Ansatz sowohl den ′subjektiven′ Aspekt der „Relation von Bedürfnissen der Menschen im Verhältnis zur faktischen Verfügbarkeit von Gütern" (ebd. 292), aber eben auch eine ′objektive Komponente′, nämlich das Faktum, dass Menschen Bedürfnisse haben und dass Güter auf Märkten angeboten werden. Damit, so meint Priddat (a.a.O., 301), solle aber nicht Mengers Beitrag zur modernen Werttheorie geschmälert, sondern lediglich darauf hingewiesen werden, dass „die Fragestellung seiner Vorgänger durch seine neuartige Konzeption nicht erledigt war". Das „Defizit" Mengers liege darin, „sich zu sehr auf bestimmte – psychologische und philosophische – Sprachspiele seiner Zeit eingelassen zu haben".

Stuart Mill zusammen mit seinen politisch liberalen Ideen vertretene ökonomische Liberalismus findet bei Adam Smith seinen systematisch-wissenschaftlichen Ausdruck, wobei es im wesentlichen um die grundlegende Forderung geht, dirigistische Steuermaßnahmen der Wirtschaft von Seiten des Staates zu unterlassen bzw. Eingriffe in das freie Spiel des Wettbewerbs nur in wenigen, wohl begründeten Fällen vorzunehmen, und – im Vertrauen auf die selbstregulierenden Kräfte des Marktes – den Einzelnen bei ihren ökonomischen Dispositionen weitgehend freie Hand zu lassen.

Die Einschätzung, dass Carl Menger als „ein klassischer Liberaler"[191] in der Nachfolge von Adam Smith einzustufen ist, lässt sich anhand zahlreicher Textstellen belegen, vor allem anhand der unpublizierten Mitschriften des Kronprinzen Rudolf nach Privatvorlesungen Mengers aus dem Jahre 1876. An vielen Stellen, vor allem jedoch in ausführlichen Passagen zur Thematik 'Über den Nutzen der staatlichen Beeinflussung der Volkswirtschaft und die Grenzen derselben' finden sich diesbezüglich anschauliche und maßgebliche Stellungnahmen[192].

Grundlegend formuliert Carl Menger die Überzeugung: „Freiheit und Selbstverantwortlichkeit der Bürger in ihren wirtschaftlichen Bestrebungen sind die Grundfesten der allgemeinen Entwicklung eines Staates; darum muss dieser diese Hauptprinzipien ermöglichen und schützen."[193] Im besonderen verbindet sich damit auch ein Plädoyer zugunsten der freien Entfaltung der Individualität der Bürger, denn bei der Verschiedenheit der Lebensumstände, so die Argumentation, kenne nur der Einzelne die Mittel, seine Ziele zu erreichen bzw. er „weiß am besten, was ihm von Nutzen ist"[194]. Ganz ähnlich hat dies bereits Smith ausgeführt[195], und auch im Hinblick auf die essentiellen Aufgaben, die der Staat zu erfüllen hat, gibt es eine Vielzahl von Übereinstimmungen zwischen den beiden Ökonomen. Neben der elementaren Funktion einer Gewährleistung von innerer und äußerer Sicherheit wird etwa unisono verwiesen auf die Notwendigkeit der Organisation von entsprechender Infrastruktur[196] und von Maßnahmen zum Schutz des Einzelnen, speziell auch gegenüber dem Egoismus und der Gewinnsucht der Anderen[197]. Menger im besonderen erwähnt des weiteren „anormale

---

191 Streissler (1997), 79.

192 Menger (1876), 104, 41r ff.

193 Ebd. 114, 46 r.

194 Menger a.a.O., 112, 45r.

195 Smith a.a.O., IV. Buch, 2, 10.

196 Vgl. Menger a.a.O., 120, 50 r bzw. Smith a.a.O., V. Buch, 1, (3) 1.

197 Wenn dies zu befürchten ist, so ist nach Menger (a.a.O., 124, 53 r) „der Moment gekommen, in dem der Staat die gleichen Rechte aller wahren soll, und zum Wohle des Ganzen kräftig in die Tätigkeiten des einzelnen eingreifen und dessen Egoismus in die gesetzlichen Schranken weisen muß". In concreto handelt es sich hierbei aber um „meistens für den Staat schwierige Fälle, besonders, wenn das Interesse des einzelnen auch scheinbar die momentanen Interessen vieler fördert, in Wirklichkeit aber sie vielleicht für lange Zeiten hinaus schä-

Fälle“[198], nämlich 'externe Effekte' nach heutiger Terminologie[199], die eine Intervention des Staates rechtfertigen, wobei eben, wie er betont, die „Kunst der Regierung“ darin bestehe, „den richtigen Augenblick zu erkennen, wo der größte Fleiß und die edelste Aufopferung der Bürger dem Drucke des hereinbrechenden Unheils erliegt“. Nur in einer derartigen Situation könne das Eingreifen des Staates „keine hindernde Bevormundung der eigenen Interessen der Bürger, sondern die notwendige Rettung derselben“[200] genannt werden. Der Appell, Sparsamkeit und Fleiß der Bürger zu unterstützen und dabei seitens der Regierung mit gutem Beispiel voranzugehen, nämlich im öffentlichen Haushalt keineswegs leichtfertig und verschwenderisch zu agieren, findet sich ebenfalls sowohl bei Adam Smith wie auch bei Carl Menger[201].

Eine weitere wichtige Aufgabe des Staates, die von beiden als solche erkannt wird, ist, wie Smith es ausdrückt, sich in angemessener Weise „um die Ausbildung der Bürger“[202] zu kümmern. Da, seiner Meinung nach, in einer zunehmend arbeitsteilig-differenzierten Gesellschaft die große Masse des Volkes auf einige wenige, sehr einfache Verrichtungen beschränkt werde[203], und sich diese eintönige und anspruchslose Tätigkeit überaus nachteilig auf den Verstand der betroffenen Menschen auswirke, solle der Staat einer zu befürchtenden bzw. in der Praxis auch feststellbaren Verkümmerung bzw. Verrohung der Persönlichkeit der arbeitenden Bevölkerung entgegenwirken, indem für eine entsprechende Ausbildung, primär der einfachen Leute, in ihrer Jugend Sorge getragen werde. Wenn Kinder aus unteren Schichten – aufgrund ökonomischer Erwägungen – auch nur wenig Zeit ihrer Erziehung bzw. schulischen Unterweisung widmen könnten, so sollte es doch möglich sein, sie zumindest die elementarsten Teile des Unterrichts, nämlich Lesen, Schreiben und Rechnen, erlernen zu lassen, wobei von Adam Smith sogar angeregt wird, eine allgemeine Schulpflicht

digen würde“. Beispielhaft herausgegriffen werden der Schutz von Fabriksarbeitern vor schlechter Behandlung durch ihre Arbeitgeber, Maßnahmen zur humanen Arbeitszeitregelung und Verhinderung einer „Zuziehung unmündiger Kinder zur Arbeit“ (a.a.O., 126, 53 r ff.).

[198] Menger a.a.O., 114, 47 r. – Angeführt werden die „Einschleppung von Viehseuchen“ oder das „Überhandnehmen der Reblaus oder des Borkenkäfers“ (a.a.O., 116, 47 r).

[199] Vgl. Streissler a.a.O., 81.

[200] Menger a.a.O., 116, 47 v.

[201] Wenn die Regierung eines Staates „mit den Staatsgeldern leichtsinnig verfährt und sie für unnütze Dinge verwende“, so ist dies für Menger (a.a.O., 70, 22 r) „ein unverantwortliches Vergehen an allen Mitgliedern des Staates und eine Versündigung an der Menschheit und ihrem Fortschritte“. Adam Smith (a.a.O., II. Buch, 3, 30) betont, dass große Nationen „bisweilen durch öffentliche Verschwendung und Mißwirtschaft“ ruiniert wurden und er bemängelt, dass England „niemals mit einer sehr sparsamen Regierung gesegnet“ und „Sparsamkeit zu keiner Zeit eine charakteristische Tugend der Engländer“ war. Könige und Minister bezeichnet er – wenig schmeichelhaft – als „die größten Verschwender im Lande“. (a.a.O., 36). – Vgl. dazu auch Streissler a.a.O., 81.

[202] Smith a.a.O., V. Buch, 1, (3.2) 49.

[203] Vgl. a.a.O., 51.

einzuführen[204]. Der rechte Gebrauch der geistigen Fähigkeiten eines Menschen wird von ihm als dermaßen essentiell erkannt, dass selbst wenn der Staat „keinen Vorteil von der Schulausbildung für Menschen aus den niederen Schichten haben sollte“ – was aber de facto keineswegs der Fall sei –, er, aus humanen Gründen, dennoch interessiert sein müsste, dass diese Menschen „nicht Analphabeten bleiben“[205]. Auch Carl Menger empfiehlt den Bau von Schulen und erkennt darin „ein schönes Gebiet für den Staat zur Kundgebung seiner Sorgen ob des Gedeihens der wirtschaftlichen Bestrebungen seiner Bürger“[206]. In „gewöhnlichen Unterrichtsanstalten“ sehe der Einzelne im Staat seinen Sohn zum gebildeten Mann heranwachsen, dem aber sodann „jede andere Laufbahn“ als die des Vaters offenstehe und der, im Sinne einer individuellen Entfaltung, erstrebenswerterweise „schwerlich in das Nest zurückkehrt, aus dem er ausgeflogen, und kaum den Beruf seines Vaters ergreifen wird“. Wegen ihres Bezuges zur ökonomischen Praxis sind insbesondere Landwirtschafts- und Gewerbeschulen zu fördern. Wird nämlich die Volkswirtschaft nicht ausreichend anwendungsbezogen gelehrt, so besteht nach Menger die Gefahr, dass das Volk hinsichtlich seiner wirtschaftlichen Bestrebungen veraltet, „und der Stillstand in diesem Zweige der Kultur wird sich wie in keinem anderen für das Gedeihen des ganzen Staates fühlbar machen“. Auch Adam Smith spricht sich für eine Praxisorientierung in der Schulbildung aus und beklagt unter anderem die Weitergabe von „überlebte(n) und veraltete(n) Theorien einer als zweckmäßig anerkannten Wissenschaft“[207] an den öffentlichen Lehranstalten seiner Zeit.

Den Schutz und die Unterstützung des Staates für den Bürger fordert Carl Menger auch für solche Fälle, in denen der Wille des Einzelnen „zu schwach ist, Hindernisse wegzuschaffen, welche den gesamten wirtschaftlichen Bestrebungen im Wege stehen, oder Maßregeln anzuwenden, welche dieselben fördern würden“[208]. An anderer Stelle heißt es dann, es sei „eine Pflicht des Staates, die wirtschaftlichen Bestrebungen seiner Bürger zu unterstützen, um durch die Hilfe, die er diesen leistet, das Gedeihen des Ganzen zu heben“[209]. Vor allem bei „einem in der Kultur sehr vorgeschrittenen Volke“ habe diese Unterstützung der wirtschaftlichen Tätigkeit Einzelner allerdings „mit großer Vorsicht“ zu geschehen, „um ja nicht in den großen Fehler der Bevormundung zu verfallen“. In diesen Ausführungen wird ein besonders origineller Beitrag Mengers zur politischen Ökonomie und gleichzeitig ein feiner Unterschied zu Adam Smith erkannt[210]. Während Letzterer die sichere Grundlage einer Privatwirtschaftsordnung, die einer Staatstätigkeit kaum bedarf, in der auf Selbstinteresse beru-

[204] Vgl. a.a.O., 58.
[205] Ebd. 62. – Vgl. dazu auch Wilke a.a.O., 376.
[206] Menger a.a.O., 120, 50 v.
[207] Smith a.a.O., 47. – Vgl. dazu auch Streissler (in: Menger a.a.O., 122), Fußnote 6.
[208] Menger a.a.O., 30, 1 v.
[209] Menger a.a.O., 108, 44 r.
[210] Streissler (in: Menger a.a.O., 30), Fußnote 3.

henden Entschlusskraft des Individuums gelegen sieht, betrachtet Menger es doch als Aufgabe des Staates, die einzelnen Bürger zu dieser Eigeninitiative zu erziehen und diese zu schützen. Stärker als von Adam Smith wird von Carl Menger auch die Bedeutung des Privat- oder Sondereigentums hervorgehoben, dessen Schutz er sogar als „eine der wichtigsten wirtschaftlichen Aufgaben jeder Regierung“[211] ansieht, wogegen Smith eindrucksvoll auf die sozialpolitisch bedenklichen Aspekte großer Vermögensunterschiede zwischen den Staatsbürgern verweist[212].

Von derart, eher geringfügigen Unterschieden abgesehen, ist ein enger Bezug zwischen den wirtschaftspolitischen Auffassungen beider Ökonomen zu konstatieren. In einer Gesamteinschätzung von berufener Stelle[213] heißt es, bei einem detaillierten Studium der Mitschriften des Kronprinzen Rudolf zeige sich „am augenfälligsten ihre starke Abhängigkeit von Adam Smith“, wobei „fast jede Passage, ja fast jeder Satz“ sich auf das Werk *Wealth of Nations* zurückverfolgen lasse.

Bei so augenfälligen Gemeinsamkeiten in den Konzeptionen der Autoren müsste nun auch ein wesentlicher Kritikpunkt, der gegen einen der beiden gerichtet ist, eo ipso auch den anderen treffen. Auf diesen Aspekt möge noch kurz anhand eines gegen Adam Smith erhobenen, ebenso schwerwiegenden wie letztlich unberechtigten Vorwurfs eingegangen werden. Ihm wurde aufgrund seines engagierten Eintretens für eine Zurückhaltung des Staates unterstellt, er hätte ein *´laissez faire´*-Prinzip in einem radikalem Sinne vertreten und sei damit in weiterer Konsequenz auch zum Urheber jener, als ´Manchester-Liberalismus´ bezeichneten wirtschaftspolitischen Haltung geworden, die trotz des Elends breiter Schichten jede staatliche Sozialpolitik mit Verweis auf die ökonomische Freiheit ablehnt. Tatsächlich können Aussagen, wie die folgende, prinzipiell in eine falsche Richtung gedeutet werden:

> „Gibt man daher alle Systeme der Begünstigung und Beschränkung auf, so stellt sich ganz von selbst das einsichtige und einfache System der natürlichen Freiheit her. Solange der einzelne nicht die Gesetze verletzt, lässt man ihm völlige Freiheit, damit er das eigene Interesse auf seine Weise verfolgen kann und seinen Erwerbsfleiß und sein Kapital mit jedem anderen oder einem anderen Stand entwickeln oder einsetzen kann.“[214]

---

[211] Menger a.a.O., 46, 8 v.

[212] Vgl. z.B. Smith (a.a.O., V. Buch, 1, (2) 2): „Überall, wo es große Vermögen gibt, ist auch die Ungleichheit groß. Auf einen sehr Reichen kommen dann wenigstens 500 Arme, denn der Überfluß weniger setzt Armut bei vielen voraus. Ein solcher Reichtum der Besitzenden reizt zur Empörung der Besitzlosen, die häufig, durch Not gezwungen und von Neid getrieben, sich deren Eigentum aneignen.“ – Vgl. auch Streissler (in: Menger a.a.O., 44, Fußnote 35).

[213] Streissler (1997), 82.

[214] Smith a.a.O., IV. Buch, 9, 51.

Bei genauerer Betrachtung ist aber unschwer zu erkennen, dass der hier vertretene Grundsatz des 'laissez faire' bei Smith keineswegs uneingeschränkt gilt, äußert er doch starke Vorbehalte sowohl gegenüber einer absolut passiven Rolle des Staates als auch etwa im Hinblick auf eine generelle Befürwortung des Freihandels. Er votiert für Verpflichtungen staatlicher Obsorge, die sich nicht nur auf die elementarsten Aufgaben der Sicherung von Leib, Leben und Eigentum der Bürger sowie der Rechtspflege beziehen, sondern, wie schon erwähnt, darüber hinaus ebenso beinhalten, die Ausbildung auch der niederen Volksklassen zu gewährleisten, – selbst wenn dies in der ökonomischen Nutzenbilanz ohne Auswirkungen bliebe. Den genannten Anschuldigungen ist somit mit allem Nachdruck zu widersprechen[215], und dies tut auch Carl Menger, der in dem Aufsatz 'Die Sozialtheorie der klassischen Nationalökonomie und die moderne Wirtschaftspolitik' betont, dass derlei Angriffe auf Adam Smith „auf Missverständnis, ja Unkenntnis“[216] beruhten. In allen Fällen eines Interessenkonflikts „zwischen den Armen und den Reichen, zwischen den Starken und den Schwachen“ stelle sich Smith „ausnahmslos“[217] auf die Seite Letzterer und befürworte staatliche Eingriffe stets dann, wenn es sich um „die Beseitigung der die Armen oder Schwachen zu Gunsten der Reichen und Mächtigen bedrückenden Gesetzgebung oder Gesetzanwendung“ handle. Letztlich sei es unwahr und „eine Geschichtsfälschung“, dass Adam Smith „ein Doctrinär des 'laisser faire, laisser aller' ist und ausschließlich von dem völlig freien Spiele der individuellen Interessen das ökonomische Heil der Gesellschaft erwartet“[218].

Damit hat Carl Menger einen, in der Fachdiskussion seiner Zeit geäußerten Vorwurf gegen Adam Smith als völlig ungerechtfertigt zurückgewiesen und gleichzeitig auch seine eigene wirtschaftspolitische Gesinnung deutlich proklamiert[219]. Die ihm zuerkannte Bezeichnung als „strenger Smithianer“[220] bzw. als ein klassischer Liberaler „von außerordentlich reinem Wasser“[221] erscheint somit als zutrefflich.

---

[215] „Smith ist schon gar kein Manchester-Liberaler“, hebt auch Recktenwald (2005, LXXVI) hervor, denn „eine Marktwirtschaft ohne einen normal funktionierenden Staat, der seine klassischen Aufgaben effizient erfüllt“, war für ihn „ebenso undenkbar wie unrealistisch“. - Vgl. auch Rothschild 2004, 43 ff.

[216] Menger 1891, 223. – Vgl. dazu Streissler a.a.O., 80.

[217] „Ich gebrauche das Wort 'ausnahmslos' mit gutem Bedachte, da sich in A. Smith's Werken nicht eine einzige Stelle findet, in welcher er die Interessen der Reichen und Mächtigen gegen die Armen und die Schwachen vertritt“, bekräftigt Menger (ebd.).

[218] Menger a.a.O., 230.

[219] Nach Hayek (1968, XXXIII) tendierte Menger „zum Konservatismus oder Liberalismus des alten Typs. Er stand der Bewegung für Sozialreformen nicht ohne Sympathie gegenüber, doch niemals beeinträchtigte sozialer Enthusiasmus seinen kühlen Verstand“.

[220] Burkhardt/Priddat a.a.O., 943.

[221] Streissler a.a.O., 79.

4. In der Weise einer, eingangs ausgeführten und begründeten – wohl nur idealtypischen – Differenzierung von explizit erklärenden und normativ-wertenden Erörterungen sollte versucht werden, exemplarisch einige Verbindungslinien zwischen Carl Menger und Adam Smith darzulegen. Im Bereich der theoretischen Analyse von Sozial- und Wirtschaftsprozessen konnte, bei prinzipiell gleicher methodologischer Positionierung der beiden, eine Unterschiedlichkeit bezüglich einiger, die Erklärung des menschlichen Verhaltens in sozialen und ökonomischen Kontexten betreffenden Implikationen festgestellt werden. Hinsichtlich der sozial- und wirtschaftspolitischen Überzeugungen ist hingegen eine weitestgehende Übereinstimmung in den Prinzipien liberaler Wirtschaftspolitik zwischen den beiden Ökonomen erkennbar geworden.

Wie hier nur andeutungsweise auszuführen ist, vollziehen sich die Reflexionen von Smith und Menger – wie selbstverständlich auch aller anderen Denker, Sozial- und Wirtschaftswissenschaftler – nicht losgelöst und unabhängig von den jeweiligen politischen bzw. sozioökonomischen Rahmenbedingungen. Während jedoch behauptet werden könnte, dass der Anstoß zu jenen fundamentalen Überlegungen bei Adam Smith ziemlich augenfällig auf dem Hintergrund eines im Zusammenhang mit der in England sich früher und rascher als in anderen Teilen der Welt vollziehenden industriellen Revolution stehenden Übergangs von feudal-agrarischen zu industriellen Gesellschaftsformen im 18. Jahrhundert steht, scheint bei Carl Menger kein ähnlich offensichtlicher Bezug gegeben zu sein, eher geradezu das Gegenteil. Wenn mitunter von einem ′Wunder′ des plötzlichen Auftretens neuer, umfassender Grenznutzentheorien in den siebziger Jahren des 19. Jahrhunderts gesprochen wird, dann wäre, wie es heißt, „ohne Zweifel das Wunder in Österreich besonders groß gewesen“[222]. Im Unterschied zu den beiden, etwa zeitgleich in England bzw. Frankreich wirkenden, „ähnlich denkenden Revolutionären der Nationalökonomie“[223], Stanley Jevons und Léon Walras, seien bei Carl Menger die äußeren Voraussetzungen für eine Entwicklung neuer ökonomischer Theorien wesentlich schlechter gewesen. Insofern ′erblühte′ „einzig und allein“ Menger „sozusagen auf ziemlich unfruchtbarem Boden, in einem Land, das ökonomische Ausbildung nur als Nebenfach für Juristen kannte und in seinen spärlichen Schriften und Diskussionen sich weitgehend auf ausländische, insbesondere deutsche, Lehrbücher und Anstöße stützte“[224]. Im Hinblick auf seine sozial- und wirtschaftspolitischen Überlegungen könne es, wie bemerkt wird, als „eine Ironie der Geschichte“ aufgefasst werden, dass „über Menger gerade im illiberalen Österreich die Österreichische Schule eine Heimstätte des ′lost cause′ des ökonomischen Liberalismus wurde

[222] Rothschild (1986), 23.
[223] Streissler (1989), 119.
[224] Rothschild ebd.

und ihn pflegte zur Zeit seiner tiefsten Ebbe, insbesondere in der Zwischenkriegszeit“[225].

Zuletzt sei noch ein Wort gesagt zur Maßgeblichkeit der Konzeptionen von Adam Smith und Carl Menger in einem größeren historischen Kontext. Die Relevanz der von ihnen dargelegten Ideen ist wohl selbstverständlich nicht in naiver Einschätzung an ihrem unmittelbaren praktischen Bezug zu virulenten Themenstellungen der Gegenwart zu messen, vielmehr an dem Bemühen dieser Ökonomen, auf der Basis ihrer zeitgenössischen Verhältnisse und Problemlagen hochwertige Lösungsansätze entwickelt zu haben, sowie an der Bedeutsamkeit dieser Analysen im Rahmen der ideengeschichtlichen Entwicklung.

Es wurde erwähnt, dass sowohl Adam Smith als auch Carl Menger einen sehr verdienstvollen Anteil an der Begründung bzw. an der weiteren Ausgestaltung jenes wichtigen wissenschaftstheoretischen Ansatzes des methodologischen Individualismus haben. Wegen der grundlegenden Annahme eines rationalen Verhaltens der Einzelnen – als deren unintendiertes Ergebnis dann wünschenswerte soziale und ökonomische Ereignisse und Prozesse zustande kommen – wurde Smith und seinen Nachfolgern fälschlich unterstellt, „das Gespenst des *'homo oeconomicus'*“[226] erfunden zu haben. Zu der weiteren, durch viele Missverständnisse und fehlgeleitete Vorstellungen geprägten Entwicklung jenes traditionellen Subjektbildes, die im 20. Jahrhundert schließlich in das sogenannte *'Rational-choice-Paradigma'* bzw. in entscheidungs- und spieltheoretische Modelle mündete, hat aber auch Carl Menger wesentlich beigetragen[227]. In seiner Konzeption finden sich, vor allem im Rahmen seiner Ausführungen zum „Zeit-Irrthum“-Topos, zahlreiche Anregungen und Vorarbeiten für die in späteren theoretischen Modifikationen so maßgeblichen Aspekte wie etwa der Rolle des Zeitfaktors[228], der generellen Unsicherheit der Zukunft, der unvollständigen Information Einzelner und der Frage der Abstimmung zukunftsträchtiger Entscheidungen zwischen rational agierenden Individuen. Interessanterweise ist für Carl Menger noch ausgeschlossen bzw. kann er im Rahmen seiner Theorie logisch nicht rechtfertigen, dass nichtwirtschaftliche – zu seiner Zeit typisch philo-

---

[225] Streissler (1997), 85. – Des weiteren sei es, wie “ Streissler (1989, 134) ergänzt, auch eine paradoxe historische Entwicklung, dass sich in den letzten Jahrzehnten des 20. Jahrhunderts „klassisch-liberale Deregulierungsbewegungen in England und den Vereinigten Staaten auf 'Austrian Economics' als ihre intellektuelle Basis, auf die Österreichische Schule als einem letzten Hort und eine theoretische Fundierung des Liberalismus berufen statt auf ihre eigene, jahrhundertealte Tradition“.

[226] Hayek (1976), 22.

[227] Vgl. Streissler a.a.O., 128 sowie Rothschild a.a.O., 26.

[228] Menger (1871), §4, 21 ff. – Streissler (1997, 75 f.) hebt die Bedeutung dieses 'Zeit-Irrthum'-Paradigmas von Menger auch für dessen wirtschaftspolitische Weltanschauung hervor: „Denn irrt der Mensch in seiner Voraussicht der Zukunft, so tut es vor allem auch der Wirtschaftspolitiker. Die Wirkungen wirtschaftspolitischer Eingriffe sind nicht vorhersehbar und daher die Eingriffe selbst zu unterlassen.“ - Vgl. auch Streissler (1989), 132.

sophische – Güter, wie etwa 'Freundschaft' oder 'Liebe', in ökonomischer Hinsicht relevant werden[229]. Dieser Schritt erfolgt spätestens bei Gary S. Becker sowie bei Richard B. McKenzie und Gordon Tullock, die ökonomisches Gedankengut ganz explizit auch auf Probleme außerhalb des traditionellen wirtschaftlichen Erfahrungsbereichs anwenden[230].

Im Hinblick auf die normativen Überlegungen zur Sozial- und Wirtschaftspolitik wurde bereits auf die „viel mißbrauchte und viel mißverstandene Phrase vom 'laissez faire'"[231] verwiesen bzw. vor allem auch darauf, dass weder Smith noch Menger als dogmatische Vertreter einer derartigen Richtung anzusehen sind. Insbesondere sind beide nicht in unmittelbare Verbindung mit den heute oft kritisierten Tendenzen einer 'neoliberalen Wirtschaftspolitik' zu bringen. Moderne Phänomene, wie sie in aktuellen Diskussionen vorrangig sind, sowohl national, etwa in Bezug auf die Frage des Sozial- und Interventionsstaates, wie auch weltpolitisch, etwa hinsichtlich der Tatsache, dass internationale Konzerne als 'global players' machtmäßig den Staaten ebenbürtig sind[232], überschritten im 19. und daher noch umso mehr im 18. Jahrhundert wohl eindeutig die antizipatorische Reichweite von Carl Menger und Adam Smith. Beide waren sie überzeugt von einer harmonisch sich vollziehenden ökonomischen Entwicklung und einem historischen Fortschritt in der Weise einer Steigerung der allgemeinen Wohlfahrt durch die moderne Marktwirtschaft, doch die heute sichtbaren, teilweise sehr bedauerlichen Folgen der enormen Wachstumsprozesse lagen außerhalb ihres Horizonts[233]. Unumstritten dürfte aber sein, dass beide in ganz maßgeblicher Weise zur Entwicklung des wissenschaftlichen Diskurses beigetragen haben und in den Ahnenreihen maßgeblicher Theoretiker wirtschaftswissenschaftlicher Forschung wie auch bedeutsamer wirtschaftsliberaler Denker ihren festen Platz einnehmen.

---

229 Vgl. Menger a.a.O., 5 bzw. 77 ff. – Vgl. auch Priddat a.a.O., 297.
230 Vgl. Wilke a.a.O., 430 ff.
231 Hayek a.a.O., 29.
232 Vgl. Rothschild (2004), 45.
233 Vgl. Burkhardt/Priddat a.a.O., 944.

III.
Menger als Erkenntnislehrer
Epistemology and Economics according to Menger

Was the Austrian School a "Psychological" School in the realm of Economics in Carl Menger's view?

Gilles Campagnolo

In the 1900's, the appellation of "Psychological School" flourished. It was used to designate the new Marginalist school of economists, especially in the German-speaking world, and to confront the "Historical School", as for example in Kraus (Oscar Kraus, 1905, *passim*). It was also meant to discard the Classical paradigm that had been dominant until then. For this purpose, the Marginalists turned to some antique schemes, like the concept of the *psyche*. Menger thus explicitly and conscientiously referred directly to Aristotle's works, *Nicomachean Ethics* and *De Anima*. Commentators like Kraus then extended the appellation to the works of other "Austrian" Marginalist economists, such as the pupils of Menger's (Böhm-Bawerk, Wieser, etc.) and, in the end, to the whole new school, so that the latter came to be known under the denomination of the "*psychologische Schule*".

Now, to what extent did Menger really ground his theory of economics upon psychology? Soon enough, Max Weber (1908, p. 384 sq.)[234], acting thus on his own behalf (but also very clearly as a careful reader of the pure economics of his times, including most of Menger's, as he himself claimed) felt the necessity to stress his disagreement with such an interpretation of the "*Grenznutzlehre*" (theory of marginal utility). That a "psychological" basis is needed for economic theory, especially in the manner that Kraus had described it – but also, along his views, other important characters of the German-speaking *Academia*, like Lujo Brentano, Kaulla, etc. – that seemed quite erroneous to Weber.

Some developers of the "*Grenznutzlehre*" seemed to base many of their views upon the so-called "*psychophysisches Grundgesetz*" (Fundamental Law of Psycho-physics, also known as the Weber-Fechner Law; from the names of its originators – including an homonym of Max Weber). They saw in the latter a possible explanation for the new style adopted in Marginalist economics and regarded it as much as a source of Marginalist reasoning: it may at first have been an unconscious one, but it seemed very applicable to it and it was also thought of as a useful explanatory device for the new creed. This chapter will deal with this popular denomination as it was discussed and rebuked by both Carl Menger and, alongside, by Max Weber, as well as then by some later heirs in the Austrian school. We shall start from the texts and try to sketch a global view of the stand they took about the hierarchy and classification of sciences.

---

[234] It is a major essay, although little known today, that the article "Die Grenznutzlehre und das psychophysische Grundgesetz", published by Weber in 1908 in the *Archiv für Staatswissenschaft und Sozialpolitik*, reprinted in *Gesammelte Aufsätze zur Wissenschaftslehre*.

1. The founder of the Austrian school and Studies in psychology

First, we shall briefly try and assess what is related in Menger's thought to both fields that were then "going on a par", and how their concepts, proper to each but apparently shared between them for the most, became a source of confusion within research in economics and in psychology, around 1900. As a matter of fact, they had to be separated for a better understanding of each field – what Weber was later to call for, that is severing fields ("*eine strenge Trennung*").[235]

What did Menger read of the psychology of his times? His Library and Archives, both in Japan and the United States, teach us that Menger had read: the following works: *Studies upon Consciousness* (*Studien über das Bewusstsein*) by Stricker, published in Vienna, by Wilhelm Braumüller (also the publisher of Menger's *Grundsätze*) in 1879; *A Study upon the Origin of the Forms and Laws of Thinking* (*Eine Untersuchung des Ursprungs den Formen und Gesetze des Denkens*), by Widemann, at Schloss-Chemnitz, 1876; and of course, several lessons and texts by Wilhelm Wundt; and some even more minor titles.

In terms of what he effectively wrote on the matter, as a matter of fact, Menger did not write much in a direct manner about psychology, even in his *Untersuchungen* of 1883 and mostly his later notebooks show a few more hints, together with manuscript annotations on the books of his Library (the Menger Archives now located in two centers: Hitotsubashi University, Japan, and Duke University, North Carolina – see our other chapter on Menger's *Nachlass* in this volume). Later notebooks, now kept in the boxes of the Perkins Library at Duke, are of interest with critical notes about Wundt.[236] Altogether, the extent of Menger's interest in psychology, which also seemed to grow at the end of his career, is clear but may leave one dubitative as to the denomination given to his school of economics, as if the original "foundational ground" was in psychology, in the same line as earlier economics may have indicated, in Classical, especially utilitarian thought, but also other promising insights like Gossen's,

---

[235] This is all the more important as economic science in the 20th century would soon get rid of psychological insights for more than a half-century: the "return of psychology" as a "source of inspiration" in pure economics is something that has only lately re- started (within the last decade) as Frey and Benz remind us [2004, subsection title p. 68, and sq.]. Both worlds of economic research and of psychology parted ways in the 1930's: that seemed to be a downright "loss of psychology in economics" due to a "revolutionary change in the concept of utility" [*ibid.*, p. 63] and it had happened when Lionel Robbins questioned the very existence of a *cardinally* measurable utility function and the possibility to directly assess it.

[236] The reference numbers of the boxes where archival work may be conducted on this topic at the Perkins Library, Duke University are: 1-3 for notebooks falling in the period 1910's; 14-20, *e.g.* material refuting Wundt. There are also proposed revised passages for the *Untersuchungen*, but altogether not much to deal with. Those may let one think that, as he rebuked it, he also probably underestimated the future of such work.

which Menger happened to know and criticize. This is where our inquiry should preferably start from, i.e. the hedonistic and/or utilitarian agent.

Now, Menger's approach to economics regarding human behavior could apparently both be seen as calling to those psychological insights and allowing to get rid of them. The main starting point can be found in Menger's famous triangle that describes the order according to which the agent would rank his "preferences" was already only ordinal, although written with figures (*Grundsätze*, 1871, p. 93).[237] While the psychology of Menger's times, in order to gain its own scientific legitimacy, was then striving away from introspection, in favor of an approach more and more experimental (Wundt being the major author), with a trend to quantify experiments, scientists in economics were discovering how they had erred alongside a purely historical approach. Menger was catalyzing the new approach, but his idea could be seen as such: that all that was needed was an ordinal ranking pattern of the revealed preferences.[238] That pattern would show itself so powerful, that no economist would need any more psychological insights considered within the "inner side", the "inner self" of the agent for more than a half-century. That evolution blatantly contradicted directly the appellation of "Psychological school". How to conciliate those two contradictory views (by commentators and by followers)? Or, rather, were they anchored in Austrian economics, and namely, in Mengerian economics?

For sure, economics in the end of the 19th century could not foresee much of the developments of the following century, but even those are not totally clear about a psychological nature of their basic principles: what about game theory? Want about its limits? It is thus only natural that it seems unclear at first, whether one must interpret Menger's early insights in favor of a psychological basis for pure economics, or rather in favor of a demand for a strict separation between sciences. We shall here try to clarify that point and assess to which extent psychology was used (or not) by Menger to put economics on a specific ground.

In questioning the nature and style of research advocated by Menger, we shall start from the issue of the basis of utility then commonly accepted, that is to say happiness in its larger sense and wonder what meaning Menger attributed to it, Aristotelian, utilitarian, or else and what subjective well-being means in Marginalism. Happiness was a basic feature of economic analysis at the time, before it disappeared from the mathematically defined models of 20th century mainstream economics.[239] How did Menger position himself towards the Bentham-Jevons tradition or the hedonistic argument put forward by Hermann

[237] For Menger's table of the theory of value in the shape of a triangle, see *Annex 1* at the end of this volume.

[238] See in this volume chapter "Cardinality or ordinality in Menger's framework" by Livet.

[239] Only to surge again recently as an issue within experimental economics (see the survey presented in Frey and Stutzer [2002]).

Heinrich Gossen's in the psychologically-oriented work where he had already, in 1854, somewhat defined marginal utility reasoning, as Walras would later recognize? We shall use here work on archives, as Menger had read Gossen and we studied his pencil-notes on the volume he owned – thus incidentally proving Pantaleoni's accusation of plagiarizing wrong. We shall also base ourselves upon archives to see how Menger reacted to the Aristotelian notion of *psyche*.

Secondly, we shall pay attention to the question raised by Weber about the marginalist theme ("*Grenznutzlehre*") at a general level and how the possible "Law of psycho-physics" might (or not) lie behind it. On the other hand, we shall also say a few words about later followers of Menger (the "Austrian School") and how they regarded the role of psychological laws. Did their interpretation strictly adhere to Menger's advocacy of a necessary division of work between specialists of both fields, and if it was the case, what did it mean about their representation of the agent and his/her action, understood as a basic property? After presenting Max Weber's critical standpoint against any psychological basis, we shall then hint at two views of "Austrianness" upon that subject, Mises' and Hayek's (in *Human Action* and in *The Sensory Order*), and try to assess whether the Austrian School was "Psychological" School in the realm of Economics in their views. Marginalists built a "new" "pure" economics; Austrians especially did so. Was their paradigm based upon psychological stands, or not? Did Menger see things otherwise?

2. The question of happiness and subjectivity: an analysis from the readings of Gossen and Aristotle by Menger

2.1. Happiness in economics as a psychological starting point

The denomination "*homo economicus*" has been used to designate a certain set of properties common to economic agents since economists have assumed some properties of the latter in order to build their science. Deriving from those properties the behavior of such an agent under given constraints (budgetary and possibly others) has been the way to understand how trade worked and prices formed. Such a fictitious "*homo economicus*" may well differ from any given person and also change according to the paradigm; whether Classical,[240] Neo-classical or, as far as we are concerned, Marginalist, the paradigm dictates what economists assume of the psychological framework of "their" economic agent. Even when, along the line proposed by Lionel Robbins in the 1930's, economists refuse to describe what happens within the minds of the agents, and if they prefer to stick to preferences only as far as revealed by external behavior, and therefore leave altogether the field of psychology out of sight, even then,

[240] Or Marxist – for the latter is in a sense part of the former, and even though that wording "*homo economicus*" has most commonly been used from a "liberal" standpoint.

economists cannot fail to encounter some psychological effects of the behavior assumed on the part of the agent.

Whether they mean not to describe it, or on the contrary, try to take them into account, that is their own choice of methods – but it is not implied within a science of economics defining "mind" as something having nothing to do with it. Conversely, one may rather stress that economics had started with attempts at understanding "human nature" (from Hume's *Treaty*, and inspiration from 18th century Sensualism down to the *Theory of Moral Sentiments* by Smith, preparing the field for the *Wealth of Nations* in our interpretation of that grounding work). In the 19th century, both in the realm of Classical economics and of its opponent, the German Historical School, such psychological insights have been taken for granted (and therefore sometimes neglected as such) or, on the contrary, undervalued as strictly individual and thus, of less portent than historical facts moving peoples as wholes (communities or classes). Individual happiness may not have been considered as a topic of enough interest.

Of course, there is a whole tradition that based itself upon that personal happiness of the individual, Bentham's utilitarianism through the "felicific calculus". It was indeed founded on an objective valuation of pleasure and pain, as the underlying bourgeois values were most of the time implicitly assumed: the well-being on the part of the individual agents was not far from what a reasonable well-fed Victorian Briton would have expected, even though the calculus was to be made individually (the thief being supposed to compute whether the robbery is worth the probability of a few years in jail). Any "I" in society was to compute how much pleasure he/she would get from his/her action, including economic ones, and how much pain he/she could supposedly immediately understand that may come from it afterwards. The utilitarian criteria ultimately tend to insure a maximum of happiness for the whole of society, and not the individual as such, as there exists, derived from the "invisible hand", a scheme harmonizing well-thought private interests with global public good. Paradoxically, in coordination with the whole of a given society, individuals are only secondary concerns of such utilitarianism, where private hedonism is deemed to insure general well-being: in this sense, individual psychological traits teach more about a global aim – political, rather than economic.

Now, in Menger's eyes, that is not the task of the theory of economics. We shall therefore deal here with the issue of a study of happiness that is important, according to Carl Menger, inasmuch as it really concerns individual needs and their satisfaction. Menger was a reader of both the Classical tradition and the German economist who had first developed a "marginal" line of reasoning, Hermann Gossen. However, as a thinker and not only an economist, his interest in Aristotle proves that Menger grounded his conception on the idea of "well-being of the *psyche*" and he combined all that in a strictly subjective approach. This is certainly why Mengerian views indeed clashed with utilitarianism in the British marginalist line of reasoning, where its role was introduced by Bentham and claimed by Jevons, too, when the latter subsequently modified substantially economic thought towards a marginalist line.[241] Against both Classics and Historicists, Menger based happiness on subjective satisfaction of needs, and his endeavor was thus labeled "psychological" by some commentators, but it was in fact neither utilitarian nor hedonistic, neither Benthamite nor Gossenian.

2.2. Menger, reader of Gossen: how Menger rebuked hedonism

Hermann Gossen is the first author in whose works the following can be found: individual needs assumed to be subjectively valued by one independent self, for the only reason that nobody else can ever know one's needs and ways of satisfaction (as well as pain) and that, alongside an intangible rule of maximizing pleasure taken in material goods. Now, if that may seem true even independently from any "marginal" reasoning, one must ponder to which extent both directions (Gossen's and Menger's) were stated within "psychology".

Menger had read Gossen's book, *Laws of Human Relations and the Rules of Human Action Derived Therefrom* (*Entwicklung der Gesetze des menschlichen Verkehrs, und der daraus fließenden Regeln für menschliches Handeln*). It is still lying on the shelves of his Library now kept in Japan.[242] The volume bears Menger's pencil-notes and one may even put a most probable date on his reading, as Menger usually wrote the date of purchase on the first page of his books, and in that case, it bears "May 8, 1886". From a philological perspective, it is also good to know, as the Italian economist Maffeo Pantaleoni, who grounded his own economics upon Gossen's, accused Menger of plagiarism in the 1900's. It is highly dubious that Menger may have read Gossen's volume before his purchase, although Walras, as is well-known, but also Kautz mentioned him.[243] Now, archives permit to answer that Pantaleoni's charge was false.

---

[241] Evidence for the results that are given in the following pages cannot be displayed at length here. Readers of the French language may look for more in Campagnolo (2004): *Critique de l'économie politique classique*, Paris, Presses Universitaires de France, p. 195-266.

[242] As reminded in the Foreword, at his Library kept at Hitotsubashi (Japan). About the history of this export, readers of French may refer to Campagnolo (2000): « La bibliothèque viennoise de Carl Menger conservée au Japon: étude des sources d'une pensée économique » in: *Austriaca*, Review of Austrian Studies, *Vienna 1900*, n° 50.

[243] Gossen's book had been published in 1854 (sec. ed. stopped by Gossen's death in 1858); the book had virtually vanished from the world. In his « Un économiste inconnu », *Journal des économistes*, Walras (1885) reintroduced Gossen both in theoretical economics and in the History of economic thought. Kautz, whose textbook, *National Economics as a Science* previously published, was used in Austria, bore a few hints at marginal reasoning, but nothing elaborated though Menger annotated the copy he owned: Kautz J. (Gyula), *Die Nationalökonomie als Wissenschaft*, Wien, 1858, p. 9; reed. 1860, p. 704

Besides the date of purchase on the opening page, Gossen's volume owned by Menger much after he had himself written his *Grundsätze* (1871), also bears annotations that can leave no doubt about the disapproval of Gossen's tenets on Menger's part. From the conceptual standpoint, as a matter of fact, Menger mostly disagreed with Gossen, except for the common basis of a marginalist line of reasoning. That is true also regarding Jevons and Walras, as far as marginalism is concerned. Is it necessary to remind here that the latter teaches that every agent appreciates himself what he/she is ready to give in exchange for a supplementary unit of any given good he/she judges adequate to his/her need. Each new unit gives less satisfaction than the former, until he/she reaches satiety (*Sättigung*). Gossen stated what he called two "Laws of Pleasure" (*Gesetze der Genießen*) which made possible his line of reasoning.

What Lexis called, in 1895, the "First Law" states: "The magnitude of a given pleasure decreases continuously if we continue to satisfy this pleasure without interruption until satiety is ultimately reached". [244] It describes the decline in the utility received from a new unit (at the "margin") of a good acquired to satisfy pleasure. Gossen demonstrated it geometrically with the following (here simplified) triangular graph:

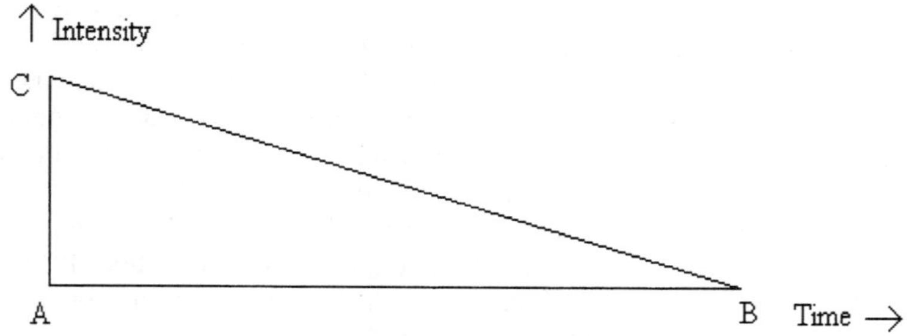

The Second Law equalizes the pleasure received "at the margin" from two (or more) different activities by the individual agent. The geometrical diagram goes as follows (in a voluntarily simplified manner):

[244] Gossen H. H., [1854], p. 4. Eng. tr. [1983], p. 6.

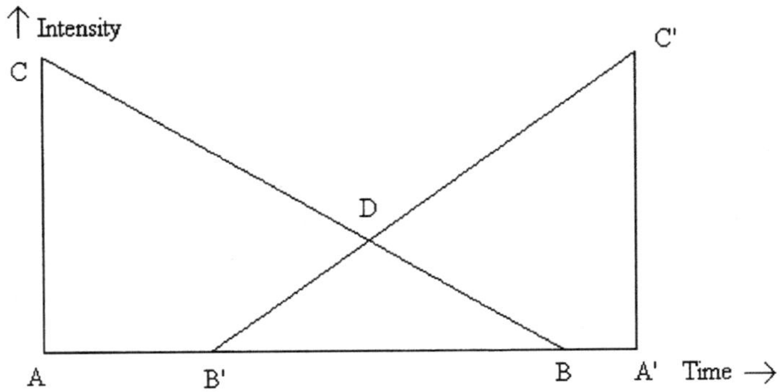

(On the abscissa is time, shown in reverse directions for triangles ABC and A'B'C'. Where both triangles intersect, that is the point of indifference between the two goods/activities on the part of the agent. In the case of more than two goods/activities, those cannot be mapped on a graph and Gossen used mathematical analysis, but Menger was to refuse it for principle reasons).

Menger's pencil-notes on the pages of the volume by Gossen show clearly that he agreed with that line of reasoning regarding the valuation of the last satisfying unit of one good against another. That would be the basic point of what the tradition was to call "Marginalism" later on and it was thus granted. But it did not mean that Menger accepted the concepts upon which Gossen based his "laws". That point is clear from a reading of Menger's opinions in his notes, and it is highly negative. Gossen's analysis is written in terms of the psychology of an egoistic agent who is in fact (and legitimately according to Gossen) interested only in pleasure. That is not the same thing as satisfaction of needs, and Gossen's point seemed unacceptable to Menger. In Gossen, Menger approved of the reasoning in terms of intensity *vs*. time (which was also after all found in older traditions), but he rebuked the egoistic-hedonistic psychology presented as grounding, which would in the end mean that economics were based upon facts that experimental psychology would discover, instead of pure economic reasoning. In Gossen's mind, there was not only what we now call "maximizing calculus", but a quest for pleasure (Genießen) in which he stated "Man must act in order that the sum of his pleasures (Genießen) be the highest possible".[245]

Menger despised such views and regarded the calculus of instantaneous derivative in satisfaction of needs as both immoral if based on a scheme lead by pleasure and inappropriate if gained from mathematics and not adequate concepts. The marginal unit scheme had to be regarded as a logical tool and not a moral stand (consciously immoral in that case) about the nature of man. A philosophy of materialistic pleasure could not be the basis for pure economics, nor

[245] In this quotation, we use our translation from the original.

an idealist philosophy: Only a causality theory of knowledge was adequate, as Menger would state in the first sentence of his *Grundsätze* ("All things in the world obey the law of cause and consequence", 1871, p. 1).[246] Gossen had not considered those matters properly. Conversely, absolute was in Gossen's eyes the fact that every man strictly followed only material satisfaction, which Menger judged as erroneous as the claim that Gossen made of his vision being the salvation of mankind through a renewed Creation.[247] Last, but not least, one must also add that, for all its novelty, Gossen kept the theory of labor and his abundant use of mathematics did not prevent the same errors of the Classics.

Hedonistic psychological foundations seemed even more than despicable to Menger, he judged them *inadequate for science*. Therefore, his opinion on Gossen is clear-cut and definitive, as the following final manuscript notes show:

> "Gossen fails: to his mind, (technical) labour has a tremendous significance. [One can see here] All the lacks of the mathematical method in the field of psychological facts. Only pleasure – and not what is truly effective in men's lives and well-being (the highest pleasure throughout life). Only labour and pleasure, like in Bastiat…"[248]

2.3. Happiness and Aristotelian views in terms of *Psyche* by Menger

Now, must happiness as a starting notion in economics necessarily call to psychological facts, as Menger judged erroneous while reading Gossen? Is happiness the ground for a psychological basis of economics? In answer to that, Menger's idea of subjective happiness is neither down-to-earth mere pleasure computing as in the way he interprets the Benthamite tradition, nor a means only to choose between alternative schemes where he finds no more palatable a mere indulging oneself in "Genießen". If psychological insights came into play, the behavior of the economic agent would cause economics to lie upon such premises: that was unacceptable, both methodologically and strategically, in order to re-establish economics as a dignified science. Within research activity, the economist must seek rational and purely economic causes. Archives show that Menger referred most preferably, rather than to Modern psychology, to the Ancient Greeks' notion of *psyche*.

---

246 In this quotation, we use our translation from the original.

247 The introduction written by Gossen to his book, as well as the last paragraphs thereof, are written in a prophetic style, Gossen claiming to play both the roles of Christ and Copernicus, passages in front of which Menger marked his deep astonishment.

248 The note is written on the back of the cover of the volume owned by Menger (our translation). Reference to Bastiat is most often very *negative* in Menger's notes – as is clearly inferred from numerous other passages. See Campagnolo (forthcoming 2008): "Origins of Menger's thought in French Liberal Economists", *Review of Austrian Economics*. Menger sums up all his criticisms on Gossen in the final judgment quoted here, with a brisk tone that he developed and documented in his notes throughout the volume.

As a matter of fact, *Psyché* appears clearly as one of Menger's basic concepts, as can be inferred from many passages, some in Menger's published texts, as stressed by commentators (some being quoted by Barry Smith [1990]) and in yet unpublished notes too (Campagnolo [2002]) [249]. In the Viennese University of Menger's times, culture of Ancient philosophy, especially of Aristotle, was still vivid, even among economists and Menger referred preferably to the notion of *Psychè* for psychological insights than to the experimental psychology of behavior that Wundt then tried to establish.[250] Menger also favored Aristotle's notion of *Psychè* to Plato's and referred to a soul that hosts both emotions and reason, opposed to a "*Psychè kai Sôma*" view of soul vs. body, the latter being both its envelope and its shroud.

Moreover, as *Psychè* is thus the seat of desires, it is also in particular that of material appetites asking for satisfaction – as in the statement: *È Psychè anapausetai* (Xenophon, *Cyropedy*, 6, 2, 28), which means that "the need for food will calm down". *Psychè* here means precisely not only that the desire for food is inherent "in the stomach" but in the whole of man, and *Psychè* conveys that meaning for man as a whole seeking satisfaction. It thus includes material needs, although not limiting them in kind: all needs ask to be satisfied and the Greek idea of *Psychè* gave, in this sense, to Menger a broader and more encompassing notion than the modern utilitarian or hedonistic views. It certainly partly inspired Menger in his account of satisfaction of material needs (Bedürfnisbefriedigung) from which his analysis starts in the first chapter of his 1871 Principles of Economics (*Grundsätze der Volkswirtschaftslehre*), that is his "Theory of goods" (*Güterlehre*). Menger also included needs higher in ranking, necessary to produce consumption goods whatever they may be (of any nature including mere "comfort" goods, like tobacco which Menger quotes), still obeying the logic of the triangle-shaped table mentioned above. In fact, there exists an order according to which the agent cannot fail to rank his "preferences" without putting his own self in danger (food comes first, etc.). The agent may judge otherwise, but cannot do so in the long term (or he shall die…)

---

[249] From Oscar Kraus on, many commentators have insisted, more generally, on Menger's Aristotelianism, opposed to the use made of Aristotle by the German Historical School as explained in Appendix VII of his *Untersuchungen* of 1883. The issue can be solved only through *documented* insights, which Emil Kauder began to do and which was pursued (for readers of French) in Campagnolo (2002): « Une source philosophique de la pensée économique de Carl Menger: l'*Éthique à Nicomaque* d'Aristote » in: *Revue de philosophie économique,* n° 6. Within the present chapter, *psyche* is the only concept we may evoke in this relation Menger – Aristotle. But it can also be shown how goods are subjectively valued and prices get fixed, for example, through a reading of Aristotelian schemes in the *Nicomachean Ethics*– Campagnolo and Lagueux (2004).

[250] Menger mentioned Wundt's works, as said above, in his notebooks now kept at the Perkins Library, Duke University Press.

The previous facts explain why Menger espoused a rigorous theory of subjective well-being and happiness but that he also started his analysis in accordance with the Greek theme of a "scale of natural satisfaction" (to be found in Aristotle in the *De Anima* as well as in the *Nicomachean Ethics*). The triadic scale that says that "survive – live – live well for higher purposes (εὖ ζῆν, that is the verb `to live´ combined with the adverb corresponding to ἀγαθός, which is good)" is regarded as a general rule of being. The economic agent does not start otherwise when considering the necessities of life, and then aiming at more and better, including in his beliefs all his subjective notions of well-being in a given social, economic and cultural world.[251] The highest goal aimed at by the agent is thus theory in its original sense (theoria, that is "contemplation of the truth"), and one may wonder whether the agent is not thus intended to become the theoretician of one's own activity – an economist... To conclude with that argument, let us stress that when Menger referred to views that he had found in Aristotle (*De Anima*, *Nicomachean Ethics*, *Politics*, *passim*), he was making the ancient notion of *Psyche* a pivotal one for his own purposes.

Oskar Kraus, a colleague of Menger, who was a Professor in the then Imperial Austrian Prague University in the 1900's, grasped well the conceptual relationship between Aristotle's philosophy and Menger's economics in his article "Die aristotelische Werttheorie in ihren Beziehungen zu den Lehren der moderner Psychologenschule". Nevertheless, Kraus may have extrapolated from that link when he wrote, as an epigraph, a quotation from the *De Anima* that tells the reader that, in order to understand human behavior, *Psychè* is the first study and only when it is properly studied, brings in other dimensions of human action. As a true understanding of behavior includes, according to Kraus as, of course, to Menger, economic phenomena, then, obviously, Kraus meant that knowledge in the latter had to be based upon the former. But that was far from the Mengerian view as expressed in the theory of the *Grundsätze* of 1871 as well as in the methodology of the *Untersuchungen* of 1883 and of later smaller texts.

But did it mean that Menger, although undoubtedly inspired by Aristotle, would draw as a consequence from the notion of *Psychè* the building of economics upon the Modern notion of mind? As said in the introduction of this chapter, although Menger clearly showed interest in volumes of the psychology of his times that archives permit to document,[252] the way he rebuked Modern notions of the mind related to hedonism and utilitarianism bore upon any experimental basis of science in his view, and that led him to use the notion of economic behavior of the agent without the psychological description that Kraus

---

[251] Including, thus, also "spiritual" needs and developing what, in the 20th century, would be called *embeddedness* (*e.g.* in the style of Karl Polanyi, Granovetter, etc.)

[252] See the list of the most annotated works given in the Introduction of this chapter. Even more than those, though, Menger annotated Aristotle's *Nicomachean Ethics* and he much preferably quoted the Ancient in his own works.

saw as its basis. To put it in a nutshell, if economics were to be based upon psychology, Menger feared that it would simply be subservient to a science (psychology) exactly in the same way it had been, until him and in German-language countries, to another, namely history.

3. Limits of any psychological laws of reasoning in terms of "marginal utility": the case argued by Max Weber, Ludwig von Mises, Friedrich Hayek

Menger was not the only author concerned with the evolution of economics, worrying about grounding the latter upon a basis of its own, rather than observe in it a sequel built of by-products taken from psychological claims. The fact that *Psychè* could be considered as the essence of the agent by Menger did not prevent him from an absolute reluctance to think that either science could serve as a ground for the other. Menger would even less agree to the idea that one science could only serve as a field of application for carrying out the essence of the other science's fundamentals!

Now, the trouble was that readers of Menger were apparently so little convinced by this dismissal that the denomination of "psychological School" became commonplace to designate him and his school. In the context of the German-speaking countries, the newly "Austrian school" came to be identified with a "*Psychologenschule*". Were then, in fact, both sciences separated? Or were they not? Or so so much so as far as to their frames, their basis, their aims and their methods, that commentators could possibly assess that building economics upon psychological fundamentals was some outcome of Menger's ideas – although he may himself have had some other intentions? A host of economists and psychologists of his time, such as Kaulla, Lujo Brentano et *alii*, could have understood things likewise. Would they disregard Menger's *opus*? Opinions such as Kraus's undoubtedly raised questions. We have no choice but to go a little beyond Menger's own works and ask again to what extent commentators were justified in calling the "Austrian" school a "*Psychologenschule*".

In doing so, commentators mainly referred to the "law of marginal utility" which they regarded as a consequence of the "psycho-physical" (and somewhat almost "physiological") law of the decrease in intensity of the quantity of pleasure received through time. Reminding much the way in which Gossen had previously presented the idea – and we have shown that Menger rebuked that hedonism, they disseminated their analysis, while Carl Menger postponed publishing the second edition of his master-work of 1871. Thus, the reply was to be made by others, of whom Max Weber may present the best example of a careful and, although not technical, deeply comprehensive reading. Now, members of the Austrian school proper (Weber still belonged to Schmoller's *Verein für*

Sozialpolitik)[253], and in particular Menger's own disciples' disciples ("*Enkel-Schüler*" in German) indeed claimed Menger's heritage: did they espouse a few psychological views in economics? A few hints shall also interest the reader of Menger, as far as later generations were concerned.

3.1. Max Weber: how to question economics and deal separately with different sciences?

The issue of a subjective notion of satisfaction of needs, but also of their availability (*Verfügbarkeit*) is obviously pivotal to the new "pure" economics. As far as happiness is now concerned, the way Kraus and others denominated the "psychological school" deserves questioning. Yet, it must be pointed out, that, at the turn of the 1900's, whereas most German academics were following Schmoller at the head of the powerful Verein für Sozialpolitik, most of those supporting Austrian Marginalism were acting in the belief of such a frame of "psychology" within "pure economics". Fighting both the British Classical school of labor-value (and Marxism, inasmuch as it inherited Ricardian concepts) and the German Historical school was a harsh task and interpreting reality through psychology might then come out of the reign of collective concepts (*Kollektivbegriffe*). Among such concepts the *Volkswirtschaftslehre* was, for instance, as is clearly expressed in the word, the doctrine (*Lehre*) of the economy (*Wirtschaft*) suited to a people (*Volk*) and preferably namely the German people. That was the most spread feature. Renouncing such concepts meant at the same time seeking methodological and institutional fights (the *Methodenstreit* combined both). Hence, there existed an interest in psychology on the part of Menger for it had already made his the "implicit" nature of the individual agent rather than the delusory *Volk*. Nevertheless, that grounding upon psychology was not acceptable in order to promote "pure economics" in Menger's eyes.

It was Max Weber who most abruptly stated why in his 1908 article: "Die Grenznutzlehre und das psychophysische Grundgesetz" (*Archiv für Staatswissenschaft und Sozialpolitik*, criticizing the way in which some confused economics with psychology. Weber had in mind those followers of Menger who did not grasp his thought correctly and claimed that the basis of the marginal utility reasoning was a mere application of a Law of Experimental Psychology. The most often elected ground by such commentators was the then well-known "Fundamental Psycho-physical Law" (*Psycho-physisches Grundgesetz*) that had first been rigorously formulated by psychologists Weber and Fechner.

It stated, much along the line of Gossen's First Law (although not as a hedonistic postulate, but rather as the result of experimental procedures) that a reverse relation existed between intensity of sensation and the time it was felt.

[253] Although Weber incarnated the "Youngest" Historical School– *die jüngste historische Schule* as opposed to Schmoller's "Young Historical School".

Obviously, the next step was to think that the individual would then value goods in accordance with his/her own desire for such good which satisfied the felt need (like hunger or thirst). Still, experimentations stopped at the results obtained. Some economists would conceive of their science as a sequel of the applied consequences of such behavior, thus pledging allegiance to psychology as such. Max Weber showed how much this was misleading in his 1908 article.

As shown earlier, Menger rebuked Gossen's hedonistic ideas that could support the idea of economics as applied findings of psychology. Max Weber had paid attention to Kraus' article of 1905,[254] to Kaulla's (1906) and to Lujo Brentano's (1908) who had more audience than the host of others tenants of the marginal utility theory of value (*Grenznutzlehre*) who interpreted Marginalism in the way of a "psychologische Schule der Nationalökonomie". Ironically, a pupil of the historicist Knies was to defend Menger's theoretical endeavors, and Weber treated the pure *Grenznutzlehre* with fairness and with arguments against a psychological foundation of economics. Max Weber pointed out that:

1). Weber-Fechner law, as purely empirical, could not fit pure economics, whose main claim it was to orientate science in a theoretical direction. Menger asked for criteria that could not be met upon any empirical basis and facts would not do for causal deduction – whatever the link between Menger's "real-types" (Realtypen) and empirical reality.[255] Menger thought it all for theory, and even though Weber wanted singularities to be considered in a science of effective reality (Wirklichkeitswissenschaft), they nevertheless agreed upon theory.

2). Although both Weber-Fechner Law and theorems found in pure economics seem to use similar concepts, like needs (Bedürfnissen) and satiety (Sättigung), a direction of inquiry lead by individual interests, etc., this is in accordance neither with the detailed contents they give them: psychologists see forms of the mind, where economists seek incentives for action; nor with the goal psychologists and economists set themselves: the ones try to understand why the mind works the way it does, the others have it as a given facts not to investigate.

3). Thus, not only methods are different, but objectives too, and therefore, sciences must be strictly separated (a *strenge Trennung* is necessary for the sake of both). Economists build a rational understanding of the process of exchange

---

[254] Kraus had sent Menger a separate copy of his article, but Menger did neither underline nor crossed out the word "psychological" in the title and it is difficult to infer a reaction from lack of any supporting indication.

[255] See in this volume chapter "Empirical Studies and Mengerian Methodology" by A. Lordon and M. Ohana.

(like Menger in his Grundsätze), whereas psychologists have experiments to do, introspective or behavioral.[256]

For Weber, as well as for Menger, theory cannot lie on empirical laws. Theory has its own concepts. And a theory for economics *needed* a strict separation from a theory for psychology. Kraus' underlying idea was that a given stratum for theoreticians in economics may be laid by other scientists. Against that view, Weber analyzed the formulas given by those who mixed psychology and economics and, along the arguments above, showed how they were driving science away from its due course through confusion. For example, the notion of "Optimum" means something in the economists' sentences and calculus (in Menger, and more at large), which the psychologists' notion of "maximization of pleasure" does not render. More generally, ontologically and methodologically, the building of a science may not depend upon changing results of another science, without impairing its own future.

As a matter of fact, Weber rebuked this latter claim not only in the case of economics, but also regarding all social sciences. He thus shared with Menger the idea that each science had to define its own standpoint, whereby it grasps the nature of reality, and issues addressed in its domain should not depend upon a given ontology, but upon an appropriate method to solve them. Along the line of Aristotle and, more generally, of a pure causality theory, sciences which are theoretical should deal with the general in phenomena of their own field, and not rely upon any results of another science. Historical sciences deal, on the contrary, with singular events and practical sciences (finance and so on) with applied theory within the realm of action. Thus, each having its proper basis, sciences teach us aspects of reality: in the case of economics, general laws of exchange. Theory has its own legitimacy, and depends neither upon historical data, nor upon results of psychology, moreover experimental. At the most, experience gives insights into what types a theoretician may be interested to forge according to the issues he should be willing to deal with. In its turn, each and every science has questions for specific facts and all of sciences show many possible approaches and facets of reality, none being the ultimate *Regina scientiarum*. Menger and Weber agree upon that, and such a point of view is universal and excludes the idea that a science may serve as basis for another.

Especially, experimental psychology cannot be the ground for sound pure economics - and the psycho-physical law was only an experimental result for most psychologists of the time. But this reasoning holds towards theoretical psychology as well, and thus, there could not be, neither in Menger's, nor in Weber's understanding of science, a whole-encompassing doctrine of human behav-

[256] Note that, the temptation to draw from experimental economics occasionally emerges again, acknowledged by the community of economists – the most recent co-Nobel Prize for Kahnemann (with Vernon L. Smith) being a strong example.

ior, even on the ground of the analysis of mind. The ontology of psychology is neither one that economics would have advantage to make its own, nor itself *a base* upon which economics could depend. Again, those scientists who believed that psychology could be the equivalent in the "sciences of the spirit" (*Geisteswissenschaften*) of what Newton's theory was in the natural sciences, those were wrong in Weber's view.

No science worthy its name could ever give up its own ontology for another one. The true fundamentals for the whole human behavior would be given neither by economics, nor by psychology, for none of them neither could, nor should encompass the whole of the *Geisteswissenschaften.* Weber was here repeating Menger. As to the latter, it is sometimes argued that he was a "realist" (because of his essentialism in an Aristotelian style), but it is also true that he carefully avoided to give an ontology, even less one which would reduce the subjectivity of the agent to a mere psychology. The agent, as described by Menger, is "really" a "type". The agent is described and understood as such, as an element of pure economic analysis. And its relationship with Weberian *ideal-types* surges from there – although it does not belong to the present chapter to discuss it in more detail.

Conversely, let us briefly go back to what was coined "psychology" in the 1900's. That was also changing, and one should insist upon the various nature of the term as a "science of mind" that was evolving from an introspective to an experimental framework. What to label "irrational" was also object of debate[257]: Windelband and Rickert, to whom Weber refers to at large, had also already criticized the naïve understanding of liberty through which "types" were regarded as "limits" put in the explanation of "whole-encompassing effectiveness of the world of phenomena" (" *die volle empirische Wirklichkeit der Erscheinungswelt*) and thus forgetting about human free behavior – making impossible to understand man mechanically, in the eyes of many, especially the Historicists.

If social reality was to become an object of rigorous study, then types were the adequate tool. In turn, medical psychiatry, and psychology, and economics, etc. were to build their own domain. Experimental psychology was in its prime heyday when Menger and Weber were writing, but this was no sufficient reason to bring all aspects of human life and all human sciences back to its own specific ground. Weber was denying psychology, and in fact any social science, the claim to be the one fundamental science of human behavior. It was erroneous to think that that study of the mind was to deliver the "true essence" from which to derive the hierarchy of all human sciences. Weber espoused

[257] Of course, Weber forges a concept of *irrationality* that fits his own theoretical goals, as a methodological concept. In Vienna the study of "non-rational" *ego* was to start soon. It was apparently not to convince Menger in any way. But here documents (on Freud for instance) are almost inexistent. Menger's era was rather that of the rise of experimental psychology.

Menger's methodological individualism (although the term was coined later). But the elementary components of social, economic phenomena and psychological events of the mind could not be considered as being the same.

Menger had also criticized psychological ground in the works of other economists, as shown in the first section, and put forward his own terminology and a new classification of the social sciences. That psychology is simply not at stake here can thus also be inferred from his tripartite division in historical, theoretical and practical sciences, as stated above.[258] To each approach, Menger recognizes its own legitimacy in its own right, as long as they do neither overlap, nor claim more than they can achieve. It is then only natural that experimental knowledge cannot give the basis to theoretical stands, and on the other hand, that psychology, even as a theory, should deal with the mind and not with the individual analysis of exchange in "social phenomena" (*Sozialerscheinungen*). Subjectivity of the economic agent was an elementary economic principle and, as such, impossible to know beforehand, anywhere else.

The kind of varieties of "type" that Menger as well as Weber were seeking were no abstract *homo economicus* with preferences modeled for mathematical treatment either, nor an experimental "inner mind" postulated by psychology, nor the "neuronal mind-man" of later cognitive sciences. Therefore, if now, one wants to take into account later evolution of the Austrian School founded by Menger, a few more hints about the role of psychology may prove useful. Two instances may be found in the way that Mises deals with psychology in *Human Action* and Hayek in his *Sensory Order*.

3.2. Psychology in later Austrian school: a few words on Mises and Hayek wondering whether subjectivity could evolve into sensory analysis and a cognitive psychology of mind?

After Menger on,[259] who had not published much on the topic of psychology after all (although his notes are plenty), both Mises and Hayek kept the idea that the subjective feeling of satisfaction of needs (*Bedürfnisbefriedigung*), rather than "happiness", was central to understanding the agent. Known as "methodological individualism", his approach would present itself as the only sensible method to a scientist in economics, who would to start from the fact that human agents act. It is well-known that Mises claims his praxeology to be based only upon that premise, and to include economics only as one of its parts. Theories

---

[258] Here, the reader may refer for the whole exposition by Menger to „Appendix IV" of his *Untersuchungen über die Methode der Socialwissenschaften und der Politischen Ökonomie insbesondere* (1883) and the article *Grundzüge einer Klassifikation der Wirtschaftswissenschaften* (1889).

[259] But, of course, a survey of the question as a whole within "the Austrian tradition" does not belong in the present chapter.

where aggregate collectivities are assumed to act are discarded from the start;[260] but again, does an individual basis, also shared by most psychological schools (in behavioral psychology, it is a defining concept) suffice to serve as a ground for economics? The same point appears, that was the source of confusion denounced by Weber as "*psychologische Schule*".

Mises clearly identified it and, from the start in *Human Action* (1949), he poses as absolute this first axiom and ultimate datum (I, 3) that agents do act. But that has nothing to do with a "psychological" tenet: it is a postulate without which the science he intends to build (which he calls praxeology) has no existence. As such, it bears no "psychological" status but a methodological one: if accepted, what follows must also be accepted (if correctly deduced). Thus, agents (those who act) are not meant to serve as elements to help solving problems of "the mind" (whatever that could mean[261]) but issues of cooperation in "trade". Through analyzing action, it is not the factual "mind events" which are taken into account, nor explained, but it is a categorical *a priori* demonstration of a "formal character and aprioristic" (*ibid.* II, 2) that is undertaken. What derives from the axiom in terms of exchange, property, contracting, etc. (most of the volume) is strictly causally linked to the original postulate.

Contrary to mainstream economics, in the Misesian scheme, truth is not checked by testing models against "reality", as reality is ultimately built-in as the object of the theory. Contrary to Menger, who had some deep interest in the *Psychè*, Mises denies the study of the "mind" any interest in the realm of his science (praxeology). But, in accordance to Menger then, we can see that psychology comes as no basis for economics. Contrary to Menger again, however, the idea of some given principle with a given content consistent for one whole-encompassing theory of the social sphere is posed. Moreover, questions that "praxeology" does not answer are simply discarded as questions which cannot be decided within any science (of social phenomena) worth of that name, but which depend upon beliefs always taken otherwise from whatever tradition or system of creed according to culture. The idea that the only universal axiom that remains true whatever the culture at stake is that men do act and act towards each other, given their needs, time, ignorance, etc., that which excludes psychology from the start.

In the case of Hayek, on the contrary, psychology plays a major role in his views on the world. As is well-known, Hayek even proposes a surprising and

---

260 They were in Menger too, as *nonsense in theory*, although not in history, etc. Frey and Benz remind us [2004, p. 65] that the question could also be raised about *markets when they are considered as ontological wholes* (as some heirs of Menger's tended to do). That may paradoxically remind us of such *Kollektivbegriffe*, like the *Volk* that Menger first denounced.

261 Mises writes, for example, that if metaphysicians have never succeeded in solving the "mind-body" problem (I,6: *Alter ego*), then one will be better off accepting the kind of linkage that we all necessarily assume in order to act at all (basing our own actions and anticipating those of others upon this principle).

innovative "renewal" of the fundamentals of theoretical psychology in *The Sensory Order*, published at a time when, in the 1950's, cognitive psychology and incipient cybernetics were open breathtaking paths to knowledge, including consequences upon the science of economics. Interest in psychology that could be found in Menger was thus re-emerging in one of his most self-claimed heirs.

What nevertheless remained quite puzzling for many economists was how little economics were to be found in the book anyway. Hayek discussed issues with so in-depth, though, that that study was clearly at the core of his thought. Moreover, as Hayek explains in the first pages of his Preface, while a young student, he had much hesitated between the career of a psychologist and that of an economist. He was so deeply interested in psychology that he wrote an essay of which he said that he always kept in mind the main points, even so many years later, and finally published some of them in *The Sensory Order*. Was that away, or near, the Mengerian perspective that he would later claim?

As a matter of fact, Hayek suggests in his presentation – and the surprising lack of economics in *The Sensory Order*, on the one hand, and lack of psychological elements in his economics, on the other hand, also tend to prove – that it is same patterns that are at work, but at different levels which do not intersect in any probing way. Where one could demonstrate truths in one field, the elements of the other would but lead to confusion. Both domains remain thus separated in their founding elements, even though the same methodology could be at work in both: Hayek wrote that, confronted with the logical problems of methodology and epistemology of the social sciences, he turned again to theoretical psychology. Not in order to ground one science in the other, but rather because the parallel he saw could contribute to convey in both fields the form adequate to represent the order which he called catallaxy.[262]

One cannot here be definitive on the inheritance of Menger's views concerning the role of psychology within economics, one must also add that the traditional question asked by Hayek later on ("what is mind"?, even the title of Chapter 1 of *The Sensory Order*), had simply no answer in economics – simply because economics does not recognize in it a question of its own. Neither the old debate of a philosophical tradition (the "mind-body dualism problem" – precisely that which Mises meant to preventively get rid of), nor the evolution in studies in psychology which had considerably changed between Menger's times and the 1950's, make the psychological field a ground for economic analysis.

---

[262] Its study does not belong here, but let it be said that even in the paragraph where he deals with the classification of sciences, Hayek concludes with the peculiarity of the finite mind as intrinsically implying that it is impossible to understand from one level, the next level of complexity. The systematic view adopted by Hayek, made of many layers, is well-known. See *The Sensory Order*, § 8.87 to the end. Commentators held the same view: see *below*.

Rather the contrary: in the economics of the 20th century, neo-classical thought conscientiously kept away from psychology until recently. [263] Austrian economics would rather be distinct because, at least Menger and Hayek displayed interest, although severely separating the fields, for that discipline, with Hayek even taking part in the new path of cognitive sciences[264] – although he used some examples that had been known already to Menger in his times, regarding a tradition still infused by his readings as a student in the 1900's: Helmholtz, Wundt, James, Müller and Mach. Wundt, Helmholtz and Mach were characters of the Old Vienna. As to Hayek, his work in psychology meant that the direction initially present in Austria could still have developments, although it had been a road parallel to the Austrian school of economics, and not its own..

Hayek, not saying much at all about economics in *The Sensory Order*, is very clear about drawing upon this other tradition where, contrary to the names of James Mill and John Stuart Mill, quoted in the volume, that of Menger does not even show up. Neuronal issues are then interesting per se and even if one wants to draw parallels with his understanding of the market, Hayek is working away from the original Austrian line, maybe announcing future developments into evolutionary/cognitive fields require another kind of clarification.[265]

Conclusion

After many commentators, but basing himself on archives (which has to be stressed), the historian of marginal utility Emil Kauder (Kauder, 1957) had

---

[263] Much later, the question has often risen again, last in Kahnemann and Tversky, for example, through observing anomalies in the behavioral patterns of the economic agents, and accounting for ignorance and time in individual action, along Menger's teachings. What is seemingly new has roots worth exhibiting when issues emerge again, roots that may provide solutions to questions of "inspirational psychology in economics". The reader may especially refer to Kahnemann and Tversky's famous works (especially since the Nobel prize) where they meant to explain how possibly expected utility maximization appeared violated – some cases as "sunk costs" being easily explained, others like "preference reversal" along different given framings were less easily so (they compelled the economists to explain the agent's inner "processing" of the information received, while not calling that agent "irrational". One key lies in the many ways in which information can be given by the markets.

[264] History of psychological thought would here be as useful as history of economic thought– in an interdisciplinary work that is indispensable.

[265] The Austrian School, as initiated by Carl Menger was our concern in those pages, and not the work of Hayek; therefore, we shall not question further whether Hayek's late attempts forged another new "Psychological" School in the realm of Economics based on his insights in theoretical psychology. The reader may want to read more upon that in the following two articles, among others: Smith, Barry, « The Connectionist Mind: A Study of Hayekian Psychology » in Frowen S.F. (ed.), 1997 *Hayek, Economist and Social Philosopher: A Critical Retrospect*, London: Macmillan, p. 9-29; Tuerck, David, 1995, "Economics as Mechanism: The Mind as Machine" in Hayek's *Sensory Order*"in *Constitutional Political Economy*, 6, p. 281-292.

shown that an Aristotelian view was underlying parts of Menger's framework. It was the case with the study of *psyche*. The more classic understanding of the mind was all the more consistent with Menger's theory of value that he rebuked both utilitarianism and hedonism. Those modern stands were not solid grounds upon which pure economics could grow and it was not up to psychology to orientate research in the social field. Not more than history. As Weber later explained, such fields may seem to bear similar concepts, but none of them could ever give the other its essential basis. The 1900's were one of the most adequate period to observe the consequences of the growing influence of psychology upon new economics, which, in the German-speaking world, meant Menger's *Grundsätze* (*Principles of Economics*-1871) and *Untersuchungen* (*Investigations in the Method of Social Sciences*-1883) with the subsequent *Methodenstreit*. Economics had to be defended in its own name, and was not a mere interpretation of a psychological kind. More than strategy in Academia, however, the status of science itself was at stake in accepting or rebuking the denomination of "Psychological school" (*Psychologenschule*).

This chapter has demonstrated that the Mengerian tradition was not to ground economics in a Law of psychology. In a sense, that was, on the contrary, what some classics, as well as a pre-marginalist like Gossen had done, and what Menger condemned in both cases as we have shown. The immediate subsequent tradition had been keen on finding similarities between theoretical foundations of the Austrian school and contemporary psychological theories to show its divergence from the Historical school, but that was not properly justified in Menger's reasoning. When, later, in the 1950's, Hayek took a cognitive approach in his atypical book, *The Sensory Order. An Inquiry into the Foundations of Theoretical Psychology* (1952), he directly linked it to Austrian origins but dealt completely separately with psychology and with economics, although he would see analogue patterns.

Psychological contents, which are truly present in the interest of the founder of the Austrian School, had been extrapolated by the early commentators and more careful readers like Weber, or heirs of the Austrian school were to denounce the confusion and advocate, like Weber a "*strenge Trennung*" of basic psychology and marginal utility theory (*Grenznutzlehre*).

To put it in a nutshell, economic theory cannot lie on empirical laws. It has its own concepts. It does not need to borrow them from the field of psychology. Last, a theory fit for economics needs to be severed from any other discipline's theory, especially if fundamentally experimental, in order to grow on its own soil. Therefore, and despite claims from a number of academics in Menger's times, and even though his analysis was centered around the individual agent as such, the founder of the Austrian school did not regard his work as psychologically grounded.

In the profession of economics, there was recently a surge and a revival of themes linking psychology and economics. On the one hand, they were mostly based upon the observation of big gaps within the analysis framework of the agent, especially in econometric models (however mathematically refined). On the other hand, impressive results that cognitive sciences have yielded in fields that may be connected with economic issues had to be acknowledged. It is not here the place to discuss whether those are along the same lines anticipated by Hayek in 1952 – but is there any link to be made further with Menger's ideas?

In the Vienna of the 1900's, theories were flourishing and there were enough to provide ideas for the whole next century – and even for our new 21st century maybe. But that is perhaps one more good reason to untangle the concepts at stake; and not to mistake Menger's endeavours with others that he knew of and respected, but did not espouse. Some claims apparently justified may be ill-founded when looked at more in-depth. Conversely, some acts of reluctance deserve explanation, especially by the philosopher with epistemological attention to the relationship between economics and psychology. Especially as today's cognitive sciences may induce some "imperialistic" claims that may be of the kind that caused the forging of the "*Psychologenschule*" denomination. But this is again another story.[266]

[266] As a matter of fact, many stories are entangled here. Let us mention only one: the debate over *qualia*, among others, has shown how philosophers, economists and cognitivists were interested in some common interdisciplinary research. It may appear only related to economics from far, but the debate was in fact intense.Less hot than ten years ago, the debate is still going on along some lines initiated by Daniel Dennett (*Consciousness Explained*, London, Penguin, 1991) and David Chalmers (*The Conscious Mind*, Oxford UP, 1996) among others.

Cardinality or ordinality in Menger's framework

Pierre Livet

1. Introduction

Usually commentators of Menger assume that when he defines the relative value of some good or the rate of exchange between supply and demand, he needs cardinal notions (for example, this is the case of the translator of the *Grundsätze* in English, who adds explicit notes about cardinality). I want to show that Menger has mainly in mind an ordinal framework, and that the assertions of *Grundsätze der Volkwirtschaftslehre* that seem to imply the use of cardinality could have a better explanation if we take them as having an ordinal one. In this sense Menger's approach of exchange value would be closer from the ordinal notions used in Arrow and Debreu's theorem about general equilibrium. On the other side, Menger was opposed to the project of the computation of a general equilibrium. He invoked the quasi-infinite variety and variation of subjective motivations. But at the same time, his notion of value based on an order is a combination of subjective evaluation – the successive degrees of satisfaction that the consumption of additional amounts of the same good provides- and of quasi-naturalistic dependence – the dependence of goods of first order upon the availability of goods of second order. As a consequence, his use of order instead of real cardinality has two faces: on one side, his preference for using formally weaker notions, suspecting computations, paying attention to qualitative aspects, and, on the other side, his reference to the natural structure of human needs. One face is relativist, or better relationalist, if we may say; the other seems reminiscent of an Aristotelian perspective. Our claim is that Menger is an ordinalist, but he is one in a complex sense which combines modernist and conservative aspects.

2. An ordinal presentation of Menger's theory

First let us remember the ordinal flavour of the basis of Menger's theory of economics. Menger begins with the distinction between goods of first order and goods of second order. Goods of first order are goods that can immediately satisfy our needs, for example, bread. Goods of second order are the ones that are needed in order to immediately produce goods of first order, for example, flour, salt, fuel, water, and labour. In the same way, goods of third order are the ones that are needed in order to immediately produce goods of second order, for example, grain mills, wheat, different labour services; goods of fourth order are in this example fields, instruments for their cultivation, labour services of farmers.

Two principles are satisfied in building this ordering. First, goods of first order can be consumed for the immediate satisfaction of the consumers, and second, there is a direct causal connexion of production between order n+1 and order n. This requirement ensures that items belonging to two different levels of order cannot be mixed. They are always separated by the causal connexion paths.

A third requirement is expressed: the elements of one level of order can be gathered in different sets, each of them assembling the elements the conjunction of which is necessary for one element of the lower order. For example flour, an element of second order with respect to bread, requires wheat, grain mill, and a specific labour. As the absence of one the conjuncts is sufficient for the good of lower order not to be produced, from each element of the lower order we have a one-to-many correspondence to the elements of the higher order, and this implies that the transition from higher to lower order implies a fusion of one set of elements of the higher order into one element of the lower order, so that the distinction between the two orders is a strong one. This gives rise to a ranked structure, in which ranks are strongly separate levels.

Nevertheless, this ranked structure may differentiate goods that could be considered otherwise as similar but are not introduced at the same level in the causal paths leading to the first order good. For example, cutting the wood can be a labour and cut wood a good of third order for making bread (if wood is needed to bake the flour) but it could be a good of sixth order (or even higher one) when used for making the iron bar that will be used for a ploughshare, which will be used for cultivating wheat, which will be used for flour, which will be used for making bread; or a good of second order if we use it to make a fire to warm us.

But according to Menger, the economical value of the two pieces of wood depends on the value either of baking the flour, or of the ploughshare, which depends eventually on need for bread or for product of cultivation, or of the need for warmth. Three different causal paths imply three different ranked structures and could lead to three different values. The global structure for one first order good is one of a tree in which similar goods can occur at different ranks in different branches. The global structure for the different first order goods could be a network of possible causal links in which each producer has to choose what tree to carve out by cutting some links of the network.

Menger uses other notions of order in his famous table of the theory of value (p. 93 in the German edition, 127 in the American-English translation, reproduced here. Also see Annex 1 at the end of the present volume).

I	II	III	IV	V	VI	VII	VIII	IX	X
10	9	8	7	6	5	4	3	2	1
9	8	7	6	5	4	3	2	1	0
8	7	6	5	4	3	2	1	0	
7	6	5	4	3	2	1	0		
6	5	4	3	2	1	0			
5	4	3	2	1	0				
4	3	2	1	0					
3	2	1	0						
2	1	0							
1	0								
0									

Here two orders are needed, an order of degrees of satisfaction, and an order of importance between the different goods. (The previous order cannot be used to say that bread is more important than flour; it could only be used to say that wood is not so important than flour, because fuel could be substituted to wood; but the order between different goods of first order has still to be specified). Our satisfaction when satisfying our greatest need (food, Menger assumes) by consuming the first unities of the relevant good is higher than our satisfaction when this need is already partially fulfilled and we go on consuming the same kind of good, and so on and so forth. This gives us decreasing degrees of satisfaction.

There is a relation between the two orders: Menger makes the hypothesis that goods of lesser importance (in his example, tobacco, to which he assigns an order of fifth importance) cannot give us the same level of satisfaction than goods of first importance. The first units of a good of second importance give us a level of satisfaction that is lower than the level given by the first units of the good of first importance. In the same way, the first unities of a good of third importance give us a level of satisfaction that is lower than the level of satisfaction than the one given to us by the first units of a good of second importance. Similarly, the second units of a good of first importance give us a level of satisfaction that is lower than the one given by the first units of this good, but higher than the level of satisfaction given by the second units of a good of second importance, and so on and so forth. According to Menger, when my need of first importance (food) is satisfied enough, I can either choose to go on consuming an additional unity of this good, decreasing my degree of satisfaction, or to shift to a good of second importance. As I have the two needs (in order) I have at some step to choose to satisfy my second order need. If I am rational, I shift to the good of lesser importance as soon as the consumption of an additional unit of the good of first importance would give me a lower degree of pleasure than the one given by the consumption of the former good.

This kind of order of degrees of satisfaction appended to a type of good is used again for reasoning about exchange. In a new table, Menger assumes that for a man who has 6 cows and one horse, the first horse does not give a degree of satisfaction lower that the one given by the first cow, and the second one would not give not a degree of satisfaction lower than the one of the second cow (similarly, mutatis mutandis, for a man who has one cow and six horses). Menger considers successively all the possible exchanges. There is a limit in this process beyond which the exchange is not to the mutual economic advantage of the two persons. "This limit is reached when one of the two bargainers has no further quantity of goods which is of less value to him than a quantity of another good at the disposal of the second bargainer who, at the same time, evaluates the two quantities of goods inversely"(167-169; 187). So for example when the man with 6 cows and one horse has exchanged three cows and gained three horses, an additional horse would give him his fourth degree of satisfaction (with respect to horses), but the lost cow would also deprive him from his fourth degree of satisfaction (with respect to cows). If we assume that the fourth degree of satisfaction related to the cows is not lower that the fourth degree of satisfaction related to the horses, then our man would not make any progress in his degrees of satisfaction by this additional exchange. Here is the limit beyond which the exchange would not be to the mutual economical advantage of the two persons (provided we can make a symmetrical reasoning for the man with one cow and six horses).

Menger makes a last use of similar orders when dealing with the price of horses and bushels of grain in trade between a monopolist who offers horses and two competitors who offer bushels of grain (181-187, 199-201). The first competitor is supposed to get from the first horse exchanged a higher degree of satisfaction than the second competitor. The degree of satisfaction given by one horse to the second competitor is supposed to be not lower than the second degree of satisfaction of the first competitor. The degree of satisfaction given by one horse to the first competitor is not lower than the one given to him by 80 bushels of grain (he has plenty of grain, so he needs a great increasing in his amount of grain in order to shift from one degree of satisfaction to a higher one). The degree of satisfaction of one horse is not lower for the second competitor than the one given to him by 30 bushels of grain.

Here, the same kind of reasoning than the one about the bargaining leads to the conclusion that the first competitor has better to exclude the second one from the market by buying horses as long as the degree of satisfaction that an additional horse gives to him is no lower than the degree of satisfaction that 30 bushels of grain would give to him. But this process gives not an equilibrium price. It only gives two limits between which the exchange would be to the economical advantage of the two traders (80 bushels and 30 bushels). Then Menger adds new competitors, with the effect that other traders make exchanges because their need of grain is lower that the one of the second competitor, but higher than the one of the first, or conversely for their need of a horse, and that the interval between the limits is reduced. No equilibrium price is fixed, but oscillations of price are constrained. But these limits need not to be defined in a cardinal way. They are just thresholds between which the relevant relations "no lower than the degree of satisfaction given by ...." are still valid.

Please notice that in this presentation of the different Menger's tables I did not have to use notions implying cardinality. Everything has been expressed in an ordinal framework, using relations like "no lower than". The consequence is that in an exchange between two people the ratio of the two goods exchanged is peculiar to this particular exchange at this place at this moment in the history of the two people, and that the ratio of several goods in an exchange between several suppliers and demanders (the price) depends on the peculiar configuration of the histories of the different people – and of the histories of production of each good, as consumers and producers have to value the goods of second, third, and higher order involved in their goods of first order (horse and cows are supposed to be at least second order goods). As nothing prevents the consumers' degree of satisfaction to be sensitive to the peculiar history of the other people, or of the production of the goods, the relation between the different scales of degrees of satisfaction might be changed in this way, so that a general equilibrium is out of reach.

But this reconstruction of Menger's theory has shown that his conceptual framework does not need any use of cardinality, and that the ordinal relation (mainly "not lower than") is sufficient for establishing his conclusions.

3. Menger's cardinal expressions

Of course, Menger does not restrict himself to such an ordinal vocabulary. In this second part, we have to take into account the passages in which Menger uses expressions that seem to imply cardinality.

The first point is that in the table of the theory of value, Menger begins by assigning numbers that can be considered only as ordinal numbers, from the best degree of satisfaction to the lowest one, for the good of first importance, but goes on assigning the very same numbers to the degrees of satisfaction of the goods of second, third order, and so on and so forth. In this way, the first degree of satisfaction of the good of first importance has rank 10, the first degree of satisfaction of the good of second importance has rank 9, and so on. Similarly, the second degree of satisfaction of the good of first importance has rank 9, which is the same figure than the one of the first degree of satisfaction of the good of second importance, and so on and so forth. In this way, the diagonals of the table are lines made of the same figures (two 9, then three 8, then four 7, etc.). As long as we take these figures just as symbols for the degree of satisfaction in each domain (degree of satisfaction in the domain of the good of first importance, distinct from degrees of satisfaction in the domain of the good of second importance, etc.) our ordinal framework is saved. But if we identify two identical figures in two different rows – that is, for two goods of different importance- we seems to belief that these two degrees of satisfaction are the very same one for the two goods. This is a step towards cardinality. And really Menger says that "consumption of tobacco begins to have the same importance (dieselbe Bedeutung) to him as further satisfaction of his need for food" (s.94, p.127). But this is still compatible with ordinality: two different goods could give two degree of satisfaction between which we are indifferent. What is required by Menger's table is only that for all the goods in the table and all the degree of comparison, we have no case of non comparability. The structure is one of an order, and not the one of a pre-order.

In order for cardinality to be needed, we have to require that it is possible to compare a difference between degree a and degree b with a difference between degree c and degree d, or that it is possible to add products of a degree a by a scalar h and product of degree b by a scalar k. The English translation seems to imply such comparison. People "*weigh* especially the relative importance of the separate acts leading to the more or less complete satisfaction of each need", so is the translation, and it goes on: "they are finally guided by the results of this *comparison* into activities directed to the fullest possible satisfaction of their needs" (p.128, italics are mine). If we combine comparison and weighing, we might interpret "weighing" as making the product of a consumed unity of good by a factor of satisfaction, and cardinality is lurking here. But Menger is only asking:

> "wie die Individuen die Bedeutung der Befriedigung ihrer verschiedenen Bedürfnisse... gegen einander *abwägen*, und sich schliesslich von dem Resultate dieser *Prüfung* in der auf die möglichst vollständige Befriediegung ihrer Bedürfnisse gerichteten Thätigkeit (Wirthschaft) bestimmen lassen" (S. 94, italics are mine).

The word „Abwägen" does not necessarily imply a product, but only a careful examination and comparison, and „Prüfung" is not a comparison, but only an examination. Each of these two operations can be done in an ordinal way.

In the same way, we have the temptation to interpret the Robinson Crusoe example of pages 99 and followings (133 and followings) as an example of non linearity of the function of satisfaction. Robinson needs only (a) one unit of water daily for the maintenance of his life, (b) nineteen units for the animals whose milk and meat provide him with the most necessary means of subsistence, (c) forty units for his health, for cleaning his body and his cloths, and for the support of some additional animals whose milk and meat he finds needful and finally (d) forty additional units for pleasure (like flower garden). The sum is 100 units. As if the spring providing water becomes partially exhausted and Robinson has only 90 units of water only, each of his left units has the value of the lost units, each of these 100 units has only the value of the last forty units (the rather superfluous ones). But if the spring is further exhausted, and gives only 20 units, one unit more lost would deprive him from his good of second importance, so that each of these 20 units has the value of this kind of good. The process is not linear. But contrary to the continuity assumption of the classical marginalism, the process is not continuous, because each good of different importance is satisfied only if a threshold is reached. Introducing degrees of satisfaction for each good would reintroduce only an apparent continuity, because degrees of satisfaction are still discrete. This is due to the fact that Menger only needs an ordinal perspective.

Other pages seem to imply a cardinal perspective. In pages 118-119, Menger examines the possibility of substituting to a good of second (or more) order (a good needed for the production of a first order good) another good of second order, but with the consequence that the quality of the final good will decrease. He says that "the value of a unit of the goods of superior quality is equal to the importance of the least important satisfaction that is provided for by the goods of superior quality minus a value quota that is greater: (1) the smaller the value of the goods of inferior quality by which the particular need in question can also be satisfied, and (2) the smaller the difference to men between the importance of satisfying the particular need with the superior good and the importance of satisfying it with the inferior one" (144-145 of the translation). Here, according to the second condition, we take into account the difference between two importances, we transform this difference into its inverse (the greater the difference, the smaller the inverse), and we substract this inverse of a difference between two importances to another importance. This seems to require a cardinal framework, as the note of the translator suggests.

But what is Menger's aim in imagining this device? As shown in pages 141 and 142, he contests that "when the diminution of the available quantity of a good of higher order is not a decrease in the quantity of product but a worsening of its quality", the value of a given quantity of this good would have to be estimated through the satisfactions provided by the *whole* product – which has been produced by a combination of a highly qualified good and a less qualified one. On the contrary, this value has to be related only "to the difference in importance (Bedeutung) between the satisfactions that can be achieved with the more highly qualified product and those that can be achieved with the less qualified product", that is the difference of importance between "the importance of the satisfactions provided for by the portion of the product that would remain unproduced if we were not in a position to command the given quantity of the good of higher order" and the importance of the product that would be produced by another less qualified mean (p.164 in the translation). But nothing prevents this difference between the importance of the two kinds of satisfaction from remaining a difference of ranks.

Menger wants to save the difference of rank between the two goods of higher order even when they are used together for bringing forth a product. But he has to take also into account the fact that the goods of higher quality can be replaced by the goods of lower quality in order to produce the good for consumption. This possibility of substitution is a challenge to the higher rank of the goods of higher quality. If something can be substituted to another one, the two things cannot be really of different ranks. Therefore if these goods of supposed higher quality can be replaced, their rank has to be decreased (first condition). But on the contrary, if the difference between the importance of the satisfaction of the need with the superior good is much higher than the importance of the satisfaction of the need with the inferior one, the difference of rank has to be maintained (this is the converse of condition 2, expressed in the vocabulary of pages 141 and 142). How to combine exactly this decreasing of rank and the resisting move of the converse of condition 2 is not specified by Menger. If he would have made his reasoning in a cardinal framework, he would have given the precise procedure. Notice that his two conditions are not independent, as the second one makes reference to the importance of the satisfaction with the inferior good, and the first one to the value of the goods of inferior quality, which depends of this very degree of satisfaction. In a cardinal framework, this ambiguity would have to be solved. But as his reasoning is a reasoning about a difference of rank, Menger has just to indicate the constraints that a shift of rank has to take into account, and not to specify the computational procedure (many procedures could be used here for changing ranks, but each has non natural aspects and remains a convention).

In another place, Menger uses a cardinal vocabulary. In a note p. 158, he defines the conditions of exchange in the following way: "let the quantity of the first good in A's possession be 10a, and let the quantity of the second good in B's possession be 10b. Assume the value of the quantity 1a to A to be W, the value of 1b to A if he should obtain command of it to be W+x, the value of 1b to B to be w, and the value of 1a to B if he should obtain command of it to be w+y. It is evident that A would gain a value of x and that B would gain a value of y from a transfer of 1a from A's possession to B's and 1b from B's possession to A's" (p. 179 in the translation). Here, Menger seems to add explicitly two values (W and x, w and y) in a cardinal way. But notice that the quantity that he adds are specific to each partner of the exchange. W is dedicated to A, as well as x. Y is dedicated to B, as well as w. Therefore, x is an addition in the scale of value of A, and y is an addition only in the scale of value of B. The whole thing boils down that by getting 1b A gets an increase in his ranking scale of value, and by getting 1a B gets an increase in his ranking value. The "quantities" x and y can be reduced to getting a higher rank in value for each partner.

Another note of Menger is ambiguous. In page 168, when explaining the figures of the table of the exchange, he says:

> "I need hardly point out that the figures in the text are not intended to express numerically the absolute but merely relative magnitudes of importance of the satisfactions in question. Thus when I designate the importance of two satisfactions with 40 and 20 for example, I am merely saying that the first of the two satisfactions has twice the importance of the second to the economizing individual concerned" (p. 183 in the translation).

This passage can be interpreted in two ways. First, Menger is using figures for cardinal quantities, but not for their absolute quantities, only for their relatives magnitudes, that is, he is using numbers as ratios between magnitudes. The figure "40" is only saying that the magnitude is twice bigger than the magnitude designed by "20". This multiplicative interpretation is strengthened by the fact that Menger a bit later says that "a cow has a value of only 10 to B while an additional horse would have a value of 30 (*three times* the value of a cow)" 164, 184, italics are mine). But just after he uses a strange periphrase if he has in mind cardinal notions: 'it can be seen that each of the two persons derived an economic gain that is *no less than if (zwar kein geringerer zugewachsen ist, als wenn)* their wealth (ihr Vermögen) had been increased by a good valued at 20" (as they gain a good that has the value of 30 while exchanging a good that had a value of 10) (p. 165, 185).

Apparently, Menger takes care of using cardinal notions in an "as if" manner, and his guarantee that the figures that he uses are not devoid of meaning is the ordinal relation "not less than". If we follow the reasoning about exchange, we can obtain the same result without using at any moment the cardinal relations between 10, 20, 30, 40, 50. We can take them as ranks (50 = rank 1rst, 40 = rank 2d, and so on). The fact that 40 is twice as big as 20 is not the interesting fact. The relevant property is that 40 has the rank above 30, and 30 the rank above 20. When Menger says that "the first of the two satisfactions has *twice* the importance of the second", what he says boils down to say that we need to decrease the importance by two ranks for passing from the rank figured by 40 to the rank figured by 20, because we have to pass through the rank figured by 30.

4. Ordinality as explanation of strange Mengerian moves

If Menger would have seriously taken for granted the cardinal property of his exchange tables, he would not have to make the rather strange move that he does. After the second exchange, it is evident from cardinal computation that the "economic positions of the two men would not be neither injured nor improved by a third exchange" (p. 165, 185), and would be damaged by a fourth one. The man who had at the beginning one horse and six cows would exchange a cow the value of which is figured by the rank assigned to 20 (the fourth rank, as rank one is 50) for a horse the value of which would be figured by the rank assigned to 20, and symmetrically for the man who had at first six horses and one cow. But Menger goes on, and gives us the table resulting from a fifth exchange and from a sixth one. Why? Apparently Menger wants to be sure that the fact that the third move is indifferent for the two partners is not due to a contingent equality between 20 in the scale for cows and 20 in the scale for horses. As he has said in the note p. 163, what he takes for validation are the relations of decreasing and increasing ranks. The optimum is not defined on a cardinal scale that would be supposed to be taken as given. It cannot be ascertained but by the fact that before this step, the ranks are always increasing, and after this step, the ranks are always decreasing. And in order to be sure of that, we have to follow each steps until we reach an end, for otherwise we could not ascertain that there were no further increase. If Menger had a cardinal framework in mind, he could have followed the whole process, but then he would have to compare the global results of each steps in order to check whether one of them was given the maximum value. On the contrary, he makes only local comparisons, always using his periphrastic way of expression:

> "seine ökonomische Lage nach diesem Tausche *ist demnach keine andere, als wäre* ein Gut von einem Werthe gleich 20 ohne jede Gegenleistung seinem Vermögen entzogen worden" (p. 166 italics are mine; the translation, as usual, has a more cardinal flavour: "is exactly the same as").

As Menger was a careful reader of Aristotle, it is possible that he had here in mind the passage of *Nicomachean Ethics*, V, 1333b in which Aristotle thinks to refute precisely this kind of step by step determination of the price in an exchange. As we know, Aristotle claims that we have to know in advance what is the right ratio between the two goods to exchange (in his example, a shoe and an house, or a shoe and a bushel of grain). His analysis of exchange has to be understood in a larger context. He wants to show that for finding justice, we have to know in advance the ratios between the qualities and values of the persons (and not only of the goods and deeds). For him, the best situation for finding justice is the context of distributive justice, in which we have precisely to know the qualities of the persons in order determine how to make the distribution. Then follows the corrective justice, which has, in order to get results, to make the hypothesis that in the beginning, the situations and goods of the two people (the victim and the thief, for example) were equal. The commutative justice, the justice of exchange, is in an even worse condition, because by definition, the starting positions of the two people are heterogeneous, as this heterogeneity is the source of the motivation for the exchange. The qualities of the persons are not only their qualities as isolated individuals, but their qualities relative to the motivations of the other. Aristotle argues in order to show that it is impossible to learn those qualities by the very process of the exchange. We cannot learn what the right ratio is by trying to make increasing or decreasing offers, by a process of excess and default. What Aristotle says is that if we do not know in advance the right ratio, then one of the two extremes (the two partners) will have both the excesses. What Aristotle takes as a demonstration of this claim is apparently the following reasoning. Suppose that we do not know the right ratio. The architect has one house, but no pair of shoes, and the shoemaker has, say, 20 pairs of shoes. A step by step exchange cannot be but unit by unit. After the first exchange, the architect has no house, one pair of shoes, and the shoemaker as 19 pairs of shoes and a house. Of course, the architect is not satisfied, so the exchange goes on. But consider the situation after this first step. Does it means that the value of one house is one pair of shoes, and symmetrically? No, it means only that if the partners extract the value of a house and a pair of shoes from this step of the exchange, the excess for the shoemaker is X-(20-1 pair of shoes) if the value of the house is X. Suppose that X= 20. Then at this step, the shoemaker has 20- 1= 19 pairs of shoes, plus a house, the value of which is supposed to be 20 pairs Therefore he has "twice the excess" as he has one house, minus one pair of shoes (corresponding to a balance of the benefit of the house and the loss of 1 pair of shoes, getting a result of 19 pairs of shoes) and 19 pairs of shoes. If X differs from the stock of shoes of the shoemaker, we have to reduce our reasoning to a stock equivalent to X. Now suppose that the shoemaker gives one more pair of shoe. Then the same reasoning applies, and the fortunate shoemaker has always twice the excess, because he has a house minus two pairs of shoes (say 18 pairs), and 18 pairs of shoes. Now let us assume that we not know in advance what the right ratio is, what X is. When the shoemaker will give all his shoes for the house, the apparent excess will be reduced to zero (and "twice the excess" is always valid, as 0 multiplied by 2 is 0). But as we do not know whether the whole set of shoes is sufficient for the house, we would not have any clue about the right ratio No step of the bargaining exchange could reveal us what it is, as we know that at each step, one of the partners has twice the excess with respect to the right price.

This reasoning of Aristotle leans on a progression in which one partner has always twice more than the other. Of course, if the progression had an end, at this end twice 0 will be equal to 0, and then, retrospectively, we could estimate what would be the functions which guides the change of the offered and the required price. But if we have no end, we could not say that the zero excess is the equilibrium or twice the excess again. In order to escape from this monotonically decreasing progression, Menger needed a non monotonic evolution. He has discovered such a reversal between an increasing evolution and a decreasing evolution, which is perfectly compatible with the monotonic progression of Aristotle. Then a step by step determination of the price becomes possible without knowing in advance the right ratio. But as we are not supposed to know in advance this ratio (as Aristotle's reasoning is supposed to have convinced us), we have to check that all along the progression we will not put into question the salient singularity of this reversal between an increasing and a decreasing in value.

One last confirmation that Menger, even when he uses cardinal expressions, has in mind an essentially ordinal framework, is given by his treatment of the transition from an exchange between a monopolist and different competitors to an exchange under bilateral competition both between sellers and between buyers. We have already seen how the ratio of exchange between the monopolist and different buyers depends on the different structures of ranks that are the ones of the different buyers in competition. Menger claims that;

> "whether a given quantity of a commodity is sold by a monopolist of by several competitors in supply,..., the effect on price formation and on the resultant distribution of the commodity among the competing buyers is exactly the same" (S. 204-205, p.219).

The competition in supply has nevertheless some effect: the suppliers cannot destroy a part of the good in order for the prices to grow, or restrict the production to the same effect. The overall effect of a competition between producers is then to increase the global quantity of the products (S. 210, p. 223). This asymmetry between sellers and buyers is a bit surprising. Of course, it is tempered by the fact that in order for the exchange to be possible, the seller has a lesser advantage to keep his last horse than to exchange it for a given amount of bushels of grain. But this fact has nothing to do with the competition between the sellers, only with the relation between the scales of value of sellers and the ones of the buyers.

Let us take Menger's example. Suppose that we have two sellers and three buyers. One of the buyer assigns a very low rank to a bushel of grain (as he has plenty of them), the second a higher rank, and the third a still higher rank. The second sellers has a bigger need of bushels of grain that the first, but also gives a higher value to his own horses, the first seller has three horses to sell, and the second two horses. There are possible structures of the different scales of value in which the first buyer buys one horse to the first seller, he and the second buyer buy two horses to the second seller, and the third buys no horse. Maybe it would be more advantageous for the first seller to decrease his price in order for the first buyer to buy him two horses, and the second buyer one. Even if the first buyer makes a worse exchange on each horse, on the three horses he would make a better gain. But this kind of reasoning, in Menger's framework, requires real cardinality, as we exchange a decrease in ranks for an increase in total gain.

Apparently, Menger refused to makes that move, and he refused, in the same way, to degrade a ranked value in order to get a better sum.

5. Conclusion: the significance of Menger's "ordinalism"

What is at stake here is the significance that this "ordinalism" has in Menger's framework. It does not seem to be reducible to formal considerations of simplicity, the ordinal relations being less axiomatically demanding than the cardinal ones. We have shown that Menger manages always to stay inside the limits of an ordinal framework at least for the content of his thought, but we have also seen that he is not reluctant to use expressions that might imply cardinality. We might use a counterfactual hypothesis in order to question the limits that Menger's "naturalism" would have put to the extension of his ordinalism. Would have Menger accepted a strategic determination of the ranked structure of economical value? He has made the step towards the relativity of the economical value of a good for one agent to the economical value of this good for another agent in an exchange between two agents and two goods. He has made the move towards the relativity of the economical value of a good for an agent to the economical value that would result from different exchanges with different agents, given their supposed scales of value. Would have he also made the move to the relativity of the economical value to the strategic moves of the agents? Apparently this move has been made by the Arrow-Debreu's notion of an abstract economy as a generalisation of the notion of a game in Nash's perspective. Then the way is opened for a strategic change of the order between goods as revealed by the exchange when this change gives to the agent the possibility of a more satisfying exchange not in the terms of his initial order but in the terms of the exchange strategically revised order. The naturalistic flavour of Menger's thought might have been an obstacle to this purely strategic and interactive notion of value, letting aside Menger's refusal of the very idea of the possibility of computing a general equilibrium.

For sure, Walras, who believes in this possibility, takes a cardinalist perspective but would also refuse the notion of such a strategical value. Here the cardinalist perspective makes us able to dispense with the question of how the demand and the supply scales of goods are determined. We have only to check whether a general equilibrium is possible. If on the contrary we try, as Menger did, to say how each agent determines his proposal in the exchange, then we are led to ask the question about how the perspective of the exchange could reveal an order of the agent which is dependent of the peculiar strategic situation of the exchange. Cardinality may mask the problem, because as we suppose that the utility function of each agent has a common measure with the utility function of each other agent, we have not to bother too much with the difference of perspective between the isolated order of the agent and his exchange order, as any order is commensurable with any other one. The problem becomes striking only when we have to tell how an order can be changed –without having the possibility of making direct inter-comparisons between the values as determined in accordance with each order. Justifying change of the order of the evaluation scale is a much more difficult problem in an ordinal perspective than in a cardinal one.

This kind of problem was not evoked in Menger's time. Ordinal perspective seemed to imply some kind of stability, while cardinal perspective was designed to compute changes. Menger wants to save the idea that in a framework in which the economical value is relative, the scale of value of each agent is dependent on his order of needs. And if he asserts repeatedly that value is subjective, orders of needs are really limited (even if not quite determined) by natural constraints, as the ones of the causal connexions that make the difference between goods of first order and goods of higher order. Subjectivism is limited by the natural connexions between the needs. The economical values are relative, but the orders themselves are not relative. In the same way, different incarnations of money have different ranks in the marketability order. Even if marketability is relative to the possibilities offered by specific markets, this order of marketability it not itself relative. It seems that Menger has kept from Aristotle the idea that some orders are more natural than some others, even if this "naturality" is relative to the context and the environment. In this respect, the "ordinalism" would not be mainly a consequence of a progressive orientation for ordinality as less demanding than cardinality, but mainly a consequence of his reluctance against the idea of a cardinal computation of a price equilibrium, and of his attachment to the idea that even if goods are subjectively appreciated, their order is submitted to constraints that are a mixture of naturality and cultural context.

Empirical studies and Mengerian methodology

Aurélien Lordon and Marc Ohana

Introduction

What strikes us when reading Carl Menger and his commentators is the diverse manners in which the commentators have analyzed his methodological work. The main cause of such a pluralism of views is the difficulty in apprehending the thought of Menger as it is presented in the Untersuchungen. Some researchers assert that Menger's writing constitutes an "epistemological obstacle" to his comprehension (Nadeau, forthcoming). Reviewers are notably divided on the question of the aim of empirical studies in Mengerian methodology. Some of them argue that he is a zealous defender of pure theoretical analysis in economics and an anti-empiricist, whereas others think that he leaves place for some empirical approaches in his work. Accordingly, the aim of this paper is precisely to investigate the place and the role that empirical methods have in a Mengerian perspective.

First, we will present the diversity of views about Menger's approach to empirical studies in the economic literature (section 1). Then, we will explain that if Menger has been considered an anti-empiricist by many authors, it is mainly because of his vehement critique of the German Historical School (GHS) during the Methodenstreit. This school is characterized by an empirical framework based on macroscopic data which contradicts the individualist Mengerian methodology (section 2). According to Menger, empirical macroscopic studies reveal only correlations and not laws. Whereas this kind of data is useless for the Mengerian "exact orientation of research", microscopic empirical studies seem to be more adequate: if they can't by themselves reveal the existence of economic *laws*, they are useful in finding universal economic *types* (section 3). The last part of the paper intends to determine which kind of microeconomic empirical studies has to be used according to Menger. We argue that qualitative studies are most suitable for this methodology (section 4).

1. The multiplicity of views about Mengerian methodology

Determining Menger's position on empiricism is not a straightforward task. Many economists have tried to give an adequate definition of his methodological point of view, but no consensus has been found. Menger himself answered such attempts: when Schmoller presented him as a pure deductivist (1883), he replied that it was a false statement as he perceived himself more as an adept of the *synthetic method.*[267] But the problem is far from being resolved, as the use of such an undefined term leaves the door open to many interpretations.

It's far from being easy to elucidate the position of Menger toward empiricism from the distinction he establishes in economics between the "empirical-realistic orientation of research" (*die exacte Richtung der Forschung*) and the "exact orientation of research" (*die realistisch-empirische Richtung der Forschung).* In fact, everybody agrees that empirical-realistic orientation lies at a more factual level and tends to show the existence of a correlation between observed events, whereas exact orientation is more theoretical and is the only way to discover the immutable laws of economics. But a problem remains: how does exact orientation work according to Menger? More precisely, do empirical studies play a part in this orientation of research? Critics are divided on that.

For some reviewers, there is no place for observations in the exact orientation of research. Gustav von Schmoller adheres to this conception when he presented Menger as a deductivist (1883). Geoffrey Hodgson (2001) also argues that Menger assigns a central role for deductive and abstract theory in economics. An empirical approach has no use in the exact orientation of research as "it cannot produce knowledge of the enduring and persisting elements" (Hodgson, 2001, p.80). Both Wade Hands (2001) and Robert Nadeau (*forthcoming*) define Menger as an apriorist. Nadeau contends that Menger is a defender of the hypothetico-deductive method and a radical opponent of induction. According to Hands, Menger adopts a deductive *a priori* approach in economics, though he is an adept of Aristotelian essentialist realism. Hands describes the standard interpretation of the *Methodenstreit* as follows:

> "Menger is viewed as a radical deductivist who wanted to deduce all of economic theory from a few basic propositions about economic behavior, while the German historical school is viewed as an equally radical, inductivist sect (…)." (Hands, 2001, p. 40)

Some authors go further and establish Menger as a precursor of Misesian praxeological method (Salerno, 1999, Smith, 1995). For Barry Smith, Menger's works rely upon non-Kantian *a priori*: the structures of the world can be grasped immediately, without observation, "in much the same way that we grasp the validity of a mathematical proof" (1995, p. 307). Smith argues that there is no need for experiments or inductive inferences in Mengerian methodology. Similarly, Max Alter argues that it could logically be deduced from Menger's works that he considers introspection as the only way to apprehend economic reality (1990, p.327).

---

[267] See Béraud, 2000, p. 306. Alain Béraud explains that Menger had mentioned in his personal copy of the book of Gustav von Schmoller (1883) that his methodology is not deductivist but synthetic. Béraud adds that this term means at this time an approach which allies induction and deduction.

Such a radical perception of Menger's works is not unanimously accepted however. For example, Böhm-Bawerk is very critical about the alleged Mengerian apriorism. He presents himself as a defender of the Mengerian "exact method", but specifies that it couldn't exactly be labeled an "abstract deductive method". In his opinion, the process that allows the discovery of laws requires some empirical observations:

> "The problems of political economy, from a technical point of view, fall into two classes. Upon those of one class the mark of the historical school is indelibly stamped. Nor would I proceed otherwise than by the historical-statistical method if I had to study, for example, the influence of retail trade upon price or the economic influence of the division of property in land. (...)With the second class of problems, however, the case is different. For them experience has already done all, or nearly all, that it can do. (...) The difficulty, and at the same time the scientific problem, is not in acquiring facts, but in mastering and correctly interpreting the facts long since acquired." (Böhm-Bawerk, 1890)

If apriorism can be used to solve some economic problems like the source of the value of goods, according to Böhm-Bawerk observation of facts proves to be essential to understand other economic phenomena. He affirms that this principle rises logically from the guiding principles of Mengerian methodology.

Mises himself shows the limits of Menger's influence on his works: "Menger was too much under the sway of John Stuart Mill's empiricism to carry his own point of view to its logical consequences." (Mises, 1969, p.12) He blames Menger for not being a pure apriorist as he himself is.

Some authors write that the goal of the *Untersuchungen* is not to discredit the use of empirical studies, but more to show the utility of theoretical analyses in social sciences (Pribram, 1986, Schumpeter, 1954). For them, Menger is neither a pure deductivist, nor an inductivist. Samuel Bostaph (1978) adds that the question of "induction versus deduction" was never really at issue during the *Methodenstreit*. In the same vein, Jack Birner explains that for Menger, "exact laws are not a priori truths, nor the result of conceptual analysis, nor are they empirical" (1990, p.251). He categorizes Menger as a justificationist-inductivist, but does not really specify the role of empirical studies in Menger's works.

Lastly, for many reviewers, the reason why Menger could not be defined as an apriorist is that in his methodology the simplest elements of economic reality – the types – are derived from empirical facts (Béraud, 2000, Bostaph, 1978, Mäki, 1997, Milford, 1990).

The divergence of opinions on this subject is therefore extensive. By presenting Mengerian methodology, we will show which conceptions are more relevant.

2. Menger's opposition to "macroscopic" empiricism

Menger's reaction against the GHS is probably the main reason why so many people consider him an anti-empiricist. It is well known that Menger wrote the *Untersuchungen*, in reaction to the theories of the GHS.[268] But fewer people are aware of the main point of the conflict. The *Methodenstreit* is in fact more an argument about "macroeconomic versus microeconomic" than about "induction versus deduction".

According to the GHS, a crucial characteristic of economic systems is that individuals do not care solely about their own interests, but also, and more essentially, about the general interest. The idea that humans accomplish what is required by society is so deeply embedded that, for the GHS, individual study in itself becomes useless. Just as the parts of the human body act for the whole organism, human beings act for the whole society. Consequently, society is thought of as an organic reality to which individuals are subordinated. Therefore, the study of isolated phenomena is irrelevant to understand social phenomena. We have instead to analyze social groups (Schmoller, 1905, p.3).

As a result, historicists claim that the most useful empirical studies for the economist are those that include macroscopic data in order to discover laws. The data that are used are essentially macroscopic statistical series, economic monographs on various subjects (institutions of Antiquity or Middle Age, social history...)[269], and anthologies on the economic and military history of nations[270]. All these data that concern transcendental entities like the nation, the communi-

[268] The GHS is not a unified school (cf. Pearson, 1999). When we speak about the GHS, we make reference essentially to the dominant tendency of the school (with authors like Wilhelm Roscher and Gustav von Schmoller) that lies essentially on the three following propositions: 1) human societies act as natural organisms; 2) nations follow the laws of historical development; 3) it does not exist any other laws that can have an universal validity in social science. The GHS has officially started since the publication of the List *National system of political economy* (1841). Roscher's book *Grundriss zu Vorlesungen über die Staatswirthschaft: nach geschichtlicher Methode* (1843) is considered as the GHS' manifesto.

[269] Schmoller works are illustrative examples (see Schefold, 1987): in *Die Strassburger Tücher- und Weberzunft* (1879), he analyses the corporations of weavers in Strasbourg. In *Umrisse und Untersuchungen zur Verfassungs* (1898), he studies the activities of the corporations of Brandeburg and Prussia in the seventeen and eighteen century. Most particularly, he insists on the cotton industry and presents an historical account of the financial politics of Prussia. In *Deutsches Städtewesen in älterer Zeit* (1922), he discusses the constitution of German cities from a historical point of view. He published also several books on social classes.

[270] Mises, one of the most vehement critics of the GHS methodology, insists that military anthologies that explains German expansion and unification are the most used, the rest being of a second interest for historicists themselves. According to him, this data's collection is an "unsystematic, poorly assorted collection of various scraps of knowledge borrowed from history, geography, technology, jurisprudence, and party politics, larded with deprecatory remarks about the errors in the "abstractions" of the Classical school" (Mises, 1969).

ties and the national economy were abundantly collected in the last part of the nineteen-century in German universities.

Menger is totally opposed to the use of these kinds of macroscopic empirical analyses that claim to discover "the laws of the development of nations". It is precisely this form of empiricism that Menger rejects and not the use of empirical data in itself. Therefore, one of the main goals of Menger in the Untersuchungen is to demonstrate the irrelevance of the parallel between the society and a social organism:

> "The nation as such is not a large subject that has needs, that works, practices economy, and consumes; and what is called "national economy" is therefore not the economy of a nation in the true sense of the word. (...) Whoever wants to understand theoretically the phenomena of "national economy", those complicated human phenomena we are accustomed to designate with this expression, must for this reason attempt to go back to their *true* elements, to the *singular economies in the nation*, and to investigate the laws by which the former are built up from the latter." (Menger, 1883, p.93)[271]

According to Menger, economists should primarily be interested in the singular elements of the economic system: individuals. Human beings, able to act freely and in their own interests – and not those of the nation – are the only cause of economic phenomena. Consequently, Menger denies categorically any research of the "law of the development of the nation" that he considers as "a methodological absurdity" (Menger, 1883, p.79): the pure observation of a historic development cannot give us a law. The only laws that can be discovered in economics are on an individual level.

What Menger condemns is definitely not the empiricist approach *per se* but the type of data historicists use in order to discover laws. No empirical macroscopic analysis can lead to the discovery of a law: in his opinion, this kind of data has another purpose. Macroscopic data can be used within the framework of the realistic-empirical orientation of theoretical research. This approach is characterized as follows by Menger:

> "Exact economics by nature has to make us aware of the *laws* holding for an analytically or abstractly conceived economic world, whereas empirical-realistic economics has to make us aware of the *regularities* in the

[271] However, Menger admits the possibility of the relevance of the analogy between organism and society in the understanding of spontaneous phenomena like Friedrich Carl Savigny's jurisprudential phenomena (1840-1849) or the process of emergence of money. Nevertheless, the analogy that can be done in this case differs totally from the one of the GHS members. Whereas the latter explain human action as imposed by society, Menger thinks that the consequences of a multitude of voluntary and independent human actions are unpredictable and can be extremely positive for the whole society.

succession and the coexistence of the real phenomena of human economy." (Menger, 1883, p. 72, italics added)

Realist-empirical orientation uses statistical data or series of historical events. It corresponds to the contemporary econometric techniques, even if, of course, it was less developed at that time. Menger argues that this means of analysis can only show the existence of a sequence of facts in a descriptive way. As it does not explain the correlation that has been found, we can infer that this kind of research cannot enable us to discover economic laws. In fact, the observed correlations are only valid for a limited period of time.

Macroscopic data are useful as soon as reality is too complex to enable us to discover the laws by the exact orientation of research. In some way, Menger heralded here the principles of the theory of complexity. The social world is too complex a system to always be known with accurateness[272]. Prediction is a very difficult task because considering the high number of agents, the number of possible states of the world is exceptionally high. The complexity of the world makes also difficult the discovery of the real causes of the economic phenomena. Thus, Menger suggests having recourse to macroeconomic analyses in certain situations, however without explaining precisely which ones. According to him, that may enable us to obtain an approximation of the social development, but in the detriment of the phenomena's real understanding. He accepts analyses that use this kind of data as long as we are aware that they only inform us about the existence of correlations corresponding to a certain period of time. Nevertheless, the discovery of universal laws must remain the primary task of the economist. And they can only be found by the exact orientation of research.

3. The utility of empirical "microscopic" studies in Mengerian methodology

Contrary to the empirical-realistic orientation of research, the object of analysis of exact orientation of research is more atomistic:

> "[Exact orientation of theoretical research] seeks to ascertain the simplest elements of everything real, elements which must be thought of as strictly typical just because they are the simplest (...). It examines how more complicated phenomena develop from the simplest, in part even unempirical elements of the real world in their (likewise unempirical) isolation from all other influences, with constant consideration of exact (likewise ideal!) measure." (Menger, 1883, pp.60-61)

---

[272] Some handwritten notes added by Manger in his own copy of the *Grundsätze* are very explicit on this subject. For exemple, in the blank page facing page 108, he has written and underlined this sentence from Rossi: "Si vous pouviez suivre à travers les milles vicissitudes du marché, les parties contractantes, en analyser rigoureusement la position, *en peser pour ainsi dire les besoins, vous auriez la solution vraie du problème.*" (thanks to G. Campagnolo)

The exact orientation of research aims at finding the historically insensitive laws that govern every human being in the world. This kind of approach intends to find the "typical empirical forms of economy" (named "type" (*Typen*) in the *Untersuchungen*, Menger, 1883, p.36) and the laws that mutually connect them.

Purchase, money, supply, demand, price, capital and rate of interest are intuitive examples of types. They are the simplest elements of reality and their combination constitutes the totality of economic phenomena. They are like the letters of an alphabet (Smith, 1995) or more precisely the elementary particles of economic reality.

Economic laws are basically universal because they connect elements that are themselves universal. For example, the law of supply and demand that presents the relation between the three existing economic types supply, demand and price, is universally valid. If this law is not empirically observed, it does not mean that it is inactive: this economic force is always at work, but other social forces can sometimes overpower it. Economic laws are thus not directly observable in reality because it is impossible to dissociate economic phenomena from other social phenomena. For example, in every individual there is one economic direction that is self-oriented and another social direction (whatever the kind) for which altruistic behavior prevails. These divergent laws of behavior are always simultaneously at work but with different degrees of intensity. *Homo economicus* is never apparent in reality: he is just an aspect of human personality. According to Menger, economists should exclusively focus their attention on this aspect of human being.

One of the main consequences for Mengerian methodology is that economic theories cannot be tested. Indeed, when confronting theory with empirical observations, the economist tests all the laws of social sciences at the same time. As Menger writes:

> "Testing the exact theory of economy by the full empirical method is simply a methodological absurdity, a failure to recognize the bases and presuppositions of exact research. (...) To want to test the pure theory of economy by experience in its full reality is a process analogous to that of the mathematician who wants to correct the principles of geometry by measuring real objects, without reflecting that the latter are indeed not identical with the magnitudes which pure geometry presumes or that every measurement of necessity implies elements of inexactitude." (Menger, 1883, p.69)

Consequently, it is impossible to verify economic axioms. Menger makes the following analogy: pure economic phenomena like pure gold in chemistry do not exist in reality. Nobody blames the chemist for working with the concept of pure gold. Similarly, the law of falling bodies is not exactly verified in the real world because of the friction forces: it only fits in a context of perfect vacuum.

In the same way, economic laws are not empirically verifiable because of the forces of social friction. As laws are not directly observable in reality, Menger considers that it requires thought experiments to discover them:

> "The nature of the exact orientation of theoretical research (...) consists in the fact that we reduce human phenomena to their most original and simplest constitutive factors. We join to the latter the measure corresponding to their nature, and finally try to investigate the laws by which more complicated human phenomena are formed from those simplest elements, *thought of in their isolation.*" (Menger, 1883, p.62, italics added)[273]

Therefore, if economic laws are not directly observable, it is nevertheless possible to think of them separately from non-economic ones. One can discover economic laws by the experience of thought because human mind has an innate knowledge of the structure of the world: because of the proximity of inter-human mental category, everybody is able to recognize the universal economic incentives that rule human behavior. According to Menger, we have a direct knowledge of economic laws that we could discover as mathematical theorem[274]. As the aim of economics is to study how humans use means to reach their given ends, the discovery of laws is accomplished with deductive analyses comparable to mathematical ones. As long as we know the situation in which people operate, their economic actions can be deduced logically.

Furthermore, Menger adds that the discovery of economic laws requires four hypotheses for the abstract representation of our pure economic world. First, humans defend their self-interest. Secondly, they are aware of the ends they pursue and of the means needed to attain them. Thirdly, the economic conditions of the situation are not unknown to them. And fourthly, there isn't any external force impairing their economic freedom. With these four assumptions and the thinking of types in isolation, economic laws become attainable via logical deduction.

---

[273] Some commentators use the term introspection to describe this Mengerian method of analysis that consists of thinking types in their isolation. According to Max Alter: " Menger's methodological and epistemological practice in the Grundsätze imposes introspection as the only logically admissible epistemology on the researcher who wants to follow the path mapped out in Menger's economic theory. Menger himself never put it in these terms, but neither did he ever publish a final, positive statement of his methodology and epistemology, nor did he himself complete the second edition of the Grundsätze. " (Alter, 1990, p.327, italics added). The expression "experience of thought" in the sense of Putnam (1975) seems to be more adequate than the wording "introspection". Indeed, introspection can make allusion to psychological concerns. As Menger thinks that the economist does not have to enter the psychological area, we will prefer the term "experience of thought", which creates no ambiguity.

[274] Menger is here a precursor of the Misesian praxeological analysis. According to Mises, only the knowledge of the essence of human action is necessary to deduce praxeological theorems and he assumes that "like logic and mathematic, praxeological knowledge is in us." (Mises, 1966, p.64).

Types are thus a necessary element for the discovery of laws in Mengerian methodology. The characterization of types according to Menger can be found in the following quotation:

> "Not every single phenomenon exhibits a particular empirical form differing from that of all the others. Experience teaches us, rather, that definite phenomena are repeated, now with greater exactitude, now with lesser, and recur in the variation of things. We call these empirical forms *types.*" (Menger, 1883, p.36)

As Menger qualifies types as "empirical forms", he explicitly suggests that types belong to the real world: they are in no way abstract concepts. They are captured through the observation in real life of concrete human behavior.

These types accessible by experience are a real part of objects or subjects. Therefore, it can be said that Menger uses an Aristotelian realist immanent approach (Bostaph, 1978, Campagnolo, 2002, Crespo, 2003, Hands, 2001, Mäki 1990, 1997, Smith, 1990, White, 1984). Contrary to transcendental Platonic ideas that lie *outside* the perceptible world, the universals that Menger is seeking are not independent of the totality of things that exist *inside* the world.

Moreover, as types are the simplest elements of the real world, Menger argues that they cannot be attainable through macroscopic studies but only through microeconomic ones. Consequently, we can argue that Menger leaves room for empiricist analysis in his methodology and particularly (even exclusively) for microscopic empirical studies:

> "For along with the historical, surely very valuable empirical basis for theoretical research, the experience of everyday life is indispensable. Or, what is the same thing, *the observation of the singular phenomena of human economy*, indeed, as must be added here, the most comprehensive possible orientation of that economy, is indispensable. It is so indispensable that we cannot imagine a highly developed theory of economic phenomena without the study of the history of economy." (Menger, 1883, p. 117)

This consideration of microscopic empirical studies proves that Menger is not the *pure* apriorist that is argued by many commentators. Our own everyday life experience is not sufficient to discover every economic type which exists. So the observation of individuals in their everyday life is useful: it is the best way to discover economic types. The Mengerian method really "begins with simplest elements that are derived from empirical reality" (Bostaph, 1978). As Uskali Mäki pertinently states:

> "Menger was not an apriorist about acquiring knowledge of exact types, since this knowledge, in his view is to be abstracted from experience. It is much more plausible to view Menger as being an apriorist about exact

> laws, since knowledge of them is derived from our experience-based abstract knowledge of exact types without any further recourse to experience." (Mäki, 1997, p.90)

So, a careful reading of Menger's methodological works shows that he does not categorically reject all empirical inquiries in the exact orientation of research. If the discovery of laws by experience of thought is attained with an aprioristic method, the discovery of types requires some microeconomic empirical studies.

4. The role of qualitative analyses in Mengerian methodology

In view of the conclusions drawn in the last section, microscopic empirical studies have a place in the Mengerian research program. The aim of this part is to determine which kinds of microscopic empirical studies are useful in Mengerian methodology. There are broadly three main categories of microscopic empirical studies.

The first category is microeconometrics. But from a Mengerian perspective, because it consists in the quantitative analysis of microeconomic characteristics, it simply enables us to discover correlations and in no way laws. For this reason, such an analysis can only help us in the realistic-empirical orientation of research.

The second category of microscopic empirical studies is experimental economics. It is clear that experimental economics does not fit well with Mengerian methodology. Indeed, its main goal is to test theories and we have seen earlier that following such an objective is absurd according to Menger. He rejects categorically the possibility of using observations to test laws because observations do not permit to isolate pure economic phenomena. As experimental economists observe real people in a real situation making a real decision (Smith, 1982, Plott, 1982), the experimentalists do not isolate the economic side of human life but take into account all the motivations and characteristics of social sciences that can impact on behavior. Therefore, an economic experimentalist does not study *pure* economic phenomena as required by Menger.

Microeconomic empirical qualitative analyses (sometimes called "case studies") form the third category. They are more in accordance with Mengerian methodology because it can be used to discover types. This form of analysis consists in collecting the greatest possible number of observations about a single case. The case studied is an original past event that has occurred naturally without any intervention of the researcher. The considered event always involves few people only in order to facilitate the study of everyone's "reasons for action". In this way, qualitative study is really an empirical analysis of microscopic order.

Qualitative studies are used to evaluate individual strategies. To do so, it is necessary to follow three steps:

1) It is necessary to describe the situation as it actually happened meticulously. The researcher presents here the physical facts after having collected enough data on the studied event.

2) Secondly, we have to present the situation as it is perceived by the agent. The researcher then describes the strategies employed by the subjects and the motivations that lead them to act in this way rather than in another one[275]. As the "reasons for action" are not directly observable, the researcher has to rebuild them rationally from the empirical data he disposes of.

3) The last step is to evaluate the individual's actions. The researcher analyses whether the subject could have behaved differently in order to obtain greater gain. Thus, he presents the mistakes that the subject made or on the contrary he shows the relevance of the subject's actions. The researcher also examines whether the action has had some positive or negative impact on the well-being of all the members of society (some welfare criteria must have previously been adopted by the researcher). During this third step the researcher presents his normative prescription.

Our everyday life experience can give us the knowledge of some types. Nevertheless, because our personal experience of the world is necessarily limited, we need another method to collect more types. It is precisely qualitative study that enables us to discover the existence of new types. Indeed, the analysis of a human's "reasons for action" in everyday life is the core of this kind of study. With original cases, it is possible to discover the existence of new elementary particles in the economic world. Many economic types that we are often confronted with (e.g. purchase, price, value, or interest rate) don't require a case study to be caught. But it is less obvious to apprehend some others (e.g. cartel ringmasters, predatory prices, hold-ups between firms, specific investments)[276]. Qualitative studies are a tool capable of presenting them in a detailed manner in order to capture them.

From a Mengerian perspective, qualitative studies do not permit us to generalize observations. They are only useful to reveal the existence of types. In fact, the first two steps of qualitative studies do precisely this. The third step, purely conceptual, that consists in drawing laws from the types, is similar to the second stage of Mengerian methodology.

To support our argument about the utility of qualitative analysis in Menger's methodology, we can claim that he himself has used a case study in the

---

[275] More often, it is considered that individuals act accordingly with "the rationality principle" in a Popperian sense. Individuals are supposed to realise their calculus and then act in hope to not commit any failure.

[276] Types that can be found respectively in Granitz and Klein (1996), McGee (1958), and in Klein (2000) for the two last.

Grundsätze. The fact that he uses such a technique in this book reinforces our analysis of his methodology. Menger's qualitative analysis appears in chapter 8 of the *Grundsätze* when he analyses the origin of money. More precisely, Menger carries out a succession of case studies in this part of his work. In each of them, Menger presents the "reasons for action" that lead individuals to choose one sort of goods rather than another as money. He starts by analyzing trade during the Neolithic revolution: he presents which goods were used as money in Europe by nomadic tribes before they settled. Then, he explains the monetary evolution that happens from Antiquity following the earlier stages of economic development and urban concentration. He gives data about commercial relations in Greece, in the Roman Empire, or in Germanic tribes among others. He then presents a more detailed analysis of trade in Aztec markets in Mexico during the 16th century. Finally, his most contemporary monetary analysis deals with commerce in Burma during the 19th century. Menger himself explains the role of these observations in his argument as follows:

> "The history of other peoples presents a picture of great differences in their economic development and hence also in their monetary institutions. When Mexico was invaded for the first time by Europeans, it appears already to have reached an unusual level of economic development, according to the reports published by eye-witnesses about the condition of the country at that time. *The trade of the ancient Aztecs is of special interest to us for two reasons*: (1) it proves to us that the economic thinking that leads men to activity directed to the fullest possible satisfaction of their needs is everywhere responsible for analogous economic phenomena, and (2) ancient Mexico presents us with the picture of a country in the state of transition from a pure barter to a money economy. We thus have the record of a situation in which we can observe the characteristic process by which a number of goods attain a greater prominence than the rest and become money." (Menger, 1871, p.268, we stressed)

Let us note that the translation of this passage by James Dingwall originates a problem. By omitting the term *aber* and translating the term "*das Verkehrswesen der alten Azteken*" by "trade of the ancient Aztecs", he is hiding the opposition that exists with the preceding sentence and therefore tends to show that the observation of facts in itself is able enough to prove the existence of an economic law[277]. However, as we saw lengthily, this idea is totally incompatible with the

[277] The original sentences are the following: "Als Mexiko das erstemal von Europäern betreten wurde, scheint dasselbe, nach den Berichten zu schliessen, welche Augenzeugen über den damaligen Zustand des Landes veröffentlicht haben, bereits einen nicht gewöhnlichen Grad wirtschaftlicher Cultur erreicht zu haben. *Es ist aber das Verkehrswesen der alten Azteken für uns aus doppeltem Grunde von besonderem Interesse*."(Menger, p. 267, we stressed). Thanks to Gilles Campagnolo for his help in translating the passage.

Mengerian methodology. The ambiguity disappears as soon as one translates the *Verkehrswesen* term with precision. This term actually means "essence of trade". It is then not the direct *observation* of those facts that where related by European in Mexico, but on the contrary the understanding of the *essence* of the fact of *Verkehr* that is useful for the author to prove his theory. Observation of facts is only useful to discover the existence of some essences, or more precisely of "types" to use the traditional Mengerian phraseology.

This fact appears clearly in the second reason advanced by Menger. He explains that qualitative studies allow us to observe what he calls a "characteristic process". The process he records in this precise case is the following: the most "marketable" economic goods in an area at one point become the area's money naturally without any intervention of the state. This could be defined as an economic law. So, does Menger want to say that we can observe such an economic law in reality? Certainly not. It would contradict what he says in the *Untersuchungen*. What he wants to explain is just that the observation of reality enables us to discover some particular economic types and that it is possible to deduce economic laws from these types by abstraction.

In the 8th chapter of the *Grundsätze*, Menger presents the type he calls "marketability" (*Absatzfähigkeit*)[278]. And all the qualitative studies he refers to bring new characteristics of this particular type. These case studies show that some goods have a higher degree of marketability than others when (1) they are very useful, (2) they are more convenient to transport, (3) they last longer, (4) they require lower maintenance costs, (5) they are a more convenient account unit, (6) their utility value is more stable, (7) they possess a higher reserve of value for a constraint volume, (8) their value is simpler to evaluate, (9) they are easier to divide and finally (10) they are surplus goods.

So, at first Menger shows that in the Neolithic era, cattle are used as currency. He explains it by the fact that this kind of good has the advantage of being easy to transport at the time – roads did not exist and cattle transports him-

---

[278] Let us note that marketability, like price, is a property of other elements of the real world: the physical goods. If certain types correspond to concrete elements of the world (gold, money, capital...), others are properties of these elements (weight, temperature, price, marketability...). Types which are properties of other types are not to be confused with the "typical relationships among economic phenomena": "The phenomena of purchase, of money, of supply and demand, of price, of capital, of rate of interest are examples of typical empirical forms of economy. On the other hand the regular drop in price of a commodity as a result of the increase in supply, the rise in price of a commodity as a result of an increase in currency, the lowering of the rate of interest as a result of considerable accumulation of capital, etc., present themselves to us as typical relationships among economic phenomena." (Menger, 1883, p.36) Thus, marketability may be considered as a type which enters into a typical relationship with the type "money" and the type "commodity": "*The theory of money necessarily presupposes a theory of the saleableness of goods.* (...) The relatively most saleable commodities become money" (Menger, 1892).

self alone –, of having low maintenance costs – this kind of animal eats the grass which grows in abundance – and finally of having a relatively long lifespan. This qualitative study is thus used to reveal characteristics (2), (3) and (4) of the type "marketability". Its qualitative study on the use of metals like gold, silver, copper or iron in their rough form as a currency among various people of Antiquity enables us to perceive the characteristics (5), (6), (7), (8) and (9). The study of the Aztecs is primarily used to reveal the characteristic (1) of the type "marketability": only useful goods in the society are used as currency. Indeed, the principal Aztec currencies are the cocoa which is the daily beverage, the cotton which is the most used material in the clothes industry, and gold, copper and tin which are the most used metals. Lastly, its analysis on the use of fur as money by tribes of hunters shows the characteristic (10): only goods that are produced in surplus in the community can become a currency.

Conclusion

To conclude on Mengerian methodology and as follow directly from the study of the type marketability, we may say that the empirical studies Menger used in the *Grundsätze* cannot directly give us the law "the most marketable goods in a given area become naturally its money". But those case studies allow us to find and understand the type "marketability". From this type and trough the use of thought experiments we can logically deduce the corresponding law. We can note that this way of designing the essences is definitely Aristotelician: types are not fixed but can evolve in the Mengerian approach. To apprehend them correctly, it is thus necessary to examine the evolution of the various empirical forms they can take in the real world:

> "The real concepts, the types of economic phenomena are only truly adequate if we make ourselves aware of the nature of the pertinent phenomena not merely at a definite moment, but in the totality of their individual development or of the development of their empirical forms." (Menger, 1883, p.107)

Thus, only the direct observation of the empirical form's evolution that the type "marketability" takes in the real world allows us to know it precisely. It is then essential to realize a great number of case studies about various historical periods. The study could be followed along characteristics that appeared after the development of paper money. Characteristics (11) and (12) could thus be added: a good will have a more important degree of marketability as (11) its production cost is low and (12) its alternative utilizations are not so important that society is penalized by using it as currency. The question of whether former characteristics are still valid (or not) is then a study of its own after the development of paper money, as well as of other types of payments systems[279]. That shows again that the type "marketability", like "the real concepts, the types of economic phenomena" evolves concurrently with the evolution of society.

Chapter 8 of the *Grundsätze* presents then a worthy great illustration of the fact that the Mengerian methodological program is divided into two parts. The first part of this program consists of discovering types and apprehending their empirical evolution by *experience of everyday life*. The second aims at discovering laws from the types by *thought experiment.* Consequently, empirical analyses, and more precisely qualitative studies, are indispensable for the first step whereas they are totally inappropriate for the second one. Thus, commentators who assert that Menger is an apriorist or an antiempiricist have neglected half of the Mengerian methodological program.

[279] For a more elaborate view on this subject, see Latzer, M. and Schmitz, *Carl Menger and the evolution of payments systems* (2002).

Comparing Menger and Böhm-Bawerk on Capital Theory

Jean Magnan de Bornier

> "...when divergence is as wide as it is on this point of capital, we are forced to the conclusion that there must be something quite unusual about this specific apple of discord... It is not the definition that is in dispute, but rather the thing itself, or better, its terminology. The definitions are so widely at variance with one another not so much because the matter to be defined appears in a different light to each framer of a definition, as because each one is defining a totally different thing." (Böhm-Bawerk, 1956c, p 31).

Controversies over capital theory seem to be among the constants of the economist's life. They extend their power and glory across national borders and schools. At the end of the nineteenth century, Böhm-Bawerk undertook a vast program involving the critical appraisal of all theoretical propositions concerning capital and interest, as well as a new body of science. His encyclopaedic *History and Critique of Interest Theories* (Böhm-Bawerk, 1956b), witnessing the extent of his knowledge of prior approaches, contains the critical part, while his ability to build a fresh theoretical corpus appears in *The Positive Theory of Capital* as well as in the *Further Essays on Capital and Interest.*

German, British, American and French economists were carefully reviewed and some of them – like Alfred Marshall or John Bates Clark – entered into lively debates with Böhm-Bawerk.

These worldlike debates which Böhm-Bawerk contributed to create will not be dealt with; instead I will concentrate on a small part of these, and try to clarify the points of divergence and of convergence between Carl Menger's and Böhm-Bawerk's positions on capital theory. All along I ask the reader to remember that these positions were at the time they were proposed only a part of a much larger discussion.

We chose here to limit the focus to only these two authors.[280] Here are the main reasons which led to confront Menger and Böhm-Bawerk on capital:

• The study we propose here doesn't already exist yet in the available literature, and it seemed to me that there was a blatant lack, sometimes misleading in that it created unclear or excessive assessments; Hayek, as well as Schumpeter, were very elliptic in referring to a Menger-Böhm disagreement on capital.[281] Some clarity – but probably not all the needed light – could hopefully be added to the question.

• A second reason is that it can be specially interesting to look at diverging opinions within a school – like the austrian school – as the lack of agreement takes

[280] Other economists will appear in this study, but not as essential contributors.

[281] See Hennings (1997) and Gloria Palermo and Palermo (2005) for various statements.

here a particular form and may have specific consequences on the future of the school.

First, I will shortly describe the texts under examination here, as well as their order of appearance. The second section is devoted to show how the very concept of capital is different in Menger's and Böhm-Bawerk's works. Then, the third section deals with the matter of the productivity of capital, and the final one with the explanation of interest.

1. Material and chronology

On Menger's side, the topic of capital, from various points of view, appears in only three texts:
• *Principles of Economics* (Menger, 1871-1950) –hereafter *Principles* – his main contribution to economic theory;
• *Zur Theorie des Kapitals* (Menger, 1888a) – hereafter *Kapital*; this important article is not yet (!) available in English, but was translated in an abbreviated from into French under the title *Contribution à la théorie du capital* (Menger, 1888b);[282]
• BBM's obituary (Menger, 1915).
Böhm-Bawerk's works on capital theory include mainly the three volumes of *Capital and Interest*:
• *History and Critique of Interest Theories* (Böhm-Bawerk, 1956b) – hereafter History – first edition 1884, second edition 1890, third edition 1914 (the year of Böhm-Bawerk's death);
• *The Positive Theory of Capital* (Böhm-Bawerk, 1956c) –hereafter *Theory* – first edition 1889, second edition 1902, third edition 1909-12;
• *Further Essays on Capital and Interest* (Böhm-Bawerk, 1956a) –hereafter Essays – added to the third edition of the *Theory*.
Other articles on capital by Böhm-Bawerk were published in his controversy with John Bates Clark (Böhm-Bawerk, 1906, 1907a,b); they have no real bearing to the problem discussed here.

An earlier text by Böhm-Bawerk[283] has been published recently by Shigeki Tomo, who worked from manuscripts of his "Innsbrück Lectures"; these lectures took place during the academic years 1882-83 and 1883-84; it seems that Böhm-Bawerk wanted to keep his first theoretical developments on capital under secrecy until he could later publish a complete treatise.[284]

Menger never referred to these lectures, and is rather unlikely that he knew their existence, so we will not make use of this interesting material here. Now we see that:

---

[282] I warmly thank Gilles Campagnolo for this reference.
[283] Schefold et al. (1998).
[284] I wish to thank Bertram Schefold for these informations.

• At the time of the first edition of Böhm-Bawerk's *History*, Menger had only published his *Principles*.
• When Menger wrote *Kapital* and published it in 1888, he knew of Böhm-Bawerk's *History* and could respond to criticisms included in it that were aimed at his positions in the *Principles*.
• One year later, Böhm-Bawerk published the first edition of the *Theory*; he had read Menger's text on capital, but had had no time to include any comment on it in his text. However, he managed to mention it in the Preface, saying

> "This book was already well through the press when Carl Menger's Contribution to the Theory of Capital appeared in Conrad's Jahrbucher (vol. xvii. part ii.) I very much regret that it was then too late for me to make full use of that most interesting and suggestive work, and, in particular, that I could not do more justice to its author in my critical notice of the historical development of the conception of capital. Unfortunately by the time it appeared the first part of my book, – that which deals with the conception and nature of capital, and touches most closely on this work of Menger, – was already printed off." (Böhm-Bawerk, 1891)

• In the second and third editions of the *History,* Böhm-Bawerk did not modify his arguments, but developed them; the criticism of Menger's position is extended to some methological arguments.
• In the second and third editions of the *Theory,* Böhm-Bawerk made full use of the contents of *Kapital.*

2. Concepts of capital

2.1 Menger on the definition of capital

A fundamental tool in Menger's approach to capital is that goods can be of different "orders". The lowest order is for goods ready for final consumption, while goods in process are of higher order, the height being a measure of distance to availability for final consumption. In the Principles (Chapter III: The theory of value), a section is devoted to *The laws governing the value of goods of higher order*. In this section we find all the book's developments on capital theory; so we could imagine Menger would define capital as "goods of high order"; but this would not be correct; this would lead to a technical, not an economical, idea of capital: The classification of goods into means of production and consumption goods (goods of higher order and goods of first order) is scientifically justified, but does not coincide with a classification of *wealth* into capital and non-capital.(Menger, 1871-1950, p 303)

In a long footnote – appearing as an appendix in the English translation – Menger gives his definition of capital.

"Correctly understood, however, capital consists only of those quantities of economic goods that are available to us in the present for future periods of time and are capable of being applied to uses whose nature and economic character I have discussed at length." (Menger, 1871- 1950, p 303).

By these words ("nature" and "economic character") Menger seems to me to refer to the productivity of capital. He goes on:

"[...] the following conditions must be met simultaneously:(1) the time period during which an economizing individual has command of the necessary quantities of economic goods must be long enough to permit a production process ... to take place; and (2) the amounts and kinds of the available quantities of goods must be such that through them, the economizing individual has either direct or indirect command of the complementary goods of higher order that are necessary for the production of goods of lower order." (Menger, 1871-1950, p 303-04)

This definition is certainly not the simplest one. The first point to note is that this is the definition of an *aggregate*; there are no capital goods, there is an addition of quantities of economic goods, so the capital is a whole. The insistence on conditions of complementarity indicates that capital is an aggregate with which the entrepreneur or "economizing individual" is (directly or indirectly) ready to produce. And secondly, this whole must be available for some period of time, because production takes time. On this second element, there will be so discrepancy with Böhm-Bawerk.

Capital then is an *organic concept*, in the meaning of the word that Menger later developed in Menger (1883-1963); that is, a whole which is more than just the sum of its parts. This non-additive view is original concerning capital, since few authors have discussed the idea that capital could be a sum of capital-goods or capital-values.

In *Kapital*, Menger wanted to deal with what he considered as an erroneous and misleading conception of capital – Adam Smith's conception, which Böhm-Bawerk at the same time also commented in his *Theory*.

"Adam Smith's error, according to Menger, is that he and his school gave the word *capital* a new meaning, and applied it to various concepts arising in the course of their analysis, and that terminological error lead them to material mistakes... Even worse, the school used this word for logically artificial constructs for which sometimes no concrete reality exists.[285]"

According to Menger, many important classifications of goods, which have been proposed as crucial for the definition of capital, cannot be retained. Let us review the main classifications he examines:

[285] My translation from the French abridged version. (Menger, 1888b, p 577)

"The opposition between *income-providing goods and consumption goods* is not clear enough, because some consumption goods can contribute to one's wealth (e.g. a house which one owns)."[286]

Another opposition exists between *goods ready for use and goods in formation* (or an process).[287] This opposition is acknowledged as important, but doesn't take into account the fact that non-economic as well as economic goods can be productive; capital should contain only «economic goods».

The last and most important conception is that of capital *as products devoted to further production*[288] 9 (or produced means of production), the main proponent of this conception being for Menger Smith. Menger first stresses that Smith's conception of capital doesn't introduce a confusion between technical production and economic production. The point of criticism is Smith's idea that capital is composed of previously produced goods. To Menger the distinction between produced and natural goods is not relevant to economics and doesn't help solving economic problems. There are no unproduced factors, because land and labor themselves are products[289]

One of the *logically artificial constructs* is the concept of national capital. If seen as a simple sum of the individual capitals, it is vacuous. One can talk of a "national capital" (Volkskapital) only insofar as one considers not only all the individual capitals but also all the relationships between these constituent parts (Menger, 1888a, p 35).[290]

Menger also studies how capital is conceived in common life, and this conception seems to appear as the "real" one[291] . By "common life" (gemeines Leben) he means the business practice (eg. accountancy) as well as the popular meaning. Both meanings, or types of meaning, mostly refer to private capital, and are not generally compatible with a national concept of capital.

In *Kapital*, Menger attacks of Smith's view of capital, seemingly for two main reasons:

---

[286] "Die Auffassung des Kapitals als des der Einkommensbildung gewidmeten Vermögens im Gegensatze zu dem Gebrauchsvorrate" (Menger, 1888a, p 4).

[287] "Die Auffassung des Kapitals als Produktionsmittel im Gegensatze zu den Genußgütern" (Menger, 1888a, p 8)

[288] "Produkte, welche der weitern Produktion gewidmet sind" (Menger, 1888a, p 11).

[289] In the language of modern economics, Menger's model of the economy would be a closed model, like (often) Marx's economics is itself modelled.

[290]Debates over the possibility of an aggregate production function (the Cambridge controversy in the sixties and seventies of the last century) turn around the same matter. Menger, Böhm-Bawerk, and later Hayek, clearly saw all the inconsistencies of a macroeconomic theory of production or growth which the Cambridge (UK) camp was later to stress (Yeager, 1979) – which doesn't imply there is a general agreement on capital theory between Austrians and cambridgians.

[291] "Der Realbegriff des Kapitals" (Menger, 1888a, p 37).

• For Menger, the natural-goods vs. produced-goods distinction is a step towards a theory of value based on the cost of production (mostly a labour theory of value), and this of course is quite contrary to Menger's own theory that the value of higher-order goods is the result of how consumers value the first-order (consumption) goods.
• As Adam Smith made use of his definition of capital to describe the whole economy as one agent and social capital as that agent's private capital, contrary to Menger's idea of what Schumpeter later was to name *methological individualism*, the definition once more is condemned for the use which Smith made of it.

In a way, one may say that *Kapital* contains for a good part developments not closely or not exclusively linked to capital theory, but allowing Menger to reassert general themes of his theory of value. On the theory of capital, Menger does not try to innovate; he mostly wants to wipe out wrong innovations from the past.

2.2 Böhm-Bawerk on the definition of capital

Böhm-Bawerk had in many respects a similar view about misuses of the word "capital"; but his approach was much more systematic; in the opening chapters of the *Theory* he carefully reviewed many definitions before proposing his own. Smith's distinction between private and public capital is described and criticized:

> "[Adam Smith] remarked that the concept of capital may be applied, not only to the affairs of the individuals, but to those of a whole economiaing society as well. In such case however, the shift in point of view brings about a shift in the nature of the things that fall within the concept of capital. (...)
> Adam Smith's observation was the initial step in the breaking down of the concept of capital into two independent concepts which were later distinguished by the names "social capital" and "private capital". (Böhm-Bawerk, 1956c, p 20)

But Böhm-Bawerk admits that, while somehow misleading, the new meaning is

> "... of extreme importance in the sphere of production (...) In the trinity "land, labor and capital", social capital gave its name to one of the three great sources of wealth or, as they were later called, the three great factors of production." (ibid)

Böhm-Bawerk's own definitions of capital consist of two elements; first, the *nature of capital*, and then, more precisely, what is to be put in the aggregate "capital". Let us recall these two points.

The nature of capital. This is perhaps the most well-known of Böhm-Bawerk's propositions: a capitalistic economy is an economy where roundabout methods of production are used. That is, capitalistic production takes time while non-capitalistic production is immediate. In the first case, intermediate goods emerge during the production process (e.g. a net to catch fish); while in the second case the only produced goods are consumption goods (the fishes). Capital is then associated with these intermediate goods:

> "Capital is nothing but the sum total of intermediate products which come into existence at the individual stages of the roundabout course of progression." (Böhm-Bawerk, 1956c, p 14)

A more technical definition. A few pages later, after reviewing several elements of "the controversy over the concept of capital", Böhm-Bawerk offers his "positive proposal"; it is based upon a few principles, like the need of consistency and Occam's razor[292]. The proposed definition is then:

> "Let us call capital, in general, an aggregate of products which serve as a means of acquiring goods" (Böhm-Bawerk, 1956c, 32).

Assessed "in general", this definition permits some flexibility, in the sense that a "narrower concept *of social capital*" can be defined; it is "an aggregate of products which serve as a means of the acquisition of economic goods by society." (ibid) It is a narrower conception because some elements of private capitals permit acquisition for their owner but not for society as a whole (painting permits; in social capital the painting would not appear, so only means of production are present. Social capital is then an *"aggregate of intermediate products"*.

Acceptance by Böhm-Bawerk of the importance of a concept of social capital reveals – if that was needed – that the macroeconomic level is an important concern for him. Böhm-Bawerk wanted to draw an image of the whole economy, and actually did it. But it is important to understand that this does not mean he viewed society as one acting agent; capital is not independent of individual entrepreneurs' decisions.

In the second and third editions of the *Theory*, Böhm-Bawerk added comments on new discussions since his first edition; comments on Menger's *Kapital* are included there. While acknowledging "that Menger has really displayed great skill and fine judgment in his determination" of the popular meaning of capital, he was certainly not convinced economists should return to that terminology. To him, the popular language does not get subjected to any objective concept of capital:

292 "[N]o terminological prodigality is to be tolerated" (Böhm-Bawerk, 1956c, 32).

> "...the language of everyday speech [...] attaches the name capital to income-producing objects which either consist in money or may be represented in terms of money. Now representation in monetary terms is a purely subjective matter dependent on fortuitous subjective impressions or motives." (...)
> "In short, the popular concept and usage in the vernacular vary with varying personalities. Popular usage does not regularly assign the term capital to a particular real category of goods marked by some individual objective characteristic, but tosses the objective categories about helter skelter and makes its classification on the basis of some purely internal factor which gives no external indication of its presence and is as unpredictable in making its appearance as are all the manifestations of the human imagination." (Böhm-Bawerk, 1956c, p 51)

On the interest for the economist of such a quite *subjective* concept, Böhm-Bawerk answers: "none at all" (ibid). The role of social capital in economic theorizing is to provide a link with the matter of production, and no subjective concept can do that.

2.3 Productivity of capital

As to the question "what constitutes the productivity of capital?", both Menger and Böhm-Bawerk seem very close. The latter views are contained in the famous expression "greater productivity of more roundabout methods of production", and are well known – although often misunderstood. The role of time, of the duration of the production processes, is emphasized in these views. But Menger has a position in which time has also a great part; in the paragraph on *The productivity of capital*, he begins by stating that

> "The transformation of goods of higher order into goods of lower order takes place, as does every process of change, in time.(...)
> While it is true [...]that the more extensive employment of goods of higher order for the satisfaction of human needs brings about a continuous expansion in the quantities of available consumption goods, this extension is only possible if the provident activities of men are extended to ever more distant time periods. (…)
> [...] by making progress in the employment of goods of higher orders for the satisfaction of their needs, economizing men can most assuredly increase the consumption goods available to them accordingly – but only on condition that they lengthen the periods of time over which their provident activity is to extend in the same degree that they progress to goods of higher order." (Menger, 1871-1950, p 152-3)

Of course, Menger did not develop the relationship of time to productivity as to make of it a central element of his system, as Böhm-Bawerk later did; but it is clear that on this point the two men were in agreement. However, it may be useful to point out some differences in focus:

• To Menger the time-productivity relation is a natural – if not a trivial – one ("as does every process of change"; but Böhm-Bawerk made of it a very special law of the economics of production and capital. Later, Ludwig von Mises was to criticize Böhm-Bawerk on that matter, stating that roundaboutness is one praxeological law, not a technological one; that is, a category of the aprioristic science: time is a category of action[293]. This would be nearer to Menger's statement, even though Menger cannot be considered an apriorist.

• The time-productivity relation has a historical dimension in Menger's hands, while for Böhm-Bawerk it is rather an element of economic choice: at any moment entrepreneurs have to choose the length of the production processes. But historical elements are present in Böhm-Bawerk's exposition, and instantaneous decisions are not quite absent in the Principles.

• Menger's words that the extent of the time necessary to produce is "in the same degree" as the progression towards goods of higher order is not clear; at any rate it suggests some kind of constant returns of roundaboutness; oppositely, Böhm-Bawerk always insisted that more roundaboutness results in more production, but at a decreasing rate (diminishing returns).

3. Explanations of interest

Much more controversial than the definition of capital is the question of why interest exists. Böhm-Bawerk made of it the quest of his life and the solution he proposed in *Theory* is still celebrated and debated.

To Menger, the matter was no less important, but he devoted much less time and energy to it; he gave his solution in the Principles, and came back to it in *Kapital*, probably partially to provide an answer to Böhm-Bawerk's criticisms in the first edition of *History*. The two men did not agree on the explanation of interest, as we shall see; but Böhm-Bawerk convinced Menger to some extent.

3.1 Menger's theory of interest

We find Menger's theory of interest in the *Principles*, in the pages following those about capital productivity (Menger, 1871-1950, p 156 ff), it actually flows from his analysis of capital productivity. What is important for this concept is that one has to have "command of quantities of economics goods for a certain period of time". Let us try here to give an account of Menger's construction.

---

293 von Mises (1966, p. 480).

The first point to emphasize is that to him capital is a *value concept*, not a technological one. Understanding the origin of interest is understanding why the *present* value of any capital is always less than the *prospective* value of the same capital. His answer is that the capital provides services:

> "The *present* value of these goods of higher order by themselves is therefore equal to the value of the prospective product minus the value of the services of the capital employed." (Menger, 1871-1950, p 158)

After developing several examples, including a theory of entrepreneurship, he summarizes his view:

> "The aggregate present value of all the complementary quantities of goods of higher order (that is, all the raw materials, labor services, services of land, tools, etc.) necessary for the production of a good of lower or first order is equal to the prospective value of the product. But it is necessary to include in the sum not only the goods of, higher order technically required for its production but also the services of capital and the activity of the entrepreneur. For these are as unavoidably necessary in every economic production as the technical requisites already mentioned." (Menger, 1871-1950, p 161)

By stating this Menger intends also to dismiss two alternative theories, the "abstinence theory" and Carey's view. Abstinence is rejected because "the abstinence of a person cannot, by itself, attain goods-character and thus value" (Menger, 1871- 1950, p 156). Carey would fall in the "opposite error", believing parsimony to be "inimical to the creation of capital" (ibid).

But Menger's theory of interest is not proposed as a complete elaboration; his proposition seems to be that other theories are wrong, so the only remaining possibility has to be the right one. In the last lines of *Kapital*, he states that

> "The explanation of *Verzinsung* which is enacted through all the categories of acquisitive goods, the accounting value of capital and aggregate capital, all that should give us but little concern, because here in science, as well as in everyday life, the question is only a simple matter of computing; the goal of our science must not be a bare theory of how to compute the interest of capital, but rather a general theory of the yield of goods overall – a theory of the yield of all things regarding its extraction from the various categories of (productive) goods[294] "

[294] Translation of: Die Erklärung der "Verzinsung" des durch die übrigen Kategorien des werbenden Vermögens dargestellen, des rechnungsmäßigen Kapitals und ihrer Maßes darf uns dann nur wenig bekümmern, da es sich hierbei in der Wissenschaft, wie im Leben, lediglich um eine einfache Berechnung handelt; nicht eine bloße Theorie des Kapitalszins, sondern eine solche des Vermögensertrages überhaupt – eine Theorie des Ertrages aller in Rücksicht auf ihre Ertragungsbildung verschiedenartigen Kategorien des (Produktiv-)Vermögens – muß

In a footnote to this sentence, Menger adds that Böhm-Bawerk is on the way of this accomplishment:

> "From this viewpoint, E. v. Böhm's endeavours in the field of the theory of interest of capital appear in their widest meaning. B. has in the first part of his comprehensive work over 'Capital and Interest' (...) undertaken "a penetrating and comprehensive critical overview of the enormous available material"; the upcoming publication of the second part of the work as announced in this journal (...) will bring forth the positive theory [of Capital] of the author"[295]

This was just before the appearance of the first edition of the *Theory*, and this was Menger's last written phrases on the theory of interest, until he wrote Böhm-Bawerk's obituary twenty-six years later.

So Menger was aware of these two elements:

1. His theory of interest was not *a complete theory*; it was a partial approach in the waiting of a more general construct, which of course had to be based upon what he proposed.

2. Böhm-Bawerk was preparing the exposition of such a theory, and *he seemed confident in his ability to propose a good theory.* What we ignore (at least what the present author ignores) is how much he knew – in 1888 – about the very theory which was to appear the next year. But he didn't hesitate to announce it as "die positive Theorie".

3.2 Böhm-Bawerk's theory of interest

It is certainly superfluous to provide a complete presentation of Böhm-Bawerk's explanation of the phenomenon of interest[296]. Let us just recall, as he himself formulated them, the three well-known sources which together constitute the basis of this theory.

Criticizing three generic kinds of explanations, viz. *the productivity theory*, the use theory, and the *abstinence theory*, he proposed these three "causes":
1. A first principal cause capable of producing a difference in value between present and future goods is inherent in the *difference between the relation of*

---

das Ziel unserer Wissenschaft sein.(Menger, 1888a, p 48-49) Thanks to Gilles Campagnolo and Herta Mayerhofer for their help.

[295] Translation of: Von diesem Gesichtspunkte aus betrachtet, erscheinen die Bestrebungen E. v. Böhm's auf dem Gebiete der Kapitalzinstheorie in ihrer großen Bedeutung. B. hat in der ersten Abteilung seines umfassenden Werkes über das 'Kapital und den Kapitalzins' (...) in der That "eine eindringende und umfassende kritische Sichtung des vorhandenen enormen Materials" vorgenommen; die in diesen Jahrbüchern (...) als demnächst bevorstehend angekündigte Veröffentlichung der zweiten Abteilung desWerkes soll die positive Theorie des Verf. bringen. (Menger, 1888a, p 48-49). Thanks to Gilles Campagnolo for his help.

[296] For a thourough and very clear account of this theory, see Hennings, chapters 7 and 9.

supply to demand as it exists at one point of time and that relation as it exists at another point of time[297].(Böhm-Bawerk, 1956c, p 266-67)
2. We *systematically undervalue our future wants and also the means which serve to satisfy them.* (Böhm-Bawerk, 1956c, p 268)
3. It is an elementary fact of human experience that time consuming roundabout methods of production are more productive. That means that, given equal quantities of the means of production, the more time a method of production consumes, will be the output it produces.(Böhm-Bawerk, 1956c, p 373)

4. Extent of the disagreement

Schumpeter, while praising without much restraint Böhm-Bawerk's accomplishments in economics (Schumpeter, 1954, 2003), drew attention to the possibility of a wide disagreement between the latter and Menger; in his *History of Economic Analysis*, he summed up Böhm-Bawerk's main thesis:

> "[...] the two propositions that the productivity of a given 'quantity' of capital can be increased by extending the period of production and that we habitually undervalue future pleasures as compared with present ones – two cornerstones as we shall see of the specifically Böhm-Bawerkian theory of capital and interest – had been indicated by Menger." (Schumpeter, 1954, p. 846-47)

Also, in a footnote to this sentence, Schumpeter adds:

> "This is the more noteworthy because Menger, far from welcoming that theory as a development of suggestions of his, severely condemned it from the first. In his somewhat grandiloquent style he told me once: 'The time will come when people will realize that Böhm-Bawerk's theory is one of the greatest error ever committed'. He deleted those hints in his 2nd edition." (Schumpeter, 1954, p. 847, note 8)

One has to be cautious with such a statement: we don't know when – if ever – it was pronounced, it is not traceable, and is associated with another fact which is obviously untrue or at least mistakenly formulated: the reference to the second edition of Menger's *Principles.* We know that this edition has been released after his death and assembled by his son Karl from personal notes, in a way which has not provoked a wide adhesion from the profession; it has not been translated into English and was not retained in Hayek's edition of Carl Menger's *Gesammelte Werke*. So this note is raising at least some reservations. Another testimony of the same is Hayek's writing – also in a footnote:

---

[297] In the translation of the first edition one reads "the different circumstances of want and provision (Bedarf und Deckung)" instead of "the relation of supply to demand". (Böhm-Bawerk, 1891)

> "Neither Carl Menger nor F. von Wieser, nor – to mention only one name from the later generation – Professor Schumpeter accepted Böhm- Bawerk's views." (Hayek, 1941, p 46, n 2)

Here again information is scarce! But these statements have been commented, and various authors attempted to figure what was the basis of the supposed disagreement; one proposition is that Böhm-Bawerk holds an objective theory of capital, whereas Menger's view is subjectivist; another hypothesis has been proposed, to the effect that Böhm-Bawerk's capital theory is technical rather than economical. We will briefly review these propositions before proposing our own.

4.1 Subjectivism vs. objectivism

Ludwig Lachmann and others (Lachmann, 1976, Gloria-Palermo, 1999, Gloria-Palermo and Palermo, 2005) proposed very imaginative developments about the disapproval by Menger of Böhm-Bawerk's theoretical contributions on the latter's alleged objectivism. Gloria-Palermo and Palermo refer to "Menger's well known criticism of the Böhmian theory of interest" (?); insisting on the rejection by Böhm-Bawerk of subjectively evaluated goods as capital, they seem to believe that Menger proposed an all-subjective view of capital, a belief which cannot be inferred from reading him. Indeed, it is quite easy to see how much Böhm-Bawerk was a subjectivism in his theory of capital and interest. Let us just look at those two texts by Böhm-Bawerk:

> "In this doctrine of Menger's the use theory finally attained full theoretical clarity and maturity. He completely avoided all relapse into ancient error, or the faintest dubious resemblance to the old productivity theories, and thus definitely transmuted the interest problem from a question of production, which it is not, into a question of value, which it is." (Böhm-Bawerk, 1956b, p 140)

Needless to say, value is a subjectively determined matter for Böhm-Bawerk.

> "Present goods have in general greater subjective value than future (and intermediate) goods of equal quantity and quality. And since results derived from the ascribing of subjective value determine objective exchange value, present goods have in general greater exchange value and a higher price than future (and intermediate) goods of the same kind and number." (Böhm-Bawerk, 1956c, p 265)

If this is not a subjectivist manifesto for capital theory, what could be? It is true that later Ludwig von Mises proposed a criticism of Böhm-Bawerk's capital theory which may appear as more subjective, if one misleads subjectivism and apriorism. This would be a misunderstanding, and would be irrelevant to deal with the Menger Böhm-Bawerk relations: Menger was not a declared apriorist, and Mises view on capital is his own[298].

4.2 Technical or economic conception of capital

In a recent research paper, Jacques-Laurent Ravix notes that

> "Schumpeter's notion of capital is quite different from that of Böhm-Bawerk and more in agreement with that of Menger. The former defines productive capital as a set of products which are means to production of goods, whereas Menger and Schumpeter define capital in economic rather than technical terms, as means of payment performing their capital role in the hands of private individuals." (Ravix, 2004, p 14-15)

This statement, although quite serious, cannot be retained: as we saw earlier, Menger as well as Böhm-Bawerk saw capital as the value of an aggregate of economic goods; reference to capital goods is present in both writers, but technical objects are never capital *per se*. Of course, the list of technical (production) or non-technical goods to include in this aggregate is not identical for them. But capital is always a value concept.

4.3 Real disagreements

Definition(s) of capital On the definition of capital, what was already said can show the extent of the dispute: Menger is reluctant (or strongly opposed) to the idea of having a concept of *social* or *national* capital, for reasons we saw. Such a concept might lead to see the whole economy as one single agent, and one can argue one way or another about Böhm-Bawerk's supposed tendency towards such a mistake vis-à-vis methological individualism. Social capital is a tool for a cost-based theory of the value of capital, and this is the very reason why later Hayek, explicitly in Böhm-Bawerk's camp, rejected[299]. Hayek, standing on Böhm-Bawerk's side in capital theory, was nevertheless approving some of Menger's reservations concerning the *definition* of capital. Capital is a sufficiently strange theoretical object that scholars can agree on its theory without agreeing on its definition!

Another point of disagreement is related to Menger's idea that economists should make use of the term "capital" as it is understood by the layman and the businessman. Böhm-Bawerk did not accept it, treating "the popular concept of

---

[298] See however 2.3

[299] "...there is another, even more fundamental, reason why the definition of capital as the produced means of production should be definitively abandoned. And this is, that it is a remnant of the cost of production theories of value..."(Hayek, 1941, p 89)

capital, which Menger would preserve as the scientific concept, to be nothing more than a development stage." (Böhm-Bawerk, 1956c, p 52)

Origin of interest On this matter we don't have a precise statement of Menger about Böhm-Bawerk's propositions, but the latter's comments on Menger's explanation are included in the *History*, and was extended in the second edition, after the *Kapital* paper appeared. Böhm-Bawerk classified Menger's theory as a "use theory", and this "theoretical movement" – also illustrated by contributions of Jean-Baptiste Say and Hermann – "reaches its highest development with Menger" (Böhm-Bawerk, 1956b, p 141). But it is unacceptable for Böhm-Bawerk; to him, there is an inconsistency in the proposition that the value of the use of capital goods has to be counted *in addition* to the value of the goods themsves, which is, as we saw earlier, the essence of Menger's explanation of interest. This position of Böhm-Bawerk's is developed in a very interesting discussion (Böhm-Bawerk, 1956b, p 170-77), and can be summarized as this: it is quite possible to attribute value to goods themselves *or* to their qualities and properties, like localization, colour or "rendition of service" (what Menger has in mind), etc. But one has, logically, to choose one way or the other, one cannot cumulate these two approaches – which Böhm-Bawerk labels "categories"; as he himself states:

> "...tangible goods and renditions of service are not two kinds of causes of our well-being, differing from each other and operating side by side, but rather, identical kinds of causes which function which function in varying degree, at times as a whole, at other times as a part, or, if preferred, now as an aggregate, and now as a constituent." (Böhm-Bawerk, 1956b, p 173)

We cannot avoid referring this discussion to two modern ways of considering consumer's choice: the usual one where utility is a function of the goods he buys, as compared to Lancaster's one where consumer is a function of the characteristics embedded in the goods; these are alternative, not cumulative, ways of looking at the question of consumer's choice[300].

This point of divergence between Menger and Böhm-Bawerk is of course important; in Böhm-Bawerk's hands, it leads to totally invalidate Menger's theory of interest; but it is a very technical matter, and it seems after all to be a small one.

In Böhm-Bawerk's obituary, Menger's appreciation of Böhm-Bawerk's contributions is quite positive on the historical account of interest theories (where his own is severely attacked – like all others) and gives a short account of his explanation of interest, then criticizes other economists (especially english and american ones[301]) for their unwarranted reactions to Böhm-Bawerk's criti-

[300] When first proposing this idea, Lancaster refered to Menger's analysis of needs.
[301] They were not named, but Alfred Marshall and John Bates Clark come to mind.

cism, reactions which led them to neglect "the important elements of truth" in his theory. This is of course a mixed statement, as one expects – if there are elements of truth here, still it not exact that the whole theory is to be considered true. It is also not impossible that in a text written shortly after Böhm-Bawerk's disappearance Menger would appear as more favourable than he really was to Böhm-Bawerk. But as this is the only text where he commented on the new "Austrian" interest theory, we can also give some credit to these words.

5. Conclusion

The Austrian School, being remarkably united on some topics, like value theory in general and methodology, is the place of strong debates on other subjects; imputation and capital (two related matters) are the most striking cases, and Wieser quite simply acknowledged that "The Austrian school does not maintain its unanimity over the theory of interest. "(von Wieser (1891)). Later, Mises, Hayek and Schumpeter all insisted on the role of non-Austrian economists in the elaboration of what they consider a good theory of capital; Jevons, as a forerunner, and Wicksell, Fetter, Fisher as continuators are often referred to.[302]

In the period extending from 1889 to Böhm-Bawerk's death in 1914, debates over capital were widespread and involved economists from many countries; but it has been much more a debate between individuals than a debate between schools of thought; Austrians were not a united front, and J.B. Clark and Marshall did not talk for more than themselves.

Can we draw from all this that there is not such a thing as an *austrian theory of capital*? Perhaps not; Menger, after all, included in his apparatus the fundamental insight of a link between capital and time – even though he did not discover it; Böhm-Bawerk and later Hayek made strong contributions, in the same direction, to capital theory, and these will stay attached to their austrian background; the austrian theory of the business cycle could not be austrian without the capital-time relationship. Such a view, however, would clearly be mostly based on accepted practice rather than detailed analysis, and it might not be convincing enough for the demanding historian.

[302] See e.g. " These observations do not detract at all from the imperishable merits of Böhm-Bawerk's contributions. It was on the foundation laid by him that later economists–foremost among them Knut Wicksell, Frank Albert Fetter and Irving Fisher–were successful in perfecting the timepreference theory." (von Mises, 1966, p. 488).

Conclusion

Gilles Campagnolo

The present book has been inspired by one major concern, that of re-establishing a more complete and more accurate image of the founder of the Austrian school. The image that is often conveyed, either by his supporters who are often also his self-claimed heirs, or by his foes and opponents, tends to confuse what original "Austrianness" was and what it has become since Menger's times, after it was intertwined with other trends of economic thought, re-interpreted in a remix of contextual frames far away from the original 1900's *Mitteleuropa* and Viennese scene. To put it in a nutshell, from *Mitteleuropa* to the *Midwest*, one may doubt whether economists may, as a matter of fact, simply talk about the same things.

Now, in order to complete such a revised portrait of Carl Menger in his works, it was purposefully intended by the Editor and the contributors that (almost) only the teachings of the Viennese professor were to be utilized in the chapters of this volume. It is with a deep consciousness of the necessary faithfulness to an author's ideas that both Menger's published works and his significant (yet insufficiently studied until nowadays) *Nachlass* were taken as sources by each contributor. There may be mistakes left here and there, and some interpretations will not satisfy all of the scholars, but our intent in raising the issues was not to give a definitive assessment of "final solutions". Our goal was to raise some points that have remained ignored because the archives were not searched for good. It was to make vivid some topics in the field of Mengerian studies that have been left into oblivion because commentators were happy with mere intuitions. Those may prove sometimes right, but also wrong at other times... Here, we have provided the reader with pieces of evidence that render a fair observer of economics more apt to decide what to think about Carl Menger.

Therefore, it appeared for sure that the way in which Menger's texts were published has created major discrepancies in the reading of his works. Hot button questions are sometimes false problems due precisely to that fact (for instance, regarding Menger's supposed "incomplete" subjectivism). Whether in plain good faith (like when his son Karl gave a second version of his father's *Grundsätze*), or somewhat more cannily when Hayek claimed the "intellectual inheritance" of Menger, it is however blatant that an approach to Menger's thought must be renewed through the use of archives ignored until recently. The contributions in this volume have shown many factual, historical and material reasons for that. They have also shown that texts by Menger unearthed partly in Japan and partly in the USA must help in overcoming prejudices born from lengthy academic traditions of oblivion of certain parts of the Viennese founder's teachings. In order to appreciate more completely and more accurately Menger's thought, the scientific community now has the indispensable tools.

True, we could neither explore here all the material that is now available, nor detail all possible ways and means. To some extent, only some domains were here studied in particular. But contributors documented their readings, each in his own way and within the branch of economic thought where most competent. We believe that they have shown how to set the issue – whether about the issue of ordinality vs. cardinality, about experimental methodology, about the theory of capital, or the role of psychology, or in the case of discussing the link between Menger and British liberalism. Because the evolution of the Austrian school has (necessarily?) deviated from the original ideas of its founder, it was necessary to retrace the history of Menger's texts as well as to describe how his works were edited. On topics of theory of knowledge as well as regarding hints at possible influences received by the Viennese, what had been left aside by commentators who neglected the *Nachlass* has been partly unearthed here. Let us remind that, in coping with those issues, it was missing until now. Because of the way texts had been edited and read, and because some precious information was missing, whether at the theoretical or at the historical level, Austrian school disciples have been diversely affected. We do not take stands; we only give evidence of what could (and should) be done to remedy that situation.

Whatever the reason (mostly political, but also academic) for which *exiles* from Austrian circles began to fill U.-K. and U.S. Faculties in the 1920's and 1930's – such as Josef Schumpeter, Gottfried Haberler, Fritz Machlup, Oscar Morgenstern, Ludwig von Mises, etc. – they participated in a historical movement that has drawn European science away from Europe. As to Karl Menger the son (one of the last academics to leave Austrian), the *Anschluss* had left no choice in March 1938. Archives too went away. It is thus not only relevant from a *philological* point of view, but also *indispensable* from historical concern, to rediscover today that "lost" heritage. The chapters in this volume have also intended to discuss contemporary commentaries through Menger's ideas in that second perspective: make known again the material that had left Europe (such as Menger's library). Our hope is that academics will end up examining anew the *Nachlass*. As a matter of fact, the *exile of* academics who left Europe was a major loss not only to the Continental (as well as to the German-speaking) *Academia*, but they obtained a different kind of recognition before. Not only did they transfer from place to place, but when they arrived to the USA, they (and many Austrian economists among them) soon understood that they should accommodate to a new academic environment and publish in English if they wanted their works to be read. When, in order to communicate, they translated their original works from German into American English, they discovered that some concepts simply did not obtain. New schools and new ideas would attract students from the whole world to the States after World War II, giving the American economic profession its world-wide dominance. But in the process, some parts were lost and some concepts did not fit in the new framework.

Moreover, besides problems of "translation", some part of the inheritance was simply materially lost during the turmoil, exile and relocation to far away places. In other cases, material was sent abroad too far to be easily reached. Those would get lost for all purposes. Therefore, whole facets of the tradition inherited from "old Vienna" fell into neglect or mere oblivion. Meanwhile, some aspects of the original thought blossomed in America, which had been of less portent in the original place. One solution is to ignore differences and, in the name of "*eternal science*", leave aside the fact that there had thus been in fact a major loss in the change of culture – after all, was it not the price to pay for newcomers? As if it were natural that a part of the inheritance be forgotten for good, because it was less adapted to the new environment. Academic benefits, as there were some (the fact that Josef Schumpeter was elected President of the American Economists' Association speaks for all) were regarded, in such hard times, as outweighing the loss. But, even if from those changes gains must be acknowledged, then the choice may legitimately be the reverse of the American mind: we may want to recognize the European heritage as such – both, for the wealth of its past and for the promise of its future.

Today, Menger's ideas (origins and contents), the nature and essence of his thoughts cannot be accounted for any more *without* recounting how his papers left Europe and disappeared for a while – for instance, precisely when the Vienna Circle and seminars (like Menger's Jr.'s *Mathematisches Kolloquium*) gave rise to "logical positivism". The fate of those books and the destiny of those men that ended in exile both explain the fact that research was deprived of many sources for decades. It is right and scientifically rigorous to check now what can be done to use again those archives. Once stressed that distortion of concepts occurred partly due to the lack of Menger's papers, what to do about it? Most chapters in this volume presented the reader with examples of such rediscoveries, whether on the theoretical or on the historical side. Besides, a study in terms of "group commitment" is possible[303]. As we gradually rediscover Menger's archives, and we go through the deciphering of the origins of his thought, many points shall re-emerge that the Viennese thinker had hinted at and which his heirs may have "forgotten". The present book was only a first step in that direction and for that purpose. Go and inquire was our motto. It is still valid for our reader.

---

[303] That is the main topic of the project „Menger and the Evolution of the Austrian school: economic theory and social epistemology" supported by the French National Center for Scientific Research (CNRS / Center for Epistemology at Aix-en-Provence) coordinated by Campagnolo. Readers of the French language may refer to one project result, Campagnolo (2007) : "*Seuls les extrémistes sont cohérents*", *Murray Rothbard et l'École austro-américaine dans la querelle de l'herméneutique,* Lyon, ENS-Éditions.

Annex 1 / Anhang 1

Table of the theory of value in the shape of a « triangle » illustrating marginal reasoning according to Carl Menger.

Carl Mengers "zehn Scalen" zum Zwecke der Erleichterung des Verständnisses der "Bedürfnissbefriedigungen".

I	II	III	IV	V	VI	VII	VIII	IX	X
10	9	8	7	6	5	4	3	2	1
9	8	7	6	5	4	3	2	1	
8	7	6	5	4	3	2	1		
7	6	5	4	3	2	1			
6	5	4	3	2	1				
5	4	3	2	1					
4	3	2	1						
3	2	1							
2	1								
1									

Carl Menger, *Grundsätze der Volkswirthschaftslehre*, 1871, Wien, Wilhelm Braumüller Verlag, *reprint: Gesammelte Werke*, volume 1, J.C.B. Mohr, Tübingen, p. 93.

Annex 2 / Anhang 2

The two versions of the *Grundsätze der Volkswirtschaftslehre* by Carl Menger:

1. ***Die allgemeine Lehre vom Gute*** **(The general Theory of good)**	**1.** ***Die Lehre von den Bedürfnissen*** **(The Theory of needs)**
2. ***Die Wirthschaft*** **[sic]** ***und die Wirthschaftlichen Güter*** **(The Economy and the economic goods)**	**2.** ***Die Lehre vom Gute*** **(The Theory of good)**
3. ***Die Lehre vom Werthe*** **[sic] (The Theory of Value)**	**3.** ***Über das Maß der menschlichen Bedürfnisse und der Güter*** **(Measuring human needs and goods)**
4. ***Die Lehre vom Tausche*** **(The Theory of Trade)**	**4.** ***Die wirthschaftlichen*** **[sic]** ***Güter*** **(The economic goods)**

5. ***Die Lehre vom Preise***
(The Theory of Price)

6. ***Gebrauchswerth und Tauschwerth*** **[sic]**
(Value-in-use and value-in-trade)

7. ***Die Lehre von der Waare*** **[sic]**
(The Theory of Wares)

8. ***Die Lehre vom Gelde***
(The Theory of Money)

In the last four chapters, there are changes in the titles of the subsections.
In den letzten vier Kapiteln, Veränderungen nur in den Untertiteln.

Literaturverzeichnis / Reference List

Alter, Max (1990): "What do we know about Menger?", in Caldwell, B. (ed.) *Carl Menger and his legacy in economics.* Duke University Press, Durham and London, p. 313-348.

Aristoteles (1975) (als unv. Nachdr. d. Ausg. v. 1921): *Lehre vom Schluss oder erste Analytik*, übers. von Eugen Rolfes, Felix Meiner Verlag, Hamburg.

Aristoteles (1975) (als unv. Nachdr. d. Ausg. v. 1922), *Lehre vom Beweis oder zweite Analytik*, übers. von Eugen Rolfes, Felix Meiner Verlag, Hamburg.

Aristoteles (2002): *Rhetorik*, Übers. u. erläutert von Christof Rapp, Erster Halbbd., Wissenschaftliche Buchgesellschaft, Darmstadt.

Aristoteles ^{2}(1981): *Politik*, Übers. und mit erkl. Anm. versehen von Eugen Rolfes, Mit einer Einleitung von Günther Bien, Felix Meiner Verlag, Hamburg.

Aristoteles ^{3}(1978): *Politik*, Übers. und hrsg. von O. Gigon, Deutscher Taschenbuch Verlag, München.

Aristoteles ^{4}(1985): *Nikomachische Ethik*, Übers. Eu. Rolfes, hrsg. G. Bien, Felix Meiner Verlag, Hamburg.

Aristoteles ^{5}(1969): *Nikomachische Ethik*, Übers. und komm. v. Franz Dirlmeier, Wissenschaftliche Buchgesellschaft, Darmstadt.

Aristoteles ^{6}(1983): *Über die Seele*, Übers. v. Willy Theiler, Berlin.

Aristoteles (1979): *Aristotelis Ethica Nicomachea*, R. b. a. c. instr. I. Bywater, SCBO, Oxford.

Aristoteles (1980): *Aristotelis Politica* R. b. a. c. instr. W. D. Ross, Scriptorum classicorum Bibliotheca Oxoniensis [im weiteren abgek. als SCBO], Oxford.

Astius, Fridericus (Fridrich Ast) (1956): (Unv. Nachdr. der Ausg. 1835–1838), *Lexicon Platonicum Sive Vocum Platonicarum Index*, Vol. 1, Wiss. Buchgesellschaft, Darmstadt.

Bellet, Michel; Gloria-Palermo, Sandye; Zouache, Abdallah (eds) (2005): *Evolution of the Market Process – Austrian and Swedish Economics.* Routledge Studies in the History of Economics. Routledge, London and New York.

Béraud, Alain (2000): "Les Autrichiens", Chapter 22, in Faccarello, G. ; Béraud, A. (eds), *Nouvelle histoire de la pensée économique*. La découverte & Syros, Paris.

Birner, Jack (1990): "A roundabout solution to a fundamental problem in Menger's methodology and beyond", in Caldwell, B. (ed.) *Carl Menger and his legacy in economics*. Duke University Press, Durham and London, p. 241-261.

Blaug, Mark (1978, 1985): *Economic Theory in Retrospect*, Cambridge University Press, Cambridge.

Böhm-Bawerk, Eugen (1891): *Positive Theory of Capital*. Macmillan and Co., London. English translation of the first edition by William A. Smart.
Available online: http: //www.econlib.org/library/BohmBawerk/bbPTC.html

Böhm-Bawerk, Eugen (1906): "Capital vs Capital Goods", *Quarterly Journal of Economics*, p. 3–21.

Böhm-Bawerk, Eugen (1907a): "A Relapse to the Productivity Theory", *Quarterly Journal of Economics*, p. 246–282.

Böhm-Bawerk, Eugen (1907b): "The Nature of Capital: a Rejoinder", *Quarterly Journal of Economics*, p. 28–47.

Böhm-Bawerk, Eugen (1956a): *Further Essays on Capital and Interest*. Libertarian Press, South Holland, Illinois. English translation of the 1921 edition by Hans F. Sennholz.

Böhm-Bawerk, Eugen (1956b): *History and Critique of Interest Theories*. Libertarian Press, South Holland, Illinois. English translation of the 1921 edition by George D Huncke and Hans F. Sennholz.

Böhm-Bawerk, Eugen (1956c): *Positive Theory of Capital*. Libertarian Press, South Holland, Illinois. English translation of the 1921 edition by George D. Huncke and Hans F. Sennholz edition.

Böhm-Bawerk, Eugen (1988): *Innsbrucker Vorlesungen über Nationalökonomie (Wiedergabe aufgrund zweier Mitschriften)* in Schefold, Bertram and Tomo, Shigeki (eds). Metropolis Verlag.

Böhm-Bawerk, Eugen (1954): *Capital and Interest: A Critical History of Economical Theory*. Macmillan and Co., London. English translation of the first edition by William A. Smart. (1890).
Available online: http://www.econlib.org/library/BohmBawerk/bbCI.html.

Boos, Margarete (1986): *Die Wissenschaftstheorie Carl Mengers.* Wien.

Burkhardt, J.; Priddat, Birner (2000): "Carl Menger. Deduktive Einfachheit: Vom Zauber axiomatischer Wertlehre", in: Burkhardt, J.; Priddat, B. (eds): *Geschichte der Ökonomie*. Frankfurt/Main, p. 937-946.

Caldwell, Bruce (1982): *Beyond Positivism: Economic Methodology in the Twentieth Century*, George Allen & Unwin.

Caldwell, Bruce (1984): "Praxeology and its critics: an appraisal", *History of Political Economy*, vol. 16/3, p. 363-379.

Caldwell, Bruce (ed.) (1990): *Carl Menger and his Legacy in Economics*, annual supplement of vol. 22, *History of Political Economy.*

Campagnolo, Gilles (2002): "Une source philosophique de la pensée économique de Carl Menger: l'Éthique à Nicomaque d'Aristote", *Revue de philosophie économique*, n° 6/2, p. 5-35.

Campagnolo, Gilles (2003): book review of Latzer, M.; Schmitz, S. (eds.) (2002): *Carl Menger and the Evolution of payments systems*. Edward Elgar,; in *European Journal of the History of Economic Thought*, vol. 10/3, p. 505-509.

Campagnolo, Gilles ; Lagueux, Maurice (2004): "Les rapports d'échange selon Aristote. *Éthique à Nicomaque* V et VIII-IX", *Dialogue, Canadian Philosophical Review*, n° 43/3, p. 443-469.

Campagnolo, Gilles (2004): *Critique de l'économie politique classique.Marx, Menger et l'École historique*. Presses Universitaires de France, Paris.

Campagnolo, Gilles (2005): «Money as Measure of Value. An English Presentation of Menger's Essay in Monetary Thought» and «Menger: *Money as Measure of Value*. Translated by G. Campagnolo », *History of Political Economy*, 37/2, p.233-262.

Campagnolo, Gilles (2006): "*Seuls les extrémistes sont cohérents*", *Murray Rothbard et l'École austro-américaine dans la querelle de l'herméneutique,* ENS-Éditions, Lyon.

Campagnolo, Gilles (forthcoming, 2008): "Origins of Menger's Thought in French Liberal Economists", *Review of Austrian Economics.*

Condillac, abbé Étienne de (1754) : *Traité des sensations*, Paris and Amsterdam.

Dolan, E. G. (1976): *The Foundations of Modern Austrian Economics* (Studies in Economic Theory). Columbia University Press, New York.

Felber, Chr. (2006): *50 Vorschläge für eine gerechtere Welt. Gegen Konzernmacht und Kapitalismus*. Deuticke im Paul Zsolnay Verlag, Wien.

Flashar, H. (1992): „Die Ökonomik als Teil der praktischen Philosophie des Aristoteles", in *Klassiker der Nationalökonomie*, geschäftsführender Editor Schefold B., p. 71–92. Wirtschaft und Finanzen Verlag, Düsseldorf.

Frey, Bruno; Stutzer, Alois (2002): *Happiness and Economics: How the Economy and Social Institutions Affect Human Well-Being*. Princeton University Press, Princeton.

Frey, Bruno; Benz, Matthias (2004): "From imperialism to inspiration: a survey of economics and psychology", in Davis J. B.; Marciano A.; Runde J. (eds). *The Elgar Companion to Economics and Philosophy*, p. 61-83. E.Elgar, Cheltenham.

Gloria-Palermo, Sandye (1999): *Evolution of Austrian Economics*. Routledge, London.

Gloria-Palermo, Sandye (2005): "To what extent is the Austrian theory of capital Austrian?", chapter 11 in Bellet *et alii* (2005).

Hack (1872): *Zeitschrift für die gesamte Staatswissenschaft*.

Haltmayer Stephan (1976): „David Hume und ein Mythos aus Platons Theaitetos", in: *Wiener Jahrbuch für Philosophie*, Bd. IX, p. 59–72.

Haltmayer, Stephan (1987): *Das Aristotelische Organon als perenne Grundlage der Wissenschaftslehre. Das Ganze des logisch-erkenntnistheoretischen Zusammenhangs*. Habilitationsschrift, angenommen an der Universität Wien.

Haltmayer, Stephan (2004): „Zum ewigen Frieden oder Krieg und Untergang", in *Die Wiederkehr des Idealismus? Festschrift für Wilhelm Lütterfelds zum 60. Geburtstag*, p. 195–212. Frankfurt am Main.

Hayek, Friedrich (1941): *The Pure Theory of Capital*. Routledge & Kegan Paul, London.

Hayek, Friedrich (1952): *The Sensory Order. An Inquiry into the Foundations of Theoretical Psychology, reed.* 1976. The University of Chicago Press, Chicago.

Hayek, Friedrich (1968): „Einleitung" in *Carl Mengers Gesammelte Werke*, vol. 1; Tübingen, p. vii-xxxvi, reprint of Menger, C. (1871): *Grundsätze der Volkswirthschaftslehre,* (1871), Wien.

Hayek, Friedrich (1976): „Wahrer und falscher Individualismus“ in Hayek, Friedrich (ed.) : *Individualismus und wirtschaftliche Ordnung*. Salzburg, p. 9-48.

Hayek, Friedrich (1979): *The Counterrevolution of Science*. Liberty Press, Indianapolis.

Hennings, Klaus (1997): *The Austrian Theory of Value and Capital: Studies in the Life and Works of Eugen Von Bohm-Bawerk by the Late Klaus H.Hennings*. Edward Elgar, Cheltenham.

Hermann, B. W. (1832): *Staatswirthschaftliche Untersuchungen*. München.

Hildebrand, Bruno (1848): *Die Nationalökonomie der Gegenwart und Zukunft*. Frankfurt am Main.

Huerta de Soto, J. (2007): *Die Österreichische Schule der Nationalökonomie – Markt und unternehmerische Kreativität,* aus der Serie: „The International Library of Austrian Economics“ Series, Bd. 12, Friedrich A. v. Hayek Institut, Wien.

Hufeland, Gottlieb (1807/1815): *Neue Grundlegung der Staatswirthschaftskunst durch Prüfung und Berichtigung ihrer Hauptbegriffe von Gut, Preis, Geld und Volksvermögen, mit ununterbrochener Rücksicht auf die bisherigen Systeme*. Tasche und Müller, Gießen und Wetzlar.

Iggers, George (1997): *Deutsche Geschichtswissenschaft*. Böhlau, Wien.

Ikeda, Yukihiro (1997): *Entstehungsgeschichte Menger Grundsätze*. Mercaturae Scriptae Verlag, Sankt-Katharinen.

Issing, O. (1992): „Aristoteles – (auch) ein Nationalökonom?”, in *Klassiker der Nationalökonomie*, geschäftsführender Editor Schefold B., p. 95–125. Wirtschaft und Finanzen Verlag, Düsseldorf.

Kauder, Emil (1957): “Intellectual and Political Roots of the Older Austrian School”, *Zeitschrift für Nationalökonomie*, vol. 17, p. 411-425.

Kauder, Emil (1963): *Carl Mengers erster Entwurf zu seinem Hauptwerk „Grundsätze“, geschrieben als Anmerkung zu den „Grundsätzen der Volkswirtschaftslehre“ von Karl Heinrich Rau*, mimeograph. Tokio.

Kaulla, Rudolf (1906): *Die geschichtliche Entwicklung der modernen Werttheorien*, Tübingen.

Kirzner, Israel (1973): *Competition and entrepreneurship*, University of Chicago Press, Chicago.

Kirzner, Israel (1978): "The entrepreneurial role in Menger's system", *Atlantic Economic Journal*, vol. 6/3, p. 31-45.

Kirzner, Israel (1997): "Entrepreneurial Discovery and the Competitive Market process: An Austrian Approach", *Journal of Economic Literature,* 35, p. 60-85.

Klein, B. (2000): "Fisher - General Motors and the nature of the firm", *Journal of Law and Economics*, vol. 43, p. 105-142.

Knies, Carl (1853): *Die Politische Oekonomie vom Standpunkt der geschichtlichen Methode*. Braunschweig.

Koslowski, P. (1979): *Zum Verhältnis von Polis und Oikos bei Aristoteles*. Donau Verlag, Straubing und München.

Koslowski, P. (1993): *Politik und Ökonomie bei Aristoteles*. J.C.B. Mohr (Paul Siebeck), Tübingen.

Kraus, Oscar (1905): „Die aristotelische Werttheorie in ihren Beziehungen zu den Lehren der moderner Psychologenschule", *Zeitschrift für die gesamte Staatswissenschaft*. Verlag der Laupp'schen Buchhandlung, Tübingen.

Kudler, Joseph (1856): *Die Grundlehren der Volkswirtschaft*. Wien.

Kuhn, H. (1973): „Das Gute", in *Handbuch philosophischer Grundbegriffe*, Krings H.; Baumgartner H. M.; Wild, Chr. (eds), vol. 3, p. 657–677. Kösel-Verlag, München.

Kuhn, H. (1975): „Werte – eine Urgegebenheit". In: Neue Anthropologie, hrsg. von H.-G. Gadamer, p. 343–373. Georg Thieme Verlag, Stuttgart.

Lachmann, Ludwig (1976): "On Austrian Capital Theory", chapter 6 in Dolan (1976).

Lachmann, Ludwig (1978): "Carl Menger and the incomplete revolution of subjectivism", *Atlantic Economic Journal*, 6/3, p. 57-59.

Latzer, Michael; Schmitz, Stefan (eds.) (2002): *Carl Menger and the evolution of payments systems*. Edward Elgar, Cheltenham.

Leser, Norbert (ed.) (1986): *Die Wiener Schule der Nationalökonomie*. Hermann Böhlaus Nachf., WienKölnGraz.

Lowry S. T.; Gordon B. (eds.) (1998): *Ancient and medieval economic ideas and concepts of social justice*. Brill, Leiden, New York, Köln.

Lowry, S. T. (1992): „Ökonomische Ideen in Aristoteles` `Politik´", in *Klassiker der Nationalökonomie*, geschäftsführender Editor Schefold B., p. 127–152, Wirtschaft und Finanzen Verlag, Düsseldorf.

Mäki, Uskali (1990): "Mengerian economics in realist perspective", in Caldwell, B. (ed.): *Carl Menger and his legacy in economics*, p. 289-312. Duke University Press, Durham and London.

Mäki, Uskali (1997): "Universals and the Methodenstreit: a re-examination of Carl Menger's conception of economics as an exact science", *Studies in the History and Philosophy of Sciences*, vol. 28/3, p. 475-495.

McGee, J. (1958): "Predatory price cutting: the Standard Oil (N.J.) case". *Journal of Law and Economics*, 1, p. 137-169.

Menger, C. (1968-1970): *Gesammelte Werke.* (ed. F.A. Hayek). Contains;
- I: *Grundsätze der Volkswirtschaftslehre*, 1871, Wien.
- II: *Untersuchungen über die Methode der Socialwissen-schaften und der politischen Œkonomie insbesondere*, 1883, Leipzig.
- III: *Kleinere Schriften über Methode und Geschichte der Volkswirtschaftslehre*
- IV: *Schriften über Geld und Währungsreform*, writings from 1886 to 1909. At the end, a complete Bibliography of Menger's published texts.

Menger, Carl (1871): *Grundsätze der Volkswirthschaftslehre*. Wilhelm Braumüller, Wien.

Menger, Carl (1883): *Untersuchungen über die Methode der Socialwissenschaften und der Politischen Oekonomie insbesondere*. Duncker & Humblot, Leipzig.

Menger, Carl (1883): „Über die sogenannte ethische Richtung der Politischen Ökonomie". Wien. In: Burkhardt; Priddat, Birner (eds) (2000): *Geschichte der Öko-nomie*. Frankfurt/Main, p. 604-608.

Menger, Carl (1888a): „Zur Theorie des Kapitals", *Jahrbücher für Nationalökonomie and Statistik.* Reprinted in *Mengers Gesammelte Werke*, vol. IV.

Menger, Carl (1888b): «Contribution à la théorie du capital» . *Revue d'Économie Politique*, adapted translation of *Zur Theorie des Kapitals* by Charles Secrétan, p. 577–94.

Menger, C. (1891): „Die Sozialtheorie der klassischen Nationalökonomie und die moderne Wirtschaftspolitik". Reprinted in *Mengers Gesammelte Werke*, vol. III.

Menger, Carl (1915): „Böhm-Bawerk, Eugen v.", *Almanach der Kaiserlichen Akademie der Wissenschaften*. Obituary. Reprinted in *Mengers Gesammelte Werke*, vol. IV.

Menger, Carl (1994): "Carl Menger's Lectures to Crown Prince Rudolf". Wien 1876. (ed. by E. Streissler; transl. by Monika Streissler and D. Good.) Hants.

Menger, Carl (1950): *Principles of Economics*. The Free Press, Glencoe, Illinois. English translation of the *Grundsätze der Volkswirtschaftslehre*, by James Dingwall and Bert F. Hoselitz.

Menger, Carl (1963): *Problems of Economics and Sociology*. University of Illinois Press. English translation of the *Untersuchungen über die Methode der Socialwissenschaften und der Politischen Ökonomie inbesondere*, by Francis J. Nock.

Menger, Karl (ed.) (1923): *Grundsätze der Volkswirthschaftslehre*, Wien. Second edition of Carl Menger's *Grundsätze der Volkswirtschaftslehre* by his son, Karl Menger.

Milford, Karl (1989): *Zu den Lösungsversuchen des Induktionsproblems und des Abgrenzungsproblems bei Carl Menger*. Verlag der Österreichischen Akademie der Wissenschaften, Wien.

Milford, Karl (1990): "Menger's methodology", in Caldwell, B. (ed.): *Carl Menger and his legacy in economics*, p. 215-240. Duke University Press, Durham and London.

Milford, Karl (1994): „Roschers historische Methode", in *Klassiker der Nationalökonomie*, geschäftsführender Editor Schefold B., S. 161–191, Verlag Wirtschaft und Finanzen, Düsseldorf.

Milford, Karl (1995): "Roscher's epistemological and methodological position and its importance for the Methodenstreit", *Journal of Economic Studies*, Vol. 22, n. 3/4/5; MCB University Press Ltd.

Milford, Karl (1997): „Hufeland als Vorläufer von Menger und Hayek" in Priddat, B.P. (ed.): *Wert, Meinung, Bedeutung. Die Tradition der subjektiven Wertlehre in der deutschen Nationalökonomie vor Menger*, p. 89-160. Marburg.

Mill, John Stuart (1843/1974): *A System of Logic Ratiocinative and Inductive*, London 1843; in: J. M. Robson (ed.), *Collected Works of John Stuart Mill*, Vols. VII, VIII. University of Toronto Press, Routledge & Kegan Paul, Toronto.

Mill, John Stuart (1848/1974): *Essays on some Unsettled Questions of Political Economy*, John W. Parker, London 1848; in J. M. Robson (ed.), *Collected Works of John Stuart Mill*, Vol. IV. University of Toronto Press, Routledge & Kegan Paul, Toronto.

Mill, John Stuart (1848/1965): *Principles of Political Economy*, London 1848; in: J. M. Robson (ed.), *Collected Works of John Stuart Mill*, Vols. II, III. University of Toronto Press, Routledge & Kegan Paul, Toronto.

Mill, John Stuart (1848/1921): *Grundsätze der politischen Ökonomie*, vol. 1, Jena 1913, vol. 2, Jena (German translation of *Principles of Political Economy*). London.

Mill, John Stuart (1976): *Einige ungelöste Probleme der politischen Ökonomie*. Frankfurt/Main.

Mises, Ludwig (1933) : *Grundprobleme der Nationalökonomie*. Fischer, Jena.

Mises, Ludwig (1949/1966): *Human Action. A Treatise on Economics*, 3rd ed. H. Regnery Co., Chicago.

Mises, Ludwig (1969/2003): *The historical setting of the Austrian School of Economics*. Ludwig von Mises Institute, Auburn.
Online edition (2003): http://www.mises.org.

Oncken, Gustav (1898): « Das Adam Smith Problem », *Zeitschrift für Sozialwissenschaft*, 1.

Pearson, H. (1999): "Was there really a German Historical School of economics?", *History of Political Economy*, vol. 31/2, p. 547-62.

Plott, C. (1982): "Industrial Organization Theory and Experimental Economics", *Journal of Economic Literature*, 20/4, p. 1485-1527.

Popper, Karl (1957/1979): *The Poverty of Historicism*, Routledge & Kegan Paul, London.

Popper, Karl (1976): *Logik der Forschung,* 6., verb. Aufl., J.C.B. Mohr (Paul Siebeck), Tübingen.

Pribram, Karl (1986): *A history of economic reasoning*. Johns Hopkins University Press.

Priddat, Birner (1997): „Wert und Bedeutung. Bruch und Kontinuität von Carl Mengers Werttheorie im Verhältnis zu seinen Vorgängern." In Priddat, B. P. (ed.): *Wert, Meinung, Bedeutung. Die Tradition der subjektiven Wertlehre in der deutschen Nationalökonomie vor Menger*, p. 287-302. Marburg.

Putnam, Hilary (1975): *Mind, Language and Reality*, Cambridge. Cambridge University Press.

Ravix, Jean-Louis (2004): "Schumpeter vs. Böhm-Bawerk on innovation and industrial dynamics". Paper of the 2004 International Schumpeter Society conference: "Innovation, Industrial Dynamics and Structural Transformation: Schumpeterian Legacies".

Recktenwald, Horst (2005): "Würdigung des Werkes". Introduction to Smith, Adam: *Der Wohlstand der Nationen. Eine Untersuchung seiner Natur und seiner Ursachen*, edition and German translation by Recktenwald, p. xv-lxxix.

Reimherr, A. (2005): *Die philosophisch-psychologischen Grundlagen der Österreichischen Wertlehre: Franz Brentano und Carl Menger,* Dissertation an der Universität Würzburg. (Unter dem Titel "Carl Menger und Franz Brentano – Ursprünge der österreichischen Wertlehre" ist die Kurzfassung davon in den Brentano-Studien (Bd. XI, 2004/05, S. 13–39) erschienen.)
Online: http://opus.bibliothek.uniwuerzburg.de/volltexte/2006/1697/.

Ricardo, David (1817/1923): *Grundsätze der Volkswirtschaft und Besteuerung.* Aus dem Englischen Original übersetzt von Heinrich Waentig. Jena.

Rizzo, Marco (ed.) (1979): *Time, Uncertainty, and Disequilibrium.* Lexington Books, Lexington.

Roscher, Wilhelm (1842): *Leben Werk und Zeitalter des Thukydides*, Vandenhoeck und Ruprecht, Göttingen.

Roscher, Wilhelm (1843): *Grundriß zu Vorlesungen über die Staatswirthschaftskunst. Nach geschichtlicher Methode.* Dieterich, Göttingen.

Rothbard, Murray (1995): *An Austrian Perspective on the History of Economic Thought*, vol. 1: *Pre-classical Economics,* vol. 2: *Classical Economics*, Edward Elgar, Aldershot.

Rothschild, K.W. (1986): „Die Wiener Schule im Verhältnis zur klassischen Nationalökonomie, unter besonderer Berücksichtigung von Carl Menger“. In Leser, Norbert (ed.): *Die Wiener Schule der Nationalökonomie*, p. 11-27. Wien.

Rothschild, K.W. (2004): *Die politischen Visionen großer Ökonomen*. Bern.

Salerno, J. (1999): “Carl Menger: the founder of the Austrian School”. In: Holcombe, R. (ed.), *Fifteen Great Austrian Economists*. Ludwig von Mises Institute; Auburn.

Savigny, F. (1840-49): *System des heutigen Römischen Rechts*. Veit und Comp., Berlin.

Schefold, Bertram (1992): „Aristoteles: Der Klassiker des antiken Wirtschaftsdenkens“, in *Klassiker der Nationalökonomie*, geschäftsführender Editor Schefold B., S. 19–69. Wirtschaft und Finanzen Verlag, Düsseldorf.

Schefold, Bertram (1999): „Antike Theoriebildungen.“ In: *Handbuch der Wirtschaftsethik*, vol. 1–4, Korff, W.; Baumgartner A. u.a. (im Auftragder Görres-Gesellschaft), vol. 1, p. 344–358. Gütersloher Verlagshaus, Gütersloh.

Schlick, Moritz (1974): *General Theory of Knowledge*, Library of Exact Philosophy Series (11). Springer Verlag , Wien & New York.

Schmidhuber, P. M. (2007): „Probleme einer Reform der Weltwirtschaftsordnung.“, *Wiener blätter zur Friedensforschung*, vol. 131.

Schumpeter, Josef (1954): *History of Economic Analysis.* Oxford University Press, New-York.

Schumpeter, Josef (2003): *Ten Great Economists.* Simon Publications.

Selgin, George (1988): *The Theory of free-banking*. Rowman and Littlefield, Totowa.

Smith, Adam (1974/2005): *„Der Wohlstand der Nationen“. Eine Untersuchung seiner Natur und seiner Ursachen (1776)*, German translation with a foreword by Horst Claus Recktenwald, München, reed. 2005.

Smith, Barry (1990): “Aristotle, Menger and Mises: an Essay in the Metaphysics of Economics”, *History of Political Economy*, n° 22, annual supplement: Caldwell B. (ed.), *Carl Menger and his Legacy in Economics*, p. 263-288.

Smith, Barry (1995): *Austrian philosophy, the legacy of Franz Brentano.* Open Court, Chicago/LaSalle.

Smith, Vernon (1982): "Microeconomic Systems as an Experimental Science", *American Economic Review*, vol. 72/5, p. 923-955.

Streissler E. W.; Streissler M. (eds) (1994): *Carl Menger`s Lectures to Crown Prince Rudolf of Austria*. Edward Elgar, Aldershot.

Streissler, E. (1989): "Carl Menger". In Starbatty, J. (ed.): *Klassiker des ökonomischen Denkens*, Volume II, p. 119-134. München.

Weber, Max (1903 – 06/1988): „Roscher und Knies und die logischen Probleme der historischen Nationalökonomie", in: *Gesammelte Aufsätze zur Wissenschaftslehre*. Tübingen, J.C.B. Mohr (Paul Siebeck).

Weber, Max (1908/1988): „Die Grenznutzlehre und das `psychophysische Grundgesetz´", in: *Gesammelte Aufsätze zur Wissenschaftslehre*. Tübingen, J.C.B. Mohr (Paul Siebeck).

White, Lawrence (1984): *The methodology of the Austrian school economists*. Ludwig von Mises Institute, Auburn.

Wieser, A. Rh. (1950): *Die Geschichte des Faches Philosophie an der Universität Wien 1848 – 1938*. Dissertation, Wien.

Wieser, F. von (1891): "The Austrian school and the theory of value". *The Economic Journal*, 1.

Wilke, W. (2002): *Zur ideengeschichtlichen Rolle des Subjekts im sozioökonomischen Prozeß. Das Spannungsverhältnis von Individuum und Gemeinschaft in ausgewählten theoretischen Entwürfen sowie deren Bezug zu den jeweiligen zeitgenössischen politischen, gesellschaftlichen und wirtschaftlichen Gegebenheiten von der griechischen Antike bis zur Gegenwart*. Dissertation, Wirtschaftsuniversität Wien.

Yagi, Kiichiro (1993): "Carl Menger's *Grundsätze* in the making", *History of Political Economy*, vol. 25/4, p. 697-724.

Yeager, L. (1979): "Capital Paradoxes and the Concept of Waiting". chapter 12 in Rizzo (1979).

Wiener Arbeiten zur Philosophie
Reihe B: Beiträge zur philosophischen Forschung

Herausgegeben von Stephan Haltmayer

Band 1 Stephan Haltmayer / Werner Gabriel (Hrsg.): Abschaffung der freien Universität? 2000.

Band 2 Heinz Krumpel: Die deutsche Philosophie in Mexiko. Ein Beitrag zur interkulturellen Verständigung seit Alexander von Humboldt. 1999.

Band 3 Friedrich F. Brezina: Die Achtung. Ethik und Moral der Achtung und Unterwerfung bei Immanuel Kant, Ernst Tugendhat, Ursula Wolf und Peter Singer. 1999.

Band 4 Stephan Haltmayer / Franz M. Wuketits / Gerhard Budin (Hrsg.): Homo pragmatico-theoreticus. Philosophie – Interdisziplinarität und Evolution – Information. Erhard Oeser zum 60. Geburtstag. 2000.

Band 5 Renate Wahsner / Thomas Posch (Hrsg.): Die Natur muß bewiesen werden. Zu Grundfragen der Hegelschen Naturphilosophie. Mit Beiträgen von Friedrich Grimmlinger, Hans-Dieter Klein, Gilles Marmasse, Thomas Posch, Urs Richli und Renate Wahsner. 2002.

Band 6 Georg Wilhelm Friedrich Hegel: Vorlesung über Naturphilosophie. Berlin 1821/22. Nachschrift von Boris von Uexküll. Herausgegeben von Gilles Marmasse und Thomas Posch. 2002.

Band 7 Heinz Krumpel: Aufklärung und Romantik in Lateinamerika. Ein Beitrag zu Identität, Vergleich und Wechselwirkung zwischen lateinamerikanischem und europäischem Denken. 2004.

Band 8 Stephan Haltmayer / Waltraud Heintel (Hrsg.): Erich Heintel: Mündiger Mensch und christlicher Glaube. Aus dem Nachlaß als teilweises Fragment herausgegeben und dabei mit Registern versehen von Stephan Haltmayer und Waltraud Heintel. 2004.

Band 9 Stephan Haltmayer / Armin Aigner (Hrsg.): Literalität und Oralität. Mit einer Einleitung von Stephan Haltmayer und mit Beiträgen von Georg Danek, Ulrich H. J. Körtner, Wilhelm Lütterfelds, Jörg Salaquarda und Detlev Thiel. 2005.

Band 10 Hisaki Hashi: Die Dynamik von Sein und Nichts. Dimensionen der vergleichenden Philosophie. 2004.

Band 11 Thomas Posch / Gilles Marmasse (Hrsg.): Die Natur in den Begriff übersetzen. Zu Hegels Kritik des naturwissenschaftlichen Allgemeinen. Mit einem Anhang: Hegels Vorlesung über Naturphilosophie von 1825/26. Einleitung. Nach der Nachschrift von H.W. Dove. 2005.

Band 12 Michael Höfler / Michael Wladika (Hrsg.): Franz Ungler: Zur antiken und neuzeitlichen Dialektik. 2005.

Band 13 Heinz Krumpel: Philosophie und Literatur in Lateinamerika – 20. Jahrhundert –. Ein Beitrag zu Identität, Vergleich und Wechselwirkung zwischen lateinamerikanischem und europäischem Denken. 2006.

Band 14 Shin-Ja Kim: Das philosophische Denken von Tasan Chong. 2006.

Band 15 Walter Methlagl / Stephan Haltmayer (Hrsg.): Hans Rochelt: Erinnerung an den künftigen Christen. Zur Pneumatologie Ferdinand Ebners. 2007.

Band 16 Thomas Auinger / Friedrich Grimmlinger (Hrsg.): Wissen und Bildung. Zur Aktualität von Hegels Phänomenologie des Geistes anlässlich ihres 200jährigen Jubiläums. Mit Beiträgen von Kurt Appel, Thomas Auinger, Walter Gartler, Wilfried Grießer, Friedrich Grimmlinger, Herbert Hrachovec, Eva L.-Waniek, Konrad Paul Liessmann, Thomas Posch, Urs Richli, Renate Wahsner, Violetta L.Waibel und Michael Wladika. 2007.

Band 17 Gilles Campagnolo (Hrsg./ed.): Carl Menger. Neu erörtert unter Einbeziehung nachgelassener Texte. Discussed on the Basis of New Findings. Mit Beiträgen von / With Contributions by G. Campagnolo, S. Haltmayer, P. Livet, A. Lordon, J. Magnan de Bornier, H. Mayerhofer, K. Milford, M. Ohana, P. Rosner, W. Wilke. 2008.

www.peterlang.de